BICENTENNIAL
1807
⊛WILEY
2007
BICENTENNIAL

THE WILEY BICENTENNIAL—KNOWLEDGE FOR GENERATIONS

*E*ach generation has its unique needs and aspirations. When Charles Wiley first opened his small printing shop in lower Manhattan in 1807, it was a generation of boundless potential searching for an identity. And we were there, helping to define a new American literary tradition. Over half a century later, in the midst of the Second Industrial Revolution, it was a generation focused on building the future. Once again, we were there, supplying the critical scientific, technical, and engineering knowledge that helped frame the world. Throughout the 20th Century, and into the new millennium, nations began to reach out beyond their own borders and a new international community was born. Wiley was there, expanding its operations around the world to enable a global exchange of ideas, opinions, and know-how.

For 200 years, Wiley has been an integral part of each generation's journey, enabling the flow of information and understanding necessary to meet their needs and fulfill their aspirations. Today, bold new technologies are changing the way we live and learn. Wiley will be there, providing you the must-have knowledge you need to imagine new worlds, new possibilities, and new opportunities.

Generations come and go, but you can always count on Wiley to provide you the knowledge you need, when and where you need it!

WILLIAM J. PESCE
PRESIDENT AND CHIEF EXECUTIVE OFFICER

PETER BOOTH WILEY
CHAIRMAN OF THE BOARD

Microsoft Certified Application Specialist (MCAS)

 | **Approved Courseware**

▪ What does this logo mean?

It means this courseware has been approved by the Microsoft® Certified Application Specialist program to be among the finest available for learning Microsoft® Office Word 2007, Microsoft® Office Excel 2007, Microsoft® Office PowerPoint 2007, Microsoft® Office Access 2007, Microsoft® Office Outlook 2007, or Microsoft® Office Project. It also means that upon completion of this courseware, you may be prepared to take an exam for Microsoft Certified Application Specialist qualification.

▪ What is a Microsoft Certified Application Specialist?

A Microsoft Certified Application Specialist is an individual who has passed exams for certifying his or her skills in one or more of the Microsoft Office desktop applications such as Microsoft Word, Microsoft Excel, Microsoft PowerPoint, Microsoft Outlook, Microsoft Access, or Microsoft Project. The Microsoft Certified Application Specialist program is the only program approved by Microsoft for testing proficiency in Microsoft Office desktop applications or the Microsoft Windows operating system. This testing program can be a valuable asset in any job search or career development.

▪ More Information

To learn more about becoming a Microsoft Certified Application Specialist and exam availability, visit www.microsoft.com/learning/msbc.

Microsoft, the Microsoft Office Logo, PowerPoint, Outlook and Windows Vista are trademarks or registered trademarks of Microsoft Corporation in the United States and/or other countries, and the Microsoft Certified Application Specialist logo is used under license from the owner.

Microsoft® Official Academic Course

Microsoft® Office Project 2007

Credits

EXECUTIVE EDITOR	John Kane
SENIOR EDITOR	Gary Schwartz
DIRECTOR OF MARKETING AND SALES	Mitchell Beaton
MICROSOFT STRATEGIC RELATIONSHIPS MANAGER	Merrick Van Dongen of Microsoft Learning
GLOBAL MOAC MANAGER	Laura McKenna
DEVELOPMENT AND PRODUCTION	Custom Editorial Productions, Inc
EDITORIAL ASSISTANT	Jennifer Lartz
PRODUCTION MANAGER	Kelly Tavares
CREATIVE DIRECTOR/COVER DESIGNER	Harry Nolan
TECHNOLOGY AND MEDIA	Lauren Sapira/Elena Santa Maria
COVER PHOTO	Corbis

Wiley 200th Anniversary logo designed by: Richard J. Pacifico

This book was set in Garamond by Aptara, Inc. and printed and bound by Bind Rite Graphics.
The covers were printed by Phoenix Color.

ISBN-13 978-0-47006953–0

Printed in the United States of America

10 9 8 7 6 5 4 3 2

Foreword from the Publisher

Wiley's publishing vision for the Microsoft Official Academic Course series is to provide students and instructors with the skills and knowledge they need to use Microsoft technology effectively in all aspects of their personal and professional lives. Quality instruction is required to help both educators and students get the most from Microsoft's software tools and to become more productive. Thus our mission is to make our instructional programs trusted educational companions for life.

To accomplish this mission, Wiley and Microsoft have partnered to develop the highest quality educational programs for Information Workers, IT Professionals, and Developers. Materials created by this partnership carry the brand name "Microsoft Official Academic Course," assuring instructors and students alike that the content of these textbooks is fully endorsed by Microsoft, and that they provide the highest quality information and instruction on Microsoft products. The Microsoft Official Academic Course textbooks are "Official" in still one more way—they are the officially sanctioned courseware for Microsoft IT Academy members.

The Microsoft Official Academic Course series focuses on *workforce development*. These programs are aimed at those students seeking to enter the workforce, change jobs, or embark on new careers as information workers, IT professionals, and developers. Microsoft Official Academic Course programs address their needs by emphasizing authentic workplace scenarios with an abundance of projects, exercises, cases, and assessments.

The Microsoft Official Academic Courses are mapped to Microsoft's extensive research and job-task analysis, the same research and analysis used to create the Microsoft Certified Application Specialist (MCAS) and Microsoft Certified Application Professional (MCAP) exams. The textbooks focus on real skills for real jobs. As students work through the projects and exercises in the textbooks they enhance their level of knowledge and their ability to apply the latest Microsoft technology to everyday tasks. These students also gain resume-building credentials that can assist them in finding a job, keeping their current job, or in furthering their education.

The concept of life-long learning is today an utmost necessity. Job roles, and even whole job categories, are changing so quickly that none of us can stay competitive and productive without continuously updating our skills and capabilities. The Microsoft Official Academic Course offerings, and their focus on Microsoft certification exam preparation, provide a means for people to acquire and effectively update their skills and knowledge. Wiley supports students in this endeavor through the development and distribution of these courses as Microsoft's official academic publisher.

Today educational publishing requires attention to providing quality print and robust electronic content. By integrating Microsoft Official Academic Course products, Wiley*PLUS*, and Microsoft certifications, we are better able to deliver efficient learning solutions for students and teachers alike.

Bonnie Lieberman
General Manager and Senior Vice President

Welcome to the Microsoft Official Academic Course (MOAC) program for Microsoft Office Project. MOAC represents the collaboration between Microsoft Learning and John Wiley & Sons, Inc. publishing company. Microsoft and Wiley teamed up to produce a series of textbooks that deliver compelling and innovative teaching solutions to instructors and superior learning experiences for students. Infused and informed by in-depth knowledge from the creators of Microsoft Office, and crafted by a publisher known worldwide for the pedagogical quality of its products, these textbooks maximize skills transfer in minimum time. With MOAC, students are hands on right away—there are no superfluous text passages to get in the way of learning and using the software. Students are challenged to reach their potential by using their new technical skills as highly productive members of the workforce.

Because this knowledgebase comes directly from Microsoft, architect of the Microsoft 2007 Office System and creator of the Microsoft Certified Application Specialist (MCAS) exams, you are sure to receive the topical coverage that is most relevant to students' personal and professional success. Microsoft's direct participation not only assures you that MOAC textbook content is accurate and current; it also means that students will receive the best instruction possible to enable their success on certification exams and in the workplace.

▪ The Microsoft Official Academic Course Program

The *Microsoft Official Academic Course* series is a complete program for instructors and institutions to prepare and deliver great courses on Microsoft software technologies. With MOAC, we recognize that, because of the rapid pace of change in the technology and curriculum developed by Microsoft, there is an ongoing set of needs beyond classroom instruction tools for an instructor to be ready to teach the course. The MOAC program endeavors to provide solutions for all these needs in a systematic manner in order to ensure a successful and rewarding course experience for both instructor and student—technical and curriculum training for instructor readiness with new software releases; the software itself for student use at home for building hands-on skills, assessment, and validation of skill development; and a great set of tools for delivering instruction in the classroom and lab. All are important to the smooth delivery of an interesting course on Microsoft software, and all are provided with the MOAC program. We think about the model below as a gauge for ensuring that we completely support you in your goal of teaching a great course. As you evaluate your instructional materials options, you may wish to use the model for comparison purposes with available products.

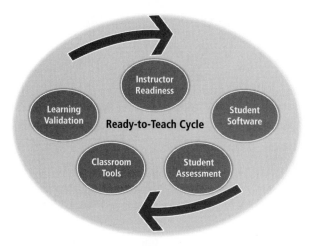

■ Pedagogical Features

MOAC is designed to cover all the learning objectives in the MCAS exams, referred to as "objective domains." The Microsoft Certified Application Specialist (MCAS) exam objectives are highlighted throughout the textbooks. Many pedagogical features have been developed specifically for *Microsoft Official Academic Course* programs. Unique features of our task-based approach include a Lesson Skill Matrix that correlates skills taught in each lesson to the MCAS objectives; Certification, Workplace, and Internet Ready exercises; and three levels of increasingly rigorous lesson-ending activities: Competency, Proficiency, and Mastery Assessment.

Presenting the extensive procedural information and technical concepts woven throughout the textbook raises challenges for the student and instructor alike. The Illustrated Book Tour that follows provides a guide to the rich features contributing to *Microsoft Official Academic Course* program's pedagogical plan. Following is a list of key features in each lesson designed to prepare students for success on the certification exams and in the workplace:

- Each lesson begins with a **Lesson Skill Matrix.** More than a standard list of learning objectives, the Skill Matrix correlates each software skill covered in the lesson to the specific MCAS "objective domain."

- Every lesson features a real-world **Business Case** scenario that places the software skills and knowledge to be acquired in a real-world setting.

- Every lesson opens with a **Software Orientation.** This feature provides an overview of the software features students will be working with in the lesson. The orientation will detail the general properties of the software or specific features, such as a ribbon or dialog box; and it includes a large, labeled screen image.

- Concise and frequent **Step-by-Step** instructions teach students new features and provide an opportunity for hands-on practice. Numbered steps give detailed, step-by-step instructions to help students learn software skills. The steps also show results and screen images to match what students should see on their computer screens.

- **Illustrations:** Screen images provide visual feedback as students work through the exercises. The images reinforce key concepts, provide visual clues about the steps, and allow students to check their progress.

- **Button images:** When the text instructs a student to click a particular toolbar button, an image of the button is shown in the margin.

- **Key Terms:** Important technical vocabulary is listed at the beginning of the lesson. When these terms are used later in the lesson, they appear in bold italic type and are defined. The Glossary contains all of the key terms and their definitions.

- Engaging point-of-use **Reader aids,** located throughout the lessons, tell students why this topic is relevant (*The Bottom Line*), provide students with helpful hints (*Take Note*), show alternate ways to accomplish tasks (*Another Way*), or point out things to watch out for or avoid (*Troubleshooting*). Reader aids also provide additional relevant or background information that adds value to the lesson.

- **Certification Ready?** features throughout the text signal students where a specific certification objective is covered. They provide students with a chance to check their understanding of that particular MCAS objective and, if necessary, review the section of the lesson where it is covered. MOAC offers complete preparation for MCAS certification.

- **New Feature:** The New Feature icon appears near any software feature that is new to Office 2007.

- **Competency, Proficiency, and Mastery Assessments** provide three progressively more challenging lesson-ending activities.

- **Internet Ready** projects combine the knowledge students acquire in a lesson with a Web-based research task.

- **Circling Back.** These integrated projects provide students with an opportunity to review and practice skills learned in previous lessons.

- **Workplace Ready.** These features preview how Microsoft Office Project is used in real-world situations.

- **Student CD:** The companion CD contains the data files needed for each lesson. These files are indicated by the CD icon in the margin of the textbook.

■ Lesson Features

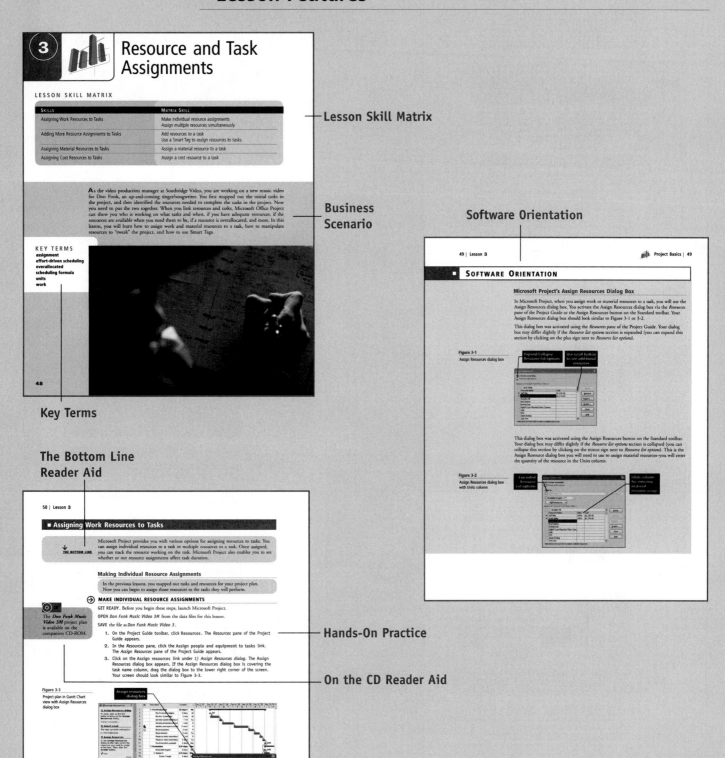

Lesson Skill Matrix

Business Scenario

Software Orientation

Key Terms

The Bottom Line Reader Aid

Hands-On Practice

On the CD Reader Aid

Project Basics | 55

The default method of scheduling in Microsoft Project is effort-driven scheduling. With **effort-driven scheduling**, the duration of a task increases or decreases as you remove resources from or assign resources to a task; the amount of work needed to complete the task does not change. Recall that in Lesson 2 you created finish-to-start relationships for the project tasks. You can now see the benefit of creating task relationships rather than setting start or finish dates. Because effort-driven scheduling resulted in decreased task durations, Microsoft Project adjusted the start dates of successor tasks that did not have a constraint such as a start or finish date.

TAKE NOTE
Although effort-driven scheduling is the default for all tasks you create in Microsoft Project, you can change the default setting for all new tasks in a project plan. On the menu bar, click Tools. On the Tools menu, select Options, and then select the Schedule tab in the Options dialog box. Clear or select the *New tasks are effort driven* check box. To change effort-driven scheduling for a single task or group of tasks, select the desired task(s). Click the Task Information button, and select the Advanced tab of the Task Information dialog box. Clear or select the *Effort driven* check box.

Take Note Reader Aid

TAKE NOTE
Look back again to Figure 3-6. Did you notice that some of the cells in the Duration, Start, and Finish columns are shaded light blue? (You may need to shift the Gantt Chart to the right so that these columns are visible.) Microsoft Project's Change Highlighting automatically highlights all items that change as a result of the most recent change you made. This helps you gain a better understanding of the impacts of your choices.

Using a Smart Tag to Assign Resources

Now that you have assigned multiple resources to several tasks, in this exercise you will use a Smart Tag to assign additional resources to a task.

USE A SMART TAG TO ASSIGN RESOURCES TO TASKS

USE the project plan you created in the previous exercise.

1. Click on the name of task 5, **Develop production layouts.** Jeff Pike is the only resource currently assigned to this task. You'd like to assign an additional resource and reduce the task's duration.

2. In the Resource Name column of the Assign Resources dialog box, click **Brenda Diaz** and then click the **Assign** button. Brenda Diaz is assigned to task 5. In addition, a small triangle appears in the top left corner of the Task Name cell. This means that there is a Smart Tag activated for this task.

3. Click again on the name of task 5, **Develop production layouts.** The Smart Tag Actions button appears in the Indicators column for task 5. Until you perform another action, you can use the Smart Tag to select how you want Microsoft Project to manage this additional resource assignment.

4. Click the **Smart Tag Actions** button. A list of options regarding how you want to handle this additional resource is displayed. This list is ONLY available until you perform another action in Microsoft Project. Your screen should look similar to Figure 3-7.

New Features

Project Basics | 13

"Apply first color overcoat." You also need a task called "Wait for undercoat to dry" because you cannot apply the color paint until the undercoat is dry. The task "Wait for undercoat to dry" will have an elapsed duration because the undercoat will dry over a contiguous range of hours, whether they are working or nonworking. If the undercoat takes 24 hours to cure, you would enter the duration for this task as 1ed (or 1 elapsed day). If you scheduled it to start at 11 A.M. on Wednesday, it would be complete at 11 A.M. on Thursday.

Table 1-1 shows abbreviations and meanings for actual and elapsed times in Microsoft Project.

Table 1-1

Abbreviations and meanings for actual and elapsed times

Easy-to-Read Tables

IF YOU ENTER THIS ABBREVIATION	IT APPEARS LIKE THIS	AND MEANS
m	min	minute
h	hr	hour
d	day	day
w	wk	week
mo	mon	month
em	emin	elapsed minute
eh	ehr	elapsed hour
ed	eday	elapsed day
ew	ewk	elapsed week
emo	emon	elapsed month

TROUBLESHOOTING
For most projects, you will use task durations of hours, days, and weeks. When estimating task durations, think carefully about the level of detail you want to apply to your project's tasks. If you have a multiyear project, it is probably not practical or even possible to track tasks that are measured in minutes or hours. You should measure task durations at the lowest level of detail or control necessary, but no lower.

Troubleshooting Reader Aid

Although the task durations are supplied for you for the exercises in this book, you will have to estimate task durations for most real-world projects. There are a number of sources of task duration estimates:

- Information from previous, similar projects
- Estimates from the people who will actually complete the tasks
- Recommendations from people who have managed similar projects
- Professional or industry organizations that deal with the project subject matter

For any project, a major source of risk is inaccurate task duration estimates. **Risk** decreases the likelihood of completing the project on time, within budget and to specification. Making good estimates is worth the time and effort.

Creating a Milestone

A milestone marks a major event in a project and can be used to monitor the project's progress. A **milestone** represents a significant event reached within the project or imposed upon the project. Milestones are often represented as a task with zero duration.

---

6 | Lesson 1

3. Click the left or right **arrow** until January 2008 is displayed, as shown in Figure 1-5.

Figure 1-5
Setting a project start date

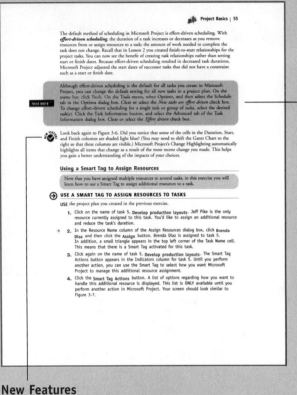

4. Click January 7.

ANOTHER WAY
You can also quickly pick the date with the calendar. First, click on the name of the month to display a menu of all months, then select the month you want. Next, click the year to display up and down arrows, and then select or key the year you want. You can also click in the Date box and key the start date in day/month/year format.

Another Way Reader Aid

Screen Images with Callouts

5. Click **Done** at the bottom of the pane.
PAUSE. LEAVE the project plan open to use in the next exercise.

In this exercise, you specified a start date for your project. You can schedule a project from either the start date or the end date, but not both. Most projects should be scheduled from a start date. Scheduling from a start date causes all tasks to start as soon as possible, and it gives you the greatest scheduling flexibility. Scheduling from a finish date can be helpful in determining when a project must start if the finish date is fixed.

Saving the Newly Created Project Plan

Once you have created a new project plan and specified the start date, you need to save the plan.

SAVE THE PROJECT PLAN

USE the project plan you created in the previous exercise.

1. On the Standard toolbar, click the **Save** button. Because you have not previously saved the project plan, the Save As dialog box appears. By default, the My Documents folder is displayed.

2. Locate and select the solutions folder for this lesson as directed by your instructor.

3. In the File name box, key **Don Funk Music Video 1.**

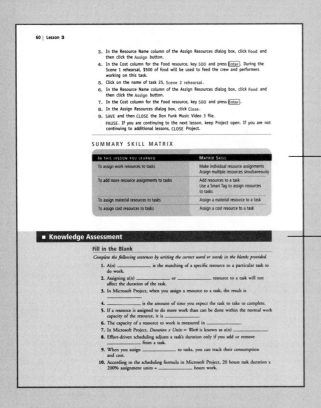

Summary Skill Matrix

Knowledge Assessment Questions

Competency Assessment Projects

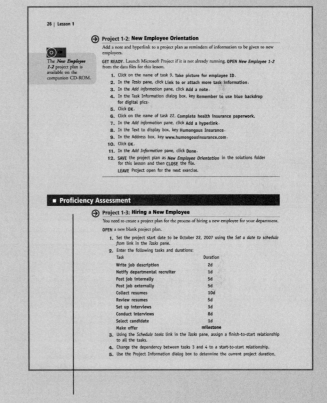

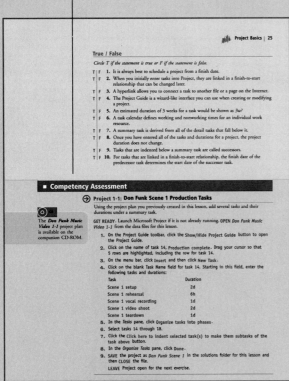

Proficiency Assessment Projects

Mastery Assessment Projects

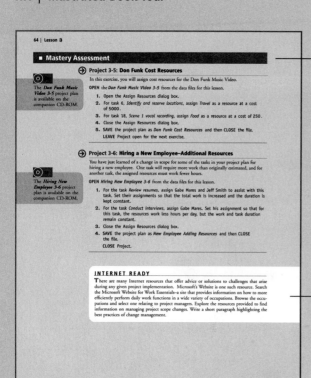

Internet Ready Project

Circling Back Projects

Workplace Ready Scenario

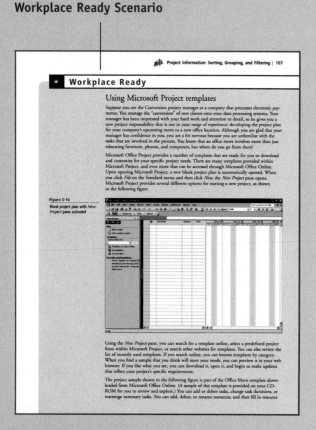

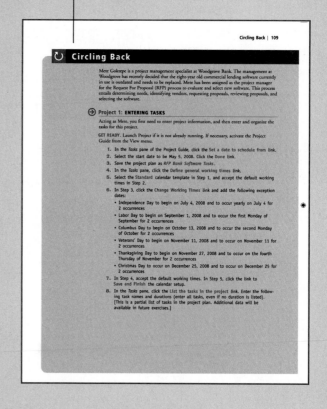

Conventions and Features Used in This Book

This book uses particular fonts, symbols, and heading conventions to highlight important information or to call your attention to special steps. For more information about the features in each lesson, refer to the Illustrated Book Tour section.

CONVENTION	MEANING
NEW FEATURE	This icon indicates a new or greatly improved Windows feature in this version of the software.
↓ **THE BOTTOM LINE**	This feature provides a brief summary of the material to be covered in the section that follows.
CLOSE	Words in all capital letters and in a different font color than the rest of the text indicate instructions for opening, saving, or closing files or programs. They also point out items you should check or actions you should take.
CERTIFICATION READY?	This feature signals the point in the text where a specific certification objective is covered. It provides you with a chance to check your understanding of that particular MCAS objective and, if necessary, review the section of the lesson where it is covered.
◎ **CD**	This indicates a file that is available on the student CD.
TAKE NOTE*	Reader aids appear in shaded boxes found in your text. *Take Note* provides helpful hints related to particular tasks or topics.
◈ **ANOTHER WAY**	*Another Way* provides an alternative procedure for accomplishing a particular task.
SHOOTING	*Troubleshooting* covers common problems and pitfalls.
X REF	These notes provide pointers to information discussed elsewhere in the textbook or describe interesting features of Project that are not directly addressed in the current topic or exercise.
SAVE 🖫	When a toolbar button is referenced in an exercise, the button's picture is shown in the margin.
Alt + Tab	A plus sign (+) between two key names means that you must press both keys at the same time. Keys that you are instructed to press in an exercise will appear in the font shown here.
A *cell* is the area where data is entered.	Key terms appear in bold italic.
Key My Name is.	Any text you are asked to key appears in color.
Click OK.	Any button on the screen you are supposed to click on or select will also appear in color.
OPEN *FitnessClasses*.	The names of data files will appear in bold, italic, and color for easy identification.

Instructor Support Program

The *Microsoft Official Academic Course* programs are accompanied by a rich array of resources that incorporate the extensive textbook visuals to form a pedagogically cohesive package. These resources provide all the materials instructors need to deploy and deliver their courses. Resources available online for download include:

- The **MSDN Academic Alliance** is designed to provide the easiest and most inexpensive developer tools, products, and technologies available to faculty and students in labs, classrooms, and on student PCs. A free 1-year membership is available to qualified MOAC adopters.

- The **Instructor's Guide** contains Solutions to all the textbook exercises, Syllabi for various term lengths, and Data Files for all the documents students need to work the exercises. The Instructor's Guide also includes chapter summaries and lecture notes. The Instructor's Guide is available from the Book Companion site (http://www.wiley.com/college/microsoft) and from Wiley*PLUS*.

- The **Test Bank** contains hundreds of multiple-choice, true-false, and short answer questions and is available to download from the Instructor's Book Companion site (http://www.wiley.com/college/microsoft) and from Wiley*PLUS*. A complete answer key is provided. It is available as a computerized test bank and in Microsoft Word format. The easy-to-use test-generation program fully supports graphics, print tests, student answer sheets, and answer keys. The software's advanced features allow you to create an exam to meet your exact specifications. The computerized test bank provides:

  - Varied question types to test a variety of comprehension levels—multiple-choice, true-false, and short answer.

  - Allows instructors to edit, randomize, and create questions freely.

  - Allows instructors to create and print different versions of a quiz or exam.

- **PowerPoint Presentations and Images.** A complete set of PowerPoint presentations is available on the Instructor's Book Companion site (http://www.wiley.com/college/microsoft) and in Wiley*PLUS* to enhance classroom presentations. Approximately 50 PowerPoint slides are provided for each lesson. Tailored to the text's topical coverage and Skills Matrix, these presentations are designed to convey key Project concepts addressed in the text.

  All figures from the text are on the Instructor's Book Companion site (http://www.wiley.com/college/microsoft) and in Wiley*PLUS*. You can incorporate them into your PowerPoint presentations, or create your own overhead transparencies and handouts.

  By using these visuals in class discussions, you can help focus students' attention on key elements of Project and help them understand how to use it effectively in the workplace.

- **Microsoft Business Certification Pre-Test and Exams (U.S. & Canada only).** With each MOAC textbook, students receive information allowing them to access a Pre-Test, Score Report, and Learning Plan, either directly from Certiport, one of Microsoft's exam delivery partners, or through links from Wiley*PLUS* Premium. They also receive a code and information for taking the certification exams.

- **The Wiley Faculty Network** lets you tap into a large community of your peers effortlessly. Wiley Faculty Network mentors are faculty like you, from educational institutions around the country, who are passionate about enhancing instructional efficiency and effectiveness through best practices. Faculty Network activities include technology training and tutorials, virtual seminars, peer-to-peer exchanges of experience and ideas, personal consulting, and sharing of resources. To register for a seminar, go to www.wherefacultyconnect.com or phone 1-866-4FACULTY (U.S. and Canada only).

Wiley*PLUS*

Broad developments in education over the past decade have influenced the instructional approach taken in the Microsoft Official Academic Course programs. The way that students learn, especially about new technologies, has changed dramatically in the Internet era. Electronic learning materials and Internet-based instruction is now as much a part of classroom instruction as printed textbooks. Wiley*PLUS* provides the technology to create an environment where students reach their full potential and experience academic success that will last them a lifetime!

Wiley*PLUS* is a powerful and highly-integrated suite of teaching and learning resources designed to bridge the gap between what happens in the classroom and what happens at home and on the job. Wiley*PLUS* provides instructors with the resources to teach their students new technologies and guide them to reach their goals of getting ahead in the job market by having the skills to become certified and advance in the workforce. For students, Wiley*PLUS* provides the tools for study and practice that are available to them 24/7, wherever and whenever they want to study. Wiley*PLUS* includes a complete online version of the student textbook; PowerPoint presentations; homework and practice assignments and quizzes; links to Microsoft's Pre-Test, Learning Plan, and a code for taking the certification exam (in Wiley*PLUS* Premium); image galleries; testbank questions; gradebook; and all the instructor resources in one easy-to-use website.

Organized around the everyday activities you and your students perform in the class, Wiley*PLUS* helps you:

- **Prepare & Present** outstanding class presentations using relevant PowerPoint slides and other Wiley*PLUS* materials—and you can easily upload and add your own.
- **Create Assignments** by choosing from questions organized by lesson, level of difficulty, and source—and add your own questions. Students' homework and quizzes are automatically graded, and the results are recorded in your gradebook.
- **Offer context-sensitive help to students, 24/7.** When you assign homework or quizzes, you decide if and when students get access to hints, solutions, or answers where appropriate—or they can be linked to relevant sections of their complete, online text for additional help whenever—and wherever they need it most.
- **Track Student Progress:** Analyze students' results and assess their level of understanding on an individual and class level using the Wiley*PLUS* gradebook, or export data to your own personal gradebook.
- **Administer Your Course:** Wiley*PLUS* can easily be integrated with another course management system, gradebook, or other resources you are using in your class, providing you with the flexibility to build your course, your way.
- **Seamlessly integrate all of the rich Wiley*PLUS* content and resources with WebCT and Blackboard**—with a single sign-on.

Please view our online demo at **www.wiley.com/college/wileyplus.** Here you will find additional information about the features and benefits of Wiley*PLUS*, how to request a "test drive" of Wiley*PLUS* for this title, and how to adopt it for class use.

MICROSOFT BUSINESS CERTIFICATION PRE-TEST AND EXAMS AVAILABLE THROUGH WILEY*PLUS* PREMIUM (US & CANADA ONLY)

Enhance your students' knowledge and skills and increase their performance on Microsoft Business Certification exams with adoption of the Microsoft Official Academic Course program for Microsoft Office Project.

With the majority of the workforce classified as *information workers*, certification on the 2007 Microsoft Office system is a critical tool in terms of validating the desktop computing knowledge and skills required to be more productive in the workplace. Certification is the primary tool companies use to validate the proficiency of desktop computing skills among employees. It gives organizations the ability to help assess employees' actual computer skills and select job candidates based on verifiable skills applying the latest productivity tools and technology.

Microsoft Pre-tests, delivered by Certiport, provide a simple, low-cost way for individuals to identify their desktop computing skill level. Pre-Tests are taken online, making the first step towards certification easy and convenient. Through the Pre-Tests, individuals can receive a custom learning path with recommended training.

To help students to study for and pass the Microsoft Certified Application Specialist, or MCAS exam, each MOAC textbook includes information allowing students to access a Pre-Test, Score Report, and Learning Plan, either directly from Certiport or through links from the Wiley*PLUS* Premium course. Students also receive a code and information for taking the certification exams. Students who do not have access to Wiley*PLUS* Premium can find information on how to purchase access to the Pre-Test and a code for taking the certification exams by clicking on their textbook at:

http://www.wiley.com/college/microsoft.

The Pre-Test can only be taken once. It provides a simple, low-cost way for students to evaluate and identify their skill level. Through the Pre-Test, students receive a recommended study plan that they can print out to help them prepare for the live certification exams. The Pre-Test is comprised of a variety of selected response questions, including matching, sequencing exercises, "hot spots" where students must identify an item or function, and traditional multiple-choice questions. After students have mastered all the certification objectives, they can use their code to take the actual Microsoft Certified Application Specialist (MCAS) exams for Office 2007.

Wiley*PLUS* Premium includes a complete online version of the student textbook, PowerPoint® presentations, homework and practice assignments and quizzes, links to Microsoft's Pre-Test, Learning Plan and a certification voucher, image galleries, test bank questions, gradebook, and all the instructor resources in one, easy-to-use website. Together, with Wiley*PLUS* and the MCAS Pre-Test and exams delivered by Certiport, we are creating the best of both worlds in academic learning and performance based validation in preparation for a great career and a globally recognized Microsoft certification—the higher education learning management system that accesses the industry-leading certification pre-test.

Contact your Wiley rep today about this special offer.

MSDN ACADEMIC ALLIANCE—FREE 1-YEAR MEMBERSHIP AVAILABLE TO QUALIFIED ADOPTERS!

MSDN Academic Alliance (MSDN AA) is designed to provide the easiest and most inexpensive way for universities to make the latest Microsoft developer tools, products, and technologies available in labs, classrooms, and on student PCs. MSDN AA is an annual membership program for departments teaching Science, Technology, Engineering, and Mathematics (STEM) courses. The membership provides a complete solution to keep academic labs, faculty, and students on the leading edge of technology.

Software available in the MSDN AA program is provided at no charge to adopting departments through the Wiley and Microsoft publishing partnership.

As a bonus to this free offer, faculty will be introduced to Microsoft's Faculty Connection and Academic Resource Center. It takes time and preparation to keep students engaged while giving them a fundamental understanding of theory, and the Microsoft Faculty Connection is designed to help STEM professors with this preparation by providing articles, curriculum, and tools that professors can use to engage and inspire today's technology students.

* Contact your Wiley rep for details.

For more information about the MSDN Academic Alliance program, go to:

http://msdn.microsoft.com/academic/

Important Web Addresses and Phone Numbers

To locate the Wiley Higher Education Rep in your area, go to the following Web address and click on the "*Who's My Rep?*" link at the top of the page.

http://www.wiley.com/college

Or Call the MOAC Toll Free Number: 1 + (888) 764-7001 (U.S. & Canada only).

To learn more about becoming a Microsoft Certified Application Specialist and exam availability, visit www.microsoft.com/learning/msbc.

Book Companion Website (www.wiley.com/college/microsoft)

The book companion site for the MOAC series includes the Instructor Resources, the student CD files, and Web links to important information for students and instructors.

Wiley*PLUS*

Wiley*PLUS* is a powerful and highly-integrated suite of teaching and learning resources designed to bridge the gap between what happens in the classroom and what happens at home and on the job. For students, Wiley*PLUS* provides the tools for study and practice that are available 24/7, wherever and whenever they want to study. Wiley*PLUS* includes a complete online version of the student textbook; PowerPoint presentations; homework and practice assignments and quizzes; links to Microsoft's Pre-Test, Learning Plan, and a code for taking the certification exam (in Wiley*PLUS* Premium); image galleries; test bank questions; gradebook; and all the instructor resources in one easy-to-use website.

Wiley*PLUS* provides immediate feedback on student assignments and a wealth of support materials. This powerful study tool will help your students develop their conceptual understanding of the class material and increase their ability to answer questions.

- A **Study and Practice** area links directly to text content, allowing students to review the text while they study and answer. Access to Microsoft's Pre-Test, Learning Plan, and a code for taking the MCAS certification exam is available in Study and Practice. Additional Practice Questions tied to the MCAS certification that can be re-taken as many times as necessary, are also available.

- An **Assignment** area keeps all the work you want your students to complete in one location, making it easy for them to stay on task. Students have access to a variety of interactive self-assessment tools, as well as other resources for building their confidence and understanding. In addition, all of the assignments and quizzes contain a link to the relevant section of the multimedia book, providing students with context-sensitive help that allows them to conquer obstacles as they arise.

- A **Personal Gradebook** for each student allows students to view their results from past assignments at any time.

Please view our online demo at www.wiley.com/college/wileyplus. Here you will find additional information about the features and benefits of Wiley*PLUS*, how to request a "test drive" of Wiley*PLUS* for this title, and how to adopt it for class use.

Student CD

The CD-ROM included with this book contains the practice files that you will use as you perform the exercises in the book. By using the practice files, you will not waste time creating the samples used in the lessons, and you can concentrate on learning how to use Microsoft Office Project. With the files and the step-by-step instructions in the lessons, you will learn by doing, which is an easy and effective way to acquire and remember new skills.

Copying the Practice Files

Your instructor might already have copied the practice files before you arrive in class. However, your instructor might ask you to copy the practice files on your own at the start of class. Also, if you want to work through any of the exercises in this book on your own at home or at your place of business, you may want to copy the practice files. Note that you can also open the files directly from the CD-ROM, but you should be cautious about carrying the CD-ROM around with you as it could become damaged.

1. Insert the CD-ROM in the CD-ROM drive of your computer.
2. Start Windows Explorer.
3. In the left pane of Explorer, locate the icon for your CD-ROM and click on this icon. The folders and files contained on the CD will appear listed on the right.
4. Locate and select the **Data** folder. This is the folder that contains all of the practice files, separated by Lesson folders.
5. Right-click on the **Data** folder and choose **Copy** from the menu.
6. In the left pane of Windows Explorer, choose the location to which you would like to copy the practice files. This can be a drive on your local PC or an external drive.
7. Right-click on the drive/location to which you want to copy the practice files and choose **Paste.** This will copy the entire Data folder to your chosen location.
8. Close Windows Explorer.

ANOTHER WAY

If you only want to copy the files for one lesson, you can open the Data folder and right-click the desired Lesson folder within the Data folder.

Deleting the Practice Files

Use the following steps when you want to delete the practice files from your hard disk or other drive. Your instructor might ask you to perform these steps at the end of class. Also, you should perform these steps if you have worked through the exercises at home or at your place of business and want to work through the exercises again. Deleting the practice files and then reinstalling them ensures that all files and folders are in their original condition if you decide to work through the exercises again.

1. Start Windows Explorer.
2. Browse through the drives and folders to locate the practice files.
3. Select the **Data** folder.
4. Right-click on the **Data** folder and choose **Delete** from the menu.
5. Close Windows Explorer.

Wiley Desktop Editions

Wiley MOAC Desktop Editions are innovative, electronic versions of printed textbooks. Students buy the desktop version for 60% off the U.S. price of the printed text, and get the added value of permanence and portability. Wiley Desktop Editions provide students with numerous additional benefits that are not available with other e-text solutions.

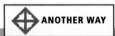

ANOTHER WAY

You can use the Search function in the Open dialog box to quickly find the specific file for which you are looking.

Wiley Desktop Editions are NOT subscriptions; students download the Wiley Desktop Edition to their computer desktops. Students own the content they buy to keep for as long as they want. Once a Wiley Desktop Edition is downloaded to the computer desktop, students have instant access to all of the content without being online. Students can also print out the sections they prefer to read in hard copy. Students also have access to fully integrated resources within their Wiley Desktop Edition. From highlighting their e-text to taking and sharing notes, students can easily personalize their Wiley Desktop Edition as they are reading or following along in class.

Preparing to Take the Microsoft Certified Application Specialist (MCAS) Exam

The Microsoft Certified Application Specialist program is part of the new and enhanced Microsoft Business Certifications. It is easily attainable through a series of verifications that provide a simple and convenient framework for skills assessment and validation.

For organizations, the new certification program provides better skills verification tools that help with assessing not only in-demand skills on the 2007 Microsoft Office system, but also the ability to quickly complete on-the-job tasks. Individuals will find it easier to identify and work towards the certification credential that meets their personal and professional goals.

To learn more about becoming a Microsoft Certified Application Specialist and exam availability, visit www.microsoft.com/learning/msbc.

Microsoft Certified Application Specialist (MCAS) Program

The core Microsoft Office Specialist credential has been upgraded to validate skills with the 2007 Microsoft Office system. The Application Specialist certifications target information workers and cover the most popular business applications such as Word 2007, PowerPoint 2007, Excel 2007, Access 2007, Outlook 2007 and Windows Vista.

By becoming certified, you demonstrate to employers that you have achieved a predictable level of skill in the use of a particular Office application or the Windows operating system. Employers often require certification either as a condition of employment or as a condition of advancement within the company or other organization. The certification examinations are sponsored by Microsoft but administered through exam delivery partners like Certiport.

Preparing to Take an Exam

Unless you are a very experienced user, you will need to use a test preparation course to prepare to complete the test correctly and within the time allowed. The *Microsoft Official Academic Course* series is designed to prepare you with a strong knowledge of all exam topics, and with some additional review and practice on your own. You should feel confident in your ability to pass the appropriate exam.

After you decide which exam to take, review the list of objectives for the exam. This list can be found in the MCAS Objectives Appendix at the back of this book. You can also easily identify tasks that are included in the objective list by locating the Lesson Skill Matrix at the start of each lesson and the Certification Ready sidebars in the margin of the lessons in this book.

To take the MCAS test, visit *www.microsoft.com/learning/msbc* to locate your nearest testing center. Then call the testing center directly to schedule your test. The amount of advance notice you should provide will vary for different testing centers, and it typically depends on the number of computers available at the testing center, the number of other testers who have already been scheduled for the day on which you want to take the test, and the number of times per week that the testing center offers MCAS testing. In general, you should call to schedule your test at least two weeks prior to the date on which you want to take the test.

When you arrive at the testing center, you might be asked for proof of identity. A driver's license or passport is an acceptable form of identification. If you do not have either of these items of documentation, call your testing center and ask what alternative forms of identification will be accepted. If you are retaking a test, bring your MCAS identification number, which will have been given to you when you previously took the test. If you have not prepaid or if your organization has not already arranged to make payment for you, you will need to pay the test-taking fee when you arrive.

Test Format

All MCAS certification tests are live, performance-based tests. There are no multiple-choice, true/false, or short-answer questions. Instructions are general: you are told the basic tasks to perform on the computer, but you aren't given any help in figuring out how to perform them. You are not permitted to use reference material other than the application's Help system.

As you complete the tasks stated in a particular test question, the testing software monitors your actions. An example question might be:

Open the file named *Wiley Guests* and select the word *Welcome* in the first paragraph. Change the font to 12 point, and apply bold formatting. Select the words *at your convenience* in the second paragraph, move them to the end of the first paragraph using drag and drop, and then center the first paragraph.

When the test administrator seats you at a computer, you will see an online form that you use to enter information about yourself (name, address, and other information required to process your exam results). While you complete the form, the software will generate the test from a master test bank and then prompt you to continue. The first test question will appear in a window. Read the question carefully, and then perform all the tasks stated in the test question. When you have finished completing all tasks for a question, click the Next Question button.

You have 45 to 60 minutes to complete all questions, depending on the test that you are taking. The testing software assesses your results as soon as you complete the test, and the test administrator can print the results of the test so that you will have a record of any tasks that you performed incorrectly. A passing grade is 75 percent or higher. If you pass, you will receive a certificate in the mail within two to four weeks. If you do not pass, you can study and practice the skills that you missed and then schedule to retake the test at a later date.

Tips for Successfully Completing the Test

The following tips and suggestions are the result of feedback received from many individuals who have taken one or more MCAS tests:

- Make sure that you are thoroughly prepared. If you have extensively used the application or operating system features for which you are being tested, you might feel confident that you are prepared for the test. However, the test might include questions that involve tasks that you rarely or never perform when you use the application at your place of business, at school, or at home. You must be knowledgeable in all the MCAS objectives for the test that you will take.

- Read each exam question carefully. An exam question might include several tasks that you are to perform. A partially correct response to a test question is counted as an incorrect response. In the example question on the previous page, you might apply bold formatting and move the words *at your convenience* to the correct location, but forget to center the first paragraph. This would count as an incorrect response and would result in a lower test score.

- You are allowed to use the application operating system's Help system, but relying on the Help system too much will slow you down and possibly prevent you from completing the test within the allotted time. Use the Help system only when necessary.

- Keep track of your time. The test does not display the amount of time that you have left, so you need to keep track of the time yourself by monitoring your start time and the required end time on your watch or a clock in the testing center (if there is one). The test program displays the number of items that you have completed along with the total number of test items (for example, "35 of 40 items have been completed"). Use this information to gauge your pace.

- If you skip a question, you cannot return to it later. You should skip a question only if you are certain that you cannot complete the tasks correctly.

- As soon as you are finished reading a question and you click in the application window, a condensed version of the instruction is displayed in a corner of the screen. If you are unsure whether you have completed all tasks stated in the test question, click the Instructions button on the test information bar at the bottom of the screen and then reread the question. Close the instruction window when you are finished. Do this as often as necessary to ensure you have read the question correctly and that you have completed all the tasks stated in the question.

If You Do Not Pass the Test

If you do not pass, you can use the assessment printout as a guide to practice the items that you missed. There is no limit to the number of times that you can retake a test; however, you must pay the fee each time that you take the test. When you retake the test, expect to see some of the same test items on the subsequent test; the test software randomly generates the test items from a master test bank before you begin the test. Also expect to see several questions that did not appear on the previous test.

Acknowledgments

MOAC Instructor Advisory Board

We would like thank to our Instructor Advisory Board, an elite group of educators who has assisted us every step of the way in building these products. Advisory Board members have acted as our sounding board on key pedagogical and design decisions leading to the development of these compelling and innovative textbooks for future Information Workers. Their dedication to technology education is truly appreciated.

Catherine Binder, Strayer University & Katharine Gibbs School–Philadelphia

Catherine currently works at both Katharine Gibbs School in Norristown, PA and Strayer University in King of Prussia, PA. Catherine has been at Katharine Gibbs School for 4 years. Catherine is currently the Department Chair/Lead instructor for PC Networking at Gibbs and the founder/advisor of the TEK Masters Society. Since joining Strayer University a year and a half ago she has risen in the ranks from adjunct to DIT/Assistant Campus Dean.

Catherine has brought her 10+ year's industry experience as Network Administrator, Network Supervisor, Professor, Bench Tech, Manager and CTO from such places as Foster Wheeler Corp, KidsPeace Inc., Victoria Vogue, TESST College, AMC Theatres, Blue Mountain Publishing and many more to her teaching venue.

Catherine began as an adjunct in the PC Networking department and quickly became a full-time instructor. At both schools she is in charge of scheduling, curricula and departmental duties. She happily advises about 80+ students and is committed to Gibbs/Strayer life, her students, and continuing technology education every day.

Penny Gudgeon, CDI College

Penny is the Program Manager for IT curriculum at Corinthian Colleges, Inc. Until January 2006, Penny was responsible for all Canadian programming and web curriculum for five years. During that time, Corinthian Colleges, Inc. acquired CDI College of Business and Technology in 2004. Before 2000 she spent four years as IT instructor at one of the campuses. Penny joined CDI College in 1997 after her working for 10 years first in programming and later in software productivity education. Penny previously has worked in the fields of advertising, sales, engineering technology and programming. When not working from her home office or indulging her passion for life long learning, and the possibilities of what might be, Penny likes to read mysteries, garden and relax at home in Hamilton, Ontario, with her Shih-Tzu, Gracie, and husband, Al.

Jana Hambruch, School District of Lee County

Ms. Hambruch currently serves as Director for the Information Technology Magnet Programs at The School District of Lee County in Ft Myers, Florida. She is responsible for the implementation and direction of three schools that fall under this grant program. This program has been recognized as one of the top 15 most innovative technology programs in the nation. She is also co-author of the grant proposal for the IT Magnet Grant prior to taking on the role of Director.

Ms. Hambruch has over ten years experience directing the technical certification training programs at many Colleges and Universities, including Barry University, the University of

South Florida, Broward Community College, and at Florida Gulf Coast University, where she served as the Director for the Center for Technology Education. She excels at developing alternative training models that focus on the tie between the education provider and the community in which it serves.

Ms. Hambruch is a past board member and treasurer of the Human Resources Management Association of SW Florida, graduate of Leadership Lee County Class of 2002, Steering Committee Member for Leadership Lee County Class of 2004 and a former board member of the Career Coalition of Southwest Florida. She has frequently lectured for organizations such as Microsoft, American Society of Training and Development, Florida Gulf Coast University, Florida State University, University of Nevada at Las Vegas, University of Wisconsin at Milwaukee, Canada's McGill University, and Florida's State Workforce Summit.

Dee Hobson, Richland College

Dee Hobson is currently a faculty member of the Business Office Systems and Support Division at Richland College. Richland is one of seven colleges in the Dallas County Community College District and has the distinction of being the first community college to receive the Malcolm Baldrige National Quality Award in 2005. Richland also received the Texas Award for Performance Excellence in 2005.

The Business Office Systems and Support Division at Richland is also a Certiport Authorized Microsoft Office testing center. All students enrolling in one of Microsoft's application software courses (Word, Excel, PowerPoint, and Access) are required to take the respective Microsoft certification exam at the end of the semester.

Dee has taught computer and business courses in K-12 public schools and at a proprietary career college in Dallas. She has also been involved with several corporate training companies and with adult education programs in the Dallas area. She began her computer career as an employee of IBM Corporation in St. Louis, Missouri. During her ten-year IBM employment, she moved to Memphis, Tennessee, to accept a managerial position and to Dallas, Texas, to work in a national sales and marketing technical support center.

Keith Hoell, Katharine Gibbs School–New York

Keith has worked in both non-profit and proprietary education for over 10 years, initially at St. John's University in New York, and then as full-time faculty, Chairperson and currently Dean of Information Systems at the Katharine Gibbs School in New York City. He also worked for General Electric in the late 80's and early 90's as the Sysop of a popular bulletin board dedicated to ASCII-Art on GE's pioneering GEnie on-line service before the advent of the World Wide Web. He has taught courses and workshops dealing with many mainstream IT issues and varied technology, especially those related to computer hardware and operating system software, networking, software applications, IT project management and ethics, and relational database technology. An avid runner and a member of The New York Road Runners, he won the Footlocker Five Borough Challenge representing Queens at the 2005 ING New York City Marathon while competing against the 4 other borough reps. He currently resides in Queens, New York.

Michael Taylor, Seattle Central Community College

Michael worked in education and training for the last 20 years in both the public and private sector. He currently teaches and coordinates the applications support program at Seattle Central Community College and also administers the Microsoft IT Academy. His experience outside the educational world is in Travel and Tourism with wholesale tour operations and cruise lines.

Interests outside of work include greyhound rescue. (He adopted 3 x-racers who bring him great joy.) He also enjoys the arts and is fortunate to live in downtown Seattle where there is much to see and do.

MOAC Office 2007 and Project Reviewers

We also thank the many reviewers who pored over the manuscript, providing invaluable feedback in the service of quality instructional materials.

Access
Susan Fry, Boise State University
Leslie Jernberg, Eastern Idaho Technical College
Dr. Deborah Jones, South Georgia Technical College
Suzanne Marks, Bellevue Community College
Kim Styles, Tri-County Technical College & Anderson School District 5
Fred Usmani, Conestoga College

Excel
Bob Gunderson, TriOS College
Christie Hovey, Lincoln Land Community College
Barbara Lave, Portland Community College
Trevor McIvor, Bow Valley College
Donna Madsen, Kirkwood Community College
James M. Veneziano, Davenport University—Caro
Dorothy Weiner, Manchester Community College

PowerPoint
Barbara Gillespie, Cuyamaca College
Caroline de Gruchy, Conestoga College
Tatyana Pashnyak, Bainbridge College
Michelle Poertner, Northwestern Michigan College
Janet Sebesy, Cuyahoga Community College

Outlook
Julie Boyles, Portland Community College
Joe LaMontagne, Davenport University—Grand Rapids
Randy Nordell, American River College
Echo Rantanen, Spokane Community College
Lyndsey Webster, TriOS College

Project
Janis DeHaven, Central Community College
Dr. Susan Jennings, Stephen F. Austin State University
Jack Maronowski, Curriculum Director, CDI College
Diane D. Mickey, Northern Virginia Community College
Linda Nutter, Peninsula College
Marika Reinke, Bellevue Community College

Vista
Gary Genereaux, Fanshawe College
Debi Griggs, Bellevue Community College
Katherine James, Seneca College
Diane Mickey, Northern Virginia Community College
Sue Miner, Lehigh Carbon Community College

Word
Diana Anderson, Big Sandy Community & Technical College
Donna Hendricks, South Arkansas Community College
Dr. Donna McGill-Cameron, Yuba Community College—Woodland Campus
Patricia McMahon, South Suburban College
Jack Maronowski, Curriculum Director, CDI College
Nancy Noe, Linn-Benton Community College
Teresa Roberts, Wilson Technical Community College

xxxii | Acknowledgments

Focus Group and Survey Participants

Finally, we thank the hundreds of instructors who participated in our focus groups and surveys to ensure that the Microsoft Official Academic Courses best met the needs of our customers.

Jean Aguilar, Mt. Hood Community College
Konrad Akens, Zane State College
Michael Albers, University of Memphis
Diana Anderson, Big Sandy Community & Technical College
Phyllis Anderson, Delaware County Community College
Judith Andrews, Feather River College
Damon Antos, American River College
Bridget Archer, Oakton Community College
Linda Arnold, Harrisburg Area Community College–Lebanon Campus
Neha Arya, Fullerton College
Mohammad Bajwa, Katharine Gibbs School–New York
Virginia Baker, University of Alaska Fairbanks
Carla Bannick, Pima Community College
Rita Barkley, Northeast Alabama Community College
Elsa Barr, Central Community College – Hastings
Ronald W. Barry, Ventura County Community College District
Elizabeth Bastedo, Central Carolina Technical College
Karen Baston, Waubonsee Community College
Karen Bean, Blinn College
Scott Beckstrand, Community College of Southern Nevada
Paulette Bell, Santa Rosa Junior College
Liz Bennett, Southeast Technical Institute
Nancy Bermea, Olympic College
Lucy Betz, Milwaukee Area Technical College
Meral Binbasioglu, Hofstra University
Catherine Binder, Strayer University & Katharine Gibbs School–Philadelphia
Terrel Blair, El Centro College
Ruth Blalock, Alamance Community College
Beverly Bohner, Reading Area Community College
Henry Bojack, Farmingdale State University
Matthew Bowie, Luna Community College
Julie Boyles, Portland Community College
Karen Brandt, College of the Albemarle
Stephen Brown, College of San Mateo
Jared Bruckner, Southern Adventist University
Pam Brune, Chattanooga State Technical Community College
Sue Buchholz, Georgia Perimeter College
Roberta Buczyna, Edison College
Angela Butler, Mississippi Gulf Coast Community College
Rebecca Byrd, Augusta Technical College
Kristen Callahan, Mercer County Community College
Judy Cameron, Spokane Community College
Dianne Campbell, Athens Technical College
Gena Casas, Florida Community College at Jacksonville
Jesus Castrejon, Latin Technologies
Gail Chambers, Southwest Tennessee Community College

Jacques Chansavang, Indiana University–Purdue University Fort Wayne
Nancy Chapko, Milwaukee Area Technical College
Rebecca Chavez, Yavapai College
Sanjiv Chopra, Thomas Nelson Community College
Greg Clements, Midland Lutheran College
Dayna Coker, Southwestern Oklahoma State University–Sayre Campus
Tamra Collins, Otero Junior College
Janet Conrey, Gavilan Community College
Carol Cornforth, West Virginia Northern Community College
Gary Cotton, American River College
Edie Cox, Chattahoochee Technical College
Rollie Cox, Madison Area Technical College
David Crawford, Northwestern Michigan College
J.K. Crowley, Victor Valley College
Rosalyn Culver, Washtenaw Community College
Sharon Custer, Huntington University
Sandra Daniels, New River Community College
Anila Das, Cedar Valley College
Brad Davis, Santa Rosa Junior College
Susan Davis, Green River Community College
Mark Dawdy, Lincoln Land Community College
Jennifer Day, Sinclair Community College
Carol Deane, Eastern Idaho Technical College
Julie DeBuhr, Lewis-Clark State College
Janis DeHaven, Central Community College
Drew Dekreon, University of Alaska–Anchorage
Joy DePover, Central Lakes College
Salli DiBartolo, Brevard Community College
Melissa Diegnau, Riverland Community College
Al Dillard, Lansdale School of Business
Marjorie Duffy, Cosumnes River College
Sarah Dunn, Southwest Tennessee Community College
Shahla Durany, Tarrant County College–South Campus
Kay Durden, University of Tennessee at Martin
Dineen Ebert, St. Louis Community College–Meramec
Donna Ehrhart, State University of New York–Brockport
Larry Elias, Montgomery County Community College
Glenda Elser, New Mexico State University at Alamogordo
Angela Evangelinos, Monroe County Community College
Angie Evans, Ivy Tech Community College of Indiana
Linda Farrington, Indian Hills Community College
Dana Fladhammer, Phoenix College
Richard Flores, Citrus College
Connie Fox, Community and Technical College at Institute of Technology West Virginia University
Wanda Freeman, Okefenokee Technical College
Brenda Freeman, Augusta Technical College

Susan Fry, Boise State University
Roger Fulk, Wright State University–Lake Campus
Sue Furnas, Collin County Community College District
Sandy Gabel, Vernon College
Laura Galvan, Fayetteville Technical Community College
Candace Garrod, Red Rocks Community College
Sherrie Geitgey, Northwest State Community College
Chris Gerig, Chattahoochee Technical College
Barb Gillespie, Cuyamaca College
Jessica Gilmore, Highline Community College
Pamela Gilmore, Reedley College
Debbie Glinert, Queensborough Community College
Steven Goldman, Polk Community College
Bettie Goodman, C.S. Mott Community College
Mike Grabill, Katharine Gibbs School–Philadelphia
Francis Green, Penn State University
Walter Griffin, Blinn College
Fillmore Guinn, Odessa College
Helen Haasch, Milwaukee Area Technical College
John Habal, Ventura College
Joy Haerens, Chaffey College
Norman Hahn, Thomas Nelson Community College
Kathy Hall, Alamance Community College
Teri Harbacheck, Boise State University
Linda Harper, Richland Community College
Maureen Harper, Indian Hills Community College
Steve Harris, Katharine Gibbs School–New York
Robyn Hart, Fresno City College
Darien Hartman, Boise State University
Gina Hatcher, Tacoma Community College
Winona T. Hatcher, Aiken Technical College
BJ Hathaway, Northeast Wisconsin Tech College
Cynthia Hauki, West Hills College – Coalinga
Mary L. Haynes, Wayne County Community College
Marcie Hawkins, Zane State College
Steve Hebrock, Ohio State University Agricultural Technical Institute
Sue Heistand, Iowa Central Community College
Heith Hennel, Valencia Community College
Donna Hendricks, South Arkansas Community College
Judy Hendrix, Dyersburg State Community College
Gloria Hensel, Matanuska-Susitna College University of Alaska Anchorage
Gwendolyn Hester, Richland College
Tammarra Holmes, Laramie County Community College
Dee Hobson, Richland College
Keith Hoell, Katharine Gibbs School–New York
Pashia Hogan, Northeast State Technical Community College
Susan Hoggard, Tulsa Community College
Kathleen Holliman, Wallace Community College Selma
Chastity Honchul, Brown Mackie College/Wright State University
Christie Hovey, Lincoln Land Community College
Peggy Hughes, Allegany College of Maryland

Sandra Hume, Chippewa Valley Technical College
John Hutson, Aims Community College
Celia Ing, Sacramento City College
Joan Ivey, Lanier Technical College
Barbara Jaffari, College of the Redwoods
Penny Jakes, University of Montana College of Technology
Eduardo Jaramillo, Peninsula College
Barbara Jauken, Southeast Community College
Susan Jennings, Stephen F. Austin State University
Leslie Jernberg, Eastern Idaho Technical College
Linda Johns, Georgia Perimeter College
Brent Johnson, Okefenokee Technical College
Mary Johnson, Mt. San Antonio College
Shirley Johnson, Trinidad State Junior College–Valley Campus
Sandra M. Jolley, Tarrant County College
Teresa Jolly, South Georgia Technical College
Dr. Deborah Jones, South Georgia Technical College
Margie Jones, Central Virginia Community College
Randall Jones, Marshall Community and Technical College
Diane Karlsbraaten, Lake Region State College
Teresa Keller, Ivy Tech Community College of Indiana
Charles Kemnitz, Pennsylvania College of Technology
Sandra Kinghorn, Ventura College
Bill Klein, Katharine Gibbs School–Philadelphia
Bea Knaapen, Fresno City College
Kit Kofoed, Western Wyoming Community College
Maria Kolatis, County College of Morris
Barry Kolb, Ocean County College
Karen Kuralt, University of Arkansas at Little Rock
Belva-Carole Lamb, Rogue Community College
Betty Lambert, Des Moines Area Community College
Anita Lande, Cabrillo College
Junnae Landry, Pratt Community College
Karen Lankisch, UC Clermont
David Lanzilla, Central Florida Community College
Nora Laredo, Cerritos Community College
Jennifer Larrabee, Chippewa Valley Technical College
Debra Larson, Idaho State University
Barb Lave, Portland Community College
Audrey Lawrence, Tidewater Community College
Deborah Layton, Eastern Oklahoma State College
Larry LeBlanc, Owen Graduate School–Vanderbilt University
Philip Lee, Nashville State Community College
Michael Lehrfeld, Brevard Community College
Vasant Limaye, Southwest Collegiate Institute for the Deaf – Howard College
Anne C. Lewis, Edgecombe Community College
Stephen Linkin, Houston Community College
Peggy Linston, Athens Technical College
Hugh Lofton, Moultrie Technical College
Donna Lohn, Lakeland Community College
Jackie Lou, Lake Tahoe Community College
Donna Love, Gaston College

Curt Lynch, Ozarks Technical Community College
Sheilah Lynn, Florida Community College–Jacksonville
Pat R. Lyon, Tomball College
Bill Madden, Bergen Community College
Heather Madden, Delaware Technical &
    Community College
Donna Madsen, Kirkwood Community College
Jane Maringer-Cantu, Gavilan College
Suzanne Marks, Bellevue Community College
Carol Martin, Louisiana State University–Alexandria
Cheryl Martucci, Diablo Valley College
Roberta Marvel, Eastern Wyoming College
Tom Mason, Brookdale Community College
Mindy Mass, Santa Barbara City College
Dixie Massaro, Irvine Valley College
Rebekah May, Ashland Community & Technical College
Emma Mays-Reynolds, Dyersburg State
    Community College
Timothy Mayes, Metropolitan State College of Denver
Reggie McCarthy, Central Lakes College
Matt McCaskill, Brevard Community College
Kevin McFarlane, Front Range Community College
Donna McGill, Yuba Community College
Terri McKeever, Ozarks Technical Community College
Patricia McMahon, South Suburban College
Sally McMillin, Katharine Gibbs School–Philadelphia
Charles McNerney, Bergen Community College
Lisa Mears, Palm Beach Community College
Imran Mehmood, ITT Technical Institute–King of
    Prussia Campus
Virginia Melvin, Southwest Tennessee Community College
Jeanne Mercer, Texas State Technical College
Denise Merrell, Jefferson Community & Technical College
Catherine Merrikin, Pearl River Community College
Diane D. Mickey, Northern Virginia Community College
Darrelyn Miller, Grays Harbor College
Sue Mitchell, Calhoun Community College
Jacquie Moldenhauer, Front Range Community College
Linda Motonaga, Los Angeles City College
Sam Mryyan, Allen County Community College
Cindy Murphy, Southeastern Community College
Ryan Murphy, Sinclair Community College
Sharon E. Nastav, Johnson County Community College
Christine Naylor, Kent State University Ashtabula
Haji Nazarian, Seattle Central Community College
Nancy Noe, Linn-Benton Community College
Jennie Noriega, San Joaquin Delta College
Linda Nutter, Peninsula College
Thomas Omerza, Middle Bucks Institute of Technology
Edith Orozco, St. Philip's College
Dona Orr, Boise State University
Joanne Osgood, Chaffey College
Janice Owens, Kishwaukee College
Tatyana Pashnyak, Bainbridge College

John Partacz, College of DuPage
Tim Paul, Montana State University–Great Falls
Joseph Perez, South Texas College
Mike Peterson, Chemeketa Community College
Dr. Karen R. Petitto, West Virginia Wesleyan College
Terry Pierce, Onandaga Community College
Ashlee Pieris, Raritan Valley Community College
Jamie Pinchot, Thiel College
Michelle Poertner, Northwestern Michigan College
Betty Posta, University of Toledo
Deborah Powell, West Central Technical College
Mark Pranger, Rogers State University
Carolyn Rainey, Southeast Missouri State University
Linda Raskovich, Hibbing Community College
Leslie Ratliff, Griffin Technical College
Mar-Sue Ratzke, Rio Hondo Community College
Roxy Reissen, Southeastern Community College
Silvio Reyes, Technical Career Institutes
Patricia Rishavy, Anoka Technical College
Jean Robbins, Southeast Technical Institute
Carol Roberts, Eastern Maine Community College
    and University of Maine
Teresa Roberts, Wilson Technical Community College
Vicki Robertson, Southwest Tennessee Community College
Betty Rogge, Ohio State Agricultural Technical Institute
Lynne Rusley, Missouri Southern State University
Claude Russo, Brevard Community College
Ginger Sabine, Northwestern Technical College
Steven Sachs, Los Angeles Valley College
Joanne Salas, Olympic College
Lloyd Sandmann, Pima Community College–Desert
    Vista Campus
Beverly Santillo, Georgia Perimeter College
Theresa Savarese, San Diego City College
Sharolyn Sayers, Milwaukee Area Technical College
Judith Scheeren, Westmoreland County
    Community College
Adolph Scheiwe, Joliet Junior College
Marilyn Schmid, Asheville-Buncombe Technical
    Community College
Janet Sebesy, Cuyahoga Community College
Phyllis T. Shafer, Brookdale Community College
Ralph Shafer, Truckee Meadows Community College
Anne Marie Shanley, County College of Morris
Shelia Shelton, Surry Community College
Merilyn Shepherd, Danville Area Community College
Susan Sinele, Aims Community College
Beth Sindt, Hawkeye Community College
Andrew Smith, Marian College
Brenda Smith, Southwest Tennessee Community College
Lynne Smith, State University of New York–Delhi
Rob Smith, Katharine Gibbs School–Philadelphia
Tonya Smith, Arkansas State University–Mountain Home
Del Spencer – Trinity Valley Community College

Jeri Spinner, Idaho State University

Eric Stadnik, Santa Rosa Junior College

Karen Stanton, Los Medanos College

Meg Stoner, Santa Rosa Junior College

Beverly Stowers, Ivy Tech Community College of Indiana

Marcia Stranix, Yuba College

Kim Styles, Tri-County Technical College

Sylvia Summers, Tacoma Community College

Beverly Swann, Delaware Technical & Community College

Ann Taff, Tulsa Community College

Mike Theiss, University of Wisconsin–Marathon Campus

Romy Thiele, Cañada College

Sharron Thompson, Portland Community College

Ingrid Thompson-Sellers, Georgia Perimeter College

Barbara Tietsort, University of Cincinnati–Raymond
    Walters College

Janine Tiffany, Reading Area Community College

Denise Tillery, University of Nevada Las Vegas

Susan Trebelhorn, Normandale Community College

Noel Trout, Santiago Canyon College

Cheryl Turgeon, Asnuntuck Community College

Steve Turner, Ventura College

Sylvia Unwin, Bellevue Community College

Lilly Vigil, Colorado Mountain College

Sabrina Vincent, College of the Mainland

Mary Vitrano, Palm Beach Community College

Brad Vogt, Northeast Community College

Cozell Wagner, Southeastern Community College

Carolyn Walker, Tri-County Technical College

Sherry Walker, Tulsa Community College

Qi Wang, Tacoma Community College

Betty Wanielista, Valencia Community College

Marge Warber, Lanier Technical College–Forsyth Campus

Marjorie Webster, Bergen Community College

Linda Wenn, Central Community College

Mark Westlund, Olympic College

Carolyn Whited, Roane State Community College

Winona Whited, Richland College

Jerry Wilkerson, Scott Community College

Joel Willenbring, Fullerton College

Barbara Williams, WITC Superior

Charlotte Williams, Jones County Junior College

Bonnie Willy, Ivy Tech Community College of Indiana

Diane Wilson, J. Sargeant Reynolds Community College

James Wolfe, Metropolitan Community College

Marjory Wooten, Lanier Technical College

Mark Yanko, Hocking College

Alexis Yusov, Pace University

Naeem Zaman, San Joaquin Delta College

Kathleen Zimmerman, Des Moines Area
    Community College

We would also like to thank Lutz Ziob, Sanjay Advani, Jim DiIanni, Merrick Van Dongen, Jim LeValley, Bruce Curling, Joe Wilson, and Naman Kahn at Microsoft for their encouragement and support in making the Microsoft Official Academic Course programs the finest instructional materials for mastering the newest Microsoft technologies for both students and instructors.

Brief Contents

Preface   ix

1   Project Basics   1

2   Establishing Resources   29

3   Resource and Task Assignments   48

4   Refining Your Project Plan   65

5   Project Information: Sorting, Grouping, and Filtering   91

     ↻ **Circling Back   109**

6   Project Plan Formatting–Fundamentals   113

7   Project Information: Customizing and Printing   132

8   Project Plan Tracking–Fundamentals   146

9   Managing Multiple Projects   165

10   Integrating Microsoft Project with Other Programs   178

     ↻ **Circling Back   192**

11   Fine-Tuning Tasks   195

12   Fine-Tuning Resources   208

13   Project Plan Optimization   228

14   Advanced Project Plan Formatting   249

15   Advanced Project Plan Tracking   266

16   Working with Resource Pools   289

17   Customizing Microsoft Project   310

     ↻ **Circling Back   325**

Glossary   330

Index   334

Contents

Lesson 1: Project Basics   1

Lesson Skill Matrix   1
Key Terms   2
Software Orientation   2
Starting Microsoft Project Standard   3
Creating a Project Plan   5
   Opening a New Project Plan   5
   Specifying the Project's Start Date   5
   Saving the Newly Created Project Plan   6
Defining Project Calendars   7
Entering Tasks and Task Details   9
   Entering Tasks   9
Software Orientation   11
   Estimating Durations   11
   Creating a Milestone   13
Organizing Tasks Into Phases   14
Linking Tasks   16
   Linking Two Tasks   17
   Linking Several Tasks   18
   Linking Milestones   19
Documenting Tasks   20
   Entering Task Notes   21
   Adding a Hyperlink   22
Reviewing the Project Plan's Duration   22
Summary Skill Matrix   24
Assessment   24
   Knowledge Assessment   24
   Competency Assessment   25
   Proficiency Assessment   26
   Mastery Assessment   27
Internet Ready   28

Lesson 2: Establishing Resources   29

Lesson Skill Matrix   29
Key Terms   29
Software Orientation   30
Establishing People Resources   31
   Establishing Individual People Resources   31
   Establishing a Group Resource   32
Establishing Equipment Resources   33
Establishing Material Resources   35

Establishing Cost Resources   36
Establishing Resource Pay Rates   37
Adjusting Resource Working Times   39
   Establishing Nonworking Times   39
   Establishing Specific Work Schedules   40
Adding Resource Notes   42
Summary Skill Matrix   42
Assessment   43
   Knowledge Assessment   43
   Competency Assessment   45
   Proficiency Assessment   46
   Mastery Assessment   47
Internet Ready   47

Lesson 3: Resource and Task Assignments   48

Lesson Skill Matrix   48
Key Terms   48
Software Orientation   49
Assigning Work Resources to Tasks   50
   Making Individual Resource Assignments   50
   Assigning Multiple Resources Simultaneously   52
Adding More Resource Assignments to Tasks   53
   Adding Resources to a Task   53
   Using a Smart Tag to Assign Resources   55
Assigning Material Resources to Tasks   58
Assigning Cost Resources to Tasks   59
Summary Skill Matrix   60
Assessment   60
   Knowledge Assessment   60
   Competency Assessment   62
   Proficiency Assessment   63
   Mastery Assessment   64
Internet Ready   64

Lesson 4: Refining Your Project Plan   65

Lesson Skill Matrix   65
Key Terms   65
Software Orientation   66

Applying a Task Calendar to an Individual Task 66

Changing Task Types 69
Using the Scheduling Formula to Change Task Types 69
Using the Task Information Dialog Box to Change
a Task Type 71

Splitting a Task 72

Establishing Recurring Tasks 74
Setting Up a Recurring Task 74
Assigning Resources to a Recurring Task 76

Applying Task Constraints 77

Reviewing the Project's Critical Path 81

Viewing Resource Allocations Over Time 83

Summary Skill Matrix 87

Assessment 87
Knowledge Assessment 87
Competency Assessment 88
Proficiency Assessment 89
Mastery Assessment 90

Internet Ready 90

Lesson 5: Project Information: Sorting, Grouping, and Filtering 91

Lesson Skill Matrix 91

Key Terms 91

Software Orientation 92

Sorting Data 92

Grouping Data 96

Filtering Data 99
Creating and Applying a Filter 99
Creating a Custom Filter 101

Summary Skill Matrix 102

Assessment 102
Knowledge Assessment 102
Competency Assessment 104
Proficiency Assessment 105
Mastery Assessment 105

Internet Ready 106

Workplace Ready 107

Circling Back 109

Lesson 6: Project Plan Formatting– Fundamentals 113

Lesson Skill Matrix 113

Key Terms 113

Software Orientation 114

Gantt Chart Formatting 114
Modifying the Gantt Chart Using the Bar Styles
Dialog Box 115
Modifying the Gantt Chart Using the Gantt
Chart Wizard 117

Drawing in a Gantt Chart 119

Changing Text Appearance in a View 121

Creating and Editing Tables 124

Creating Custom Views 126

Summary Skill Matrix 127

Assessment 127
Knowledge Assessment 127
Competency Assessment 128
Proficiency Assessment 129
Mastery Assessment 130

Internet Ready 131

Lesson 7: Project Information: Customizing and Printing 132

Lesson Skill Matrix 132

Key Terms 132

Software Orientation 133

Customizing and Printing a View 133

Customizing and Printing Reports 137

Summary Skill Matrix 140

Assessment 140
Knowledge Assessment 140
Competency Assessment 142
Proficiency Assessment 143
Mastery Assessment 144

Internet Ready 145

Lesson 8: Project Plan Tracking– Fundamentals 146

Lesson Skill Matrix 146

Key Terms 146

Software Orientation 147

Establishing a Project Baseline 147

Tracking a Project as Scheduled 150

**Entering the Completion Percentage for
a Task** 151

**Tasks and Assignments: Tracking Timephased
Actual Work** 153

Identifying Over Budget Tasks and Resources   156
Identifying Time and Schedule Problems   159
Summary Skill Matrix   161
Assessment   161
Knowledge Assessment   161
Competency Assessment   162
Proficiency Assessment   163
Mastery Assessment   164
Internet Ready   164

Lesson 9: Managing Multiple Projects   165

Lesson Skill Matrix   165
Key Terms   165
Software Orientation   166
Managing Consolidated Projects   166
Creating Dependencies Between Projects   169
Summary Skill Matrix   172
Assessment   173
Knowledge Assessment   173
Competency Assessment   174
Proficiency Assessment   175
Mastery Assessment   176
Internet Ready   177

Lesson 10: Integrating Microsoft Project with Other Programs   178

Lesson Skill Matrix   178
Key Terms   178
Software Orientation   179
Using a GIF Image to Display Project Information   179
Copying and Pasting with Microsoft Project   182
Using Other File Formats in Microsoft Project   184
Summary Skill Matrix   186
Assessment   187
Knowledge Assessment   187
Competency Assessment   188
Proficiency Assessment   189
Mastery Assessment   190
Internet Ready   191

Circling Back   192

Lesson 11: Fine-Tuning Tasks   195

Lesson Skill Matrix   195
Key Terms   195
Software Orientation   196
Managing Task Constraints and Dependencies   196
Setting Deadline Dates   199
Establishing Task Priorities   201
Summary Skill Matrix   202
Assessment   203
Knowledge Assessment   203
Competency Assessment   205
Proficiency Assessment   205
Mastery Assessment   206
Internet Ready   207

Lesson 12: Fine-Tuning Resources   208

Lesson Skill Matrix   208
Key Terms   208
Entering Material Resource Consumption Rates   209
Entering Costs Per Use for Resources   210
Assigning Multiple Pay Rates for a Resource   211
Apply Different Cost Rates to Assignments   213
Specifying Resource Availability at Different Times   214
Resolving Resource Overallocations Manually   216
Software Orientation   220
Leveling Overallocated Resources   221
Summary Skill Matrix   224
Assessment   224
Knowledge Assessment   224
Competency Assessment   225
Proficiency Assessment   226
Mastery Assessment   227
Internet Ready   227

Lesson 13: Project Plan Optimization   228

Lesson Skill Matrix   228
Key Terms   228
Software Orientation   229

Making Time and Date Adjustments 229

Viewing the Project's Critical Path 231

Delaying the Start of Assignments 234

Applying Contours to Assignments 235
Applying a Contour to a Resource Assignment 235
Manually Editing a Task Assignment 237

Optimizing the Project Plan 238
Identifying the Project Finish Date and Total Cost 239
Compressing the Project Plan 240

Summary Skill Matrix 244

Assessment 244
Knowledge Assessment 244
Competency Assessment 246
Proficiency Assessment 247
Mastery Assessment 248

Internet Ready 248

Lesson 14: Advanced Project Plan Formatting 249

Lesson Skill Matrix 249

Key Terms 249

Software Orientation 250

Customizing the Calendar View 250

Using Task IDs and WBS Codes 253

Formatting the Network Diagram 257

Customizing and Printing Reports 260

Summary Skill Matrix 262

Assessment 262
Knowledge Assessment 262
Competency Assessment 263
Proficiency Assessment 264
Mastery Assessment 265

Internet Ready 265

Lesson 15: Advanced Project Plan Tracking 266

Lesson Skill Matrix 266

Key Terms 266

Software Orientation 267

Recording Actual Start, Finish, and Duration Values of Tasks 268

Adjusting Remaining Work or Duration of Tasks 271

Rescheduling Uncompleted Work 274

Saving an Interim Plan 275

Comparing Baseline, Interim, and Actual Plans 276

Reporting Project Status 278

Evaluating Performance With Earned Value Analysis 280

Summary Skill Matrix 284

Assessment 284
Knowledge Assessment 284
Competency Assessment 286
Proficiency Assessment 287
Mastery Assessment 287

Internet Ready 288

Lesson 16: Working with Resource Pools 289

Lesson Skill Matrix 289

Key Terms 289

Software Orientation 290

Developing a Resource Pool 290

Viewing Assignment Details in a Resource Pool 294

Revising Assignments in a Sharer Plan 295

Updating Resource Information in a Resource Pool 297

Updating Working Time for All Projects in a Resource Pool 299

Adding New Project Plans to a Resource Pool 301

Revising a Sharer Plan and Updating a Resource Pool 302

Summary Skill Matrix 304

Assessment 305
Knowledge Assessment 305
Competency Assessment 306
Proficiency Assessment 307
Mastery Assessment 308

Internet Ready 309

Lesson 17: Customizing Microsoft Project 310

Lesson Skill Matrix 310

Key Terms 310

Software Orientation 311

Defining General Preferences 311

Working with Templates 313

Working with the Organizer 314

Working with Macros   318

Summary Skill Matrix   320

Assessment   320

   Knowledge Assessment   320

   Competency Assessment   321

   Proficiency Assessment   322

   Mastery Assessment   323

Internet Ready   323

Workplace Ready   324

Circling Back   325

Appendix A   329

Glossary   330

Index   334

www.wiley.com/college/microsoft *or*

call the MOAC Toll-Free Number: 1+(888) 764-7001 (U.S. & Canada only)

The first person to invent a car that runs on water…

… may be sitting right in your classroom! Every one of your students has the potential to make a difference. And realizing that potential starts right here, in your course.

When students succeed in your course—when they stay on-task and make the breakthrough that turns confusion into confidence—they are empowered to realize the possibilities for greatness that lie within each of them. We know your goal is to create an environment where students reach their full potential and experience the exhilaration of academic success that will last them a lifetime. WileyPLUS can help you reach that goal.

WileyPLUS is an online suite of resources—including the complete text—that will help your students:

- come to class better prepared for your lectures
- get immediate feedback and context-sensitive help on assignments and quizzes
- track their progress throughout the course

CERTIPORT
Achieve · Distinguish · Advance

And now, through WileyPLUS, Wiley is partnering with Certiport to create the best preparation possible for the Microsoft Certified Application Specialist (MCAS) examination. By combining the Microsoft Official Academic Course program for the 2007 Microsoft Office System with Microsoft's Assessment, Learning Plan, and Certification Examination Vouchers delivered by Certiport and WileyPLUS Premium, we are creating the best environment in academic learning for future success in the workplace. Together, Wiley and Certiport are supplying online performance-based training to help students prepare for the globally recognized Microsoft certification exams so they get that job they want.

www.wiley.com/college/wileyplus

80% of students surveyed said it improved their understanding of the material.*

FOR INSTRUCTORS

WileyPLUS is built around the activities you perform in your class each day. With WileyPLUS you can:

Prepare & Present

Create outstanding class presentations using a wealth of resources such as PowerPoint™ slides, image galleries, interactive simulations, and more. You can even add materials you have created yourself.

Create Assignments

Automate the assigning and grading of homework or quizzes by using the provided question banks, or by writing your own.

Keep track of your students' progress and analyze individual and overall class results.

Now Available with WebCT and Blackboard!

"It has been a great help, and I believe it has helped me to achieve a better grade."

Michael Morris,
Columbia Basin College

Track Student Progress

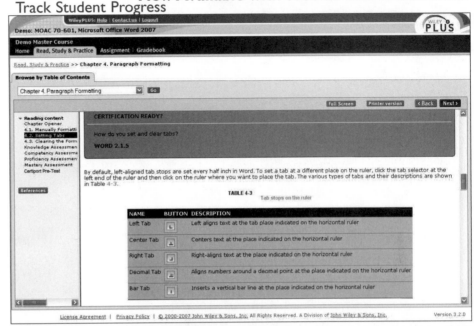

FOR STUDENTS

You have the potential to make a difference!

WileyPLUS is a powerful online system packed with features to help you make the most of your potential and get the best grade you can!

With WileyPLUS you get:

A complete online version of your text and other study resources.

•

Problem-solving help, instant grading, and feedback on your homework and quizzes.

•

The ability to track your progress and grades throughout the term.

•

Access to Microsoft's Assessment, Learning Plan, and MCAS examination voucher.

For more information on what WileyPLUS can do to help you and your students reach their potential, please visit www.wiley.com/college/wileyplus.

76% of students surveyed said it made them better prepared for tests.*

*Based on a survey of 972 student users of WileyPLUS

www.wiley.com/college/microsoft *or*
call the MOAC Toll-Free Number: 1+(888) 764-7001 (U.S. & Canada only)

Project Basics

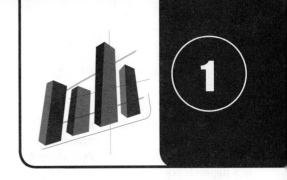

LESSON SKILL MATRIX

SKILLS	MATRIX SKILL
Starting Microsoft Project Standard	Start Microsoft Project
Creating a Project Plan	Open a new project plan Specify a start date Save the project plan
Defining Project Calendars	Define the project calendar
Entering Tasks and Task Details	Enter tasks Enter task durations Create a milestone
Organizing Tasks Into Phases	Create summary tasks
Linking Tasks	Link two tasks Link several tasks at once Link the milestone tasks
Documenting Tasks	Enter a task note Add a hyperlink
Reviewing the Project Plan's Duration	Check the project's duration

KEY TERMS

bottom-up planning
calendar
deliverable
dependency
duration
elapsed duration
Entry table
Gantt Chart view
hyperlink
link
milestone
note

phase
predecessor
Project Guide
project plan
risk
sequence
subtasks
successor
summary task
task
Task ID
top-down planning

Southridge Video is a video production and editing agency that works primarily with clients in the music industry to produce promotional videos for tours and full-length music videos for television play. Video production managers must identify the production tasks, plan and manage the schedule, and communicate project information to all the members of the production team. Microsoft Office Project is the perfect tool for managing a project such as this. In this lesson, you will learn how to create a new project plan, enter tasks, durations, and milestones into the plan, and organize the tasks in the plan.

■ SOFTWARE ORIENTATION

Microsoft Project's Opening Screen

Before you begin working in Project, you will need to be familiar with the primary user interface. When you first launch Microsoft Project, you will see a screen similar to that shown in Figure 1-1.

Figure 1-1

Project Opening Screen

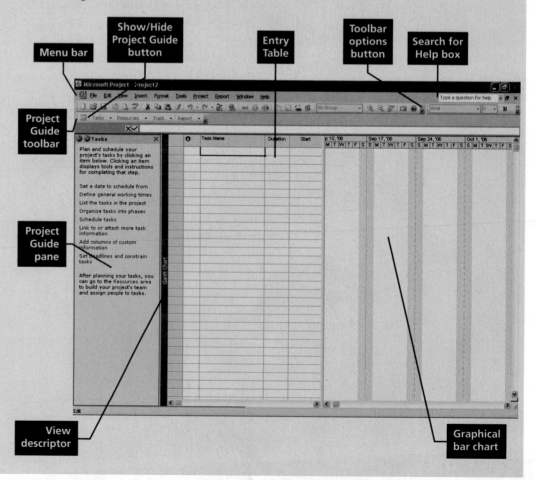

The features and options on this screen are those that are typically seen when you start Microsoft Project. Your screen may be different if default settings have been changed or if other preferences have been set. Use this figure as a reference for this lesson and through the rest of this book.

The view on this screen is known as the **Gantt Chart view**. It consists of a table (the **Entry table** by default) on the left side and a graphical bar chart on the right side.

The Project Guide and Project Guide Toolbar are vital to successful navigation in Microsoft Project. If they are not visible on your screen, click View on the menu bar and then click Turn on Project Guide.

■ Starting Microsoft Project Standard

THE BOTTOM LINE

In Microsoft Project, the documents that you use are referred to as projects or project plans.

➔ START MICROSOFT PROJECT

GET READY. Before you begin these steps, be sure to turn on or log on to your computer.

1. On the Windows taskbar, click the **Start** button. The Start menu appears.

2. On the Start menu, point to **All Programs** (in Microsoft Windows XP), point to **Microsoft Office**, and then click **Microsoft Office Project 2007**. Microsoft Project Standard opens.

3. On the menu bar, click **File,** and then click **New.** The *New Project* task pane opens. The *New Project* task pane contains a list of recently opened files as well as other means of creating new files. Your screen should look similar to Figure 1-2.

Figure 1-2

Microsoft Project *New Project* task pane

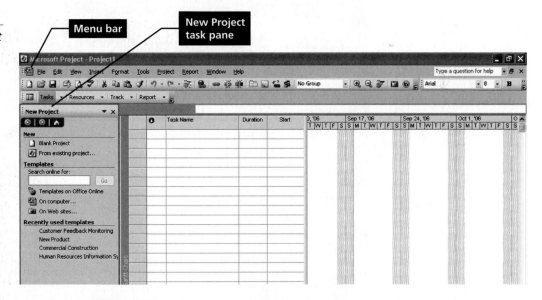

If the Project Guide toolbar and *Project Guide* pane are not visible on your screen, you may need to manually activate them. On the menu bar, click on View and then click Turn On Project Guide. Also, if a button you need is not immediately visible on the Standard toolbar, you may need to use the Toolbar Options button to bring a button into view. On the Standard toolbar, click on the Toolbar Options button to display a list of additional buttons, and then click on the desired button to add it to the Standard toolbar.

SHOOTING

4. In the *New Project* task pane, under the Templates heading, click **On computer**. The Templates dialog box appears.

5. Click the **Project Templates** tab. The Templates dialog box should look similar to Figure 1-3.

Figure 1-3

Microsoft Project 2007 Templates dialog box

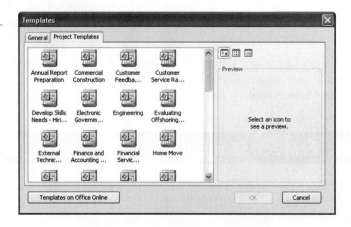

6. Click **Customer Feedback Monitoring**, and then click **OK**. Microsoft Project opens a project based on the Customer Feedback Monitoring template, closes the *New Project* task pane, and displays the Tasks activity list in the *Project Guide* pane. Your screen should look similar to Figure 1-4.

Figure 1-4

Project Plan based on Customer Feedback Monitoring template

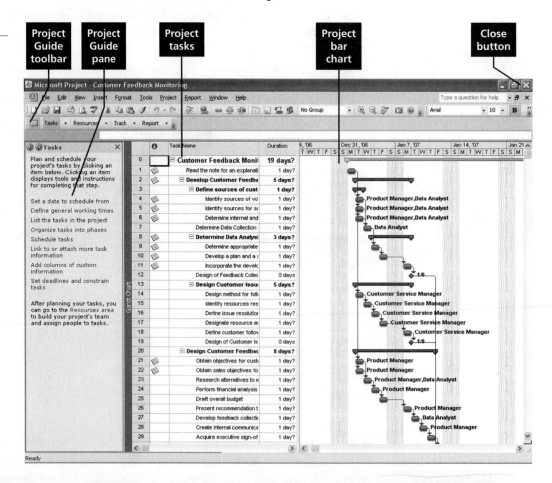

TAKE NOTE

The *Project Guide* is a wizard-like interface you can use when creating or modifying a project.

PAUSE. LEAVE Microsoft Project open for the next exercise.

You have just opened a project plan from a template in Microsoft Project. A ***project plan*** is a model of a real project–what you want to happen or what you think will happen. The plan contains tasks, resources, time frames, and costs that might be associated with such a project. You can modify this plan (or any other project template) to fit your specific project needs. Later in this lesson you will learn how to create a project plan from a blank template.

■ Creating a Project Plan

THE BOTTOM LINE

Microsoft Project is an active scheduling tool. You can create a new project plan using the Project Guide, specify the project's start date, and save the project plan.

Opening a New Project Plan

Rather than use a project plan template, you can create a new, blank project plan that you can fine-tune to your specific project.

⊕ OPEN A NEW PROJECT PLAN

GET READY. Before you begin these steps, **CLOSE** the Customer Feedback Monitoring project plan by clicking on the small black **X** in the upper right-hand corner of your screen and click **NO** when prompted to save. **LEAVE** Microsoft Project open.

1. On the menu bar, click **File** and then click **New**. The *New Project* task pane appears.
2. Under New, click **Blank Project**. A new blank project plan appears, and the *Tasks* pane of the Project Guide is activated.

ANOTHER WAY

If the Project Guide and *Tasks* pane are not active on your screen, Project automatically activates them when you click the New button.

PAUSE. LEAVE the project plan open to use in the next exercise.

In this exercise, you created a new project plan. Now you will begin to add details to the project plan, such as start date, tasks, and calendars. As you work through these exercises, you will frequently use the Project Guide to build your project. The **Project Guide** is a wizard-like interface that is divided into four subject areas: Tasks, Resources, Track, and Report. Each area guides you through the steps to create or update your project plan. Pay careful attention to the instructions, hints, and information provided in the Project Guide, as they will help you to build and manage your project effectively and efficiently.

Specifying the Project's Start Date

The first step of creating a new project plan is to specify the start date for the project.

⊕ SPECIFY A START DATE

TAKE NOTE

By default, Microsoft Project uses the current date as the project start date.

USE the project plan you opened in the previous exercise.

1. In the *Tasks* pane, click the **Set a date to schedule from** link. The *Enter project information* pane appears and displays a Date box.
2. Click the **arrow** next to the Date box. A small monthly calendar appears. For this exercise, you will change the project start date to January 7, 2008.

3. Click the left or right **arrow** until January 2008 is displayed, as shown in Figure 1-5.

Figure 1-5

Setting a project start date

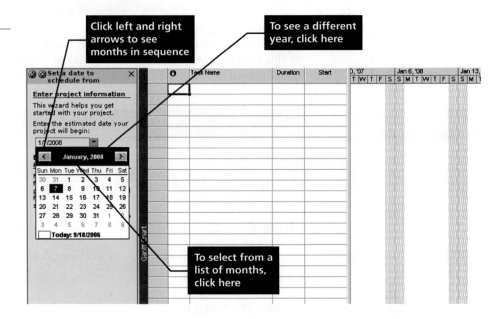

4. Click January 7.

 **ANOTHER WAY**

You can also quickly pick the date with the calendar. First, click on the name of the month to display a menu of all months, then select the month you want. Next, click the year to display up and down arrows, and then select or key the year you want. You can also click in the Date box and key the start date in day/month/year format.

5. Click **Done** at the bottom of the pane.

PAUSE. LEAVE the project plan open to use in the next exercise.

In this exercise, you specified a start date for your project. You can schedule a project from either the start date or the end date, but not both. Most projects should be scheduled from a start date. Scheduling from a start date causes all tasks to start as soon as possible, and it gives you the greatest scheduling flexibility. Scheduling from a finish date can be helpful in determining when a project must start if the finish date is fixed.

Saving the Newly Created Project Plan

Once you have created a new project plan and specified the start date, you need to save the plan.

→ SAVE THE PROJECT PLAN

USE the project plan you created in the previous exercise.

1. On the Standard toolbar, click the **Save** button. Because you have not previously saved the project plan, the Save As dialog box appears. By default, the My Documents folder is displayed.

2. Locate and select the solutions folder for this lesson as directed by your instructor.

3. In the File name box, key **Don Funk Music Video 1**.

4. Click **Save**. The Save As dialog box closes and the project plan is saved as *Don Funk Music Video 1*.

   PAUSE. LEAVE the project plan open to use in the next exercise.

In this exercise, you named and saved your project plan. It is important to get into the habit of saving your file frequently so that minimal information is lost should you experience a software or hardware malfunction.

 TAKE NOTE You can also have Microsoft Project save your project plan at specified intervals. On the Tools menu, click Options. In the Options dialog box, click the Save tab. Select the Save every check box and then specify the time interval at which you want Microsoft Project to automatically save your file.

■ Defining Project Calendars

↓ **THE BOTTOM LINE** Calendars determine how tasks and resources assigned to these tasks are scheduled. You can set your project calendar to reflect the working days and hours of your project, as well as nonworking times such as evenings, weekends, and holidays.

⊕ DEFINE THE PROJECT CALENDAR

USE the project plan you created in the previous exercise.

1. In the *Tasks* pane, click the **Define general working times** link. The *Project Working Times* task pane is displayed.

2. Click on the arrow next to the calendar template dropdown box. Select **Standard**, if necessary. Your screen should look similar to Figure 1-6.

Figure 1-6

Project Working times

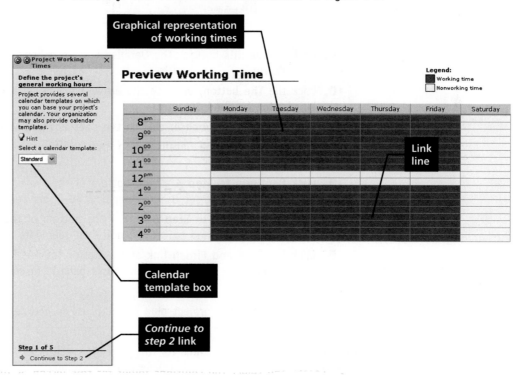

3. Click the **Continue to Step 2** link at the bottom of the pane. Checkboxes for Monday through Friday are selected under *Define the work week*. You will use these workdays for this project. You will also use the hours as shown in the preview window.

4. Click the **Continue to Step 3** link at the bottom of the pane.

5. Click the **Change Working Time** link under *Set Holidays and Days Off.* The Change Working Time dialog box appears.

6. Slide the button next to the calendar until the calendar is on January, 2008. Click the date box for **January 21**.

7. Click in the first **Name field** under the Exceptions tab and key **Martin Luther King Jr. Birthday Observed**.

8. Click the first **Start field.** The date 1/21/2008 will be displayed. Your screen should look similar to Figure 1-7.

Figure 1-7

Change Working Time
dialog box

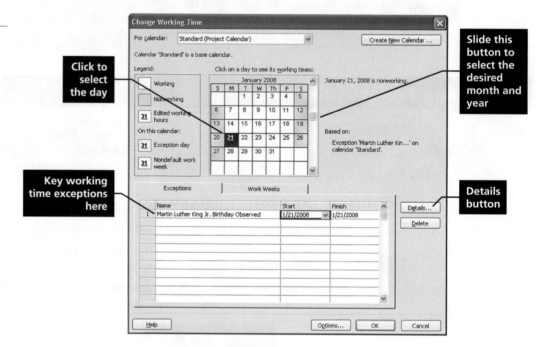

9. Click the **Details** button. The Details dialog box appears. Under *Recurrence pattern*, click **Yearly**.

10. Click the **The** button, and use the arrows next to each selection box to select **Third, Monday,** and **January**.

11. Under *Range of recurrence*, change the date in the **End by** box to **Mon 1/21/15**.

12. Click **OK** to close the Details dialog box, and then click **OK** to close the Change Working Time Box.

13. Click **Continue to Step 4** at the bottom of the *Project Working Times* pane. You will use the pre-set 8 hours per day, 40 hours per week, 20 days per month.

14. Click the **Continue to Step 5** link at the bottom of the *Project Working Times* pane. You do not need to define additional calendars now.

15. Click the **Save and Finish** link at the bottom of the *Project Working Times* pane. Your project plan is saved and the *Tasks* pane is displayed.

16. **SAVE** the project plan.

PAUSE. LEAVE the project plan open to use in the next exercise.

You have just defined the calendar for this project, as well as set up exception time (a holiday). A *calendar* is a scheduling tool that determines the standard working time and nonworking time (such as evening or holidays) for the project, resources, and tasks. Calendars are used to determine how tasks and resources assigned to these tasks are scheduled. Project uses four types of calendars:

- A *base calendar* specifies default working and nonworking times for a set of resources. It can serve as a project calendar or a task calendar. Microsoft Project provides three base calendars: Standard, 24-Hours, and Night Shift.
- A *project calendar* is the base calendar that is used for an entire project. It defines the normal working and nonworking times.
- A *resource calendar* defines working and nonworking times for an individual work resource.
- A *task calendar* is the base calendar you can use for individual tasks to manage the scheduling of these tasks. A task calendar defines working and nonworking times for a task, regardless of the settings in the project calendar.

X REF

You will learn more about base calendars, project calendars, and resource calendars in Lesson 2. You'll learn about task calendars in Lesson 4.

Project and task calendars are used in scheduling tasks. If resources are assigned to tasks, resource calendars are also used.

■ Entering Tasks and Task Details

 THE BOTTOM LINE

Tasks represent the actual individual work activities that must be done to accomplish the final goal, or *deliverable*, of a project. The tasks contain the details about each activity or event that must occur in order for your project to be completed. These details include the order and duration of tasks, critical tasks, and resource requirements.

Entering Tasks

Once you have created and saved a new project plan and defined the project's working times, you can begin to enter tasks. Tasks are the most basic building blocks of any project plan. You will enter a single task in each row of the Entry table.

→ ENTER TASKS

USE the project plan you created in the previous exercise.

1. In the *Tasks* pane of the Project Guide, click the **List the tasks in the project** link. The *List Tasks* pane appears.
2. Click the cell directly below the Task Name column heading.
3. Key **Review Screenplay** and press (Enter). Your screen should look similar to Figure 1-8.

Figure 1-8

Task list for Don Funk
Music Video 1

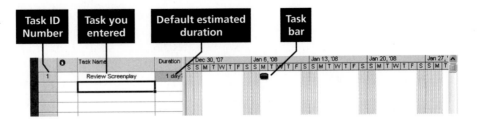

4. Enter the following task names below the Review Screenplay task name. Press Enter after each task name.

Develop scene blocking and schedule

Develop production layouts

Identify and reserve locations

Book musicians

Book dancers

Reserve audio recording equipment

Reserve video recording equipment

TAKE NOTE* The question mark behind the duration of the task (1 day?) indicates that this is an estimated duration.

As you enter new tasks, they will be assigned a default duration of one day, and they will not be linked. Your screen should look similar to Figure 1-9.

Figure 1-9

Task list for Don Funk Music Video 1

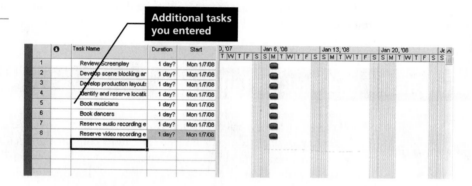

5. SAVE the project plan.

PAUSE. LEAVE the project plan open to use in the next exercise.

You have just added eight tasks to your project plan. Note that as you entered a task on each row of the Entry table, Microsoft Project assigned a Task ID (see Figure 1-8). The *Task ID* is a unique number that is assigned to each task in the project. It appears on the left side of the task's row.

SOFTWARE ORIENTATION

Calendar Tab in Options Dialog Box

Microsoft Project uses standard values of minutes and hours for durations: one minute equals 60 seconds, and one hour equals 60 minutes. However, you can define the duration of days, weeks, and months for your project. See Figure 1-10.

Figure 1-10

Calendar tab in Options dialog box

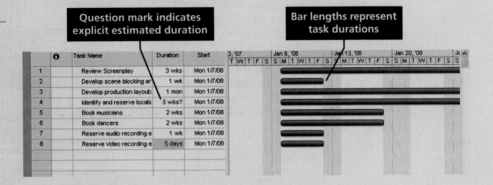

Click the **Tools** menu, click the **Options** command, and then click the **Calendar** tab.

Calendar Option	Function
Week starts on	Changes the day on which the project week starts
Fiscal year starts in	Changes the month in which the project fiscal year begins
Default start time	Changes the default start time for scheduled tasks
Default end time	Changes the default end time for scheduled tasks
Hours per day	Changes how many hours are scheduled for one day
Hours per week	Changes how many hours are scheduled for one week
Days per month	Changes how many days are scheduled for one month

Estimating Durations

A task's *duration* is the amount of working time required to complete a task. Because different tasks usually take different amounts of time to complete, each task is assigned a separate duration.

⊕ ENTER TASK DURATIONS

USE the project plan you created in the previous exercise.

1. Click the first cell in the Duration column, next to the task Review Screenplay. The Duration field for task 1 is selected.
2. Key **3w** and then press [Enter]. The value 3 wks appears in the Duration field.

3. Enter the following durations for the remaining tasks.

Task ID	Task Name	Duration
2	Develop scene blocking and schedule	1w
3	Develop production layouts	1mo
4	Identify and reserve locations	5w?
5	Book musicians	2w
6	Book dancers	2w
7	Reserve audio recording equipment	1w
8	Reserve video recording equipment	5d

Your screen should look similar to Figure 1-11.

Figure 1-11

Gantt Chart showing task durations entered

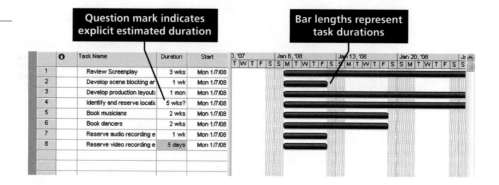

4. SAVE the project plan.

PAUSE. LEAVE the project plan open to use in the next exercise.

Recall that when you set up your project calendar in the previous exercise, the working times for your project were Monday through Friday from 8:00 A.M.–5:00 P.M. with an hour off for lunch each day. Microsoft Project differentiates between working and nonworking time, so the duration of a task doesn't always correspond to elapsed time. If you estimate that a task will take 24 hours of working time, you would enter its duration as 3d to schedule the task over three 8-hour workdays. If this task were to start at 8:00 A.M. on Thursday, it would not be completed until 5:00 P.M. on Monday. No work is scheduled on evenings or weekends because these have been defined as nonworking times.

You can also schedule tasks to occur over working and nonworking time by assigning an elapsed duration to a task. ***Elapsed duration*** is the total length of working and nonworking time you expect it will take to complete a task. Suppose you own an automobile body shop. In the process of repainting a car, you have the tasks "Apply rustproof undercoat" and

"Apply first color overcoat." You also need a task called "Wait for undercoat to dry" because you cannot apply the color paint until the undercoat is dry. The task "Wait for undercoat to dry" will have an elapsed duration because the undercoat will dry over a contiguous range of hours, whether they are working or nonworking. If the undercoat takes 24 hours to cure, you would enter the duration for this task as 1ed (or 1 elapsed day). If you scheduled it to start at 11 A.M. on Wednesday, it would be complete at 11 A.M. on Thursday.

Table 1-1 shows abbreviations and meanings for actual and elapsed times in Microsoft Project.

Table 1-1

Abbreviations and meanings for actual and elapsed times

IF YOU ENTER THIS ABBREVIATION	IT APPEARS LIKE THIS	AND MEANS
m	min	minute
h	hr	hour
d	day	day
w	wk	week
mo	mon	month
em	emin	elapsed minute
eh	ehr	elapsed hour
ed	eday	elapsed day
ew	ewk	elapsed week
emo	emon	elapsed month

SHOOTING

For most projects, you will use task durations of hours, days, and weeks. When estimating task durations, think carefully about the level of detail you want to apply to your project's tasks. If you have a multiyear project, it is probably not practical or even possible to track tasks that are measured in minutes or hours. You should measure task durations at the lowest level of detail or control necessary, but no lower.

Although the task durations are supplied for you for the exercises in this book, you will have to estimate task durations for most real-world projects. There are a number of sources of task duration estimates:

- Information from previous, similar projects
- Estimates from the people who will actually complete the tasks
- Recommendations from people who have managed similar projects
- Professional or industry organizations that deal with the project subject matter

For any project, a major source of risk is inaccurate task duration estimates. **Risk** decreases the likelihood of completing the project on time, within budget and to specification. Making good estimates is worth the time and effort.

Creating a Milestone

A milestone marks a major event in a project and can be used to monitor the project's progress. A **_milestone_** represents a significant event reached within the project or imposed upon the project. Milestones are often represented as a task with zero duration.

⊕ CREATE A MILESTONE

USE the project plan you created in the previous exercise.

1. In the Task Name column, click on the empty cell below the name of task 8, Reserve video recording equipment.

2. Key **Pre-Production complete** and press Right Arrow to move to the Duration field.

3. In the *List Tasks* pane, under Indicate milestones, click the checkbox next to *Make selected task a milestone*. The duration is set at 0 days and the milestone is added to your project plan.

4. In the Task Name column, click on the name of task 1, **Review Screenplay**.

5. On the menu bar, click **Insert** and then click **New Task**. Microsoft Project inserts and numbers a new task (1). Notice that the other tasks after the new task insertion point have been renumbered.

ANOTHER WAY

You can also press **Insert to add a new task above the selected task**. To insert multiple new tasks, select multiple tasks and then press **Insert**. The same number of new tasks will be inserted as the number you selected.

6. Key **Pre-Production begins** and press the Right Arrow to move to the Duration field.

7. In the *List Tasks* pane, under Indicate milestones, click the checkbox next to *Make selected task a milestone*. The duration is set at 0 days and the milestone is added to your project plan. Your screen should look similar to Figure 1-12.

Figure 1-12

Gantt Chart showing milestone added

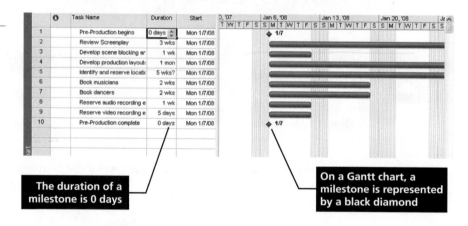

The duration of a milestone is 0 days

On a Gantt chart, a milestone is represented by a black diamond

8. At the bottom of the *List Tasks* pane, click the **Done** link.

9. **SAVE** the project plan.

   PAUSE. LEAVE the project plan open to use in the next exercise.

■ Organizing Tasks into Phases

THE BOTTOM LINE

After you enter tasks in your project, it can be helpful to organize your project by grouping related tasks into phases. The phases, represented by summary tasks, identify the major phases and subphases in your project.

➔ CREATE SUMMARY TASKS

USE the project plan you created in the previous exercise.

1. In the *Tasks* pane of the Project Guide, click the **Organize tasks into phases** link. The *Organize Tasks* pane appears.

2. Click the name of task 1, **Pre-Production begins**.

3. In the *Organize Tasks* pane, click the **Click here to insert a new row** button. A new row is inserted and subsequent tasks are shifted down and renumbered.

4. In the Task Name field for the new task, key **Pre-Production** and press ⎡Enter⎤.

5. Key the following task names below task 11, Pre-Production complete. Press ⎡Enter⎤ after each task name.

   Production

   Post-Production

6. Click on the name of task 13, **Post-Production**, and press ⎡Insert⎤ twice. Two blank tasks are inserted above the Post-Production task.

7. Key the following task names and durations below task 12, Production.

Task Name	Duration
Production begins	**0d**
Production complete	**0d**

8. Key the following tasks names and durations below task 15, Post-Production.

Task Name	Duration
Post-Production begins	**0d**
Post-Production complete	**0d**

9. Click on the task name for task 2, **Pre-Production begins**. Drag your cursor to task 11, **Pre-Production complete**, to highlight and select tasks 2 through 11.

ANOTHER WAY

To quickly select a range of tasks to be indented under a summary task, click on the name of the first task to be indented, hold down the **Shift** key, and then click the name of the last task to be indented. All of the tasks between the two will be selected.

10. In the *Organize Tasks* pane, click the **Click here to indent selected tasks to make them subtasks of the task above** button. Tasks 2 through 11 are indented and task 1 becomes a summary task. Notice the summary task name is in bold type.

11. Click on the name of task 13, **Production begins**. Drag your cursor to the name of task 14, **Production complete**. Tasks 13 and 14 are highlighted and selected.

12. In the *Organize Tasks* pane, click the **Click here to indent selected tasks to make them subtasks of the task above** button. Tasks 13 and 14 are indented and task 12 becomes a summary task.

13. Click on the name of task 16, **Post-Production begins**. Drag your cursor to the name of task 17, **Post-Production complete**. Tasks 16 and 17 are highlighted and selected.

14. In the *Organize Tasks* pane, click the **Click here to indent selected tasks to make them subtasks of the task above** button. Tasks 16 and 17 are indented and task 15 becomes a summary task. Your screen should look similar to Figure 1-13.

Figure 1-13

Gantt Chart showing summary and indented tasks

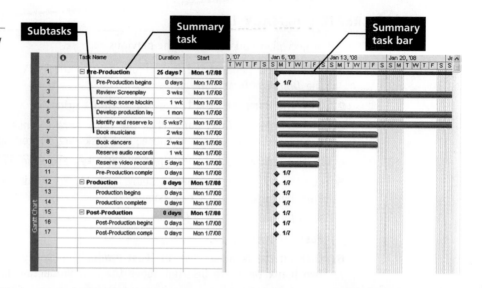

The Production and Post-Production summary tasks appear as milestones because they have no subtasks with a positive duration below them (only milestones with zero duration). The appearance of the Production and Post-production summary tasks will change once additional tasks are added in later lessons.

15. At the bottom of the *Organize Tasks* pane, click the **Done** link. The *Tasks* pane reappears.

16. **SAVE** the project plan.

PAUSE. LEAVE the project plan open to use in the next exercise.

You have just organized your tasks into ***phases,*** or a group of closely related tasks that encompass a major section of your project. Working with phases and tasks in Microsoft Project is similar to working with an outline in Microsoft Word. You can create phases by indenting and outdenting tasks, and you can collapse an entire task list into its phase components.

A ***summary task*** is made up of and summarizes all of the detail tasks, or ***subtasks,*** that fall below it. You cannot directly edit a summary task's duration, start date, or other calculated values.

Most complex projects require a combination of both top-down and bottom-up planning in order to create accurate tasks and phases:

- ***Top-down planning*** develops a project plan by identifying the highest level phases or summary tasks before breaking them into lower level components or subtasks. This approach works from general to specific.

- ***Bottom-up planning*** develops a project plan by starting with the lowest level tasks before organizing them into higher level phases or summary tasks. This approach works from specific to general.

■ Linking Tasks

THE BOTTOM LINE

You can create task relationships by creating links between tasks. The links create a dependency in which one task depends on the start or completion of another task in order to begin or end.

Linking Two Tasks

You will create a dependency between, or link, two tasks to correctly reflect the order in which work must be completed.

⊕ LINK TWO TASKS

USE the project plan you created in the previous exercise.

1. In the *Tasks* pane of the Project Guide, click the **Schedule tasks** link. The *Schedule Tasks* pane appears.

2. Select the names of tasks 3 and 4.

3. In the *Schedule Tasks* pane, click the **Click here to create a finish to start link** button. Tasks 3 and 4 are now linked with a finish-to-start relationship. Microsoft Project changed the start date of task 4 to the next working day following the completion of task 3. Note that because January 21 was a nonworking day (the Martin Luther King holiday you set up), task 3 does not finish until January 28 and task 4 does not start until January 29. If necessary, scroll the Gantt Chart to January 28 so that the link you just created is visible. Your screen should look similar to Figure 1-14.

Figure 1-14

Tasks 3 and 4 linked in a finish-to-start relationship

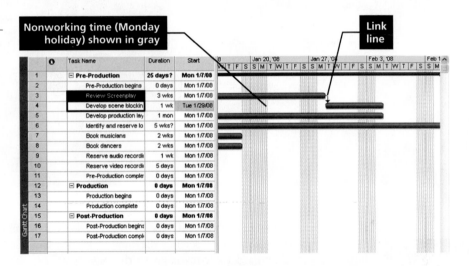

Nonworking time (Monday holiday) shown in gray

Link line

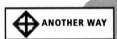 **ANOTHER WAY**   You can also click the Link Tasks button on the Standard toolbar or click Link Tasks on the Edit menu to create a finish-to-start dependency.

4. **SAVE** the project plan.

PAUSE. LEAVE the project plan open to use in the next exercise.

When you started the exercise in this section, all of the tasks in the project plan were scheduled to start on the same date—the project start date. You have just linked two tasks to reflect the actual order in which they will occur. A *link* is a logical connection between tasks that controls sequence and dependency. These two tasks have a finish-to-start relationship, or dependency. Note the following characteristics of the task relationship:

- The second task must occur after the first task. This is called a *sequence*, or the chronological order in which tasks must occur.

- The second task can occur only if the first task is completed, known as a dependency. A *dependency* controls the start or finish of one task relative to the start or finish of another task. There are four types of dependencies in Microsoft Project: finish-to-start, start-to-start, finish-to-finish, and start-to-finish.

In Microsoft Project, the first task is called the **_predecessor_**, a task whose start or end date determines the start or finish of another task or tasks. Any task can be a predecessor for one or more tasks. The second task is called the **_successor_**, a task whose start or finish is driven by another task or tasks. Again, any task can be a successor to one or more predecessor tasks. Tasks can have only one of four types of task relationships, as shown in Table 1-2.

Table 1-2

The four types of task relationships

THIS TASK RELATIONSHIP	MEANS	LOOKS LIKE THIS IN THE GANTT CHART	EXAMPLE
Finish-to-start (FS)	The finish date of the predecessor task determines the start date of the successor task.		A music track must be recorded before it can be edited.
Start-to-start (SS)	The start date of the predecessor task determines the start date of the successor task.		Booking musicians and Booking dancers are related tasks and can occur simultaneously.
Finish-to-finish (FF)	The finish date of the predecessor task determines the finish date of the successor task.		Tasks that require the use of specific equipment must end when the equipment rental ends.
Start-to-finish (SF) (This type of relationship is rarely used.)	The start date of the predecessor task determines the finish date of the successor task.		The time when the production sound studio becomes available determines when rehearsals must end.

SHOOTING

If you need to change the type of link between tasks, you should break the original link between the tasks before setting the new link. You can use the Unlink tasks button on the Standard toolbar, or go to the *Schedule Tasks* pane (under Tasks) in the Project Guide.

Linking Several Tasks

You can also use Microsoft Project to link several tasks at once.

⊖ LINK SEVERAL TASKS AT ONCE

USE the project plan you created in the previous exercise.

1. Select the names of tasks 4 through 11.
2. In the *Schedule Tasks* pane, click the **Click here to create a finish to start link** button. Tasks 4 through 11 are now linked with a finish-to-start relationship. Your screen should look similar to Figure 1-15.

Figure 1-15

Tasks 4 through 11 linked in a finish-to-start relationship

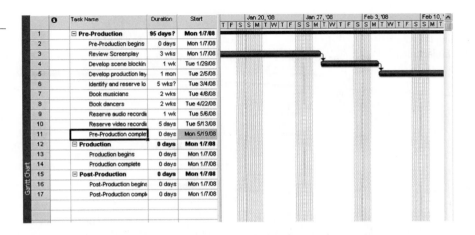

You can also set finish-to-start links using the Task Information dialog box. Click on the name of the task that you wish to set as the successor, click the Task Information button, and click the Predecessors tab. Click the first cell in the Task Name column, and then click the arrow to select the task you wish to set as the predecessor.

3. **SAVE** the project plan.

   PAUSE. LEAVE the project plan open to use in the next exercise.

Linking Milestones

Now that you have linked some of the tasks in the project plan, you will link milestones across summary tasks. Linking milestones to each other reflects the sequential nature of the overall phases.

⊖ LINK THE MILESTONE TASKS

USE the project plan you created in the previous exercise.

1. Select the name of task 11, **Pre-Production complete**, and, while holding down the control key, select the name of task 13, **Production begins**. This is how you select nonadjacent tasks in a table in Microsoft Project.

2. In the *Schedule Tasks* pane, click the **Click here to create a finish to start link** button to link the two milestone tasks. Tasks 11 and 13 are linked with a finish-to-start relationship.

3. Select the name of task 14, **Production complete**, and, while holding down the control key, select the name of task 16, **Post-Production begins**.

4. In the *Schedule Tasks* pane, click the **Click here to create a finish to start link** button to link the two milestone tasks. Tasks 14 and 16 are linked with a finish-to-start relationship.

5. Scroll the chart section of the Gantt Chart view to the right until the later portion of the project plan is visible. Your screen should look similar to Figure 1-16.

Figure 1-16

Gantt Chart showing linked
milestones in the project plan

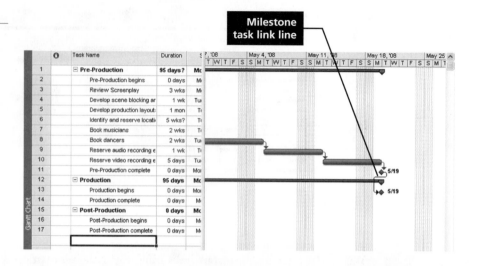

TAKE NOTE

Because you have not yet entered and linked actual tasks under the Production and Post-Production summary tasks, the milestones for these phases (tasks 13, 14, 16, and 17) remain at the beginning (left end) of the Gantt bar chart. They will move to the right side of the Gantt bar chart once you add and link more subtasks in a future lesson.

6. Click **Done** in the *Schedule Tasks* pane.
7. **SAVE** the project plan.

ANOTHER WAY

You can also create finish-to-start relationships between tasks directly in the Gantt Chart. Point to the predecessor task until the pointer changes to a four-arrow star. Drag the pointer up or down to the task bar of the successor task. Microsoft Project will link the two tasks. Notice that while you are dragging, the pointer image changes to a chain link.

PAUSE. LEAVE the project plan open to use in the next exercise.

In this exercise, you linked milestones across summary tasks. When you link milestones in this way, you set up the natural flow of the project—when one phase finishes, the next phase begins. In this particular project, you have not yet entered all of the subtasks for the Production and Post-Production phases, so the graphical representation of the milestones and links on the Gantt Chart may have looked a bit strange. Once you begin to enter and link these tasks, the project will begin to look more like the Pre-Production section of the Gantt Chart.

■ Documenting Tasks

THE BOTTOM LINE

You should keep the tasks in a project plan simple and specific. Additional task information that is important to the project can be recorded in a note. You can also provide more information about a task by linking it to another file, an intranet page, or an Internet page through a hyperlink.

Entering Task Notes

Attaching a note to a task in a project plan allows you to document important information while keeping your project plan succinct.

⊕ ENTER A TASK NOTE

USE the project plan you created in the previous exercise.

1. In the *Tasks* pane, click the **Link to or attach more task information** link. The *Add Information* pane appears.
2. Select task 7, Book musicians, by clicking on the task number (**7**).
3. In the *Add Information* pane, click the **Add a note** link. The Task Information dialog box appears with the Notes tab displayed.

 **ANOTHER WAY** You can also add a note by clicking the Task Notes button in the Standard toolbar, or by right-clicking on the task name and selecting Task Notes from the shortcut menu.

4. In the Notes box, key **Call Andy Teal for the mandolin** and click **OK**. A note icon appears in the Indicators column for task 7.
5. Point to the note icon. The note appears in a Screen Tip. For longer notes, or to see other task information, you can double-click the note icon and the Task Information box will display the full text of the note. The note and Screen Tip are shown in Figure 1-17.

Figure 1-17

Task note displayed
as a screen tip

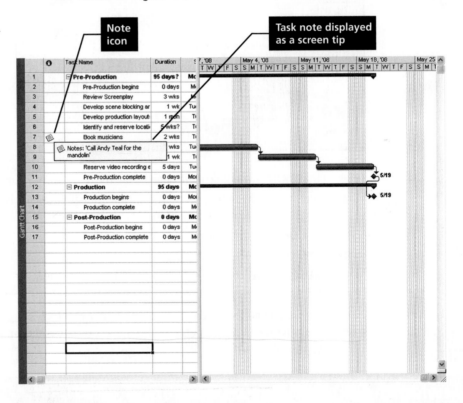

6. **SAVE** the project plan.

   PAUSE. LEAVE the project plan open to use in the next exercise.

A ***note*** is supplemental text that you can attach to a task, resource, or assignment. As you saw in this activity, you enter and review task notes on the Notes tab in the Task Information dialog box. You can enter a wide variety of additional information to help clarify or enhance your project plan. Some options for attaching files are text and graphics from Microsoft programs, sound or video files, photos (to link faces with resource names), company logos, PowerPoint slides or presentations, and organizational charts.

Adding a Hyperlink

A hyperlink is another method of attaching important information to a task.

 **ADD A HYPERLINK**

USE the project plan you created in the previous exercise.

1. Select task 6, Identify and reserve locations, by clicking on the task number (**6**).
2. In the *Add Information* pane, click the **Add a hyperlink** link. The Insert Hyperlink dialog box appears.

ANOTHER WAY You can also add a hyperlink by clicking the Insert Hyperlink button on the Standard toolbar.

3. In the *Text to display* box, key **Web site of a good location for a video shoot**.
4. In the address box, key **www.alpineskihouse.com**. The Insert Hyperlink dialog box should look similar to Figure 1-18.

Figure 1-18

Completed Insert Hyperlink dialog box

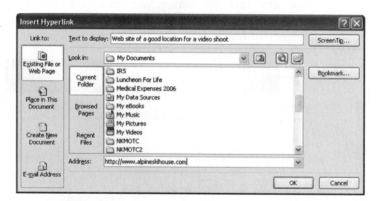

5. Click **OK**. A hyperlink icon appears in the Indicators column for task 5.
6. Point to the hyperlink icon. The informational text you keyed in step 3 appears in a Screen Tip. Clicking on the hyperlink icon opens the Web page in your browser.
7. Click **Done** in the *Add Information* pane.
8. **SAVE** the project plan.

   PAUSE. LEAVE the project plan open to use in the next exercise.

In this exercise you added a hyperlink to a task. A ***hyperlink*** is a portion of text that contains a link to another file, a portion of a file, a page on the Internet, or a page on an intranet.

■ Reviewing the Project Plan's Duration

 THE BOTTOM LINE Microsoft Project calculates both the current project duration and the scheduled finish date based on the task durations and relationships you entered. You can view both the project statistics and the Gantt Chart for the entire project.

➔ CHECK THE PROJECT'S DURATION

USE the project plan you created in the last exercise.

1. On the menu bar, click **Project,** and then click **Project Information**. The Project Information dialog box appears. Your screen should look similar to Figure 1-19.

Figure 1-19

Project Information dialog box

2. Click the **Statistics** button. The Project Statistics dialog box appears and displays information such as the project start and finish dates and duration. Other information on this screen will be covered in later chapters.

3. Click the **Close** button to close the Project Statistics dialog box.

4. Click the **Show/Hide Project Guide** button on the Project Guide toolbar. The Project Guide closes.

5. Click **View** on the Standard toolbar, then click **Zoom**. The Zoom dialog box appears.

6. Click **Entire project**, then click **OK**. The graphical portion of the Gantt Chart is compressed so the entire project is visible on the screen. Your screen should look similar to Figure 1-20.

Figure 1-20

Gantt Chart view of entire project

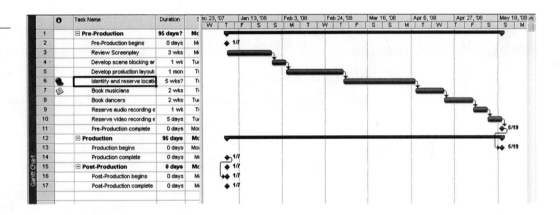

7. **SAVE** the project plan.

8. **CLOSE** the *Don Funk Music Video 1* file.

PAUSE. If you are continuing to the next lesson, keep Project open. If you are not continuing to additional lessons, **CLOSE** Project.

SUMMARY SKILL MATRIX

IN THIS LESSON YOU LEARNED	MATRIX SKILL
To start Microsoft Project Standard	Start Microsoft Project
To create a project plan	Open a new project plan Specify a start date Save the project plan
To define project calendars	Define the project calendar
To enter tasks and task details	Enter tasks Enter task durations Create a milestone
To organize tasks into phases	Create summary tasks
To link tasks	Link two tasks Link several tasks at once Link the milestone tasks
To document tasks	Enter a task note Add a hyperlink
To review the project plan's duration	Check the project's duration

■ Knowledge Assessment

Fill in the Blank

Complete the following sentences by writing the correct word or words in the blanks provided.

1. A(n) _____ is a model of a real project–what you want to happen or what you think will happen.

2. A(n) _____ is a logical connection between tasks that controls sequence and dependency.

3. A group of closely related tasks that encompass a major section of your project is a(n) _____.

4. A(n) _____ is a scheduling tool that determines the standard working time and nonworking time for the project, resources, and tasks.

5. _____ is the total length of working and nonworking time you expect it will take to complete a task.

6. A(n) _____ is supplemental text that you can attach to a task, resource, or assignment.

7. A(n) _____ controls the start or finish of one task relative to the start or finish of another task.

8. A task whose start or end date determines the start or finish of another task or tasks is a(n) _____.

9. A(n) _____ represents a significant event reached within the project or imposed upon the project.

10. A(n) _____ represents the actual individual work activities that must be done to accomplish the final goal.

True / False

Circle T if the statement is true or F if the statement is false.

T | F **1.** It is always best to schedule a project from a finish date.

T | F **2.** When you initially enter tasks into Project, they are linked in a finish-to-start relationship that can be changed later.

T | F **3.** A hyperlink allows you to connect a task to another file or a page on the Internet.

T | F **4.** The Project Guide is a wizard-like interface you can use when creating or modifying a project.

T | F **5.** An estimated duration of 3 weeks for a task would be shown as *3w?*

T | F **6.** A task calendar defines working and nonworking times for an individual work resource.

T | F **7.** A summary task is derived from all of the detail tasks that fall below it.

T | F **8.** Once you have entered all of the tasks and durations for a project, the project duration does not change.

T | F **9.** Tasks that are indented below a summary task are called successors.

T | F **10.** For tasks that are linked in a finish-to-start relationship, the finish date of the predecessor task determines the start date of the successor task.

■ Competency Assessment

→ Project 1-1: Don Funk Scene 1 Production Tasks

Using the project plan you previously created in this lesson, add several tasks and their durations under a summary task.

The *Don Funk Music Video 1-1* project plan is available on the companion CD-ROM.

GET READY. Launch Microsoft Project if it is not already running. **OPEN** *Don Funk Music Video 1-1* from the data files for this lesson.

1. On the Project Guide toolbar, click the **Show/Hide Project Guide** button to open the Project Guide.

2. Click on the name of task 14, **Production complete.** Drag your cursor so that 5 rows are highlighted, including the row for task 14.

3. On the menu bar, click **Insert** and then click **New Task.**

4. Click on the blank Task Name field for task 14. Starting in this field, enter the following tasks and durations:

Task	Duration
Scene 1 setup	2d
Scene 1 rehearsal	6h
Scene 1 vocal recording	1d
Scene 1 video shoot	2d
Scene 1 teardown	1d

5. In the *Tasks* pane, click **Organize tasks into phases.**

6. Select tasks 14 through 18.

7. Click the **Click here to indent selected task(s) to make them subtasks of the task above** button.

8. In the *Organize Tasks* pane, click **Done.**

9. **SAVE** the project as *Don Funk Scene 1* in the solutions folder for this lesson and then **CLOSE** the file.

   LEAVE Project open for the next exercise.

The *New Employee 1-2* project plan is available on the companion CD-ROM.

➔ Project 1-2: New Employee Orientation

Add a note and hyperlink to a project plan as reminders of information to be given to new employees.

GET READY. Launch Microsoft Project if it is not already running. **OPEN** *New Employee 1-2* from the data files for this lesson.

1. Click on the name of task 9, **Take picture for employee ID.**
2. In the *Tasks* pane, click **Link to or attach more task information.**
3. In the *Add information* pane, click **Add a note.**
4. In the Task Information dialog box, key **Remember to use blue backdrop for digital pics.**
5. Click **OK.**
6. Click on the name of task 22, **Complete health insurance paperwork.**
7. In the *Add information* pane, click **Add a hyperlink.**
8. In the Text to display box, key **Humongous Insurance.**
9. In the Address box, key **www.humongousinsurance.com.**
10. Click **OK.**
11. In the *Add Information* pane, click **Done.**
12. **SAVE** the project plan as *New Employee Orientation* in the solutions folder for this lesson and then **CLOSE** the file.

    LEAVE Project open for the next exercise.

■ Proficiency Assessment

➔ Project 1-3: Hiring a New Employee

You need to create a project plan for the process of hiring a new employee for your department.

OPEN a new blank project plan.

1. Set the project start date to be October 22, 2007 using the *Set a date to schedule from* link in the *Tasks* pane.
2. Enter the following tasks and durations:

Task	Duration
Write job description	2d
Notify departmental recruiter	1d
Post job internally	5d
Post job externally	5d
Collect resumes	10d
Review resumes	5d
Set up interviews	3d
Conduct interviews	8d
Select candidate	1d
Make offer	milestone

3. Using the *Schedule tasks* link in the *Tasks* pane, assign a finish-to-start relationship to all the tasks.
4. Change the dependency between tasks 3 and 4 to a start-to-start relationship.
5. Use the Project Information dialog box to determine the current project duration.

6. **SAVE** the project plan in the solutions folder for this lesson as *Hiring Employee* xx*d* where the xx in the file name is the duration (in days) of the project. (For example, if the project is 13 days long, save the file as *Hiring Employee 13d*.) **CLOSE** the file.

LEAVE Project open for the next exercise.

➔ Project 1-4: Don Funk Video: New Task Dependencies

The *Don Funk Music Video 1-4* project plan is available on the companion CD-ROM.

After reviewing your project plan, you have determined that some of the tasks could be linked in a different way to make your project more efficient.

OPEN *Don Funk Music Video 1-4* from the data files for this lesson.

1. If necessary, turn on the Project Guide. Using the *Schedule tasks* link, change tasks 9 and 10 so that they have a start-to-start relationship. (Hint: you need to break the existing link before changing the type of link.)
2. Change tasks 7 and 8 so that they have a start-to-start relationship.
3. Adjust the Gantt bar section of your screen so that the Gantt bars for these new relationships are visible.
4. **SAVE** the project plan as *Don Funk Revised Links* in the solutions folder for this lesson and then **CLOSE** the file.

LEAVE Project open to use in the next exercise.

■ Mastery Assessment

➔ Project 1-5: Setting Up a Home Office

The *Home Office 1-5* project plan is available on the companion CD-ROM.

You are ordering equipment and setting up a home office and need to create a schedule to minimize the amount of time it takes to do this.

OPEN *Home Office 1-5* from the data files for this lesson.

1. Set tasks 6, 9, 10, and 14 as milestones.
2. Assign a start-to-start relationship for tasks 1, 2, and 3.
3. Assign a finish-to-start relationship for tasks 1 and 6, 3 and 9, and 2 and 10.
4. Assign a finish-to-start relationship for tasks 4, 5, 7, and 8.
5. Assign a finish-to-start relationship for tasks 10 through 14.
6. **SAVE** the project plan as *Home Office* in the solutions folder for this lesson and then **CLOSE** the file.

LEAVE Project open for the next exercise.

➔ Project 1-6: Don Funk All Scenes Production

The *Don Funk Music Video 1-6* project plan is available on the companion CD-ROM.

You need to enter and organize the tasks for producing the four scenes in the Don Funk music video.

OPEN *Don Funk Music Video 1-6* from the data files for this lesson.

1. Insert a new row after task 13. Name this new task **Scene 1**.
2. Indent tasks 15 through 21 under the Scene 1 summary task you just created.
3. Add two more sets of summary and subtasks (including durations) for Scenes 2 and 3 under the Production summary task. They will be identical to the Scene 1 tasks and durations except for the scene number.

4. Assign the subtasks for Scenes 2 and 3 finish-to-start relationships.

5. Assign a finish-to-start relationship between the *Scene 1 complete* milestone and the *Scene 2 begin* milestone. Assign a finish-to-start relationship between the *Scene 2 complete* milestone and the *Scene 3 begin* milestone.

6. Link the *Scene 3 complete* milestone and the *Production Complete* milestone with a finish-to-start dependency.

7. Link the *Production Complete* milestone and the *Post-Production begins* milestone with a finish-to-start dependency.

8. **SAVE** the project plan as ***Don Funk 3 Scenes*** in the solutions folder for this lesson and then **CLOSE** the file.

   CLOSE Project.

INTERNET READY

Many companies find their beginnings with an entrepreneur and an idea for a product or service that satisfies a customer need. Use Web search tools to find information about the basics of starting your own business. Identify 15 to 20 tasks that you would need to do to begin setting up your own business. Develop a simple project plan with these tasks, and include a start date, working times, task durations, and task dependencies. Add notes and hyperlinks where appropriate.

Establishing Resources

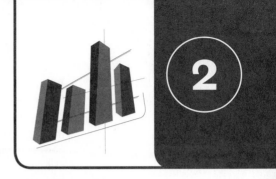

2

LESSON SKILL MATRIX

SKILLS	MATRIX SKILL
Establishing People Resources	Establish individual people resources Establish a resource that represents multiple people
Establishing Equipment Resources	Establish equipment resources
Establishing Material Resources	Establish material resources
Establishing Cost Resources	Establish cost resources
Establishing Resource Pay Rates	Enter resource cost information
Adjusting Resource Working Times	Establish nonworking times for an individual resource Establish a specific work schedule for a resource
Adding Resource Notes	Attach a note to a resource

KEY TERMS
availability
base calendar
cost
cost resource
material resource
maximum units
project calendar
resource calendar
resources
work resource

Now that Southridge Video has laid out the initial project plan for Don Funk's latest music video, the next step for the video production manager is to identify the people, equipment, and materials needed to complete the tasks in this project. He must also determine when these resources are available, how much work they can do, and their cost. One of the most powerful tools in Microsoft Office Project is the ability to manage resources effectively. In this lesson, you will learn how to set up basic resource information for people, equipment, and materials, how to set up cost information for a resource, and how to change a resource's availability for work.

■ SOFTWARE ORIENTATION

Microsoft Project's Resource Sheet View

You have several views available when working in Microsoft Project. One view you will use in this lesson is the Resource Sheet view, as shown in Figure 2-1.

Figure 2-1

Resource Sheet view

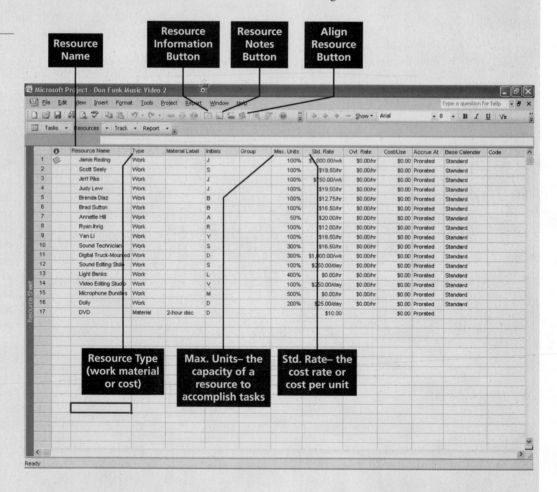

In this lesson, you will be working on establishing your project resources. Some of the features you will use in this lesson are shown on this screen. Your screen may be different if default settings have been changed or if other preferences have been set. Use this figure as a reference for this lesson.

■ Establishing People Resources

THE BOTTOM LINE

When you set up people resources in Microsoft Project, you are able to track who is available to work, the type of work they can do, and when they are available to do it.

Establishing Individual People Resources

You can set up resource information for the individual people who will perform the tasks on the project.

CD

The **Don Funk Music Video 2A** project plan is available on the companion CD-ROM.

⊕ ESTABLISH INDIVIDUAL PEOPLE RESOURCES

GET READY. Before you begin these steps, launch Microsoft Project.
OPEN Don Funk Music Video 2A from the data files for this lesson.
SAVE the file as **Don Funk Music Video 2**.

1. Click **Resources** on the Project Guide toolbar. The *Resources* pane of the Project Guide appears.

2. In the *Resources* pane, click the **Specify people and equipment for the project** link. The *Specify Resources* pane appears and the Project Guide: Simple Resource Sheet view replaces the Gantt Chart view.

3. Select **Enter resources manually**.

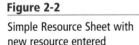
ANOTHER WAY

If your resource information for your own project exists on your network, such as in a Microsoft Outlook address book, you can quickly import the resource information into Microsoft Project. This saves the time and effort of retyping the information and reduces the possibility of data entry errors.

4. In the Simple Resource Sheet view, click the empty cell directly below the Resource Name column heading.

5. Key **Jamie Reding** and press **Enter**. Microsoft Project adds Jamie Reding as a resource. Your screen should look similar to Figure 2-2.

Figure 2-2

Simple Resource Sheet with new resource entered

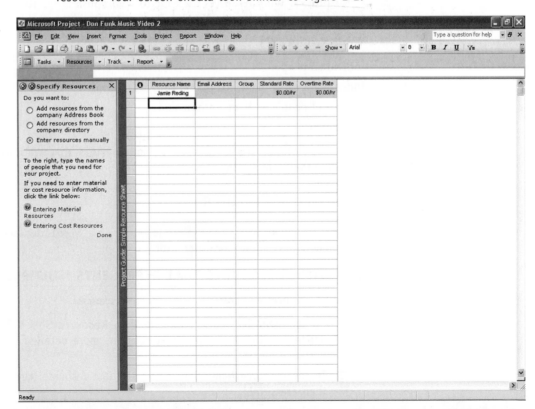

6. Enter the remaining resource names into the Simple Resource Sheet. Enter the first column of names (Scott Seely, Jeff Pike, etc.), and then the second column.

Scott Seely	Brad Sutton
Jeff Pike	Annette Hill
Judy Lew	Ryan Ihrig
Brenda Diaz	Yan Li

Your screen should look similar to Figure 2-3.

Figure 2-3

Simple Resource Sheet with all resources added

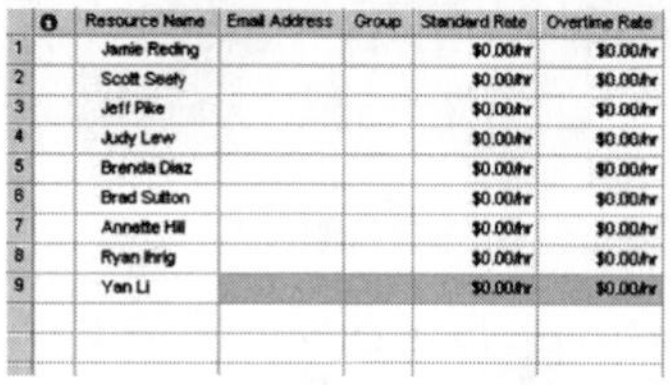

	Resource Name	Email Address	Group	Standard Rate	Overtime Rate
1	Jamie Reding			$0.00/hr	$0.00/hr
2	Scott Seely			$0.00/hr	$0.00/hr
3	Jeff Pike			$0.00/hr	$0.00/hr
4	Judy Lew			$0.00/hr	$0.00/hr
5	Brenda Diaz			$0.00/hr	$0.00/hr
6	Brad Sutton			$0.00/hr	$0.00/hr
7	Annette Hill			$0.00/hr	$0.00/hr
8	Ryan Ihrig			$0.00/hr	$0.00/hr
9	Yan Li			$0.00/hr	$0.00/hr

7. Click **Done** at the bottom of the *Specify Resources* pane.

8. Click the close button in the upper right corner of the Project Guide to close the project guide.

9. SAVE the project plan.

PAUSE. LEAVE the project plan open to use in the next exercise.

You are beginning to set up some of the basic resource information for the people who will work on this project. *Resources* are the people, equipment, and materials used to complete the tasks in a project. As you are entering this information, keep in mind two important aspects of resources: availability and cost. *Availability* determines when and how much of a resource's time can be assigned to work on tasks. *Cost* refers to how much money will be needed to pay for the resources on a project. Although setting up resource information in Microsoft Project may take a little extra time and effort, entering this information will provide you with more control over your project.

You will work with two types of resources in Microsoft Project: work resources and material resources. *Work resources* are the people and equipment that do work to accomplish the tasks of the project. Work resources use time to accomplish tasks. You will learn about material resources later in this lesson. Work resources can be in many different forms:

Work Resource	Example
Individual people	Yan Li; Jeff Pike
Individual people identified by job title or function	editor; camera person
Groups of people with a common skill	sound technician; dancer
Equipment	keyboard; digital recorder

When establishing your resources, use resource names that will make sense to you and anyone else using the project plan.

Establishing a Group Resource

In the previous exercise, you set up resources that were individuals. Now, you will set up a single resource that represents multiple people.

➔ ESTABLISH A RESOURCE THAT REPRESENTS MULTIPLE PEOPLE

USE the worksheet you created in the previous exercise.

1. On the menu bar, click **View** and then **Resource Sheet**. The Resource Sheet view appears. Notice that this sheet contains more detailed fields than the Simple Resource Sheet.

2. In the Resource Name field below the last resource, key **Sound Technician** and then press Tab.

3. In the Type field, make sure that *Work* is selected. Press `Tab` four times to move to the Max. Units field.

TAKE NOTE *Maximum units* is the maximum capacity of a resource to accomplish tasks. The default value for maximum units is 100%. For example, specifying that a resource has 75% maximum units means that 75 percent of the resource's time is available to work on tasks assigned to it. Microsoft Project will warn you if you assign a resource to more tasks than it can accomplish at its maximum units.

4. In the Max. Units field for the sound technician, key or select **300%** and then press `Tab`.

ANOTHER WAY When you tab into or click a numeric field, up and down arrows appear in the field. You can simply click these arrows to scroll to the number you want displayed.

5. Click the Max. Units field for Annette Hill, key or select **50%** and then press `Enter`. Your screen should look similar to Figure 2-4.

Figure 2-4

Resource Sheet showing adjusted Max. Units for several resources

	0	Resource Name	Type	Material Label	Initials	Group	Max. Units	Std. Rate	Ovt. Rate	Cost/Use	Accrue At	Base Calendar	Code
1		Jamie Reding	Work		J		100%	$0.00/hr	$0.00/hr	$0.00	Prorated	Standard	
2		Scott Seely	Work		S		100%	$0.00/hr	$0.00/hr	$0.00	Prorated	Standard	
3		Jeff Pike	Work		J		100%	$0.00/hr	$0.00/hr	$0.00	Prorated	Standard	
4		Judy Lew	Work		J		100%	$0.00/hr	$0.00/hr	$0.00	Prorated	Standard	
5		Brenda Diaz	Work		B		100%	$0.00/hr	$0.00/hr	$0.00	Prorated	Standard	
6		Brad Sutton	Work		B		100%	$0.00/hr	$0.00/hr	$0.00	Prorated	Standard	
7		Annette Hill	Work		A		50%	$0.00/hr	$0.00/hr	$0.00	Prorated	Standard	
8		Ryan Ihrig	Work		R		100%	$0.00/hr	$0.00/hr	$0.00	Prorated	Standard	
9		Yan Li	Work		Y		100%	$0.00/hr	$0.00/hr	$0.00	Prorated	Standard	
10		Sound Technician	Work		S		300%	$0.00/hr	$0.00/hr	$0.00	Prorated	Standard	

ANOTHER WAY You can also enter maximum units as a decimal rather than a percentage. To change to this format, on the menu bar click Tools, then Options, and then click the Schedule tab. In the *Show assignment units as a* box, select Decimal.

6. SAVE the project plan.

PAUSE. LEAVE the project plan open to use in the next exercise.

In this exercise, you established a group resource. The resource named Sound Technician does not represent a single person. It actually represents a group of people called sound technicians. By setting the Max. Units for this resource at 300%, you are indicating that three sound technicians will be available to work full time on every workday. You might not know specifically who the sound technicians will be at this point, but you can still proceed with more planning.

■ Establishing Equipment Resources

THE BOTTOM LINE Setting up equipment resources in Microsoft Project is very similar to setting up people resources. There are key differences, however, in the way equipment resources can be scheduled.

⊙ ESTABLISH EQUIPMENT RESOURCES

USE the project plan you created in the previous exercise.

1. In the Resource Sheet, click the next empty cell in the Resource Name column.

2. On the menu bar, click **Project** and then **Resource Information**. The Resource Information dialog box appears.

ANOTHER WAY You can also activate the Resource Information dialog box by clicking the Resource Information button ▣ on the Standard toolbar, or by double-clicking a resource name or an empty cell in the Resource Name column.

3. If it is not already displayed, click the **General** tab.

4. In the Resource Name field, key **Digital Truck-Mounted Video Camera**.

5. In the Type field, select **Work** from the dropdown menu. Your screen should look similar to Figure 2-5. Notice that the Resource Information dialog box contains many of the same fields as the Resource Sheet.

Figure 2-5

Resource Information Dialog box showing Digital Truck-Mounted Video Camera

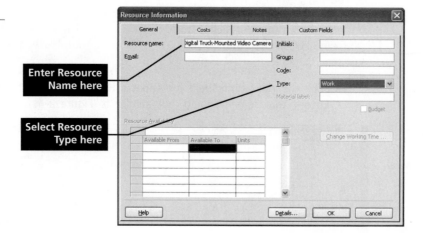

6. Click **OK**. The Resource Information dialog box closes and the Resource Sheet is visible. Notice that the Max. Units field for the new resource is at the default of 100%.

7. In the Max. Units field for the Digital Truck-Mounted Video Camera, key **200** or press the arrows until the value shown is 200%, and then press **Tab**. This indicates that you will have two truck cameras available every workday.

8. Add the following additional equipment resources to the project plan. You can use the Resource Sheet or the Resource Information dialog box to enter your information. Make sure that **Work** is selected in the *Type* field for each resource.

Resource Name	Max. Units
Sound Editing Studio	**100%**
Light Banks	**400%**
Video Editing Studio	**100%**
Microphone Bundles	**500%**
Dolly	**200%**

Your screen should look similar to Figure 2-6.

Figure 2-6

Resource Sheet showing equipment resources added

	❶	Resource Name	Type	Material Label	Initials	Group	Max. Units	Std. Rate	Ovt. Rate	Cost/Use	Accrue At	Base Calendar	Code	
1		Jamie Reding	Work		J		100%	$0.00/hr	$0.00/hr	$0.00	Prorated	Standard		
2		Scott Seely	Work		S		100%	$0.00/hr	$0.00/hr	$0.00	Prorated	Standard		
3		Jeff Pike	Work		J		100%	$0.00/hr	$0.00/hr	$0.00	Prorated	Standard		
4		Judy Lew	Work		J		100%	$0.00/hr	$0.00/hr	$0.00	Prorated	Standard		
5		Brenda Diaz	Work		B		100%	$0.00/hr	$0.00/hr	$0.00	Prorated	Standard		
6		Brad Sutton	Work		B		100%	$0.00/hr	$0.00/hr	$0.00	Prorated	Standard		
7		Annette Hill	Work		A		50%	$0.00/hr	$0.00/hr	$0.00	Prorated	Standard		
8		Ryan Ihrig	Work		R		100%	$0.00/hr	$0.00/hr	$0.00	Prorated	Standard		
9		Yan Li	Work		Y		100%	$0.00/hr	$0.00/hr	$0.00	Prorated	Standard		
10		Sound Technician	Work		S		300%	$0.00/hr	$0.00/hr	$0.00	Prorated	Standard		
11		Digital Truck-Mounted	Work		D		300%	$0.00/hr	$0.00/hr	$0.00	Prorated	Standard		
12		Sound Editing Stdio	Work		S		100%	$0.00/hr	$0.00/hr	$0.00	Prorated	Standard		
13		Light Banks	Work		L		400%	$0.00/hr	$0.00/hr	$0.00	Prorated	Standard		
14		Video Editing Studio	Work		V		100%	$0.00/hr	$0.00/hr	$0.00	Prorated	Standard		
15		Microphone Bundles	Work		M		500%	$0.00/hr	$0.00/hr	$0.00	Prorated	Standard		
16		Dolly	Work		D		200%	$0.00/hr	$0.00/hr	$0.00	Prorated	Standard		

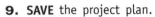

9. SAVE the project plan.

PAUSE. LEAVE the project plan open to use in the next exercise.

It is important to notice the differences between scheduling equipment resources and scheduling people resources. Equipment resources tend to be more specialized than people resources. For example, a microphone can't be used as a video recorder, but an audio technician might be able to fill in as an "extra" in a video shoot. Also, some equipment resources might work 24 hours a day, but most people resources don't work more than 8 or 12 hours in a day. You don't need to track every piece of equipment that will be used in your project. It will be helpful, though, to track equipment resources when

- you need to plan and track the costs of the equipment
- the piece of equipment might be needed by several people or groups simultaneously, and there is a possibility that it will be overbooked

■ Establishing Material Resources

↓
THE BOTTOM LINE
Just as you established people and equipment resources in your project plan, you can also set up material resources in Microsoft Project to track the rate of use of the particular resource and its related cost.

⊕ ESTABLISH MATERIAL RESOURCES

USE the project plan you created in the previous exercise.

1. In the Resource Sheet, click the next empty cell in the Resource Name column.
2. Key **DVD** and press `Tab`.
3. In the Type field, click the **arrow** and select **Material**, then press `Tab`.
4. In the Material Label field, key **2-hour disc** and press `Enter`. This means you will use 2-hour discs as the unit of measure to track consumption during the project. Your screen should look similar to Figure 2-7.

Figure 2-7

Resource Sheet showing DVD material resource

	🛈	Resource Name	Type	Material Label	Initials	Group	Max. Units	Std. Rate	Ovt. Rate	Cost/Use	Accrue At	Base Calendar	Code
1		Jamie Reding	Work		J		100%	$0.00/hr	$0.00/hr	$0.00	Prorated	Standard	
2		Scott Seely	Work		S		100%	$0.00/hr	$0.00/hr	$0.00	Prorated	Standard	
3		Jeff Pike	Work		J		100%	$0.00/hr	$0.00/hr	$0.00	Prorated	Standard	
4		Judy Lew	Work		J		100%	$0.00/hr	$0.00/hr	$0.00	Prorated	Standard	
5		Brenda Diaz	Work		B		100%	$0.00/hr	$0.00/hr	$0.00	Prorated	Standard	
6		Brad Sutton	Work		B		100%	$0.00/hr	$0.00/hr	$0.00	Prorated	Standard	
7		Annette Hill	Work		A		50%	$0.00/hr	$0.00/hr	$0.00	Prorated	Standard	
8		Ryan Ihrig	Work		R		100%	$0.00/hr	$0.00/hr	$0.00	Prorated	Standard	
9		Yan Li	Work		Y		100%	$0.00/hr	$0.00/hr	$0.00	Prorated	Standard	
10		Sound Technician	Work		S		300%	$0.00/hr	$0.00/hr	$0.00	Prorated	Standard	
11		Digital Truck-Mounted	Work		D		300%	$0.00/hr	$0.00/hr	$0.00	Prorated	Standard	
12		Sound Editing Stdio	Work		S		100%	$0.00/hr	$0.00/hr	$0.00	Prorated	Standard	
13		Light Banks	Work		L		400%	$0.00/hr	$0.00/hr	$0.00	Prorated	Standard	
14		Video Editing Studio	Work		V		100%	$0.00/hr	$0.00/hr	$0.00	Prorated	Standard	
15		Microphone Bundles	Work		M		500%	$0.00/hr	$0.00/hr	$0.00	Prorated	Standard	
16		Dolly	Work		D		200%	$0.00/hr	$0.00/hr	$0.00	Prorated	Standard	
17		DVD	Material	2-hour disc	D			$0.00		$0.00	Prorated		

Material Resource unit of measure

5. SAVE the project plan.

PAUSE. LEAVE the project plan open to use in the next exercise.

In this exercise, the DVD you entered as a resource is a material resource. ***Material resources are consumable items used up as the tasks in a project are completed.*** Unlike work resources, material resources have no effect on the total amount of work scheduled to be performed on a task. For example, in a remodeling project, material resources may include drywall, nails, and paint. For your music video project, DVDs are the consumable that interests you most.

■ Establishing Cost Resources

THE BOTTOM LINE

Cost resources are financial obligations to your project. A cost resource enables you to apply a cost to a task by assigning a cost item (such as travel) to that task. The cost resource has no relationship to the work assigned to the task.

(→) ESTABLISH COST RESOURCES

USE the project plan you created in the previous exercise.

1. In the Resource Sheet, click the next empty cell in the Resource Name column.
2. Key **Travel** and then press [Tab].
3. In the Type field, click on the **arrow** and select **Cost**. The travel resource has now been established as a cost resource.
4. In the Resource Name field below Travel, key **Food** and press [Tab].
5. In the Type field, select **Cost** and press [Tab]. Your screen should look like Figure 2-8.

Figure 2-8

Resource Sheet with cost resources entered

		❶	Resource Name	Type	Material Label	Initials	Group	Max. Units	Std. Rate	Ovt. Rate	Cost/Use	Accrue At	Base Calendar	Code
	1		Jamie Reding	Work		J		100%	$0.00/hr	$0.00/hr	$0.00	Prorated	Standard	
	2		Scott Seely	Work		S		100%	$0.00/hr	$0.00/hr	$0.00	Prorated	Standard	
	3		Jeff Pike	Work		J		100%	$0.00/hr	$0.00/hr	$0.00	Prorated	Standard	
	4		Judy Lew	Work		J		100%	$0.00/hr	$0.00/hr	$0.00	Prorated	Standard	
	5		Brenda Diaz	Work		B		100%	$0.00/hr	$0.00/hr	$0.00	Prorated	Standard	
	6		Brad Sutton	Work		B		100%	$0.00/hr	$0.00/hr	$0.00	Prorated	Standard	
	7		Annette Hill	Work		A		50%	$0.00/hr	$0.00/hr	$0.00	Prorated	Standard	
	8		Ryan Ihrig	Work		R		100%	$0.00/hr	$0.00/hr	$0.00	Prorated	Standard	
	9		Yan Li	Work		Y		100%	$0.00/hr	$0.00/hr	$0.00	Prorated	Standard	
	10		Sound Technician	Work		S		300%	$0.00/hr	$0.00/hr	$0.00	Prorated	Standard	
	11		Digital Truck-Mounted	Work		D		200%	$0.00/hr	$0.00/hr	$0.00	Prorated	Standard	
	12		Sound Editing Studio	Work		S		100%	$0.00/hr	$0.00/hr	$0.00	Prorated	Standard	
	13		Light Banks	Work		L		400%	$0.00/hr	$0.00/hr	$0.00	Prorated	Standard	
	14		Video Editing Studio	Work		V		100%	$0.00/hr	$0.00/hr	$0.00	Prorated	Standard	
	15		Microphone Bundles	Work		M		500%	$0.00/hr	$0.00/hr	$0.00	Prorated	Standard	
	16		Dolly	Work		D		200%	$0.00/hr	$0.00/hr	$0.00	Prorated	Standard	
	17		DVD	Material	2-hour disc	D			$0.00		$0.00	Prorated		
	18		Travel	Cost		T						Prorated		
	19		Food	Cost		F						Prorated		

Cost resources entered on Resource Sheet

TAKE NOTE

Cost resources differ from fixed costs in that cost resources are created as a type of resource and then assigned to a task. Also, unlike work resources, cost resources cannot have a calendar applied to them and therefore do not affect the scheduling of the task. The dollar value of cost resources doesn't depend on the amount of work done on the task to which they are assigned.

6. **SAVE** the project plan.

PAUSE. LEAVE the project plan open to use in the next exercise.

In this exercise, you added cost resources to the resource sheet for your project. *A cost resource* is a resource that doesn't depend on the amount of work on a task or the duration of a task. Some examples of cost resources are airfare, lodging, and asset costs. Unlike fixed costs, you can apply as many cost resources to a task as necessary. Cost resources give you more control when applying various types of costs to tasks.

■ Establishing Resource Pay Rates

THE BOTTOM LINE Although you might not track costs on small or personal projects, managing cost information is a key part of most project managers' job descriptions. When you enter the cost information for resources, tracking the finances of a project becomes a more manageable task.

➔ ENTER RESOURCE COST INFORMATION

USE the project plan you created in the previous exercise.

1. In the Resource Sheet, click the Std. (Standard) Rate field for resource 1, Jamie Reding.
2. Key **1000/w** and press **Enter**. Jamie's standard weekly rate of $1,000 per week appears in the Std. rate column.
3. In the Std. Rate column for resource 2, Scott Seely, key **19.50/h** and press **Enter**. Scott's standard hourly rate of $19.50 appears in the Std. Rate column. Your screen should look similar to Figure 2-9.

Figure 2-9

Resource Sheet showing standard rates for first two resources

	❶	Resource Name	Type	Material Label	Initials	Group	Max. Units	Std. Rate	Ovt. Rate	Cost/Use	Accrue At	Base Calendar	Code
1		Jamie Reding	Work		J		100%	$1,000.00/wk	$0.00/hr	$0.00	Prorated	Standard	
2		Scott Seely	Work		S		100%	$19.50/hr	$0.00/hr	$0.00	Prorated	Standard	
3		Jeff Pike	Work		J		100%	$0.00/hr	$0.00/hr	$0.00	Prorated	Standard	
4		Judy Lew	Work		J		100%	$0.00/hr	$0.00/hr	$0.00	Prorated	Standard	
5		Brenda Diaz	Work		B		100%	$0.00/hr	$0.00/hr	$0.00	Prorated	Standard	
6		Brad Sutton	Work		B		100%	$0.00/hr	$0.00/hr	$0.00	Prorated	Standard	
7		Annette Hill	Work		A		50%	$0.00/hr	$0.00/hr	$0.00	Prorated	Standard	
8		Ryan Ihrig	Work		R		100%	$0.00/hr	$0.00/hr	$0.00	Prorated	Standard	
9		Yan Li	Work		Y		100%	$0.00/hr	$0.00/hr	$0.00	Prorated	Standard	
10		Sound Technician	Work		S		300%	$0.00/hr	$0.00/hr	$0.00	Prorated	Standard	
11		Digital Truck-Mounted	Work		D		200%	$0.00/hr	$0.00/hr	$0.00	Prorated	Standard	
12		Sound Editing Studio	Work		S		100%	$0.00/hr	$0.00/hr	$0.00	Prorated	Standard	
13		Light Banks	Work		L		400%	$0.00/hr	$0.00/hr	$0.00	Prorated	Standard	
14		Video Editing Studio	Work		V		100%	$0.00/hr	$0.00/hr	$0.00	Prorated	Standard	
15		Microphone Bundles	Work		M		500%	$0.00/hr	$0.00/hr	$0.00	Prorated	Standard	
16		Dolly	Work		D		200%	$0.00/hr	$0.00/hr	$0.00	Prorated	Standard	
17		DVD	Material	2-hour disc	D			$0.00		$0.00	Prorated		
18		Travel	Cost		T						Prorated		
19		Food	Cost		F						Prorated		

4. Enter the following standard pay rates for the remaining resources

Resource Name	Standard Rate
Jeff Pike	750/w
Judy Lew	19.50/h
Brenda Diaz	12.75/h
Brad Sutton	16.50/h
Annette Hill	20.00/h
Ryan Ihrig	12.00/h
Yan Li	18.50/h
Sound Technician	16.50/h
Digital Truck-Mounted Video Camera	1000/w
Sound Editing Studio	250/d
Light Banks	0/h

Video Editing Studio	250/d
Microphone Bundles	0/h
Dolly	25/d
DVD	10

5. Widen the Std. Rate column by moving the mouse pointer to the vertical divider line between the Std. Rate column and Ovt. Rate column. Double click on the divider line. Your screen should look similar to Figure 2-10.

Figure 2-10

Resource Sheet with standard pay rates for all resources

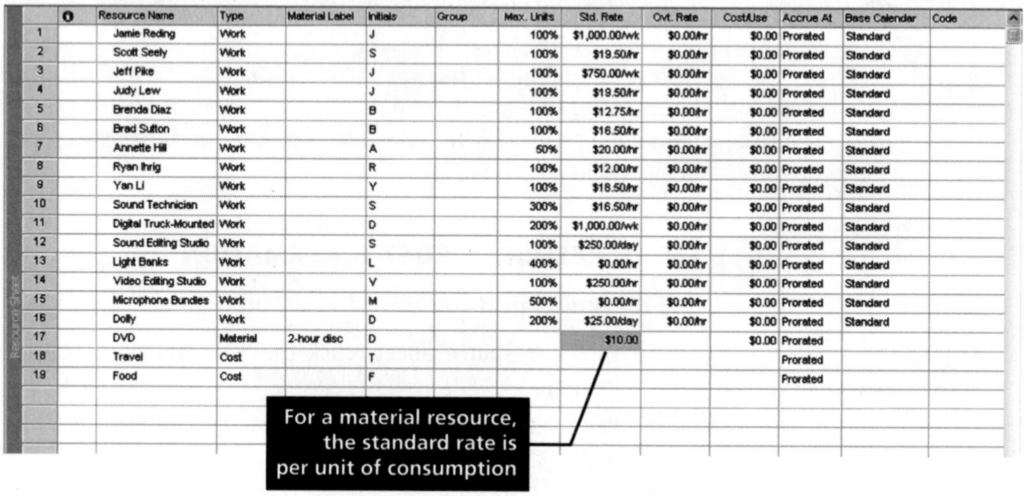

		Resource Name	Type	Material Label	Initials	Group	Max. Units	Std. Rate	Ovt. Rate	Cost/Use	Accrue At	Base Calendar	Code
1		Jamie Reding	Work		J		100%	$1,000.00/wk	$0.00/hr	$0.00	Prorated	Standard	
2		Scott Seely	Work		S		100%	$19.50/hr	$0.00/hr	$0.00	Prorated	Standard	
3		Jeff Pike	Work		J		100%	$750.00/wk	$0.00/hr	$0.00	Prorated	Standard	
4		Judy Lew	Work		J		100%	$19.50/hr	$0.00/hr	$0.00	Prorated	Standard	
5		Brenda Diaz	Work		B		100%	$12.75/hr	$0.00/hr	$0.00	Prorated	Standard	
6		Brad Sutton	Work		B		100%	$16.50/hr	$0.00/hr	$0.00	Prorated	Standard	
7		Annette Hill	Work		A		50%	$20.00/hr	$0.00/hr	$0.00	Prorated	Standard	
8		Ryan Ihrig	Work		R		100%	$12.00/hr	$0.00/hr	$0.00	Prorated	Standard	
9		Yan Li	Work		Y		100%	$18.50/hr	$0.00/hr	$0.00	Prorated	Standard	
10		Sound Technician	Work		S		300%	$16.50/hr	$0.00/hr	$0.00	Prorated	Standard	
11		Digital Truck-Mounted	Work		D		200%	$1,000.00/wk	$0.00/hr	$0.00	Prorated	Standard	
12		Sound Editing Studio	Work		S		100%	$250.00/day	$0.00/hr	$0.00	Prorated	Standard	
13		Light Banks	Work		L		400%	$0.00/hr	$0.00/hr	$0.00	Prorated	Standard	
14		Video Editing Studio	Work		V		100%	$250.00/hr	$0.00/hr	$0.00	Prorated	Standard	
15		Microphone Bundles	Work		M		500%	$0.00/hr	$0.00/hr	$0.00	Prorated	Standard	
16		Dolly	Work		D		200%	$25.00/day	$0.00/hr	$0.00	Prorated	Standard	
17		DVD	Material	2-hour disc	D			$10.00		$0.00	Prorated		
18		Travel	Cost		T						Prorated		
19		Food	Cost		F						Prorated		

For a material resource, the standard rate is per unit of consumption

TAKE NOTE * Notice that you didn't enter a rate (weekly, hourly, or daily) for the cost of the DVD. For a material resource, the standard rate is per unit of consumption. For this exercise, that is a 2-hour DVD. Also note that you did not assign a cost to the cost resources; this is done when the cost resources are assigned to a task (covered in Lesson 3).

6. SAVE the project plan.

PAUSE. LEAVE the project plan open to use in the next exercise.

You have just entered cost information for both work and material resources. For this exercise, knowing this information will help you to take full advantage of the cost management features of Microsoft Project. In the real world, however, it is often difficult to get cost information for people resources because this information is usually considered confidential. As a project manager, it is important that you are aware of the limitations of your project plan because of the information that is available to you, and that you communicate these limitations to your project team and management.

As a project manager, tracking and managing cost information may be a significant part of your project responsibilities. Understanding the cost details of your project will allow you to stay on top of such key information as

- the expected total cost of the project
- resource costs over the life of the project
- possible cost savings from using one resource versus another
- the rate of spending in relation to the length of the project

These and other cost limits often drive the scope of your project and may become critical to project decisions that you will make.

■ Adjusting Resource Working Times

THE BOTTOM LINE   Working times for resources can be adjusted in a number of ways.

Establishing Nonworking Times

Now that you have entered resources and their associated pay rates in your project plan, you can specify the working and nonworking times for some of these resources.

⊕ ESTABLISH NONWORKING TIMES FOR AN INDIVIDUAL WORK RESOURCE

USE the project plan you created in the previous exercise.

1. On the menu bar, click **Tools** and then click **Change Working Time**. The Change Working Time dialog box appears.

2. In the *For calendar* box, select **Jamie Reding**. Jamie Reding's resource calendar appears in the Change Working Time dialog box.

3. Slide the button next to the calendar until the calendar is on January, 2008.

4. Select the dates January **30** and **31**.

5. In the first Name field under the Exceptions tab, key **Vacation Days**.

6. Click on the first field in the Start column. The Start field displays 1/30/2008 and the Finish field displays 1/31/2008. Microsoft Project will not schedule Jamie Reding to work on these two days. Your screen should look similar to Figure 2-11.

Figure 2-11

Change Working Time dialog box showing exception time for Jamie Reding

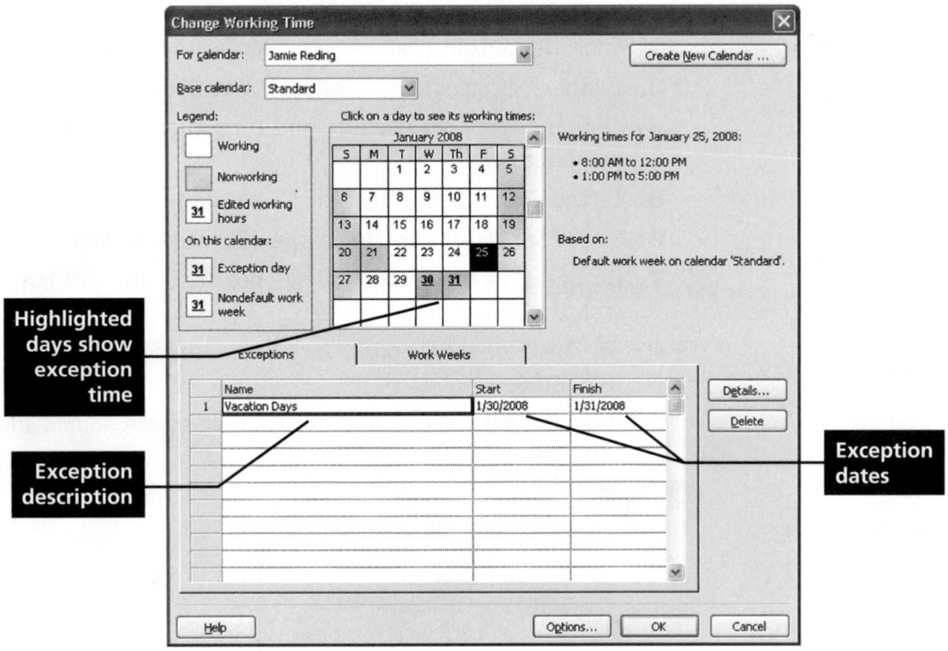

7. Click **OK** to close the Change Working Time dialog box.

8. **SAVE** the project plan.

   PAUSE. LEAVE the project plan open to use in the next exercise.

A *resource calendar* defines the working and nonworking time for an individual resource. A resource calendar applies only to people and equipment (work) resources–not to material resources. When you establish resources in your project plan, a resource calendar is created for each resource. Initially in Microsoft Project, the resource calendar is identical to the *project calendar*, or the base calendar that provides default working times for an entire project. However, as you saw in this exercise, you will usually need to make changes to individual resource calendars to reflect differences from the project calendar such as vacation, flex-time work schedules, or conference attendance.

REF

Refer back to Lesson 1 for a quick refresher on the types of calendars used by Microsoft Project.

Keep in mind that when you make changes to the project calendar, the changes are reflected in all resource calendars that are based on the project calendar. However, any changes you have made to the working times of an individual resource are not changed.

Establishing Specific Work Schedules

In addition to specifying exception times for resources, you can also set up a specific work schedule for any given resource.

➔ ESTABLISH A SPECIFIC WORK SCHEDULE FOR A RESOURCE

USE the project plan you created in the previous exercise.

1. On the menu bar, click **Tools** and then click **Change Working Time** to open the Change Working Time dialog box.
2. Slide the button next to the calendar until the calendar is on January, 2008.
3. In the *For calendar* box, select **Scott Seely**.
4. Click the **Work Weeks** tab, and then click the **Details** button. The Details dialog box appears.
5. In the *Select day(s)* box, click and drag to select Monday through Thursday.
6. Select **Set day(s) to these specific working times**.
7. On line 1 of the Working Times box, click the **8:00AM** box and replace it with **7:00AM**.
8. On line 2 of the Working Times box, click the **5:00PM** box and replace it with **6:00PM**.
9. Press **Enter** to set your changes. Your screen should look similar to Figure 2-12.

Figure 2-12

Details dialog box showing modified working times for Scott Seely

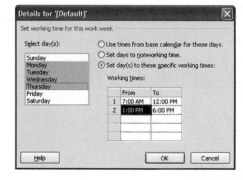

10. In the *Select day(s)* box, click **Friday**.

11. Select **Set day(s) to nonworking time**.

12. Click **OK** to close the Details dialog box. Microsoft Project can now schedule Scott Seely to work as early as 7:00AM and as late as 6:00PM on Monday through Thursday, but it will not schedule him to work on Friday. Your screen should look similar to Figure 2-13.

Figure 2-13

Change Working Time dialog box showing modified resource calendar for Scott Seely

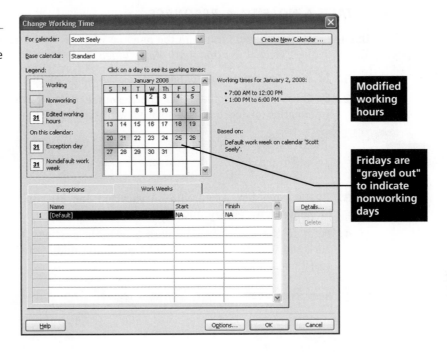

13. Click **OK** to close the Change Working Time dialog box.

14. **SAVE** the project plan.

PAUSE. LEAVE the project plan open to use in the next exercise.

In this exercise, you made a change to the resource calendar for an individual resource. If you need to edit several resource calendars in the same way (to handle a flex-time schedule or night shift, for example), you might find it easier to assign a different base calendar to this group of resources. A ***base calendar*** can be used as both a task and project calendar and specifies default working and nonworking times for a set of resources. Assigning a different base calendar is quicker than editing each individual resource calendar, and it allows you to make future project-wide changes to a single base calendar (rather than editing each resource calendar again). You can change a resource's base calendar by opening the Change Working Time dialog box from the Tools menu. In the *For* box, select the desired resource and then in the *Base Calendar* box, select the desired base calendar. For a group of resources that will be using the same calendar, you can change the calendar directly in the Base Calendar column of the Entry table in the Resource Sheet view. Microsoft Project includes three base calendars: Standard, 24 Hours, and Night Shift. You can customize these or use them as a basis for your own base calendar.

■ Adding Resource Notes

↓ THE BOTTOM LINE

At times, you may want to provide the details regarding how (and why) a resource is scheduled the way that it is. You can add this additional information about a resource by attaching a note.

➔ ATTACH A NOTE TO A RESOURCE

USE the project plan you created in the previous exercise. Make sure you are still in the Resource Sheet view of the ***Don Funk Music Video 2*** file.

1. In the Resource Name column, select the name of the resource 1, **Jamie Reding**.

2. On the Standard toolbar, click the **Resource Notes** button 🗒 . The Resource Information dialog box is displayed with the Notes tab visible.

TROUBLESHOOTING

Remember that if a button is not visible on your toolbar, use the Toolbar Options button to add the desired button to your Standard toolbar.

3. In the Notes box, key **Jamie on vacation Jan 30 and 31; available for consult at home if necessary** and click **OK**. A note icon appears in the indicator column.

4. Point to the note icon. The note appears in a Screen Tip. For longer notes, double-click the icon to display the full text of the note. Your screen should look similar to Figure 2-14.

Figure 2-14

Resource note displayed as a Screen Tip

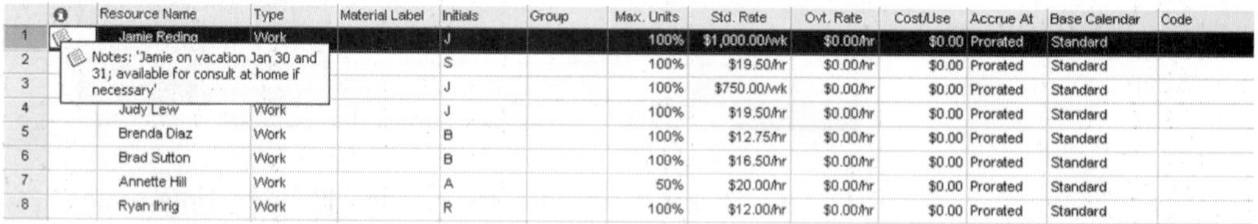

	❶	Resource Name	Type	Material Label	Initials	Group	Max. Units	Std. Rate	Ovt. Rate	Cost/Use	Accrue At	Base Calendar	Code
1		Jamie Reding	Work		J		100%	$1,000.00/wk	$0.00/hr	$0.00	Prorated	Standard	
2		Notes: 'Jamie on vacation Jan 30 and 31; available for consult at home if necessary'			S		100%	$19.50/hr	$0.00/hr	$0.00	Prorated	Standard	
3					J		100%	$750.00/wk	$0.00/hr	$0.00	Prorated	Standard	
4		Judy Lew	Work		J		100%	$19.50/hr	$0.00/hr	$0.00	Prorated	Standard	
5		Brenda Diaz	Work		B		100%	$12.75/hr	$0.00/hr	$0.00	Prorated	Standard	
6		Brad Sutton	Work		B		100%	$16.50/hr	$0.00/hr	$0.00	Prorated	Standard	
7		Annette Hill	Work		A		50%	$20.00/hr	$0.00/hr	$0.00	Prorated	Standard	
8		Ryan Ihrig	Work		R		100%	$12.00/hr	$0.00/hr	$0.00	Prorated	Standard	

5. **SAVE** the project plan.

6. **CLOSE** the **Don Funk Music Video 2** file.

7. **PAUSE**. If you are continuing to the next lesson, keep Project open. If you are not continuing to additional lessons, **CLOSE** Project.

SUMMARY SKILL MATRIX

IN THIS LESSON YOU LEARNED	MATRIX SKILL
To establish people resources	Establish individual people resources Establish a resource that represents multiple people
To establish equipment resources	Establish equipment resources
To establish material resources	Establish material resources
To establish cost resources	Establish cost resources
To establish resource pay rates	Enter resource cost information
To adjust resource working times	Establish nonworking times for an individual resource Establish a specific work schedule for a resource
To add resource notes	Attach a note to a resource

■ Knowledge Assessment

Matching

Match the term in column 1 to its description in column 2.

	Column 1		Column 2
1.	resource calendar	a.	the maximum capacity of a resource to accomplish tasks
2.	Max. Units	b.	specifies default working and nonworking times for a set of resources
3.	material resource	c.	when and how much of a resource's time can be assigned to work on tasks
4.	project calendar	d.	the people and equipment that do work to accomplish the tasks of the project
5.	cost	e.	the people, equipment, and materials used to complete the tasks in a project
6.	work resource	f.	a financial obligation to the project that doesn't depend on the amount of work on a task
7.	base calendar	g.	consumable items used up as the tasks in a project are accomplished
8.	availability	h.	how much money will be needed to pay for the resources on a project
9.	resources	i.	the base calendar that provides default working times for an entire project
10.	cost resource	j.	defines the working and nonworking time for an individual resource

Multiple Choice

Select the best response for the following statements.

1. Which of the following is NOT an example of a work resource?
   a. Yan Li
   b. keyboard
   c. DVD
   d. electrician

2. It is helpful to assign a base calendar to a group of resources when they all
   a. have the same pay rate.
   b. work night shift.
   c. have the same Max. units.
   d. do the same job function.

3. A resource calendar does not apply to
   a. material resources.
   b. people resources.
   c. equipment resources.
   d. work resources.

4. You can view information for the individual people who will perform the tasks on the project in the
   a. Calendar view.
   b. Gantt Chart view.
   c. Task Usage view.
   d. Resource Sheet view.

5. You can provide additional information about how a resource is scheduled by
   a. changing the Max. Units.
   b. establishing a project calendar.
   c. adding a resource note.
   d. setting constraints.

6. For which resource is the standard rate listed per unit of consumption?
   a. material
   b. equipment
   c. people
   d. all of the above

7. If you have four electricians who can each work part-time (4 hours rather than 8), what value should you assign to Max. Units for the resource "electrician"?
   a. 50%
   b. 25%
   c. 100%
   d. 200%

8. If you assign a resource to more tasks than it can accomplish at its maximum units, the resource is
   a. maxed out.
   b. overallocated.
   c. constrained.
   d. in default.

9. To add vacation days to the calendar for an individual work resource, which dialog box would you use?
   a. Resource Information
   b. Resource Notes
   c. Change Working Times
   d. none of the above

10. It is often difficult to get cost information for people resources because
    a. the information is often confidential.
    b. the information is too complex to calculate.
    c. the information changes too frequently.
    d. the costs are large in comparison with other resource costs.

■ Competency Assessment

➔ Project 2-1: Hiring a New Employee

The *Hiring New Employee 2-1* project plan is available on the companion CD-ROM.

In the previous lesson, you entered the tasks of a project plan for hiring a new employee. Now you need to add some of the people resources that will be responsible for performing those tasks.

GET READY. Launch Microsoft Project if it is not already running. **OPEN** *Hiring New Employee 2-1* from the data files for this lesson.

1. Click **Resources** on the Project Guide toolbar.
2. In the *Resources* pane, click the **Specify people and equipment for the project** link.
3. Select **Enter resources manually.**
4. In the Simple Resource Sheet view, click the empty cell directly below the Resource Name column heading.
5. Enter the following resource names into the Simple Resource Sheet.

   Gabe Mares

   Barry Potter

   Amy Rusko

   Jeff Smith
6. Click **Done** in the *Specify Resources* pane.
7. Click the close button in the upper right corner of the Project Guide to close the project guide.
8. **SAVE** the project as *Hire New Employee* and then **CLOSE** the file.

   LEAVE Project open for the next exercise.

➔ Project 2-2: Office Remodel

The *Office Remodel 2-2* project plan is available on the companion CD-ROM.

You are in charge of the remodel for the kitchen and lunchroom for your office. Your facilities manager has just provided you with the resource pay rates for this project. You need to enter the pay rates in the project plan.

OPEN *Office Remodel 2-2* from the data files for this lesson.

1. On the menu bar, click **View** and then click **Resource Sheet.**
2. In the Type field for Drywall, click the arrow in the dropdown box and select **Material**, then press Tab. In the Type field for Nails, click the arrow in the dropdown box and select **Material**, then press Tab.
3. In the Resource Sheet, click the Std. (Standard) Rate field for resource 1, Toby Nixon.
4. Key 500/w and press Enter.
5. Enter the following standard pay rates for the remaining resources.

Resource Name	Standard Rate
Lori Kane	500/w
Run Liu	20/h
Electrician	30/h
Plumber	30/h
Drywall	11
Nails	5
John Emory	450/w
Scaffolding	50/d
Table saw	35/d

6. **SAVE** the project as *Remodel-2* and then **CLOSE** the file.

LEAVE Project open for the next exercise.

■ Proficiency Assessment

⊕ Project 2-3: Resource Note for Hiring New Employee

The *Hiring Empl-Note 2-3* project plan is available on the companion CD-ROM.

You have created a project plan for hiring a new employee. Now you need to add a note to one of the resources on the project.

OPEN *Hiring Empl–Note 2-3* from the data files for this lesson.

1. Select the name of resource 3, **Amy Rusko**.
2. Click the **Resource Notes** button.
3. Add the following note: **Amy will be at the SHRM conference on July 18-20. Not available for any interviews.**
4. Close the Resource Information box.
5. Select the name of resource 4, **Jeff Smith**.
6. Click the **Resource Notes** button.
7. Add the following note: **Jeff will be at the SHRM conference on July 18-19. Available for interviews on July 20.**
8. Close the Resource Information box.
9. **SAVE** the project plan as **Hiring Employee Note** and then **CLOSE** the file.

LEAVE Project open for the next exercise.

⊕ Project 2-4: Equipment Resources for New Employee Orientation

The *Employee Orientation 2-4* project plan is available on the companion CD-ROM.

You have already developed a project plan for a New Employee Orientation in your department. Now you need to add several equipment resources to make sure that your plan flows smoothly.

OPEN *Employee Orientation 2-4* from the data files for this lesson.

1. Activate the *Resources* pane of the Project Guide.
2. Change the view to Resource Sheet.
3. Add the following equipment resources to the project plan.

Resource Name	Max. Units
DVD/TV Combo	100%
Digital Camera	50%
Laminating Machine	50%
Laptop Computer	600%
Large Conference Room	100%

4. **SAVE** the project plan as *Employee Orientation Resources* and then **CLOSE** the file.

LEAVE Project open for the next exercise.

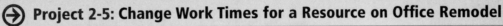

■ Mastery Assessment

→ Project 2-5: Change Work Times for a Resource on Office Remodel

The *Office Remodel 2-5* project plan is available on the companion CD-ROM.

You have just been told that one of your resources on your office remodel project is planning to take a week of vacation. You need to add this information to your project plan.

OPEN *Office Remodel 2-5* from the data files for this lesson.

1. Open the Change Working Times dialog box.
2. Change Lori Kane's resource calendar to reflect her vacation from August 20-24, 2007.
3. **SAVE** the project plan as **Office Remodel Vacation** and then **CLOSE** the file.

   LEAVE Project open to use in the next exercise.

→ Project 2-6: Don Funk Music Video Problems

The *Don Funk Incorrect 2-6* project plan is available on the companion CD-ROM.

A student who is interning with your company made some updates to the music video project plan. Unfortunately, he is still learning about Microsoft Project and has entered some information incorrectly. You need to correct the problems with the project plan before distributing it to your team.

OPEN *Don Funk Incorrect 2-6* from the data files for this lesson.

1. Review the Resource Sheet for this project plan.
2. Based on what you have learned in this lesson about Resource Types, Maximum Units, and Standard Rates, find the resource errors in this project plan and make corrections to them. (Hint: There are three resource errors in the project plan.)
3. Study the last three resources on the sheet. If dry ice is a material resource and bottled water is a cost resource, make corrections to the information given for these resources (estimate the rate if necessary).
4. **SAVE** the project plan as **Don Funk Corrected** and then **CLOSE** the file.

   CLOSE Project.

INTERNET READY

Search the Internet for information on summer camps for children. Review locations, facilities, equipment, activities, and staffing for several well-developed camp programs. Based on your research, develop a Resource table in Microsoft Project of the resources (people, equipment, cost, and material) that are necessary for running a summer camp. Include at least 20 resources. For each resource, include the type, maximum units, standard rate, and material label if appropriate. (Make estimates of the maximum units and standard rate.)

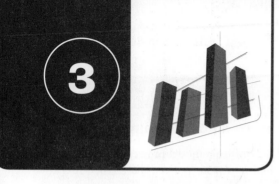

3

Resource and Task Assignments

LESSON SKILL MATRIX

SKILLS	MATRIX SKILL
Assigning Work Resources to Tasks	Make individual resource assignments Assign multiple resources simultaneously
Adding More Resource Assignments to Tasks	Add resources to a task Use a Smart Tag to assign resources to tasks
Assigning Material Resources to Tasks	Assign a material resource to a task
Assigning Cost Resources to Tasks	Assign a cost resource to a task

As the video production manager at Southridge Video, you are working on a new music video for Don Funk, an up-and-coming singer/songwriter. You first mapped out the initial tasks in the project, and then identified the resources needed to complete the tasks in the project. Now you need to put the two together. When you link resources and tasks, Microsoft Office Project can show you who is working on what tasks and when, if you have adequate resources, if the resources are available when you need them to be, if a resource is overallocated, and more. In this lesson, you will learn how to assign work and material resources to a task, how to manipulate resources to "tweak" the project, and how to use Smart Tags.

■ SOFTWARE ORIENTATION

Microsoft Project's Assign Resources Dialog Box

In Microsoft Project, when you assign work or material resources to a task, you will use the Assign Resources dialog box. You activate the Assign Resources dialog box via the *Resources* pane of the Project Guide or the Assign Resources button on the Standard toolbar. Your Assign Resources dialog box should look similar to Figure 3-1 or 3-2.

This dialog box was activated using the *Resources* pane of the Project Guide. Your dialog box may differ slightly if the *Resource list options* section is expanded (you can expand this section by clicking on the plus sign next to *Resource list options*).

Figure 3-1

Assign Resources dialog box

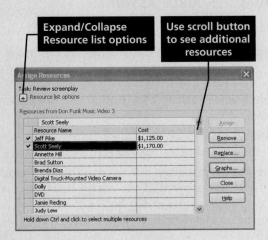

This dialog box was activated using the Assign Resources button on the Standard toolbar. Your dialog box may differ slightly if the *Resource list options* section is collapsed (you can collapse this section by clicking on the minus sign next to *Resource list options*). This is the Assign Resource dialog box you will need to use to assign material resources–you will enter the quantity of the resource in the Units column.

Figure 3-2

Assign Resources dialog box with Units column

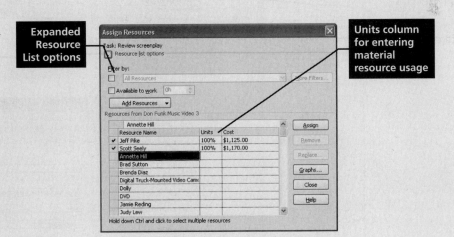

▪ Assigning Work Resources to Tasks

<table>
<tr><td>↓
THE BOTTOM LINE</td><td>Microsoft Project provides you with various options for assigning resources to tasks. You can assign individual resources to a task or multiple resources to a task. Once assigned, you can track the resource working on the task. Microsoft Project also enables you to see whether or not resource assignments affect task duration.</td></tr>
</table>

Making Individual Resource Assignments

In the previous lessons, you mapped out tasks and resources for your project plan. Now you can begin to assign those resources to the tasks they will perform.

➔ MAKE INDIVIDUAL RESOURCE ASSIGNMENTS

The **Don Funk Music Video 3M** project plan is available on the companion CD-ROM.

GET READY. Before you begin these steps, launch Microsoft Project.

OPEN *Don Funk Music Video 3M* from the data files for this lesson.

SAVE the file as *Don Funk Music Video 3*.

1. On the Project Guide toolbar, click **Resources**. The *Resources* pane of the Project Guide appears.

2. In the *Resources* pane, click the **Assign people and equipment to tasks** link. The *Assign Resources* pane of the Project Guide appears.

3. Click on the **Assign resources** link under *1) Assign Resources dialog*. The Assign Resources dialog box appears. If the Assign Resources dialog box is covering the task name column, drag the dialog box to the lower right corner of the screen. Your screen should look similar to Figure 3-3.

Figure 3-3

Project plan in Gantt Chart view with Assign Resources dialog box

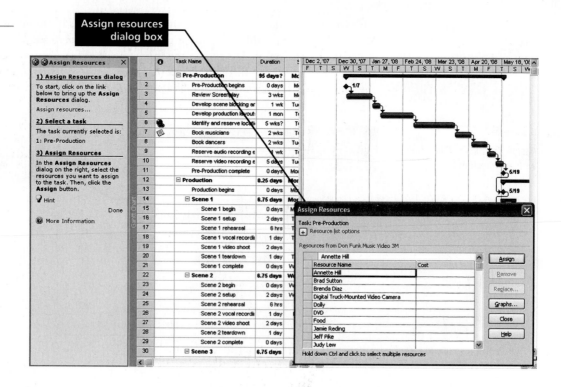

4. In the Task Name column of the Gantt Chart, click the name of task 3, **Review Screenplay**.

5. In the Resource Name column of the Assign Resources dialog box, scroll down and click **Scott Seely** and then click the **Assign** button. A check appears next to Scott Seely's name, indicating that you have assigned him to the task of reviewing the screenplay. Also, the fourth step of the process (Review Information) appears in the *Assign Resources* pane. Your screen should look similar to Figure 3-4.

TAKE NOTE

Resources are sorted alphabetically in the Assign Resources dialog box. Once the resource has been assigned, it is moved to the top of the list.

Figure 3-4

Project plan showing Scott Seely assigned to task 3, and *Assign Resources* pane showing Step 4, Review Information

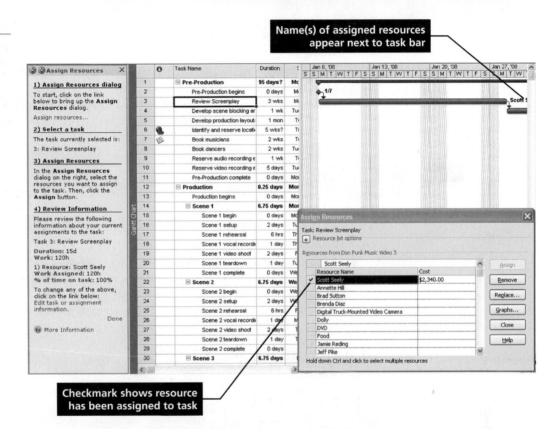

Name(s) of assigned resources appear next to task bar

Checkmark shows resource has been assigned to task

TAKE NOTE

Step 4 of the *Assign Resources* pane, Review Information, summarizes the key scheduling information for this task–duration, work, resource(s) assigned, and assignment units (shown as % of time on task).

6. In the Task Name column, click the name of task 5, **Develop production layouts**.
7. In the Assign Resources dialog box, click **Jeff Pike** and then click the **Assign** button. A check appears next to Jeff's name to show that you have assigned him to task 5.
8. **SAVE** the project plan.

   PAUSE. LEAVE the project plan open to use in the next exercise.

An ***assignment*** is the matching of a specific resource to a particular task to do work. Depending on your perspective, you might call it a resource assignment or you might call it a task assignment. In either case, a task paired with a resource results in an assignment. Once you have assigned a resource to a task, Microsoft Project tracks the progress of the resource in working on the task. If you have entered cost information, Project can also track resource and task costs.

■ Assigning Multiple Resources Simultaneously

THE BOTTOM LINE

You have just assigned one resource to a task. Sometimes it is necessary to assign multiple resources simultaneously to a task.

→ ASSIGN MULTIPLE RESOURCES SIMULTANEOUSLY

USE the project plan you created in the previous exercise.

1. In the Task Name column, click the name of task 4, **Develop scene blocking and schedule**. The *Assign Resources* pane of the Project Guide and the Assign Resources dialog box are both refreshed.

2. In the Assign Resources dialog box, scroll down and click **Scott Seely**. Scroll up or down in the list until the name Judy Lew is visible. Hold down [Ctrl], click **Judy Lew**, and then click the **Assign** button. Check marks appear next to Scott Seely's and Judy Lew's names, indicating that you have assigned them both to task 4.

TAKE NOTE

If you want to remove or unassign a resource from a selected task, click the resource name and then click the Remove button.

3. In the Task Name column, click the name of task 6, **Identify and reserve locations**.

4. In the Assign Resources dialog box, click **Jeff Pike**. Scroll up or down in the list until the name Yan Li is visible. Hold down [Ctrl], click **Yan Li**, and then click the **Assign** button. Check marks appear next to Jeff Pike's and Yan Li's names, indicating that you have assigned them both to task 6. Your screen should look similar to Figure 3-5.

Figure 3-5

Project plan showing Jeff Pike and Yan Li assigned to task 6

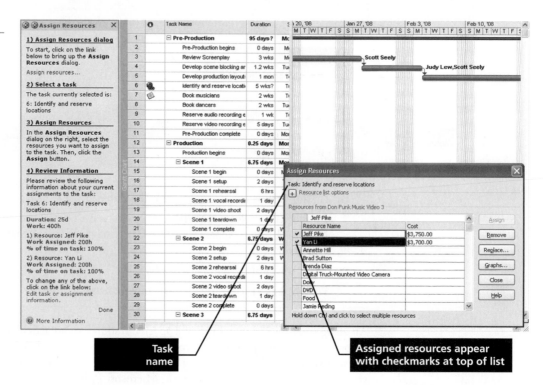

5. **SAVE** the project plan.

PAUSE. LEAVE the project plan open to use in the next exercise.

REF

Recall that in Lesson 2 you learned that *Max. Units* referred to the maximum capacity of a resource to accomplish tasks.

The capacity of a resource to work when you assign that resource to a task is measured in *units*. Units are recorded in the Max. Units field on the Resource Sheet view. One full-time resource has 100% (or 1.0) resource units. As you are assigning resources, you need to be careful that you do not overallocate a resource. A resource is **overallocated** when it is assigned to do more work than can be done within the normal work capacity of the resource. This may happen if you assign a resource to a task with more units than the resource has available. Another possibility is that you assign the resource to multiple tasks with schedules that overlap and with combined units that exceed those of the resource. Keep in mind that Microsoft Project assumes that all of a resource's work time can be allotted to an assigned task unless you specify otherwise. If the resource has less than 100 percent maximum units, Microsoft Project assigns the value of the resource's maximum units.

■ Adding More Resource Assignments to Tasks

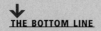

THE BOTTOM LINE

Microsoft Project applies a default scheduling called effort-driven scheduling when you assign resources to or remove resources from tasks. With effort-driven scheduling, the task's initial work value remains constant, no matter how many additional resources are assigned. The most obvious effect of effort-driven scheduling is that as you add or remove resources, a task's duration decreases or increases.

Adding Resources to a Task

You have started to define resource assignments for several tasks in your project plan. Now you will assign additional resources to those tasks. Pay close attention to the results in relation to task duration and work.

⊖ ADD RESOURCES TO A TASK

USE the project plan you created in the previous exercise.

1. Click the name of task 3, **Review Screenplay**. In the *Assign Resources* pane on the left side of your screen, take note of the Review Information section, particularly the values for Work and Duration.

2. In the Assign Resources dialog box, click **Jeff Pike** and then click the **Assign** button. Microsoft Project assigns Jeff Pike to task 3. Your screen should look similar to Figure 3-6. If necessary, expand the *Duration* column so that the durations for all tasks can be fully seen.

Figure 3-6

Assign Resources pane and
Assign Resources dialog box
showing details for task 3

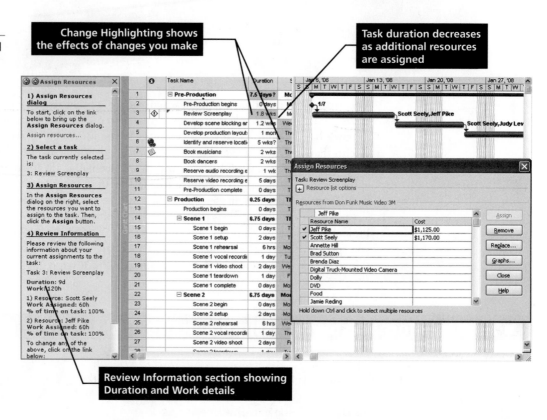

Change Highlighting shows
the effects of changes you make

Task duration decreases
as additional resources
are assigned

Review Information section showing
Duration and Work details

3. **SAVE** the project plan.

PAUSE. LEAVE the project plan open to use in the next exercise.

X REF
If you noticed a small triangle in the corner of the name of task 3, this is a SmartTag. You can find more information on SmartTags in the next section of this lesson.

In Lesson 1, you created tasks that had a *duration,* or the amount of time you expected the task to take to complete. In Lesson 2, you created resources that would be responsible for the tasks. Now, in Lesson 3, when you assigned resources to tasks, the result is work. **Work** is the total amount of effort a resource or resources will spend to complete a task. Microsoft Project calculates work using a ***scheduling formula***: Duration × Units = Work.

LOOKING AHEAD
You can find more information on the scheduling formula in Lesson 4.

In general, if you have one resource working full-time on a task, the amount of work will match the duration. If your resource is not working full-time, or if you assign more than one resource to a task, then work and duration will not be equal. You saw this in the exercise you just completed. When only Scott Seely was assigned to task 3, the work and duration were the same (15d or 120h). However, when you assigned Jeff Pike to help on this task, the duration decreased (9d) but the work stayed the same (120h, or 60h each to Jeff and Scott).

TAKE NOTE
Click the More Information link at the bottom of the *Assign Resources* pane for a review of work and assignment units.

The default method of scheduling in Microsoft Project is effort-driven scheduling. With *effort-driven scheduling*, the duration of a task increases or decreases as you remove resources from or assign resources to a task; the amount of work needed to complete the task does not change. Recall that in Lesson 2 you created finish-to-start relationships for the project tasks. You can now see the benefit of creating task relationships rather than setting start or finish dates. Because effort-driven scheduling resulted in decreased task durations, Microsoft Project adjusted the start dates of successor tasks that did not have a constraint such as a start or finish date.

TAKE NOTE

Although effort-driven scheduling is the default for all tasks you create in Microsoft Project, you can change the default setting for all new tasks in a project plan. On the menu bar, click Tools. On the Tools menu, select Options, and then select the Schedule tab in the Options dialog box. Clear or select the *New tasks are effort driven* check box. To change effort-driven scheduling for a single task or group of tasks, select the desired task(s). Click the Task Information button, and select the Advanced tab of the Task Information dialog box. Clear or select the *Effort driven* check box.

 Look back again to Figure 3-6. Did you notice that some of the cells in the Duration, Start, and Finish columns are shaded light blue? (You may need to shift the Gantt Chart to the right so that these columns are visible.) Microsoft Project's Change Highlighting automatically highlights all items that change as a result of the most recent change you made. This helps you gain a better understanding of the impacts of your choices.

Using a Smart Tag to Assign Resources

Now that you have assigned multiple resources to several tasks, in this exercise you will learn how to use a Smart Tag to assign additional resources to a task.

⊕ USE A SMART TAG TO ASSIGN RESOURCES TO TASKS

USE the project plan you created in the previous exercise.

1. Click on the name of task 5, **Develop production layouts**. Jeff Pike is the only resource currently assigned to this task. You'd like to assign an additional resource and reduce the task's duration.

2. In the Resource Name column of the Assign Resources dialog box, click **Brenda Diaz** and then click the **Assign** button. Brenda Diaz is assigned to task 5. In addition, a small triangle appears in the top left corner of the Task Name cell. This means that there is a Smart Tag activated for this task.

3. Click again on the name of task 5, **Develop production layouts**. The Smart Tag Actions button appears in the Indicators column for task 5. Until you perform another action, you can use the Smart Tag to select how you want Microsoft Project to manage this additional resource assignment.

4. Click the **Smart Tag Actions** button. A list of options regarding how you want to handle this additional resource is displayed. This list is ONLY available until you perform another action in Microsoft Project. Your screen should look similar to Figure 3-7.

Figure 3-7

Entry Table showing Smart Tag
Actions list

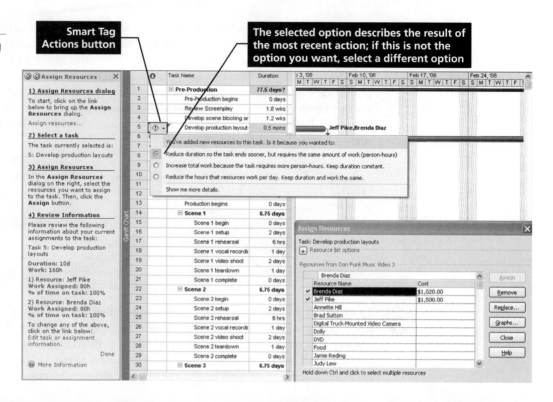

TAKE NOTE

Although Microsoft Project assumes that you want to use effort-driven scheduling, the Smart Tag Actions list lets you choose the scheduling option you need. You can change the task's duration, the resource's work, or the assignment units. The default setting in the Smart Tag Actions list is to reduce the task's duration.

5. You want to reduce the task's duration. Because this option is already selected, you do not need to make any changes. Click the **Smart Tags Action** button again to close the list.

6. Click the name of task 6, **Identify and reserve locations**.

7. In the Resource Name column of the Assign Resources dialog box, click **Annette Hill**.

8. Scroll down until Ryan Ihrig's name is visible. Hold down Ctrl, click **Ryan Ihrig**, and then click the **Assign** button. Microsoft Project assigns Annette and Ryan to the task. Because effort-driven scheduling is the default, Microsoft Project also reduces the task duration and adjusts the start date of all successor tasks. However, you do not want the additional resources to change the task's duration. You have determined that the original scope of this task was underestimated and that Annette and Ryan must perform additional work on this task. Take note of the data in the Review Information section of the *Assign Resources* pane.

9. Select task 6 again. Your screen should look similar to Figure 3-8.

Figure 3-8

Assign Resources pane and Assign Resources dialog box showing details for task 6

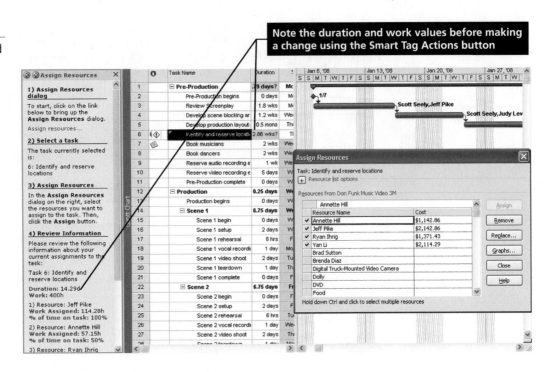

10. Click the Smart Tag Actions button. In the Smart Tag Actions List, select *Increase total work because the task requires more person-hours. Keep duration constant*. Microsoft Project changes the task's duration back to 5 weeks and adjusts the start dates of successor tasks. It also resets the work values back to the values that the initially assigned resources had, resulting in an increase in total work on the task. Your screen should look similar to Figure 3-9.

Figure 3-9

Task duration stays the same but total work for the task increases

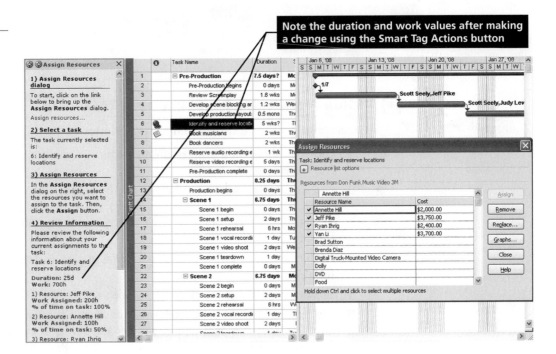

TROUBLESHOOTING

Exercise caution when determining the extent to which effort-driven scheduling should apply to the tasks in your project. Although applying more resources to your tasks may reduce their duration on paper, this may not be possible in a real-world situation. For example, if one resource could complete a task in 20 hours, could 20 resources complete the task in one hour? What about 40 resources in 30 minutes? In reality, the resources would probably get in each other's way, and productivity may even decrease. Additional coordination might be needed. For complex tasks, a resource might need specialized training before it could be productive. There is no exact rule about when you should or should not apply effort-driven scheduling. As a project manager, you need to review the requirements of your project tasks and use your best reasoning.

11. Click the **Close** button in the Assign Resources dialog box. Click **Done** at the bottom of the *Assign Resources* pane.

12. **SAVE** the project plan.

   PAUSE. LEAVE the project plan open to use in the next exercise.

It is important to remember that effort-driven scheduling adjusts task duration only if you add or delete resources from a task. For example, if you initially assign a resource to a task with a duration of 16 hours and later add a second resource, effort-driven scheduling will cause Microsoft Project to schedule each resource to work 8 hours at the same time, resulting in 16 hours of work on the task. However, if you initially assign two resources to a task with a duration of 16 hours, Microsoft Project schedules each resource to work 16 hours, for a total of 32 hours of work on the task. Keep this in mind as you are assigning resources.

■ Assigning Material Resources to Tasks

THE BOTTOM LINE

In a previous lesson, you entered material resources. In this exercise, you will assign material resources to tasks. Most projects use at least some material resources. When you assign material resources to tasks, Microsoft Project can track their consumption and cost.

➔ ASSIGN A MATERIAL RESOURCE TO A TASK

USE the project plan you created in the previous exercise.

1. Click the **Show/Hide Project Guide** button on the Project Guide toolbar. The Project Guide closes.

2. Click the **Assign Resources** button on the Standard toolbar. The Assign Resources dialog box appears. Although this dialog box is similar to the one you used through the Project Guide, this version contains the Units (assignment units) column.

3. In the Task Name column, click the name of task 6, **Identify and reserve locations**.

4. In the Assign Resources dialog box, click on the Units field for the DVD resource.

5. Key **8**, and then click the **Assign** button. Scroll the Gantt bar portion of your screen so that the right end of the bar for task 6 is visible. You will use eight DVDs while identifying locations for this video. Remember that a DVD is a material resource and cannot do work, so assigning it to a task does not affect the task's duration. Your screen should look similar to Figure 3-10.

Figure 3-10

Material resource assigned
to task 6

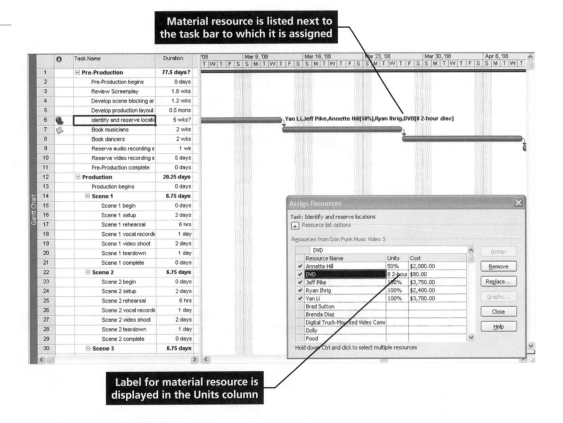

**Material resource is listed next to
the task bar to which it is assigned**

**Label for material resource is
displayed in the Units column**

6. In the Assign Resources dialog box, click **Close**.

7. **SAVE** the project plan.

   PAUSE. LEAVE the project plan open to use in the next exercise.

When you assign a material resource to a task, there are two ways in which you can handle their consumption and cost:

- Assign a fixed unit quantity of the material resource. This is what you did in the exercise above. Microsoft Project then multiplied the unit cost of the resource by the number of units to calculate the total cost.

- Assign a variable rate quantity of the material resource. For example, if two DVDs will be used per day, you would enter 2/day as the assignment unit. Microsoft Project will adjust the quantity and cost of the resource as the duration of the task changes.

■ Assigning Cost Resources to Tasks

THE BOTTOM LINE

A cost resource is another type of resource that you can assign to a task. A cost resource represents a financial obligation to your project. Once you assign the cost resource to the task, you can then assign the cost for the resource.

⊙ ASSIGN A COST RESOURCE TO A TASK

USE the project plan you created in the previous exercise.

1. Click the **Assign Resources** button on the Standard toolbar. The Assign Resources dialog box appears.

2. In the Task Name column, click the name of task 17, **Scene 1 rehearsal.**

3. In the Resource Name column of the Assign Resources dialog box, click **Food** and then click the **Assign** button.

4. In the Cost column for the Food resource, key **500** and press Enter. During the Scene 1 rehearsal, $500 of food will be used to feed the crew and performers working on this task.

5. Click on the name of task 25, **Scene 2 rehearsal.**

6. In the Resource Name column of the Assign Resources dialog box, click **Food** and then click the **Assign** button.

7. In the Cost column for the Food resource, key **500** and press Enter.

8. In the Assign Resources dialog box, click **Close.**

9. **SAVE** and then **CLOSE** the Don Funk Music Video 3 file.

   PAUSE. If you are continuing to the next lesson, keep Project open. If you are not continuing to additional lessons, **CLOSE** Project.

SUMMARY SKILL MATRIX

IN THIS LESSON YOU LEARNED	MATRIX SKILL
To assign work resources to tasks	Make individual resource assignments Assign multiple resources simultaneously
To add more resource assignments to tasks	Add resources to a task Use a Smart Tag to assign resources to tasks
To assign material resources to tasks	Assign a material resource to a task
To assign cost resources to tasks	Assign a cost resource to a task

■ Knowledge Assessment

Fill in the Blank

Complete the following sentences by writing the correct word or words in the blanks provided.

1. A(n) _____ is the matching of a specific resource to a particular task to do work.

2. Assigning a(n) _____ or _____ resource to a task will not affect the duration of the task.

3. In Microsoft Project, when you assign a resource to a task, the result is _____.

4. _____ is the amount of time you expect the task to take to complete.

5. If a resource is assigned to do more work than can be done within the normal work capacity of the resource, it is _____.

6. The capacity of a resource to work is measured in _____.

7. In Microsoft Project, *Duration x Units = Work* is known as a(n) _____.

8. Effort-driven scheduling adjusts a task's duration only if you add or remove _____ from a task.

9. When you assign _____ to tasks, you can track their consumption and cost.

10. According to the scheduling formula in Microsoft Project, 20 hours task duration x 200% assignment units = _____ hours work.

Multiple Choice

Select the best response for the following statements.

1. If you assign a resource to a task with more units than the resource has available, then the resource is
   a. maximized.
   b. overutilized.
   c. compromised.
   d. overallocated.

2. The _____ lets you choose the scheduling option you need.
   a. Smart Tag Action list
   b. scheduling formula
   c. Assign Resources dialog box
   d. effort-driven scheduler

3. A task plus a resource equals
   a. work.
   b. an assignment.
   c. overallocation.
   d. duration.

4. If, after an initial assignment, you assign more resources to a task, the task's duration
   a. is doubled.
   b. decreases.
   c. is reduced by half.
   d. increases.

5. The difference between activating the Assign Resources dialog box from the Project Guide versus from the Standard toolbar is that the dialog box from the Standard toolbar
   a. allows you to assign multiple resources.
   b. contains only work resources.
   c. includes the Units column.
   d. enables you to remove resources.

6. If you assign two resources, each at 100% assignment units, to a task with 24 hours duration, then each resource will work on the task for
   a. 12 hours.
   b. 24 hours.
   c. 36 hours.
   d. 48 hours.

7. To assign more than one resource to a task using the Assign Resources dialog box, click on the first resource name, hold down _____, click the second resource name, and then click Assign.
   a. Alt
   b. Shift
   c. Ctrl
   d. none of the above

8. Which of the following is an advantage of assigning resources to tasks?

    a. You can see if the resource assignment affects task duration.

    b. You can track the progress of the resource in working on the task.

    c. You can track resource and task costs.

    d. All of the above.

9. If you assign a(n) _____ quantity of a material resource to a task, Microsoft Project will adjust the quantity and cost of the resource as the task's duration changes.

    a. variable-rate

    b. open-ended

    c. fixed unit

    d. declining rate

10. With effort-driven scheduling, if you initially assign multiple resources to a task and later remove one of those resources from the task, the amount of *work* for the task

    a. decreases.

    b. increases.

    c. stays constant.

    d. It is not possible to determine with the information given.

■ Competency Assessment

➔ Project 3-1: Hiring a New Employee–Resource Assignments

The *Hiring Employee 3-1* project plan is available on the companion CD-ROM.

You have a project plan for hiring a new employee that contains tasks and resources. Now you will assign some of the resources to perform specific tasks.

GET READY. Launch Microsoft Project if it is not already running. **OPEN** *Hiring Employee 3-1* from the data files for this lesson.

1. Click **Resources** on the Project Guide toolbar, if necessary.
2. In the *Resources* pane, click the **Assign people and equipment to tasks** link.
3. Click the **Assign resources** link in the *Assign Resources* pane.
4. In the Task Name column, click name of task 1, **Write job description**.
5. In the Resources Name column of the Assign Resources dialog box, click **Amy Rusko** and then click **Assign**.
6. In the Task Name column, click the name of task 6, **Review resumes**.
7. In the Resources Name column of the Assign Resources dialog box, click **Barry Potter** and then click **Assign**.
8. Click **Close** in the Assign Resources dialog box.
9. **SAVE** the project as *Hiring Employee-Resources* and then **CLOSE** the file.

    LEAVE Project open for the next exercise.

➔ Project 3-2: Office Remodel

The *Office Remodel 3-2* project plan is available on the companion CD-ROM.

You are in charge of the remodel for the kitchen and lunchroom of your office. You need to assign resources to tasks. It is necessary to assign several of these resources simultaneously to a task.

OPEN *Office Remodel 3-2* from the data files for this lesson.

1. Click **Resources** on the Project Guide toolbar, if necessary.
2. In the *Resources* pane, click the **Assign people and equipment to tasks** link.
3. Click the **Assign resources** link in the *Assign Resources* pane.
4. In the Task Name column, click the name of task 5, **Remove drywall from main walls**.
5. In the Assign Resources dialog box, select **John Emory** and **Toby Nixon** and then click **Assign**.
6. In the Task Name column, click the name of task 12, **Paint walls and woodwork**.
7. In the Assign Resources dialog box, select **Run Liu** and **Toby Nixon** and then click **Assign**.
8. Click **Close** in the Assign Resources dialog box.
9. **SAVE** the project as *Office Remodel Multiple Resources* and then **CLOSE** the file.
   LEAVE Project open for the next exercise.

■ Proficiency Assessment

⊕ Project 3-3: Office Remodel Material Resources

The *Office Remodel 3-3* project plan is available on the companion CD-ROM.

You now need to assign material resources to tasks in your office remodel project plan.

OPEN *Office Remodel 3-3* from the data files for this lesson.

1. Close the Project Guide.
2. Open the Assign Resources dialog box using the button on the Standard toolbar.
3. Select task 9, **Install drywall**.
4. In the Assign Resources dialog box, assign drywall as a resource and then assign **50** units for the drywall resource.
5. In the Assign Resources dialog box, assign nails as a resource and then assign **5** units for the nails resource.
6. Close the Assign Resources dialog box.
7. **SAVE** the project as **Office Remodel Material Resources** and then **CLOSE** the file.
   LEAVE Project open for the next exercise.

⊕ Project 3-4: Don Funk Video–Assigning Resources Using a Smart Tag

The *Don Funk Music Video 3-4* project plan is available on the companion CD-ROM.

Although you have already assigned most of the resources for your music video, you have realized that you need to assign additional resources for a few of the tasks. You can use a Smart Tag to do this.

OPEN *Don Funk Music Video 3-4* from the data files for this lesson.

1. Select task 7, **Book Musicians**.
2. Activate the Assign Resources dialog box through either the Project Guide or the Standard toolbar.
3. Click on **Brenda Diaz**, and then assign her to the task.
4. Use the Smart Tag to indicate that you want to increase the total work for this task.
5. Close the Assign Resources dialog box.
6. **SAVE** the project plan as **Don Funk Smart Tag** and then **CLOSE** the file.
   LEAVE Project open to use in the next exercise.

■ Mastery Assessment

The *Don Funk Music Video 3-5* project plan is available on the companion CD-ROM.

⊕ Project 3-5: Don Funk Cost Resources

In this exercise, you will assign cost resources for the Don Funk Music Video.

OPEN the *Don Funk Music Video 3-5* from the data files for this lesson.

1. Open the Assign Resources dialog box.
2. For task 6, *Identify and reserve locations*, assign *Travel* as a resource at a cost of **5000**.
3. For task 18, *Scene 1 vocal recording*, assign *Food* as a resource at a cost of **250**.
4. Close the Assign Resources dialog box.
5. **SAVE** the project plan as *Don Funk Cost Resources* and then **CLOSE** the file.
   LEAVE Project open for the next exercise.

The *Hiring New Employee 3-6* project plan is available on the companion CD-ROM.

⊕ Project 3-6: Hiring a New Employee–Additional Resources

You have just learned of a change in scope for some of the tasks in your project plan for hiring a new employee. One task will require more work than originally estimated, and for another task, the assigned resources must work fewer hours.

OPEN *Hiring New Employee 3-6* from the data files for this lesson.

1. For the task *Review resumes*, assign Gabe Mares and Jeff Smith to assist with this task. Set their assignments so that the total work is increased and the duration is kept constant.
2. For the task *Conduct interviews*, assign Gabe Mares. Set his assignment so that for this task, the resources work less hours per day, but the work and task duration remain constant.
3. Close the Assign Resources dialog box.
4. **SAVE** the project plan as *New Employee Adding Resources* and then **CLOSE** the file.
   CLOSE Project.

INTERNET READY

There are many Internet resources that offer advice or solutions to challenges that arise during any given project implementation. Microsoft's Website is one such resource. Search the Microsoft Website for Work Essentials—a site that provides information on how to more efficiently perform daily work functions in a wide variety of occupations. Browse the occupations and select one relating to project managers. Explore the resources provided to find information on managing project scope changes. Write a short paragraph highlighting the best practices of change management.

Refining Your Project Plan

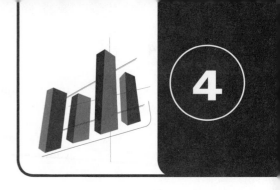

LESSON SKILL MATRIX

SKILLS	MATRIX SKILL
Applying a Task Calendar to an Individual Task	Apply a task calendar to an individual task
Changing Task Types	Change scheduling formula values to change task types
	Change a task type using the Task Information dialog box
Splitting a Task	Split a task
Establishing Recurring Tasks	Set up a recurring task
	Assign resources to a recurring task
Applying Task Constraints	Apply a Start No Earlier Than constraint to a task
Reviewing the Project's Critical Path	Review the project's critical path
Viewing Resource Allocations Over Time	Explore resource allocations and identify overallocated resources

You are Southridge Video's production manager and have been working on a project plan for a new music video for Don Funk. You have developed the three key building blocks for the project—tasks, resources, and assignments. By setting up tasks and resources, and then assigning one to the other, the plan is beginning to take shape. Now, you need to fine-tune your plan to reflect some of the details and exceptions of these building blocks. Some tasks

KEY TERMS
allocation
constraint
critical path
fixed duration
fixed units
fixed work
flexible constraint
free slack
fully allocated
inflexible constraint
negative slack
noncritical tasks
recurring task
semi-flexible constraint
slack
split
task calendar
task type
total slack
underallocated

cannot occur during normal working hours, other tasks will have interruptions, and still others will repeat on a regular basis throughout the project. There are also tasks that have limits on when or by whom they can be performed. In this lesson, you will learn how to create task calendars, change task types, split tasks, set up and apply resources to recurring tasks, apply constraints, and identify the critical path of your project.

■ SOFTWARE ORIENTATION

Microsoft Project's Change Working Time and Create New Base Calendar Dialog Boxes

In Microsoft Office Project, there may be times when you want specific tasks to occur at times that are outside the project calendar's working time. To do this, you need to create a new base calendar, a function that is accessed through the Change Working Time dialog box.

Figure 4-1

Change Working Time dialog box with Create New Base Calendar dialog box displayed

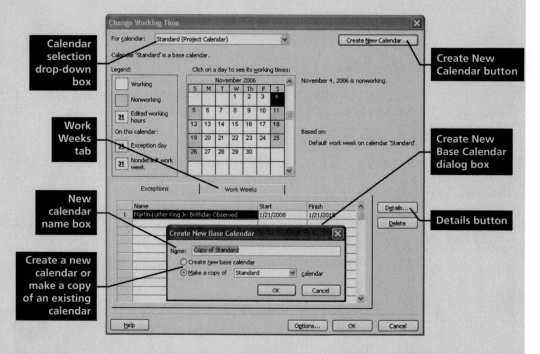

This dialog box is accessed by clicking the Create New Calendar button in the Change Working Time dialog box. The Create New Base Calendar dialog box enables you to name the new calendar, create a totally new calendar, or make a copy of an existing calendar on which to base your new calendar.

■ Applying a Task Calendar to an Individual Task

THE BOTTOM LINE

When you set up resources in your project plan, Microsoft Project created the corresponding resources calendar. As you saw in Lesson 2, you were able to adjust a resource calendar to reflect exception working times. However, this is not the case for tasks and task calendars. Sometimes, you need a specific task to occur at a time that is outside the project calendar's working time (such as overnight or on a weekend). To do this, you can assign a task calendar to this task. You can use one of Project's base calendars, or you can create a new base calendar that fits your task requirements.

APPLY A TASK CALENDAR TO AN INDIVIDUAL TASK

The ***Don Funk Music Video 4M*** project plan is available on the companion CD-ROM.

GET READY. Before you begin these steps, launch Microsoft Project.

OPEN *Don Funk Music Video 4M* from the data files for this lesson.

SAVE the file as ***Don Funk Music Video 4*** in the solutions folder for this lesson as directed by your instructor.

1. On the menu bar, click **Tools** and then click **Change Working Time**. The Change Working Time dialog box is activated as shown in Figure 4-1.

2. In the Change Working Time dialog box, click **Create New Calendar**. The Create New Base Calendar dialog box appears.

3. In the Name box, key **Overnight Beach Filming**. One of the scenes for the video will be shot during the overnight hours on a public beach.

4. If it is not already selected, click the **Make a copy of** button. In the dropdown menu, select **Standard**, and then click **OK**. (Refer back to the Software Orientation at the beginning of this lesson for more details on this screen.)

5. Click on the **Work Weeks** tab in the Change Working Time dialog box, and then click the **Details** button. The Details dialog box appears.

6. In the *Select days* box, drag your pointer to select **Tuesday** through **Friday**. Click the **Set day(s) to these specific working times** button.

7. Click the cell in row 1 of the *From* column and key **12:00 AM**. Click the cell in row 1 of the *To* column and key **3:00 AM**. Click the cell in row 2 of the *From* column and key **9:00 PM**. Click the cell in row 2 of the *To* column and key **12:00 AM**. Press **Enter**. Your screen should look similar to Figure 4-2. Click **OK**.

Figure 4-2

Change Working Time and Details dialog boxes showing evening working times

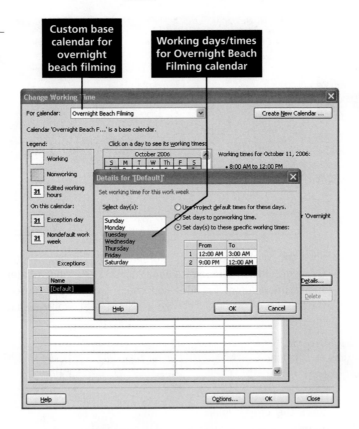

8. Click the **Details** button again. In the *Select days* box, select **Monday**. Click the **Set day(s) to these specific working times** button. Click the cell in row 1 of the *From* column and key **9:00 PM**. Click the cell in row 1 of the *To* column and key **12:00 AM**. Click the cell in row 2 of the *From* column and press **Delete**.

TROUBLESHOOTING Microsoft Project will not allow you to set a timeframe that spans two days. For instance, you cannot specify a working time for Monday of 9PM–3AM because 3AM is on Tuesday. You must set the time intervals for each specific day, as you did in this exercise.

9. Select **Saturday**. Click the **Set day(s) to these specific working times** button. Click the cell in row 1 of the *From* column and key **12:00 AM**. Click the cell in row 1 of the *To* column and key **3:00 AM**. Press [Enter]. You have now set the working times for this calendar from 9:00 PM to 3:00 AM from Monday night through Friday night (Saturday morning). Click **OK** to close the Details dialog box. Click **OK** to close the Change Working Time dialog box.

10. Select the name of task 35, **Scene 3 video shoot**. If the Gantt bar of this task is not visible, click the **Scroll To Task** button.

TROUBLESHOOTING If the Scroll to Task button is not visible on your Standard toolbar, click Toolbar Options to display a list of additional buttons, and then click the Scroll To Task button to add it to your Standard toolbar.

11. On the Standard toolbar, click the **Task Information** button. The Task Information dialog box appears.

12. Click the **Advanced** tab.

13. In the Calendar box, select **Overnight Beach Filming** from the dropdown list. Click the **Scheduling ignores resource calendars** check box. Your screen should look like Figure 4-3.

Figure 4-3

Task Information dialog box

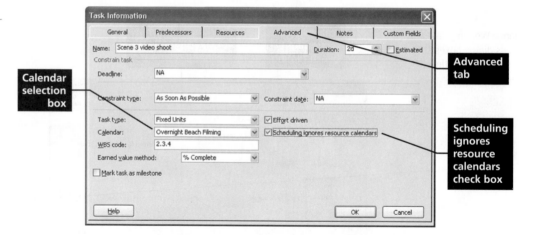

14. Click **OK** to close the Task Information dialog box. Microsoft Project applies the Overnight Beach Filming calendar to task 35, and a calendar icon appears in the Indicators column. Because you chose to ignore resource calendars, the resources for this task will be scheduled at times that would usually be nonworking times for them.

TAKE NOTE To remove a calendar from a task, select the task and open the Task Information dialog box. On the advanced tab, click None in the Calendar box.

15. SAVE the project plan.

PAUSE. LEAVE the project plan open to use in the next exercise.

You have just created and assigned a task calendar to a task that occurs outside normal working times–an overnight video shoot. A ***task calendar*** is the base calendar that is used by a single task. It defines working and nonworking times for a task, regardless of settings in the project calendar. Task calendars are often used when a task must run overnight, occur on a specific weekday, or occur over a weekend. Task calendars are beneficial when other base calendars–such as the 24 Hours or Night Shift–are too broad or too specific for the task requirements. For tasks that have both a task calendar and resource assignments (and therefore a resource calendar), Microsoft Project will schedule work in the working time that is common between the task and resource calendar(s). If there is no common time, Project will alert you when you assign a resource to the task or when you apply the task calendar. As you saw in this exercise, you can specifically choose to ignore resource calendars.

■ Changing Task Types

THE BOTTOM LINE

As you learned in lesson 3, Microsoft Project uses the scheduling formula *Duration* × *Units* = *Work*. The task type specifies which value in the scheduling formula remains fixed if the other two values change. The three task types are fixed units, fixed duration, and fixed work. To determine which task type is the right one to apply to each task in your project plan, you need to determine how you want Project to schedule that task.

Using the Scheduling Formula to Change Task Types

In an earlier Lesson, you learned that Microsoft Project uses the scheduling formula to determine a task's work value. In this exercise, you will examine the relationship between scheduling formula and task type.

⊕ CHANGE SCHEDULING FORMULA VALUES TO CHANGE TASK TYPES

USE the project plan you created in the previous exercise.

1. Click the **Track** button on the Project Guide toolbar. The *Track* pane appears.
2. In the *Track* pane, click the **Make changes to the project** link. The *Change Project* pane appears and the *Project Guide: Edit Assignments View* replaces the Gantt Chart view. This view is called a usage view. It lists the assigned resources below each task. It also shows you each task's and assignment's duration, work, and assignment units values–the three variables in the scheduling formula.
3. On the menu bar, click **Edit**, then click **Go To**.
4. In the ID box, key **4**, and then click **OK**. Microsoft Project shifts the project plan so that task 4, *Develop scene blocking and schedule*, and its assignments are visible. Note that task 4 has a total work value of 80 hours, 40 work hours and 100 percent resource units for each of two resources, and duration of 1.2 weeks. Your team has determined that this task's duration should be two weeks, but the work necessary to complete the task should remain the same.
5. In the Duration field for task 4, select or key **2w**, and press **Enter**. Microsoft Project changes the duration of task 4 to two weeks and increases the work for each resource. You want to increase the duration but keep the work the same.

TAKE NOTE

If a task type is fixed, this doesn't mean that its units, work, or duration values are unchangeable. You can change any value for any task type.

6. Point to the Duration field for task 4, and then click on the **Smart Tag** button. Your screen should look similar to Figure 4-4. Review the options in the Smart Tag list. The task type for task 4 is fixed units (the default task type), so the default selection in the Smart Tag is to increase work as the duration increases. Based on your team's discussions, you want to keep the work value constant and decrease assignment units for the task's new duration.

Figure 4-4

Smart Tag Action List for task 4

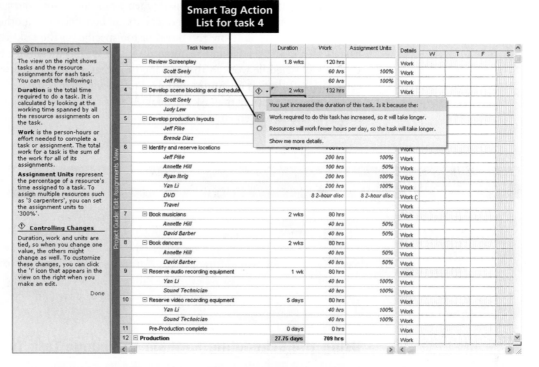

7. Click **Resources will work fewer hours per day, so the task will take longer** in the Smart Tag actions list. The total work on the task is still 80 hours, but the assignment units value of each resource decreases. Another way to think of this is that the resources will put in the same total effort over a longer period of time. Figure 4-5 shows the adjusted scheduling formula values for task 4.

Figure 4-5

Adjusted scheduling formula values for task 4

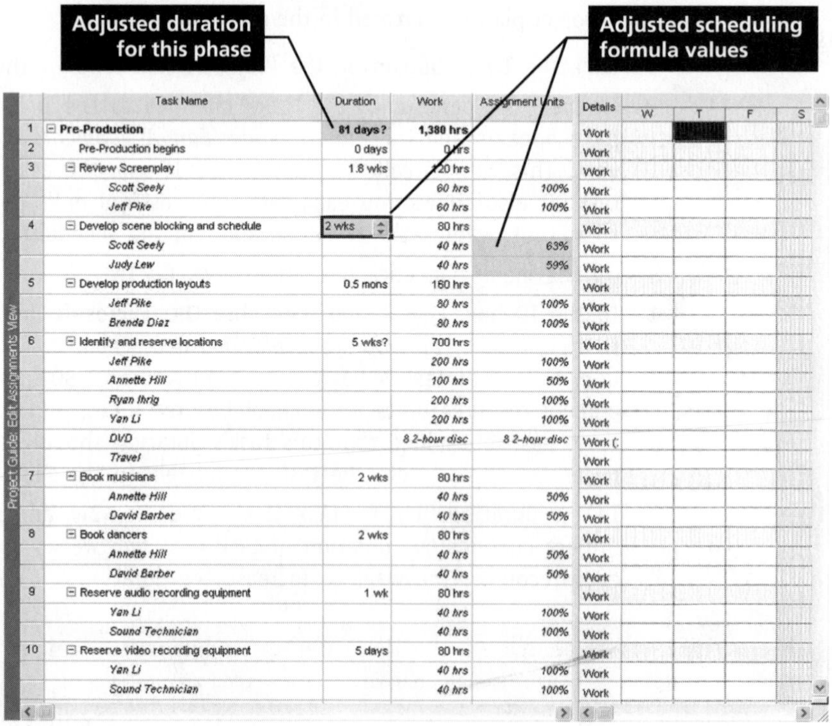

8. **SAVE** the project plan.

   PAUSE. LEAVE the project plan open to use in the next exercise.

You have just changed the task type by changing two values in the scheduling formula: the duration of the task and the assignment units of the assigned resources. Recall again that Microsoft Project uses the scheduling formula *Duration × Units = Work.* A **task type** determines which of the three scheduling formula variables remains the same if the other two values change.

There are three task types: fixed units, fixed duration, and fixed work. The default task type is *fixed units*, a task type in which the units value does not change. With the fixed units task type, if you change a task's duration, Microsoft Project recalculates work. If you change work, duration is recalculated. A *fixed duration* task is one in which the duration value is fixed. If you change the task's work or units value, Project recalculates the other value. A *fixed work* task is one in which the work value is held constant. You can change the duration or units and Project will determine the other value.

TROUBLESHOOTING

As you fine-tune your project plan, keep in mind that you cannot turn off effort-driven scheduling for a fixed work task.

The following table highlights the effect of changing any scheduling formula variable for any task type.

Table 4-1

Task types and scheduling formula values

IF THE TASK TYPE IS....	...AND YOU CHANGE THE		
	DURATION	**UNITS**	**WORK**
Fixed Duration	Project recalculates work	Project recalculates units	Project recalculates work
Fixed Units	Project recalculates work	Project recalculates duration	Project recalculates duration
Fixed Work	Project recalculates units	Project recalculates duration	Project recalculates duration

TAKE NOTE

To see the task type of a task you have selected, click the Task Information button on the Standard toolbar, and then click the Advanced tab in the Task Information dialog box. You can also see the task type when you are in the Gantt Chart view via the Task Form. On the menu bar, click Window, then click Split. The Task form will appear in the lower portion of your screen.

Using the Task Information Dialog Box to Change a Task Type

In the previous exercise, you changed the task type using Smart Tag actions. In this exercise, you will change the task type using the Task Information dialog box.

⊕ CHANGE A TASK TYPE USING THE TASK INFORMATION DIALOG BOX

USE the project plan you created in the previous exercise.

TAKE NOTE

You cannot change the task type on a *summary* task—it is always fixed duration. This is because the summary task is based on the earliest start date and the latest finish date of its subtasks.

1. On the menu bar, click **Edit**, then click **Go To**.
2. In the ID box, key **6**, and then click **OK**.
3. On the Standard toolbar, click the **Task Information** button. The Task Information dialog box appears.
4. Click the **Advanced** tab if it is not already selected. Note that in the *Task type* box the task has a Fixed Units task type. For this particular task, you need to make adjustments to some of the resources who will work less time, but you want the duration of the task to remain fixed at the estimated 5 weeks.

5. Select **Fixed Duration** from the dropdown menu in the *Task type* box.

6. Click the **Resources** tab on the Task Information dialog box.

7. In the Units column, set the units value for Jeff Pike to **50%** and for Ryan Ihrig to **75%**. Your screen should look similar to Figure 4-6.

Figure 4-6

Task Information dialog box showing adjusted resource units

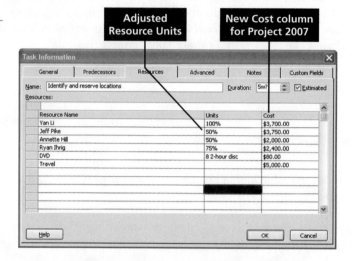

8. Click **OK** to close the Task Information dialog box. The updated work values of the two resources are reflected in the Project Guide: Edit Assignments View (your current screen). The duration did not change.

9. **SAVE** the project plan.

PAUSE. LEAVE the project plan open to use in the next exercise.

In this exercise, you changed the task type by using the Task Information dialog box. You now know two ways to change the task type and adjust scheduling formula values. As you are fine-tuning your project plan, keep in mind that it is easy to confuse task type and effort-driven scheduling. They are similar in that they both affect work, duration, and units values. The key difference is that effort-driven scheduling affects your schedule only when you add or remove resources from tasks, while modifying the task type affects only the resources that are assigned to the task when the change is made.

Also, look back to the Task Information dialog box in Figure 4-6. Note the Cost column on the right-hand side of the dialog box. This is a new feature to Microsoft Project and is beneficial in cost estimation and tracking. This field provides immediate feedback regarding individual cost items in your project plan. Look for this new cost field in various task and resource dialog boxes throughout Microsoft Project.

■ Splitting a Task

THE BOTTOM LINE

Sometimes, work on certain tasks in a project plan will stop and then start again. This may be planned or unplanned. A task can be split to show that work has been interrupted and restarted.

⊕ SPLIT A TASK

USE the project plan you created in the previous exercise.

1. On the menu bar, click **View**, and then click **Gantt Chart**.

2. On the menu bar, click **Edit**, and then click **Go To**.

3. Key 5 in the ID box, and then click **OK**. Microsoft Project shifts the view to task 5, *Develop production layouts*. Your screen should look similar to Figure 4-7. You have just been told that work on this task will be interrupted on January 31 and February 1 (no work will occur on these days).

Figure 4-7

Gantt Chart view of task 5

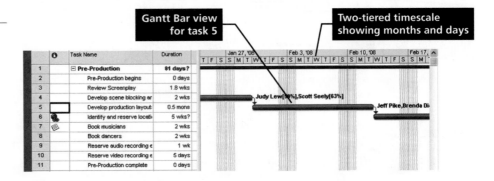

> The timescale at the top of the right half of the Gantt Chart (above the graphical bars) determines at what level of time (months, weeks, days, etc.) you can split a task. The calibration of the bottom tier of the timescale is the smallest increment into which you can split a task. In this exercise, you can split a task into one-day increments because days are on the bottom tier. If you wanted to split a task at the hourly level, you would need to adjust the tiers via the Timescale option on the Format menu.

TAKE NOTE

4. On the Standard toolbar, click the **Split Task** button. A ScreenTip appears and the mouse pointer changes.

5. Move the mouse pointer over the Gantt bar of task 5. Watch the ScreenTip as you move the pointer–the date changes. The ScreenTip reflects the date on which you will begin to split the task. Your screen should look similar to Figure 4-8.

Figure 4-8

Gantt Chart with Screen Tip for splitting a task

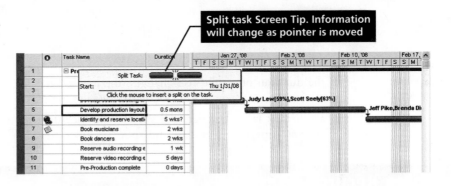

6. Move (but don't click the mouse pointer) over the Gantt bar until the Start date of Thursday, 1/31/08, appears in the ScreenTip.

7. Click and drag the mouse pointer to the right until the Start date of Saturday, 2/02/08, appears in the ScreenTip, and then release the mouse button. Microsoft Project inserts a task split between the two parts of the task. The split, or interruption in work, is represented by a dotted line in the Gantt Chart. Your screen should look similar to Figure 4-9.

Figure 4-9

Task 5 shown as a split task

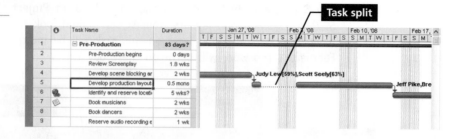

TROUBLESHOOTING

Splitting tasks using the mouse pointer takes a little practice. If you split a task on the wrong date, there are two ways you can correct it. First, you can click the Undo button on the menu bar to remove the incorrect split. Another option is to point to the second segment of the task again. When the mouse pointer changes to a circle with four arrows, drag the segment to the correct start date. You can drag multiple times.

8. SAVE the project plan.

PAUSE. LEAVE the project plan open to use in the next exercise.

You have just split a task to represent some nonworking time in the middle of the task. A **split** is an interruption in a task, represented in the Gantt bar by a dotted line between the two segments of the task. Keep the following points in mind when splitting a task:

- You can split a task into as many parts as necessary.

- You can drag a segment of a split task either right or left to reschedule the split.

- The time of the actual task split, represented by the dotted line, does not count in the duration of the task unless the task type is fixed duration. Work does not occur during the split.

LOOKING AHEAD

Resource leveling or manually contouring assignments can also cause tasks to split. You can find out more about resource leveling in Lesson 13 and about contouring assignments in Lesson 14.

- If the duration of a split task changes, the last segment of the task is lengthened or shortened.

- If a split task is rescheduled, the whole task, including the splits, is rescheduled. The same pattern of segments and splits is preserved.

■ Establishing Recurring Tasks

THE BOTTOM LINE

Many projects require repetitive tasks, such as attending a status meeting or cleaning a production line. Even though these may seem like negligible tasks, you should account for them in your project plan because they require time from project resources–time that your resources could spend on other key assignments.

Setting Up a Recurring Task

In this exercise, you will learn how to set up a task that will repeat at a specified interval during the project.

→ SET UP A RECURRING TASK

USE the project plan you created in the previous exercise.

1. Select the name of task 11, **Pre-Production complete**. You want to insert the recurring tasks as the last items in the Pre-Production phase.

2. On the menu bar, click **Insert**, and then click **Recurring Task**. The Recurring Task Information dialog box appears.

3. In the Task Name box, key **Status Meeting**.

4. In the Duration box, key **1h**.

5. Under *Recurrence pattern*, make sure that **Weekly** is selected, and then select the **Monday** check box.

6. In the Start box, key or select **1/14/08**. The first occurrence of your weekly meeting will be on January 14, 2008.

> **TAKE NOTE**
>
> Microsoft Project schedules a recurring task to start at the Default Start Time value you established at the beginning of your project (on the menu bar, click Tools, then Options, then click the Calendar tab). If you want to schedule a recurring task to begin at a different time, enter that time along with the start date in the Start box of the Recurring Task Information dialog box. For instance, if you want the status meeting to start at 9 A.M. on January 14, you would enter *1/14/08 9AM* in the Start box.

7. Under *Range of recurrence*, select **End after**, and then key or select **15** occurrences. Your screen should look like Figure 4-10.

Figure 4-10

Completed Recurring Task
Information dialog box

8. Click **OK** to create the recurring task. A Microsoft Office Project dialog box appears to notify you that one of the instances of the recurring task will occur during nonworking times (the holiday on January 21).

9. Review the options presented in the dialog box. You want to skip the status meeting for this particular week. Click **No** to not schedule this occurrence of the task. Microsoft Project inserts the recurring tasks within the Pre-Production phase. A recurring task icon appears in the Indicators column. Your screen should look similar to Figure 4-11.

Figure 4-11

Gantt Chart showing
recurring task

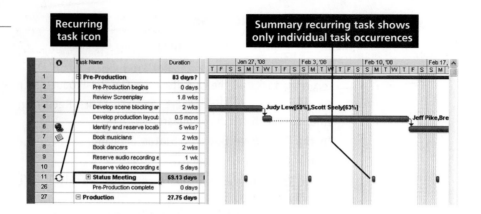

10. Click on the name of task 11, **Status Meeting**, and then click the **Scroll to Task** button on the Standard toolbar. The Gantt Chart displays the first occurrences of the recurring meeting's Gantt bars. Notice that the summary Gantt bar for the recurring task is different from other summary bars. A summary bar for a recurring task shows only the individual occurrences of the tasks.

11. **SAVE** the project plan.

PAUSE. LEAVE the project plan open to use in the next exercise.

You have just added a recurring task to your project plan. A **recurring task** is a task that is repeated at specified intervals, such as daily, weekly, or monthly. When you create a recurring task, Microsoft Project creates a series of tasks with Start No Earlier Than constraints, no task relationships, and effort-driven scheduling turned off.

Assigning Resources to a Recurring Task

In the previous exercise, you established a recurring task in your project plan. Now you will assign resources to it.

➔ ASSIGN RESOURCES TO A RECURRING TASK

USE the project plan you created in the previous exercise.

1. If it is not already selected, click on the name of task 11, **Status Meeting**.

2. On the Standard toolbar, click **Assign Resources**.

3. In the Assign Resources dialog box, click **Brad Sutton**. Then hold down [Ctrl] while clicking **Chris Preston, Eva Corets, Jamie Reding, Jane Clayton**, and **Judy Lew**.

4. Click **Assign**, and then click **Close**. Microsoft Project assigns the selected resources to the recurring task.

5. Click the plus sign (+) next to task 11's title to expand and show the subtasks. Your screen should look similar to Figure 4-12.

Figure 4-12

Gantt Chart showing all occurrences and resources for recurring task

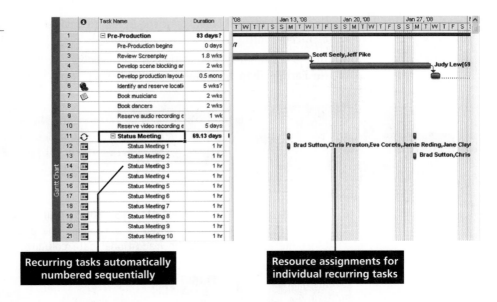

Recurring tasks automatically numbered sequentially

Resource assignments for individual recurring tasks

6. Click the minus sign (−) next to task 11's title to collapse the subtasks under the summary task.

7. **SAVE** the project plan.

   PAUSE. LEAVE the project plan open to use in the next exercise.

You have now assigned resources to the recurring task you established for your project plan. Keep the following points in mind when establishing a recurring task:

- You should always use the Assign Resources dialog box when assigning resources to recurring tasks. If you enter resource names in the Resource Name field of the summary task, the resources will only be assigned to the summary task, not to the individual occurrences.

- If you schedule a recurring task to end on a specific date, Microsoft Project will suggest the current project end date. If you select the project end date, you will need to manually change it later if the project end date changes.

- As you saw in this exercise, Microsoft Project will alert you if an occurrence of a recurring task will take place during nonworking time. You can choose to skip that occurrence or to schedule it for the next working day.

■ Applying Task Constraints

THE BOTTOM LINE

Every task that you enter into your project plan has some type of limit, or constraint, applied to it. The constraint controls the start or finish date or the extent to which the task can be adjusted. There are three categories of constraints: flexible, inflexible, and semi-flexible. These three categories of constraints have very different effects on the scheduling of tasks. (A table showing all of the different task categories and constraints can be found after this exercise.) The type of constraint you apply to the tasks in your project plan will depend on what you need from Microsoft Project.

➔ APPLY A START NO EARLIER THAN CONSTRAINT TO A TASK

USE the project plan you created in the previous exercise.

1. Click **Tasks** on the Project Guide toolbar, if necessary. The *Tasks* pane appears.

2. In the *Tasks* pane, click the **Set deadlines and constrain tasks** link. The *Deadlines and Constraints* pane appears.

3. Select task 38, **Scene 2 begin**. This scene will be shot at a location that is not available until May 15, 2008.

4. On the Standard toolbar, click the **Scroll to Task** button. The Gantt bars for this task come into view.

5. In the *Constrain a task* section of the *Deadlines and Constraints* pane, select **Start No Earlier Than** from the dropdown box.

> **TAKE NOTE**
>
> Unless you specify otherwise, Microsoft Project schedules the start or finish time of a constraint date using the Default Start Time or Default End Time value you established at the beginning of your project (on the menu bar, click Tools, then Options, then click the Calendar tab).

6. In the date box, key or select **May 15, 2008**. Your screen should look similar to Figure 4-13. Note the highlighted cells showing the effect of this change. Widen the table as necessary to view additional data columns.

Figure 4-13

Deadlines and Constraints pane and Gantt Chart showing *Start No Earlier Than* (SNET) constraint

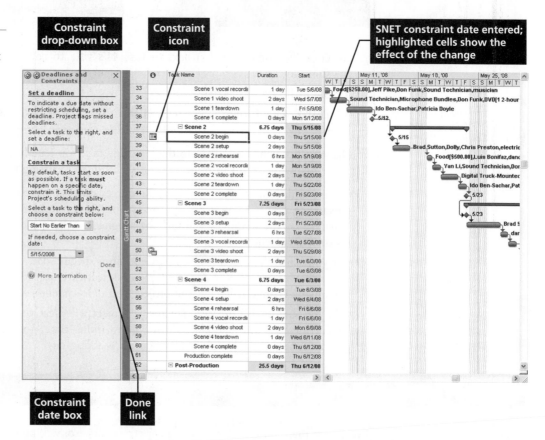

7. At the bottom of the *Deadlines and Constraints* pane, click the **Done** link. The constraint is applied and a constraint icon appears in the Indicators column. When you point to the icon, constraint details will be shown in a ScreenTip. The task is rescheduled to start on May 15, and all other tasks that depend on task 38 are also rescheduled.

8. Click the **Show/Hide Project Guide** button on the Project Guide toolbar. The Project Guide closes.

9. **SAVE** the project plan.

PAUSE. LEAVE the project plan open to use in the next exercise.

You have just added a Start No Earlier Than (SNET) constraint to a task in your project plan. A *constraint* is a restriction that you or Microsoft Project set which controls the start or finish date of a task. As indicated at the beginning of this exercise, there are three categories of constraints:

- A *flexible constraint* is a constraint type that gives Microsoft Project the flexibility to change start and finish dates of a task. No constraint date is associated with a flexible constraint. The flexible constraint As Soon As Possible (ASAP) is the default constraint type in Microsoft Project. Use these constraint types whenever possible.

- An *inflexible constraint* is a constraint type that forces a task to begin or end on a certain date, completely preventing the rescheduling of a task. Inflexible constraints are sometimes called hard constraints. Use these constraint types only when absolutely necessary.

- A *semi-flexible constraint* is a constraint type that gives Microsoft Project the flexibility to change the start and finish dates (but not the duration) of a task within one date boundary.

The table below shows the eight types of task constraints within these three categories.

Table 4-2

Constraint categories and constraint types

CONSTRAINT CATEGORY	CONSTRAINT TYPES	PROPERTIES
Flexible	As Soon As Possible (ASAP)	Project will schedule a task to occur as soon as it can happen. The default constraint type applied to new tasks when scheduling from the project start date.
	As Late As Possible (ALAP)	Project will schedule a task to occur as late as it can occur. The default constraint type applied to all new tasks when scheduling from the project finish date.
Semi-Flexible	Start No Earlier Than (SNET)	Project will schedule a task to start on or after the specified constraint date. Use this type to make sure a task will not start before a specific date.
	Start No Later Than (SNLT)	Project will schedule a task to start on or before the specified constraint date. Use this type to make sure a task will not start after a specific date.
	Finish No Earlier Than (FNET)	Project will schedule a task to finish on or after the specified constraint date. Use this type to ensure a task will not finish before a specific date.
	Finish No Later Than (FNLT)	Project will schedule a task to finish on or before the specified constraint date. Use this type to ensure that a task will not finish after a specific date.
Inflexible	Must Start On (MSO)	Project will schedule a task to start on the specified constraint date. Use this type to ensure that a task will start on an exact date.
	Must Finish On (MFO)	Project will schedule a task to finish on the specified constraint date. Use this type to ensure that a task will finish on an exact date.

SHOOTING

One of the most common scheduling problems that people encounter in Microsoft Project results when they enter start or finish dates for tasks. However, when start or finish dates are entered, semi-flexible constraints such as Start No Earlier Than or Finish No Earlier Than are applied, preventing the project manager from taking advantage of the Microsoft Project scheduling engine. You should avoid entering start and finish dates unless absolutely necessary. Keep in mind that by entering dates in the Start or Finish columns, you are applying SNET or FNET constraints (without using the *Deadlines and Constraints* pane).

Keep the following points in mind when setting constraints for tasks:

- To remove a constraint, click Project on the menu bar, and then click Task Information. In the Task Information dialog box, click the Advanced tab. In the Constraint Type box, select As Soon As Possible (if scheduling from start date) or As Late As Possible (if scheduling from finish date).

- If you try to apply inflexible or semi-flexible constraints to tasks in addition to task links, you might create what is known as **negative slack**–the amount of time that tasks overlap due to a conflict between task relationships and constraints. For example, a task with a Must Start On (MSO) constraint for April 24 and a finish-to-start relationship to another task will always be scheduled for April 24, no matter when its predecessor finishes. To set Microsoft Project to honor relationships over constraints, select Tools on the menu bar, click Options, and then click the Schedule tab. Clear the *Tasks will always honor their constraint dates* check box.

- Some constraint behaviors change if you must schedule a project from a finish date rather than a start date. For instance, the ALAP constraint type becomes the default for new tasks, rather than ASAP. Pay close attention to the constraints you apply in this case to make sure the results are what you expected.

A new feature in Microsoft Project 2007 that is helpful in reviewing constraints, assignments, and dependencies is Task Drivers. Task Drivers show the factors that drive a task's start times and help you backtrack to analyze the constraints. You can use Task Drivers to determine the factor(s) driving the start date of a task or follow a chain of factors to find the cause of a delay you are tracking. You can access Task Drivers in two ways:

- Click the Task Drivers button on the Standard toolbar. The *Task Drivers* pane will appear on the left side of your screen.

- Click Track on the Project Guide menu, and then click the See what is driving the start date of a task link. The *Task Drivers* pane will appear on the left side of your screen.

Figure 4-14 shows the *Task Drivers* pane activated for task 50.

Figure 4-14

Task Drivers pane activated for task 50

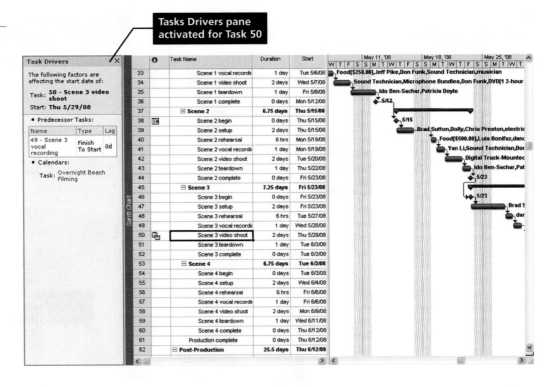

■ Reviewing the Project's Critical Path

THE BOTTOM LINE

In every project, there is a series of tasks that directly affect the finish date of the project, known as the critical path. If any of these tasks is delayed, the finish date of the project will be delayed. The term "critical" refers not to the importance of these tasks but rather to the impact that the scheduling of these tasks has on the finish date of the project. If you want to decrease the duration of the project, you must shorten the critical path.

⊙ REVIEW THE PROJECT'S CRITICAL PATH

USE the project plan you created in the previous exercise.

1. Click **View** on the menu bar, and then click **More Views**. The More Views dialog box appears.

2. In the More Views dialog box, select **Detail Gantt**, and then click the **Apply** button. The project plan is displayed in the Detail Gantt view.

3. On the menu bar, click **Edit**, and then click **Go To**.

4. In the ID box, key **51**, and then click **OK**. The view shifts so that the Gantt bar for task 51 is visible. Scroll down so that most of the tasks after task 51 are visible, and you can see more of the critical path. Your screen should look similar to Figure 4-15.

Figure 4-15

Detail Gantt view showing
critical path at task 51

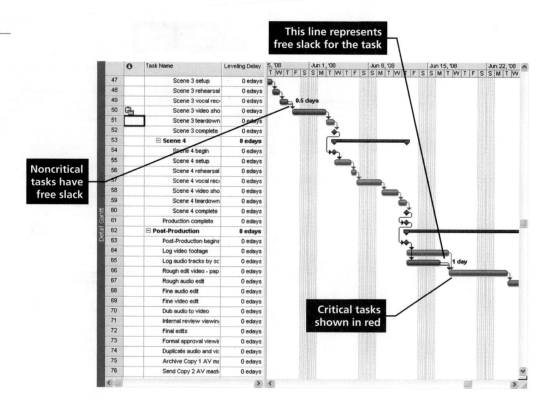

Almost all of the tasks that fall after task 50, Scene 3 video shoot, are on the critical path, which is shown in red. Noncritical tasks are displayed in blue and also show free slack. (Free slack is shown as the thin bar that extends to the right of the task bar.)

5. SAVE the project plan.

PAUSE. LEAVE the project plan open to use in the next exercise.

In this exercise you learned how to view the critical path for a project. The ***critical path*** is the series of tasks whose scheduling directly affects the project's finish date. It is not unusual for the project's critical path to change as the project moves along, since some tasks will be completed early and others will be delayed. Once a task on the critical path is complete, it is no longer considered critical since it cannot affect the finish date of the project.

To fully understand the critical path concept, there are a few other terms with which you need to become familiar. ***Slack*** is the amount of time a task can be delayed without causing a delay to a task or the overall project. Slack is also known as float. ***Free slack*** is the amount of time a task can be delayed before it will delay another task. ***Total slack*** is the amount of time a task can be delayed without delaying the project end date. A task is considered to be on the critical path if its total slack is zero (or occasionally, less than some specified amount). Conversely, ***noncritical tasks*** have slack greater than zero. Their start or finish dates can vary within their slack amounts without affecting the finish date of the project. The best way to manage the overall duration of a project is via its critical path.

■ Viewing Resource Allocations Over Time

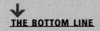
THE BOTTOM LINE

As a project manager, you are responsible for distributing work among the people and equipment resources of the project. Allocation is how you manage these resources and their assignments over time. You need to be able to review each resource's allocation, identify any problems that are evident, and adjust allocations as needed.

⊕ EXPLORE RESOURCE ALLOCATIONS AND IDENTIFY OVERALLOCATED RESOURCES

USE the project plan you created in the previous exercise.

1. Click **View** on the menu bar, and then click **Gantt Chart**.

2. On the Project Guide toolbar, click the **Report** button. In the *Report* pane, click the **See how resources' time is allocated** link. A split view appears: the Resource Usage view is on the top and the Gantt Chart view is on the bottom. Your screen should look similar to Figure 4-16.

Figure 4-16

Split screen showing Resource Usage and Gantt Chart views

On the left side of the Resource Usage view is the Usage Table, which shows the assignments grouped by resource, the total work assigned to each resource, and the work for each assignment. The outline format can be expanded and collapsed. The right side of the view contains assignment details (default setting is work) displayed on a timescale.

3. In the Usage Table, click the **Resource Name** column heading.

4. On the Formatting Toolbar, click the **Hide Subtasks** button. Microsoft Project collapses the Resource Usage view. The resources' total work values over the project timescale appear in the grid on the right. In the Resource Name column, click **Unassigned**. Your screen should look similar to Figure 4-17.

Figure 4-17

Collapsed Resource Usage view

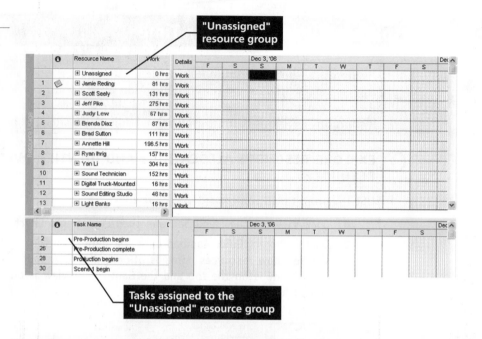

"Unassigned" resource group

Tasks assigned to the "Unassigned" resource group

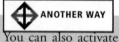
TAKE NOTE

Don't worry if you see a resource group titled Unassigned. Sometimes there are tasks that have no specific resources assigned to them. These tasks are grouped together in this view and listed as a resource named Unassigned.

5. In the Resource Name column, click on the name of resource 3, **Jeff Pike**.

6. Click the **Scroll to Task** button on the Standard toolbar. Project scrolls the grid to show Jeff Pike's earliest assignment: 8 hours on Monday, January 7. At the bottom of the screen, the Gantt Chart view shows the actual tasks to which Jeff is assigned.

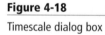
ANOTHER WAY

You can also activate the Timescale dialog box by clicking Format on the menu bar, and then clicking Timescale.

7. At the bottom of the *Resource Allocation* pane, click the **Change Timescale** link. The Timescale dialog box appears. The timescale can display up to three tiers, usually shown in descending order of detail (months, days, hours). By default, the top tier is disabled.

8. Select the **Middle Tier** tab if it is not already selected. Under *Middle tier formatting* in the Units box, select **Months**.

9. Under *Timescale options* in the Show box, select **One tier (Middle)**. Your screen should look similar to Figure 4-18.

Figure 4-18

Timescale dialog box

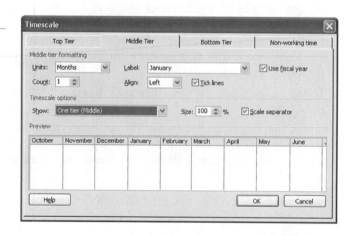

10. Click **OK** to close the Timescale dialog box. The timescaled grid now shows work values per month. Your screen should look similar to Figure 4-19.

Figure 4-19

Timescaled grid showing work values by month

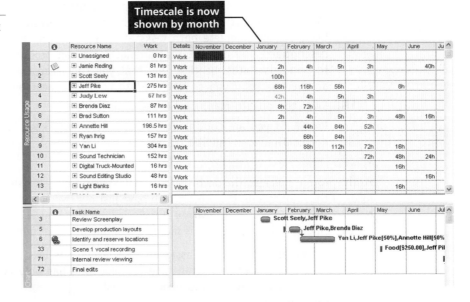

Use the arrow on the right side of the Resource Usage view to scroll down and review the resources listed. Some of the names are formatted in red, indicating that these resources are overallocated–at some point(s) in the schedule, their assigned tasks are greater than their capacity to work.

 ANOTHER WAY

Instead of using the Timescale command to change the tiers of the timescale, you can click the Zoom In and Zoom Out buttons on the Standard toolbar. If this method doesn't give you the level of detail you need, then you can use the Timescale command.

11. On the Standard toolbar, click the **Undo** button to undo the timescale change you just made. You want to look at resources in more detail now.

12. In the Resource Name column, click the name of resource 4, **Judy Lew**.

13. Click the **Scroll to Task** button on the Standard toolbar. Project scrolls the grid to show Judy Lew's earliest assignments. Using the arrows at the bottom of the timescaled section of the view, scroll over until you see the week of January 27, 2008. On Monday, January 28, Judy Lew's 5.7 hours of work are formatted in red, indicating that she is overallocated on that day. You need to take a closer look at her assignments to determine exactly what is causing this.

14. Click the plus sign (+) next to Judy Lew's name in the Resource Name column. The Resource Usage view expands to show Judy Lew's individual assignments. Your screen should look similar to Figure 4-20.

Figure 4-20

Expanded Resource Usage view with Judy Lew's assignments

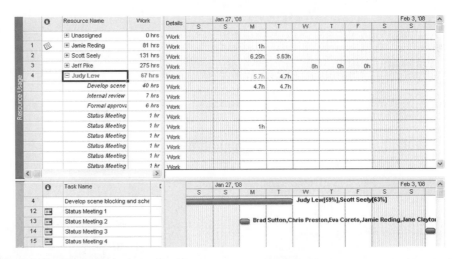

There are two assignments on January 28: *Develop scene blocking and schedule* (4.7h) and *Status Meeting 2* (1h). This is a true overallocation–Judy Lew most likely cannot complete both tasks at once. However, after reviewing the task descriptions, you can tell that arrangements can probably be made for Judy Lew to skip this status meeting, and that you can make this adjustment later. It is an overallocation you do not need to be very concerned with right now.

15. SAVE the project plan. **CLOSE** the project plan.

PAUSE. If you are continuing to the next lesson, keep Project open. If you are not continuing to additional lessons, **CLOSE** Project.

As the project manager, the decisions you make regarding task assignments affect the workloads of the resources on the project. You have just reviewed your resources to identify resource allocation issues. ***Allocation*** is the portion of a resource's capacity devoted to work on a specific task. Every resource is said to be in one of three states of allocation:

1. ***Underallocated***–the work assigned to a resource is less than the resource's maximum capacity. For example, a full-time resource who has only 20 hours of work assigned in a 40-hour work week is underallocated.

2. ***Fully allocated***–the condition of a resource when the total work of its task assignments is exactly equal to that resource's work capacity. For example, a full-time resource assigned to work 40 hours per week is fully allocated.

3. ***Overallocated***–the work assigned to a resource is more than the resource's maximum capacity. For example, a full-time resource who has 55 hours of work assigned in a 40-hour work week is overallocated.

Allocating resources takes a combination of skill and common sense. It might seem straightforward to say that all resources should be fully allocated all of the time, but this is not always possible, practical, or even desirable. There are situations in which overallocation or underallocation is quite acceptable. As the project manager, you must learn how to identify allocation problems and how to handle them.

You might want to also keep the following points in mind when reviewing resource allocation:

- In the Resource Usage view, the default table is the Usage table. You can display other table views by clicking View on the menu bar, then click Table: Usage, and then select the table you want to display.

- Work values are the default in the timescaled grid of the Resource Usage view. To display other assignment values, such as cost, click Format on the menu bar, then click Details, and select the value you want to display.

SUMMARY SKILL MATRIX

IN THIS LESSON YOU LEARNED	MATRIX SKILL
To apply a task calendar to an individual task	Apply a task calendar to an individual task
To change task types	Change scheduling formula values to change task types Change a task type using the Task Information dialog box
To split a task	Split a task
To establish recurring tasks	Set up a recurring task Assign resources to a recurring task
To apply task constraints	Apply a Start No Earlier Than constraint to a task
To review the project's critical path	Review the project's critical path
To view resource allocations over time	Explore resource allocations and identify overallocated resources

■ Knowledge Assessment

Matching

Match the term in column 1 to its description in column 2.

Column 1	Column 2
1. critical path	**a.** the amount of time a task can be delayed before it will delay another task
2. free slack	**b.** a restriction that is set which controls the start or finish date of a task
3. split	**c.** the condition of a resource when the total work of its task assignments is exactly equal to that resource's work capacity
4. underallocated	**d.** the amount of time a project can be delayed without delaying the project end date
5. recurring task	**e.** the series of tasks whose scheduling directly affects the project's finish date
6. fixed units	**f.** forces a task to begin or end on a certain date, completely preventing the rescheduling of a task
7. constraint	**g.** an interruption in a task
8. fully allocated	**h.** the work assigned to a resource is less than the resource's maximum capacity
9. inflexible constraint	**i.** a task that is repeated at specific intervals
10. total slack	**j.** a task type in which the units value does not change

True / False

Circle T if the statement is true or F if the statement is false.

T **F** 1. It is always best to enter a start or finish date for every task.

T F 2. By default, critical path tasks are shown in red on the Detail Gantt view.

T F 3. It is never acceptable to have an overallocated resource.

T **F** 4. It is not possible to split a task over a weekend.

T **F** 5. Effort-driven scheduling and changing a task type both affect all resources in the same way.

T F 6. You cannot change the task type for a summary task.

T F 7. You can use a task calendar to schedule a task that will occur during a time that is not on the project calendar.

T F 8. It is acceptable to have a resource group named *Unassigned*.

T F 9. It is not possible to set a specific time of day for a recurring task.

T **F** 10. You can split a task only three times.

■ Competency Assessment

➔ Project 4-1: Adjusting Working Time for Office Remodel

You are in charge of the kitchen and lunchroom remodel for your office. Based on feedback from your associates, you have decided to schedule the drywall installation after working hours due to the noise. You need to set up a task calendar that reflects the different working hours.

GET READY. Launch Microsoft Project if it is not already running.

OPEN *Office Remodel 4-1* from the data files for this lesson.

The *Office Remodel 4-1* project plan is available on the companion CD-ROM.

1. On the menu bar, click **Tools**, and then click **Change Working Time**.
2. In the Change Working Time dialog box, click **Create New Calendar**.
3. In the Name box, key **Evening Drywall Install**.
4. If it is not already selected, click the **Make a copy of** button. In the dropdown menu, select **Standard**, and then click **OK**.
5. Click on the **Work Weeks** tab in the Change Working Time dialog box, and then click the **Details** button.
6. In the *Select days* box, drag your pointer to select **Monday** through **Friday**. Click the **Set day(s) to these specific working times** button.
7. Click the cell in row 1 of the *From* column and key **4:00 PM**. Click the cell in row 1 of the *To* column and key **12:00 AM**. Click the cell in row 2 of the *From* column, and press **Delete**. Click **OK**. Click **OK** again to close the Change Working Time dialog box.
8. Select the name of task 9, **Install drywall**.
9. On the Standard toolbar, click the **Task Information** button.
10. Click the **Advanced** tab.
11. In the Calendar box, select **Evening Drywall Install** from the dropdown list.
12. Click the **Scheduling ignores resource calendars** check box, and then click **OK**.
13. **SAVE** the project plan as *Office Remodel Drywall Install*, and then **CLOSE** the file.

    LEAVE Project open for the next exercise.

→ Project 4-2: Weekly Meeting for Hiring a New Employee

You have developed a project plan for hiring a new employee. You now need to add a recurring weekly status meeting to your tasks.

The *Hiring New Employee 4-2* project plan is available on the companion CD-ROM.

OPEN *Hiring New Employee 4-2* from the data files for this lesson.

1. Select the name of task 5, **Collect resumes**.
2. On the menu bar, click **Insert**, and then click **Recurring Task**.
3. In the Task Name box, key **Status Meeting**.
4. In the Duration box, key **1h**.
5. Under *Recurrence pattern*, select **Daily.**
6. In the *Every* box, key or select **3** and then select **workdays**.
7. In the Start box, key or select **11/1/07**.
8. Under *Range of recurrence*, select **End after**, and then key or select **10** occurrences.
9. Click **OK**.
10. **SAVE** the project plan as *Hiring New Employee Recurring* and then **CLOSE** the file.

    LEAVE Project open for the next exercise.

■ Proficiency Assessment

→ Project 4-3: Splitting a Task for Setting Up a Home Office

You are in the process of setting up a home office, but have just been notified that you will need to be out of town from Wednesday, October 11 through Friday, October 13 for some training. You need to adjust your project plan to reflect this out-of-town time.

The *Home Office 4-3* project plan is available on the companion CD-ROM.

OPEN *Home Office 4-3* from the data files for this lesson.

1. Change the view to the Gantt Chart view.
2. Select the name of task 13. Scroll to the bar chart view for this task.
3. Use the Split Task Button to shift the task from Wednesday, October 11 to Monday, October 16 (you will not be in town from Wed.–Fri.).
4. **SAVE** the project plan as *Home Office Split Task*, and then **CLOSE** the file.

   LEAVE Project open to use in the next exercise.

→ Project 4-4: Setting a Constraint for the Don Funk Music Video

You have just been informed that Don Funk is not available for the Formal approval viewing until July 21, 2008. You need to set a constraint for this task so that it cannot start until July 21.

The *Don Funk Music Video 4-4* project plan is available on the companion CD-ROM.

OPEN *Don Fun Music Video 4-4* from the data files for this lesson.

1. Switch to the *Tasks* pane in the Project Guide.
2. Select **Set deadlines and constrain tasks**.
3. Select the name of task 73. Scroll the Gantt bars to this task.
4. Use the Project Guide to set a Start No Earlier Than constraint with a date of July 21, 2008.
5. **SAVE** the project plan as *Don Funk Constraint* and then **CLOSE** the file.

   LEAVE Project open to use in the next exercise.

■ Mastery Assessment

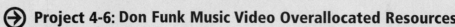

➔ Project 4-5: Hiring a New Employee–Adding Resources to the Recurring Status Meeting

The *Hiring New Employee Recurring 4-5* project plan is available on the companion CD-ROM.

In Project 4-2, you established a recurring status meeting for the Hiring a New Employee project plan. Now you will add resources to that task.

OPEN *Hiring New Employee Recurring 4-5* from the data files for this lesson.

1. Assign the resources Amy Rusko, Barry Potter, Gabe Mares, and Jeff Smith to the Status Meeting recurring task.

2. Expand the subtasks for the recurring task to visually confirm that the resources have been assigned.

3. **SAVE** the project plan as *Hiring New Employee Recurring Resources* and then **CLOSE** the file.

   LEAVE Project open to use in the next exercise.

➔ Project 4-6: Don Funk Music Video Overallocated Resources

The *Don Funk Music Video 4-6* project plan is available on the companion CD-ROM.

Review the resource allocations for the Don Funk Music Video. Pay close attention to overallocated resources.

OPEN *Don Funk Music Video 4-6* from the data files for this lesson.

1. Use the *Report* panes of the Project Guide to review resource assignments for this project.

2. Locate Yan Li and then review his task assignments for the weeks of April 13 and 20, 2008.

3. In a separate Word document, write a brief paragraph detailing Yan Li's assignments for those weeks. Include any times that he is overallocated, and discuss whether or not you think the overallocation is critical or can be left as is.

4. **SAVE** the project plan as *Don Funk-Yan Li* and then **CLOSE** the file. **SAVE** the Word document as *Don Funk-Yan Li Discussion* and then **CLOSE** the file.

   CLOSE Project.

INTERNET READY

Many sites on the Internet provide Microsoft Project templates for public use. You can download a template that someone else has created and modify it to fit your specific needs. One such place to find a large variety of templates is Microsoft Office Online.

Open Microsoft Project. Click on *File*, then *New*. Under the Templates section, click on the *Search on Office Online* link. Search Microsoft Office Online for a Project template that is of some personal interest to you. Download the template. Using the skills you learned in this lesson, change the view so that you can review the critical path of the project. Study how the tasks are linked and why some tasks are not on the critical path. Make changes to some of the start dates to see the effect of your changes on the critical path.

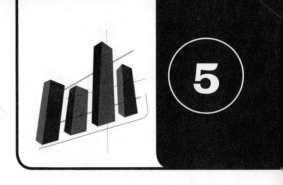

Project Information: Sorting, Grouping, and Filtering

LESSON SKILL MATRIX

SKILLS	MATRIX SKILL
Sorting Data	Sort data in a resource view
Grouping Data	Group data in a resource view
Filtering Data	Create and apply a filter in a view Create a custom filter

KEY TERMS
AutoFilter
filter
group
sort

As a video production manager for Southridge Video and the project manager for the new Don Funk music video, you have invested much time and effort into assembling your project plan. You have entered and linked tasks, created work and material resources, and assigned these resources to the project tasks. Now that the key elements of the project plan have been established, you need to be able to view and analyze the project plan information in different ways. The best project plan is only as good as the data you are able to get out of it. In this lesson, you will learn to use some of the tools in Microsoft Office Project, such as views, tables, and reports, to modify the way your data is organized. You will also learn about some features that enable you to make custom changes to your data to suit your own specific needs.

■ SOFTWARE ORIENTATION

Microsoft Project's Sort dialog box

In Microsoft Project, you can use the Sort dialog box to sort task or resource information in the current view by a specified field or fields.

Figure 5-1

Sort dialog box

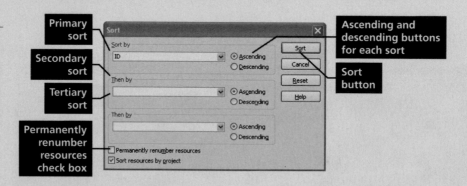

The Sort dialog box enables you to select up to three fields for three levels of sorts within sorts, to choose whether the view should be sorted in ascending or descending order, and to indicate whether items should be permanently renumbered according to the sort.

■ Sorting Data

THE BOTTOM LINE

It is easiest to review and utilize data in Microsoft Project when you have organized it so that it fits your needs. The simplest way to reorganize task and resource data in Project is by sorting.

⊕ SORT DATA IN A RESOURCE VIEW

GET READY. Before you begin these steps, launch Microsoft Project.

OPEN the *Don Funk Music Video 5M* from the data files for this lesson.

SAVE the file as *Don Funk Music Video 5* in the solutions folder for this lesson as directed by your instructor.

The *Don Funk Music Video 5M* project plan is available on the companion CD-ROM.

1. On the menu bar, click **View**, and then click **Resource Sheet**. The Resource Sheet view appears. The default view in the Resource Sheet is the Entry table. However, you want to look at the cost per resource, which is not displayed in the Entry table.

2. On the menu bar, click **View**, point to **Table: Entry**, and then click **Summary**. The Summary table appears in the Resource Sheet view. Your screen should look similar to Figure 5-2.

Figure 5-2

Resource Sheet view showing Summary Table

Cost per resource displayed in the summary table

Recall that resources listed in red are overallocated

	Resource Name	Group	Max. Units	Peak	Std. Rate	Ovt. Rate	Cost	Work
1	Jamie Reding	Production	100%	100%	$1,000.00/wk	$0.00/hr	$2,025.00	81 hrs
2	Scott Seely	Production	100%	100%	$19.50/hr	$0.00/hr	$2,554.50	131 hrs
3	Jeff Pike	Production	100%	100%	$750.00/wk	$0.00/hr	$5,156.25	275 hrs
4	Judy Lew	Production	100%	159%	$19.50/hr	$0.00/hr	$1,306.50	67 hrs
5	Brenda Diaz	Production	100%	100%	$12.75/hr	$0.00/hr	$1,109.25	87 hrs
6	Brad Sutton	Production	100%	100%	$16.50/hr	$0.00/hr	$1,831.50	111 hrs
7	Annette Hill	Production	50%	50%	$20.00/hr	$0.00/hr	$3,930.00	196.5 hrs
8	Ryan Ihrig	Production	100%	100%	$12.00/hr	$0.00/hr	$1,884.00	157 hrs
9	Yan Li	Production	100%	100%	$18.50/hr	$0.00/hr	$5,624.00	304 hrs
10	Sound Technician	Crew	300%	100%	$16.50/hr	$0.00/hr	$2,508.00	152 hrs
11	Digital Truck-Mounted	Equipment	200%	100%	$1,000.00/wk	$0.00/hr	$400.00	16 hrs
12	Sound Editing Studio	Lab	100%	100%	$250.00/day	$0.00/hr	$1,500.00	48 hrs
13	Light Banks	Equipment	400%	100%	$0.00/hr	$0.00/hr	$0.00	16 hrs
14	Video Editing Studio	Lab	100%	100%	$250.00/hr	$0.00/hr	$0.00	98 hrs
15	Microphone Bundles	Equipment	500%	100%	$0.00/hr	$0.00/hr	$0.00	16 hrs
16	Dolly	Equipment	200%	100%	$25.00/day	$0.00/hr	$100.00	32 hrs
17	DVD	Materials			c/day	$10.00		$120.00	2 2-hour disc
18	Travel	Cost		0%			$5,000.00	
19	Food	Cost		0%			$1,250.00	
20	Don Funk	Talent	100%	100%	1,000.00/day	$0.00/hr	$13,625.00	109 hrs
21	Bjorn Rettig	Production	50%	50%	$18.00/hr	$0.00/hr	$360.00	20 hrs
22	Frank Zhang	Production	50%	50%	$16.50/hr	$0.00/hr	$181.50	11 hrs
23	Florian Voss	Production	100%	100%	$13.00/hr	$0.00/hr	$728.00	56 hrs
24	Chris Preston	Production	100%	100%	$17.00/hr	$0.00/hr	$1,326.00	78 hrs
25	Shu Ito	Production	100%	100%	$16.00/hr	$0.00/hr	$1,792.00	112 hrs
26	Jim Kim	Production	100%	100%	$16.50/hr	$0.00/hr	$759.00	46 hrs
27	Greg Guzik	Production	100%	100%	$18.50/hr	$0.00/hr	$740.00	40 hrs
28	Maria Hammond	Production	100%	100%	$18.00/hr	$0.00/hr	$720.00	40 hrs
29	Patricia Doyle	Production	100%	100%	$17.50/hr	$0.00/hr	$700.00	40 hrs
30	Eva Corets	Production	100%	100%	$13.50/hr	$0.00/hr	$270.00	20 hrs
31	Luis Bonifaz	Production	100%	100%	$14.00/hr	$0.00/hr	$308.00	22 hrs

3. On the menu bar, click on **Project**, point to **Sort**, and then click **Sort by**. The Sort dialog box appears (as displayed in Figure 5-1).

TAKE NOTE *

Notice that in the Sort box, you can utilize up to three nested levels of sort criteria. Also, you can sort by any field, not just the fields that are visible in the active view.

4. In the *Sort by* section, select **Cost** from the dropdown menu. Next to that, click on **Descending**. Make sure that the *Permanently renumber resources* check box at the bottom of the Sort dialog box is NOT checked.

SHOOTING

The *Permanently renumber resources* check box (or when in a task view, *Permanently renumber tasks*) is a Project-level setting. If you check this box, Project will permanently renumber resources or tasks in ANY Microsoft Project file in which you sort. Since you may not want to permanently renumber tasks or resources every time you sort, it is a good idea to have this option turned off.

5. Click the **Sort** button. The Summary table is sorted from the highest to lowest value in the Cost column. Your screen should look similar to Figure 5-3. This sort enables you to look at resource costs across the entire project.

Figure 5-3

Summary Table sorted by Cost
(descending)

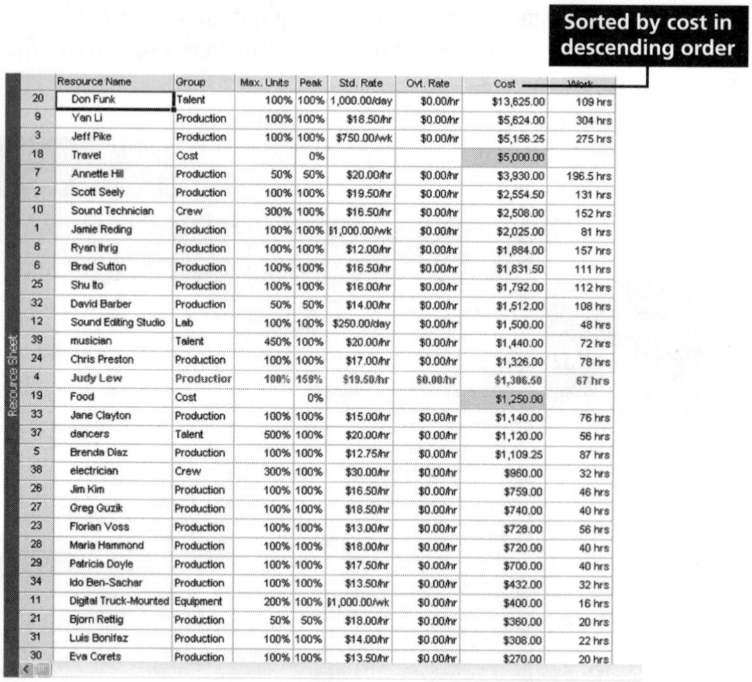

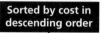

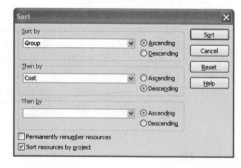

	Resource Name	Group	Max. Units	Peak	Std. Rate	Ovt. Rate	Cost	Work
20	Don Funk	Talent	100%	100%	1,000.00/day	$0.00/hr	$13,625.00	109 hrs
9	Yan Li	Production	100%	100%	$18.50/hr	$0.00/hr	$5,624.00	304 hrs
3	Jeff Pike	Production	100%	100%	$750.00/wk	$0.00/hr	$5,156.25	275 hrs
18	Travel	Cost		0%			$5,000.00	
7	Annette Hill	Production	50%	50%	$20.00/hr	$0.00/hr	$3,930.00	196.5 hrs
2	Scott Seely	Production	100%	100%	$19.50/hr	$0.00/hr	$2,554.50	131 hrs
10	Sound Technician	Crew	300%	100%	$16.50/hr	$0.00/hr	$2,508.00	152 hrs
1	Jamie Reding	Production	100%	100%	$1,000.00/wk	$0.00/hr	$2,025.00	81 hrs
8	Ryan Ihrig	Production	100%	100%	$12.00/hr	$0.00/hr	$1,884.00	157 hrs
6	Brad Sutton	Production	100%	100%	$16.50/hr	$0.00/hr	$1,831.50	111 hrs
25	Shu Ito	Production	100%	100%	$16.00/hr	$0.00/hr	$1,792.00	112 hrs
32	David Barber	Production	50%	50%	$14.00/hr	$0.00/hr	$1,512.00	108 hrs
12	Sound Editing Studio	Lab	100%	100%	$250.00/day	$0.00/hr	$1,500.00	48 hrs
39	musician	Talent	450%	100%	$20.00/hr	$0.00/hr	$1,440.00	72 hrs
24	Chris Preston	Production	100%	100%	$17.00/hr	$0.00/hr	$1,326.00	78 hrs
4	Judy Lew	Production	100%	159%	$19.50/hr	$0.00/hr	$1,306.50	67 hrs
19	Food	Cost		0%			$1,250.00	
33	Jane Clayton	Production	100%	100%	$15.00/hr	$0.00/hr	$1,140.00	76 hrs
37	dancers	Talent	500%	100%	$20.00/hr	$0.00/hr	$1,120.00	56 hrs
5	Brenda Diaz	Production	100%	100%	$12.75/hr	$0.00/hr	$1,109.25	87 hrs
38	electrician	Crew	300%	100%	$30.00/hr	$0.00/hr	$960.00	32 hrs
26	Jim Kim	Production	100%	100%	$16.50/hr	$0.00/hr	$759.00	46 hrs
27	Greg Guzik	Production	100%	100%	$18.50/hr	$0.00/hr	$740.00	40 hrs
23	Florian Voss	Production	100%	100%	$13.00/hr	$0.00/hr	$728.00	56 hrs
28	Maria Hammond	Production	100%	100%	$18.00/hr	$0.00/hr	$720.00	40 hrs
29	Patricia Doyle	Production	100%	100%	$17.50/hr	$0.00/hr	$700.00	40 hrs
34	Ido Ben-Sachar	Production	100%	100%	$13.50/hr	$0.00/hr	$432.00	32 hrs
11	Digital Truck-Mounted	Equipment	200%	100%	$1,000.00/wk	$0.00/hr	$400.00	16 hrs
21	Bjorn Rettig	Production	50%	50%	$18.00/hr	$0.00/hr	$360.00	20 hrs
31	Luis Bonifaz	Production	100%	100%	$14.00/hr	$0.00/hr	$308.00	22 hrs
30	Eva Corets	Production	100%	100%	$13.50/hr	$0.00/hr	$270.00	20 hrs

Sorted by cost in descending order

TAKE NOTE When you sort data in your project, the sort applies to the active view, no matter which table is currently displayed in the view. For example, if you sort the Task Usage view by finish date while the Entry table is visible, and then switch to the Cost table, you will see that the tasks are still sorted by finish date in the Cost column.

6. On the menu bar, click on **Project**, point to **Sort**, and then click **Sort by**. The Sort dialog box appears.

7. In the *Sort by* section, select **Group** from the dropdown menu. Next to that, click **Ascending**.

8. In the *Then by* section, select **Cost** from the dropdown menu. Next to that, click **Descending**. Make sure the *Permanently renumber resources* box is not checked. Your screen should look similar to Figure 5-4.

Figure 5-4

Sort dialog box with two-level sort choices

9. Click the **Sort** button. The Resource Sheet view is sorted to display resources sorted first by Group (Equipment, Talent, etc.) and then by Cost within each group. Your screen should look similar to Figure 5-5.

Figure 5-5

Summary table sorted first by Group and then by Cost

| | Sorted first by group . . . | | | | | | . . . and then by cost in descending order | |

	Resource Name	Group	Max. Units	Peak	Std. Rate	Ovt. Rate	Cost	Work
18	Travel	Cost		0%			$5,000.00	
19	Food	Cost		0%			$1,250.00	
10	Sound Technician	Crew	300%	100%	$16.50/hr	$0.00/hr	$2,508.00	152 hrs
38	electrician	Crew	300%	100%	$30.00/hr	$0.00/hr	$960.00	32 hrs
11	Digital Truck-Mounted	Equipment	200%	100%	$1,000.00/wk	$0.00/hr	$400.00	16 hrs
16	Dolly	Equipment	200%	100%	$25.00/day	$0.00/hr	$100.00	32 hrs
13	Light Banks	Equipment	400%	100%	$0.00/hr	$0.00/hr	$0.00	16 hrs
15	Microphone Bundles	Equipment	500%	100%	$0.00/hr	$0.00/hr	$0.00	16 hrs
12	Sound Editing Studio	Lab	100%	100%	$250.00/day	$0.00/hr	$1,500.00	48 hrs
14	Video Editing Studio	Lab	100%	100%	$250.00/hr	$0.00/hr	$0.00	98 hrs
17	DVD	Materials		c/day	$10.00		$120.00	2 2-hour disc
35	Dry Ice	Materials		k/day	$12.00		$24.00	2 10 lb block
36	Bottled Water	Materials		e/day	$5.00		$20.00	4 bottle case
9	Yan Li	Production	100%	100%	$18.50/hr	$0.00/hr	$5,624.00	304 hrs
3	Jeff Pike	Production	100%	100%	$750.00/wk	$0.00/hr	$5,156.25	275 hrs
7	Annette Hill	Production	50%	50%	$20.00/hr	$0.00/hr	$3,930.00	196.5 hrs
2	Scott Seely	Production	100%	100%	$19.50/hr	$0.00/hr	$2,554.50	131 hrs
1	Jamie Reding	Production	100%	100%	$1,000.00/wk	$0.00/hr	$2,025.00	81 hrs
8	Ryan Ihrig	Production	100%	100%	$12.00/hr	$0.00/hr	$1,884.00	157 hrs
6	Brad Sutton	Production	100%	100%	$16.50/hr	$0.00/hr	$1,831.50	111 hrs
25	Shu Ito	Production	100%	100%	$16.00/hr	$0.00/hr	$1,792.00	112 hrs
32	David Barber	Production	50%	50%	$14.00/hr	$0.00/hr	$1,512.00	108 hrs
24	Chris Preston	Production	100%	100%	$17.00/hr	$0.00/hr	$1,326.00	78 hrs
4	Judy Lew	Production	100%	159%	$19.50/hr	$0.00/hr	$1,306.50	67 hrs
33	Jane Clayton	Production	100%	100%	$15.00/hr	$0.00/hr	$1,140.00	76 hrs
5	Brenda Diaz	Production	100%	100%	$12.75/hr	$0.00/hr	$1,109.25	87 hrs
26	Jim Kim	Production	100%	100%	$16.50/hr	$0.00/hr	$759.00	46 hrs
27	Greg Guzik	Production	100%	100%	$18.50/hr	$0.00/hr	$740.00	40 hrs
23	Florian Voss	Production	100%	100%	$13.00/hr	$0.00/hr	$728.00	56 hrs
28	Maria Hammond	Production	100%	100%	$18.00/hr	$0.00/hr	$720.00	40 hrs
29	Patricia Doyle	Production	100%	100%	$17.50/hr	$0.00/hr	$700.00	40 hrs

When you sort data in this way, it is easy to identify the most and least expensive resources in each group on your project. You can sort your data in any way that is beneficial to the analysis of your project. The sort order you most recently specified will remain in effect until you re-sort the view. Now you will restore the data to its original order.

10. On the menu bar, click the **Undo** button one time. The Undo button reverses the last sort you performed, restoring the data to the original sort order (by Cost only).

11. Now click the **Undo** button again. The data is restored to the original order in the Summary table of the Resource Sheet view (as displayed previously in Figure 5-2). The Multiple Level Undo enables you to undo actions or sets of actions while you are working on your project plan.

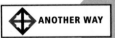 **ANOTHER WAY** You can also "unsort" your data by clicking Project on the menu bar, pointing to Sort, and then clicking By ID.

12. **SAVE** the project plan.

PAUSE. LEAVE the project plan open to use in the next exercise.

You have just performed several sorts on your project data to allow you to more closely examine certain aspects of your project. A **sort** is a way of ordering task or resource information in a view by the criteria you specify. You can sort tasks or resources using predefined criteria, or you can create your own sort order with up to three levels (a group within a group within a group).

Except for one instance, sorting does not change the actual data of your project plan, but rather just reorders your data. Sorting allows you to arrange data in an order that answers a question you may have, or in a way that makes more sense or is more user-friendly to your project team. Note that there is no visual indicator that a task or resource view has been sorted other than the order in which the rows of data appear. Furthermore, unlike grouping and filtering, which you will learn about later in this lesson, you cannot save custom sort settings that you have specified.

The one instance in which the actual data of your project is changed by sorting is the option that Project offers to renumber resource or task IDs after sorting. Once resources or tasks are renumbered by sorting, you can't restore their original numeric order. Sometimes, you might want to permanently renumber tasks or resources. For instance, at the beginning of a project, you might enter resource names as they are needed on the project. When you are finished entering resources, you might want to sort then alphabetically and permanently renumber them.

The Multiple Level Undo function you used in this exercise is a very valuable new tool in Microsoft Project. As you saw, this feature allows you to easily undo sets of actions you have performed in Microsoft Project. You can undo changes that you purposely made (as in this exercise), or reverse "mistakes" that you make while working on your project plan. However, the functionality of Multiple Level Undo doesn't stop there. It enables you to make, undo, and redo changes to views, data, and options–giving you the ability to experiment with different scenarios without causing permanent undesired effects. You can test several approaches to resolving a problem or optimizing a project plan in order to fully understand the implications of each choice. (You can also use the Visual Change Highlighting as you are making changes to see the effects of your actions.)

■ Grouping Data

THE BOTTOM LINE

Another way to organize, view, and analyze the data in your project plan is through grouping. Grouping enables you to organize the task and resource criteria in your plan according to various criteria that you select.

➔ GROUP DATA IN A RESOURCE VIEW

USE the project plan you created in the previous exercise.

1. On the menu bar, click **Project**, point to **Group by: No Group**, and then click **Resource Group**. Microsoft Project reorganizes the data into resource groups and presents it in an expanded outline form. It also adds summary costs by group. Your screen should look similar to Figure 5-6.

Figure 5-6

Project data grouped by resource group, with summary fields

Summary data rows shaded yellow

	Resource Name	Group	Max. Units	Peak	Std. Rate	Ovt. Rate	Cost	Work
	⊟ **Group: Cost**	**Cost**		**0%**			**$6,250.00**	
18	Travel	Cost		0%			$5,000.00	
19	Food	Cost		0%			$1,250.00	
	⊟ **Group: Crew**	**Crew**	**600%**	**200%**			**$3,468.00**	**184 hrs**
10	Sound Techniciar	Crew	300%	100%	$16.50/hr	$0.00/hr	$2,508.00	152 hrs
38	electrician	Crew	300%	100%	$30.00/hr	$0.00/hr	$960.00	32 hrs
	⊟ **Group: Equipment**	**Equipment**	**1,300%**	**400%**			**$500.00**	**80 hrs**
11	Digital Truck-Moun	Equipment	200%	100%	$1,000.00/wk	$0.00/hr	$400.00	16 hrs
13	Light Banks	Equipment	400%	100%	$0.00/hr	$0.00/hr	$0.00	16 hrs
15	Microphone Bund	Equipment	500%	100%	$0.00/hr	$0.00/hr	$0.00	16 hrs
16	Dolly	Equipment	200%	100%	$25.00/day	$0.00/hr	$100.00	32 hrs
	⊟ **Group: Lab**	**Lab**	**200%**	**200%**			**$1,500.00**	**146 hrs**
12	Sound Editing Stu	Lab	100%	100%	$250.00/day	$0.00/hr	$1,500.00	48 hrs
14	Video Editing Stuc	Lab	100%	100%	$250.00/hr	$0.00/hr	$0.00	98 hrs
	⊟ **Group: Materials**	**Materials**					**$164.00**	
17	DVD	Materials		disc/day	$10.00		$120.00	2 2-hour disc
35	Dry Ice	Materials		lock/day	$12.00		$24.00	2 10 lb block
36	Bottled Water	Materials		ase/day	$5.00		$20.00	4 bottle case
	⊟ **Group: Production**	**Production**	**2,100%**	**2,159%**			**$36,389.50**	**2,110.5 hrs**
1	Jamie Reding	Production	100%	100%	$1,000.00/wk	$0.00/hr	$2,025.00	81 hrs
2	Scott Seely	Production	100%	100%	$19.50/hr	$0.00/hr	$2,554.50	131 hrs
3	Jeff Pike	Production	100%	100%	$750.00/wk	$0.00/hr	$5,156.25	275 hrs
4	Judy Lew	Production	100%	159%	$19.50/hr	$0.00/hr	$1,306.50	67 hrs
5	Brenda Diaz	Production	100%	100%	$12.75/hr	$0.00/hr	$1,109.25	87 hrs
6	Brad Sutton	Production	100%	100%	$16.50/hr	$0.00/hr	$1,831.50	111 hrs
7	Annette Hill	Production	50%	50%	$20.00/hr	$0.00/hr	$3,930.00	196.5 hrs
8	Ryan Ihrig	Production	100%	100%	$12.00/hr	$0.00/hr	$1,884.00	157 hrs
9	Yan Li	Production	100%	100%	$18.50/hr	$0.00/hr	$5,624.00	304 hrs
21	Bjorn Rettig	Production	50%	50%	$18.00/hr	$0.00/hr	$360.00	20 hrs
22	Frank Zhang	Production	50%	50%	$16.50/hr	$0.00/hr	$181.50	11 hrs
23	Florian Voss	Production	100%	100%	$13.00/hr	$0.00/hr	$728.00	56 hrs

The summary data rows are set off with a colored background (yellow in this case). Because the data in the summary rows is derived from subordinate data, it cannot be changed directly. To have more control over how your data is presented, you can create custom groups.

2. On the menu bar, click **Project**, point to **Group by: Resource Group**, and then click **More Groups**. The More Groups dialog box appears, displaying all of the predefined groups for tasks and resources available to you. You will create a new group that is similar to the Resource Group.

The Project Guide can also be used to apply a group (or a filter) to a table. On the Project Guide toolbar, click *Report*. In the *Reports* pane, click the *Change the content or order of information in a view* link.

3. Select **Resource Group** (if it is not already selected), and then click the **Copy** button. The Group Definition dialog box appears.

4. In the Names box, key **Resource Groups by Cost**.

5. In the Field Name column, click the first empty cell below Group.

6. Key or select **Cost**.

7. In the Order column for the Cost field, click on **Ascending** to select it and then select **Descending** from the dropdown menu. The resources will be sorted within their groups by descending cost. The Group Definition dialog box should look similar to Figure 5-7.

Figure 5-7

Group Definition dialog box with custom selections

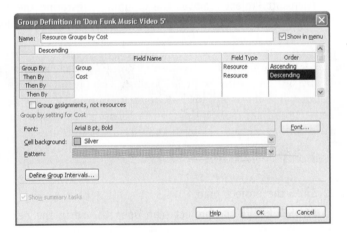

8. In the Group Definition dialog box, click the **Define Group Intervals** button. The Define Group Intervals dialog box appears.

9. In the *Group on* box, select **Interval** from the dropdown menu.

10. Key **500** in the *Group interval* box, and then click the **OK** button.

11. Click the **OK** button in the Group Definition dialog box to close it. Resource Groups by Cost appears as a new group in the More Groups dialog box.

12. Click the **Apply** button in the More Groups dialog box. Microsoft Project applies the new group to the Resource Sheet view.

13. Double-click the Resource Name column heading. The Column Definition dialog box appears. You want to widen the Resource Name column.

14. Click the **Best Fit** button in the Column Definition dialog box. The Resource Name column is widened. Your screen should look similar to Figure 5-8.

Figure 5-8

Resource sheet view showing two-level grouping

Data grouped first by resource and then by cost

Resource Name	Group	Max. Units	Peak	Std. Rate	Ovt. Rate	Cost	Work
⊟ Group: Cost	Cost		0%			$6,250.00	
⊟ Cost: $5,000.00 - <$5,500.00	Cost		0%			$5,000.00	
Travel	Cost		0%			$5,000.00	
⊟ Cost: $1,000.00 - <$1,500.00	Cost		0%			$1,250.00	
Food	Cost		0%			$1,250.00	
⊟ Group: Crew	Crew	600%	200%			$3,468.00	184 hrs
⊟ Cost: $2,500.00 - <$3,000.00	Crew	300%	100%			$2,508.00	152 hrs
Sound Technician	Crew	300%	100%	$16.50/hr	$0.00/hr	$2,508.00	152 hrs
⊟ Cost: $500.00 - <$1,000.00	Crew	300%	100%			$960.00	32 hrs
electrician	Crew	300%	100%	$30.00/hr	$0.00/hr	$960.00	32 hrs
⊟ Group: Equipment	Equipment	1,300%	400%			$500.00	80 hrs
⊟ Cost: $0.00 - <$500.00	Equipment	1,300%	400%			$500.00	80 hrs
Digital Truck-Mounted Video Camera	Equipment	200%	100%	$1,000.00/wk	$0.00/hr	$400.00	16 hrs
Light Banks	Equipment	400%	100%	$0.00/hr	$0.00/hr	$0.00	16 hrs
Microphone Bundles	Equipment	500%	100%	$0.00/hr	$0.00/hr	$0.00	16 hrs
Dolly	Equipment	200%	100%	$25.00/day	$0.00/hr	$100.00	32 hrs
⊟ Group: Lab	Lab	200%	200%			$1,500.00	146 hrs
⊟ Cost: $1,500.00 - <$2,000.00	Lab	100%	100%			$1,500.00	48 hrs
Sound Editing Studio	Lab	100%	100%	$250.00/day	$0.00/hr	$1,500.00	48 hrs
⊟ Cost: $0.00 - <$500.00	Lab	100%	100%			$0.00	98 hrs
Video Editing Studio	Lab	100%	100%	$250.00/hr	$0.00/hr	$0.00	98 hrs
⊟ Group: Materials	Materials					$164.00	
⊟ Cost: $0.00 - <$500.00	Materials					$164.00	
DVD	Materials		disc/day	$10.00		$120.00	2 2-hour disc
Dry Ice	Materials		lock/day	$12.00		$24.00	2 10 lb block
Bottled Water	Materials		ase/day	$5.00		$20.00	4 bottle case
⊟ Group: Production	Production	2,100%	2,159%			$36,389.50	2,110.5 hrs
⊟ Cost: $5,500.00 - <$6,000.00	Production	100%	100%			$5,624.00	304 hrs
Yan Li	Production	100%	100%	$18.50/hr	$0.00/hr	$5,624.00	304 hrs
⊟ Cost: $5,000.00 - <$5,500.00	Production	100%	100%			$5,156.25	275 hrs
Jeff Pike	Production	100%	100%	$750.00/wk	$0.00/hr	$5,156.25	275 hrs

The resources are grouped by Resource Group (the yellow shaded cells) and within each group by cost values at $500 increments (the gray shaded cells).

15. After you have reviewed the groupings you created, click on **Project** on the menu bar. Point to **Group By: Resource Groups by Cost** and then click **No Group**. Microsoft Project removes the groupings, restoring the original data. Displaying or removing a group has no effect on the data in the project.

ANOTHER WAY

The predefined groups and any custom groups you create are also available via the Group By button on the Standard toolbar. The button appears as a box with a drop-down list. Click the arrow in the Group By button to see all group names. The name of the active group appears on this button. If no group is applied to the table, No Group is visible on the button. (Note: If the Group By button is not visible on your Standard toolbar, you may have to use the Toolbar Options button to activate it.)

16. **SAVE** the project plan.

PAUSE. LEAVE the project plan open to use in the next exercise.

In this exercise, you have just reorganized your project data using grouping. A *group* is a way to reorder task or resource information in a table and to display summary values for each group according to various criteria you can choose. Grouping goes a step beyond sorting in that grouping your project data will add summary values, called "roll-ups," at customized intervals.

Grouping the data in a project plan enables you to view your information from a variety of perspectives. It also allows for a more detailed level of data analysis and presentation. In your role as project manager, your project plan helps you track the work and costs associated with your project. By using grouping, you also have the ability to look at more details—to understand not just what is happening on your project, but also why.

As with sorting, grouping does not change the fundamental structure of your project plan but rather just reorganizes and summarizes it. Also like sorting, grouping applies to all tables you can display in the view. You can use any of the predefined groups, customize these predefined groups, or create your own.

■ Filtering Data

THE BOTTOM LINE

The Microsoft Project feature called filtering allows you to look only at specific task or resource data that meet specific criteria. Filtering hides task or resource data that does not meet the criteria you specify and displays only the data in which you are interested. You can use a predefined filter, use AutoFilters, or create a custom filter.

Creating and Applying a Filter

In this exercise, you will create a filter that allows you to focus on tasks related to the video shoot.

⊕ CREATE AND APPLY A FILTER IN A VIEW

USE the project plan you created in the previous exercise.

1. On the menu bar, click **View**, and then click **Gantt Chart**. The Gantt Chart view appears.

2. On the Formatting toolbar, click the **AutoFilter** button. When AutoFilter is turned on, Microsoft Project displays arrows to the right of each column heading. You can use these arrows to select the AutoFilter option you want to use. Adjust the width of the Gantt Chart so that the Task Name, Duration, and Start columns are visible. Your screen should look similar to Figure 5-9.

Figure 5-9

Gantt Chart view with AutoFilter turned on

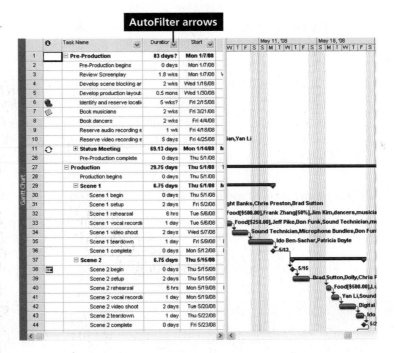

3. Click the down arrow in the Task Name column heading and then click (**Custom . . .**). The Custom AutoFilter dialog box appears. You want to see just the tasks that contain the word *shoot*, so you need to set up the Custom AutoFilter this way.

4. In the Name section, select **contains** from the dropdown list in the first box if it is not already visible. In the adjacent box, key **shoot**. The Custom AutoFilter dialog box should look similar to Figure 5-10.

Figure 5-10

Custom AutoFilter dialog box
with criteria entered

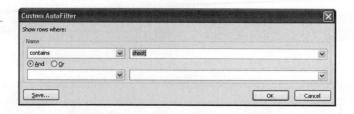

5. Click the **OK** button to apply the filter and close the Custom AutoFilter dialog box. Microsoft Project filters the task list to show only the tasks that contain the word *shoot*, as well as their summary tasks. Your screen should look similar to Figure 5-11.

Figure 5-11

Gantt Chart view with custom
AutoFilter applied.

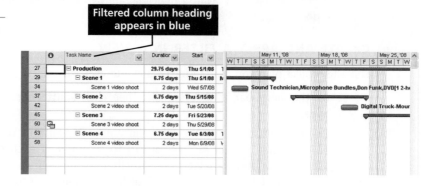

Note that the Task Name column heading appears in blue. This is a visual indicator that an AutoFilter has been applied to this view.

6. On the Formatting menu, click the **AutoFilter** button. The AutoFilter is turned off and all the tasks in the project plan are displayed.

7. **SAVE** the project plan.

PAUSE. LEAVE the project plan open to use in the next exercise.

ANOTHER WAY

You can also use the Undo button to remove the filter you just applied.

In this exercise, you created and applied a filter to the project plan to enable you to look at only the tasks dealing with scene shoots. A *filter* is a tool that enables you to see or highlight in a table only the task or resource information that meets criteria you choose. Filtering doesn't change the data in your project plan–it only changes the data's appearance.

There are two ways to apply filters to a view: predefined filters or an AutoFilter.

- Predefined or custom filters allow you to see or highlight only the task or resource information that meets the criteria of the filter. For example, the Milestones filter displays only tasks that are milestones. Some predefined filters, such as the Date Range filter, require you to enter criteria (a date) to set up the filter.

TAKE NOTE

If a task or a resource sheet view has a filter applied to it, the name of the filter will be displayed in the Filter button on the Formatting toolbar.

- AutoFilters are used for more informal or impromptu filtering. An *AutoFilter* is a quick way to view only the task or resource information that meets the criteria you choose. When the AutoFilter feature is turned on, small down arrows are visible adjacent to the column heading name. Clicking the arrow activates a list of criteria that can be used to filter the data. The criteria is appropriate for the type of data in the column.

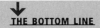

■ Creating a Custom Filter

THE BOTTOM LINE In the previous exercise, you used AutoFilter to apply a filter to the data of interest. Now, you will create a custom filter.

⊕ CREATE A CUSTOM FILTER

USE the project plan you created in the previous exercise.

1. On the menu bar, click **Project**, point to **Filtered for: All Tasks**, and then click **More Filters**. The More Filters dialog box appears. This dialog box shows you all of the predefined filters for tasks or resources that are available to you.

2. Click the **New** button. The Filter Definition dialog box appears.

3. In the Name box, key **Unfinished Shoots**.

4. In the first row of the Field Name column, key or select **Name**.

5. In the first row of the Test column, key or select **contains**.

6. In the first row of the Value(s) column, key **shoot**. You have now finished entering the first criterion for the filter. Next you will enter the second criterion.

7. In the second row of the And/Or column, select **And**.

8. In the second row of the Field Name column, key or select **Actual Finish**.

9. In the second row of the Test column, key or select **equals**.

10. In the second row of the Value(s) column, key **NA**. NA means "not applicable" and is how Microsoft Project marks some fields that do not yet have a value. In other words, any shooting task that does not yet have a value must be uncompleted. Your screen should look similar to Figure 5-12.

Figure 5-12

Filter Definition dialog box with custom criterion entered

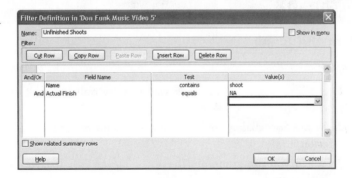

11. Click the **OK** button to close the Filter Definition dialog box. The new filter you have just created, Unfinished Shoots, appears in the More Filters dialog box.

12. Click the **Apply** button. Microsoft Project applies the new filter to your project plan in the Gantt Chart view. Your screen should look similar to Figure 5-13.

Figure 5-13

Gantt Chart view with Unfinished Shoots filter applied

Take note of the gaps in the task IDs. This is one visual way you can tell that a filter has been applied. The tasks are filtered to show uncompleted tasks (and since you haven't started tracking actual work yet, all the shooting tasks are currently uncompleted).

13. On the menu bar, click **Project**, point to **Filtered for: Unfinished Shoots**, and then click **All Tasks**. Microsoft Project removes the filter.

14. **SAVE** the project plan. **CLOSE** the project plan.

   PAUSE. If you are continuing to the next lesson, keep Project open. If you are not continuing to additional lessons, **CLOSE** Project.

In this exercise, you learned how to create and apply a custom filter. A custom filter works in the same way as a predefined filter, except that *you* have selected the filtering criterion rather than Microsoft Project. Remember that after filtering, you might see gaps in the task or resource ID numbers. The data has not been deleted–it is only hidden until you remove the filter. Also, as with sorting and grouping, the filtering applies to all the tables you can display in the active view. Some views that do not support tables, such as the Calendar view, do support filtering but not AutoFilters.

SUMMARY SKILL MATRIX

IN THIS LESSON YOU LEARNED	MATRIX SKILL
To sort data	Sort data in a resource view
To group data	Group data in a resource view
To filter data	Create and apply a filter in a view Create a custom filter

■ Knowledge Assessment

Fill in the Blank

Complete the following sentences by writing the correct word or words in the blanks provided.

1. _____ is a quick way to view only the task or resource information you choose.

2. In the Sort dialog box, you can utilize up to _____ nested levels of sort criteria.

3. When you use grouping, the _____ data rows are set off by a colored background.

4. When AutoFilter is turned on, small _____ are visible next to the column headings.

5. A way to reorder task or resource information in a table and to display summary values according to various criteria you can choose is called a(n) _____.

6. The _____ dialog box shows you all of the predefined filters that are available to you for tasks or resources.

7. A(n) _____ is a way of ordering task or resource information in a view by the criteria you specify.

8. When you apply a filter, you may see gaps in the _____.

9. When you sort data in your project, the sort applies to the active _____, no matter which table is displayed.

10. A tool that enables you to see or highlight in a table only the task or resource information that meets criteria you choose is a(n) _____.

Multiple Choice

Select the best response for the following statements.

1. The simplest way to reorganize data in Microsoft Project is by
   a. filtering.
   b. sorting.
   c. grouping.
   d. AutoFiltering.

2. The _____ function lets you reverse sets of actions you have performed in Microsoft Project.
   a. Task Drivers
   b. Reverse Filtering
   c. Multiple Level Undo
   d. Ungrouping

3. The one instance in which the actual data of your project is changed by sorting is when
   a. the *Permanently renumber resources* check box is selected.
   b. the Multiple Level Undo function is disabled.
   c. the project is saved before the sorting is reversed.
   d. all of the above.

4. When you apply a group to your project plan, the data in the summary rows cannot be changed directly because
   a. it will cause the grouping to become permanent.
   b. it will alter the data in your project plan.
   c. it is derived from subordinate data.
   d. it will cause an error in the grouping function.

5. When AutoFilter is on, clicking on the down arrow next to the column heading
   a. sorts the data in descending order.
   b. turns the AutoFilter off.
   c. automatically adjusts the column width.
   d. activates a list of criteria that can be used to filter the data.

6. Multiple Level Undo can be used
   a. as many times as desired, until the original data is restored.
   b. up to two consecutive times.
   c. up to five consecutive times.
   d. up to three consecutive times.

7. If a view has a filter applied to it, the name of the filter will be displayed in the Filter button on the _____ toolbar.
   a. Standard
   b. Formatting
   c. Project Guide
   d. Resource Management

8. There is no visual indicator that a task or resource view has been sorted other than
   a. the shaded summary rows.
   b. the small "s" at the top of each data column.
   c. the order in which the rows of data appear.
   d. There is no visual indicator to show a view has been sorted.

9. Grouping might be helpful if you are trying to see
   a. only the tasks that contain the word "Weekly."
   b. the critical path tasks.
   c. the tasks ordered from highest to lowest cost.
   d. the total cost of each resource group.

10. You cannot save custom settings that you have specified for
    a. sorting.
    b. grouping.
    c. filtering.
    d. all of the above.

■ Competency Assessment

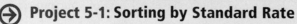

→ Project 5-1: Sorting by Standard Rate

You have some additional setup work that needs to be completed before the shooting of one of the Don Funk Music Video scenes can begin. Because you will need to pay overtime (time and one-half) for this additional work, you would like to get a volunteer who has a low standard rate. Sort your resources according to Standard Rate and Max Units so that you can make your request from the least-cost group of employees.

GET READY. Launch Microsoft Project if it is not already running.

OPEN *Don Funk Music Video 5-1* from the data files for this lesson.

1. On the menu bar, click **View** and then click **Resource Sheet**.
2. On the menu bar, click **Project**, point to **Sort**, and then click **Sort by**.
3. In the *Sort by* section, select **Standard Rate** from the dropdown menu. Next to that, click on **Descending**.
4. In the first *Then by* section, select **Max Units** from the dropdown menu. Next to that, click on **Descending**. Make sure the *Permanently renumber resources* box is not checked.
5. Click the **Sort** button.
6. **SAVE** the project plan as *Don Funk Standard Rate Sort* and then **CLOSE** the file.
   LEAVE Project open for the next exercise.

The *Don Funk Music Video 5-1* project plan is available on the companion CD-ROM.

→ Project 5-2: Apply HR Filter

You are reviewing your project plan for hiring a new employee. You want to specifically review the staff members from the Human Resources (HR) department who are involved with this project. You need to apply a filter that will screen out any staff except HR.

OPEN *Hiring New Employee 5-2* from the data files for this lesson.

1. On the menu bar, click **View** and then click **Resource Sheet**.
2. On the Formatting toolbar, click the **AutoFilter** button.
3. Click the down arrow in the Group column heading, and then click (**Custom . . .**).
4. In the Group section, select **contains** from the dropdown list in the first box if it is not already visible. In the adjacent box, key **HR**.
5. Click the **OK** button.
6. **SAVE** the project plan as *Hiring New Employee HR Filter* and then **CLOSE** the project plan.
   PAUSE. LEAVE Project open to use in the next exercise.

The *Hiring New Employee 5-2* project plan is available on the companion CD-ROM.

■ Proficiency Assessment

➔ Project 5-3: Resource Groups by Standard Rate for Don Funk Music Video

You are working on employee reviews and pay increases for your staff for the upcoming year. You have decided it would be beneficial to be able to look at the standard rate variation within resource groups working on this project. You need to set up a custom group that will enable you to do this.

OPEN *Don Funk Music Video 5-3* from the data files for this lesson.

1. Change the view to a resource sheet view.
2. From the Project menu, select **Group by: More Groups**.
3. Select **Resource Group**, and then make a copy of this group.
4. In the Group Definition box, name the new group **Resource Groups by Standard Rate**.
5. On the first *Then By* line, set up the grouping by Standard Rate in descending order.
6. Click **Define Group Intervals**, then set up this dialog box so that the grouping is done on Intervals of 5.
7. Select the group you have created and apply it to your project plan.
8. Widen the Resource Name field so that you can see the Standard Rate groupings.
9. **SAVE** the project plan as *Don Funk Resource Groupings* and then **CLOSE** the file.
   PAUSE. LEAVE Project open to use in the next exercise.

The *Don Funk Music Video 5-3* project plan is available on the companion CD-ROM.

➔ Project 5-4: Duration Sort for Office Remodel

You are responsible for the kitchen and lunchroom remodel for your office. Your manager has asked you which tasks on the project are scheduled to take the longest. You need to do a quick sort on the tasks to respond to his question.

OPEN *Office Remodel 5-4* from the data files for this lesson.

1. Change the view to the Gantt Chart view.
2. Change the table view to Summary.
3. From the Project menu, select **Sort**, and then **Sort by**.
4. Set up the dialog box to sort by Duration in descending order. Make sure that the resources are not permanently renumbered.
5. Perform the sort.
6. **SAVE** the project plan as *Office Remodel Duration Sort* and then **CLOSE** the file.
   PAUSE. LEAVE Project open to use in the next exercise.

The *Office Remodel 5-4* project plan is available on the companion CD-ROM.

■ Mastery Assessment

➔ Project 5-5: Don Funk Filter for Don Funk Music Video

You are the project manager for the Don Funk Music Video. You need to review all of the Production tasks to which Don Funk, the musical star, is assigned so that you can make sure his dressing room is prepared properly for him on those days. (Hint: Note that all of the Production tasks contain the word "Scene.") You need to apply a filter to show only the Production tasks with Don Funk assigned to them.

The *Don Funk Music Video 5-5* project plan is available on the companion CD-ROM.

OPEN *Don Funk Music Video 5-5* from the data files for this lesson.

1. Open the More Filters dialog box.
2. Begin to build a new filter based on the Using Resource task filter.
3. Name the new filter Don Funk Production Tasks.
4. Build the first level of the filter based on Name, which contains **Scene**.
5. Using **And** to link the levels, add a second level of the filter based on Resource Names, which contains Don Funk.
6. Run the filter.
7. **SAVE** the project plan as *Don Funk Filter* and then **CLOSE** the file.

   PAUSE. LEAVE Project open to use in the next exercise.

Project 5-6: Costs and Durations for Hiring a New Employee

You want to compare the cost of tasks that have the same duration in your project plan to hire a new employee. You need to set up a custom group in order to group the data by duration and then by cost.

The *Hiring New Employee 5-6* project plan is available on the companion CD-ROM.

OPEN *Hiring New Employee 5-6* from the data files for this lesson.

1. Switch to the Task Usage view.
2. Use the Duration group to set up a new custom group called Duration-Cost.
3. Set up the new group so that it groups by descending Duration and then descending Cost.
4. Apply the Duration-Cost group.
5. **SAVE** the project plan as *Hiring Duration Cost Group* and then **CLOSE** the file.

   CLOSE Project.

INTERNET READY

Over the last five lessons, you have become familiar with the basics of Microsoft Project: tasks, resources, assignments, constraints, resource allocation, and project plan monitoring. You have learned that even the best project plan is only as good as the information that you can get out of it.

Search the Internet for current events in your city or state, and identify a story on a project that has not gone according to schedule (construction of a road or building, production of a new product, opening of a restaurant, etc). Review the article on the event you choose. Then, using what you have learned about Microsoft Project so far, write a short paragraph on what you believe went "wrong" with the project you selected. Make suggestions on how these problems could be avoided in the future. If necessary, perform additional Internet research on your selected current event.

✳ Workplace Ready

Using Microsoft Project templates

Suppose you are the Conversion project manager at a company that processes electronic payments. You manage the "conversion" of new clients onto your data processing systems. Your manager has been impressed with your hard work and attention to detail, so he gives you a new project responsibility that is not in your range of experience—developing the project plan for your company's upcoming move to a new office location. Although you are glad that your manager has confidence in you, you are a bit nervous because you are unfamiliar with the tasks that are involved in the process. You know that an office move involves more than just relocating furniture, phones, and computers, but where do you go from there?

Microsoft Office Project provides a number of templates that are ready for you to download and customize for your specific project needs. There are many templates provided within Microsoft Project, and even more that can be accessed through Microsoft Office Online. Upon opening Microsoft Project, a new blank project plan is automatically opened. When you click *File* on the Standard menu and then click *New*, the *New Project* pane opens. Microsoft Project provides several different options for starting a new project, as shown in the following figure.

Figure 5-14

Blank project plan with *New Project* pane activated

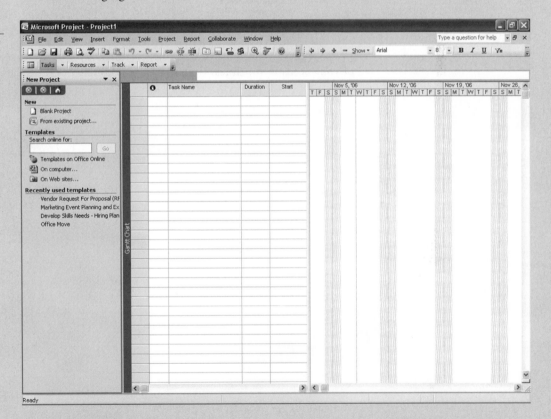

Using the *New Project* pane, you can search for a template online, select a predefined project from within Microsoft Project, or search other websites for templates. You can also review the list of recently used templates. If you search online, you can browse templates by category. When you find a sample that you think will meet your needs, you can preview it in your web browser. If you like what you see, you can download it, open it, and begin to make updates that reflect your project's specific requirements.

The project sample shown in the following figure is part of the Office Move template downloaded from Microsoft Office Online. (A sample of this template is provided on your CD-ROM for you to review and explore.) You can add or delete tasks, change task durations, or rearrange summary tasks. You can add, delete, or rename resources, and then fill in resource details such as cost and assignment units. You can change dependencies, constraints, and calendars, all based on your actual project requirements.

Figure 5-15

Office Move project plan

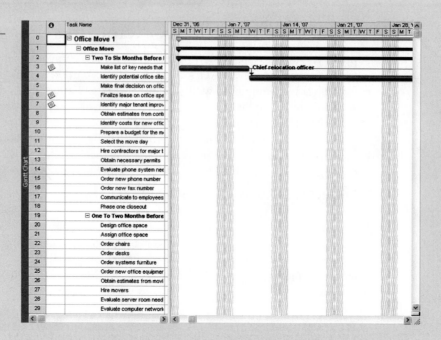

You can see that by starting with a Project template, you can create a project plan that fits all of your needs in much less time than it would take to create the project from scratch.

↻ Circling Back

Mete Goktepe is a project management specialist at Woodgrove Bank. The management at Woodgrove has recently decided that the eight-year old commercial lending software currently in use is outdated and needs to be replaced. Mete has been assigned as the project manager for the Request For Proposal (RFP) process to evaluate and select new software. This process entails determining needs, identifying vendors, requesting proposals, reviewing proposals, and selecting the software.

⊕ Project 1: ENTERING TASKS

Acting as Mete, you first need to enter project information, and then enter and organize the tasks for this project.

GET READY. Launch Project if it is not already running. If necessary, activate the Project Guide from the View menu.

1. In the *Tasks* pane of the Project Guide, click the Set a date to schedule from link.
2. Select the start date to be May 5, 2008. Click the Done link.
3. Save the project plan as *RFP Bank Software Tasks*.
4. In the *Tasks* pane, click the Define general working times link.
5. Select the Standard calendar template in Step 1, and accept the default working times in Step 2.
6. In Step 3, click the Change Working Times link and add the following exception dates:
   - Independence Day to begin on July 4, 2008 and to occur yearly on July 4 for 2 occurrences
   - Labor Day to begin on September 1, 2008 and to occur the first Monday of September for 2 occurrences
   - Columbus Day to begin on October 13, 2008 and to occur the second Monday of October for 2 occurrences
   - Veterans' Day to begin on November 11, 2008 and to occur on November 11 for 2 occurrences
   - Thanksgiving Day to begin on November 27, 2008 and to occur on the fourth Thursday of November for 2 occurrences
   - Christmas Day to occur on December 25, 2008 and to occur on December 25 for 2 occurrences
7. In Step 4, accept the default working times. In Step 5, click the link to Save and Finish the calendar setup.
8. In the *Tasks* pane, click the List the tasks in the project link. Enter the following task names and durations (enter all tasks, even if no duration is listed). [This is a partial list of tasks in the project plan. Additional data will be available in future exercises.]

Task Name	Duration
RFP Solicitation Process	
RFP solicitation process begins	0d
RFP Creation	
RFP creation begins	0d
Document software requirements	8d
Define evaluation criteria	2d
Identify evaluation team	1d
Draft RFP	5d
Review RFP with management and commercial lending representatives	1d
Refine RFP	1d
RFP ready to release	0d
RFP Release	
RFP release begins	0d
Identify software suppliers	5d
Determine deadline dates for vendor responses	2h
Finalize RFP with time frames and points of contact	6h
Release RFP to target companies	2d
Conduct RFP briefing	1d
RFP release complete	0d
RFP Solicitation Process Complete	0d

9. **SAVE** the project plan.

10. In the *Tasks* pane, click the **Organize tasks into phases** link.

11. Using the outline structure in the table above, indent and outdent tasks as necessary to organize the tasks into phases.

12. **SAVE** the project plan.

13. In the *Tasks* pane of the Project Guide, click the **Schedule tasks** link.

14. Select tasks 2, 4 through 11, and 13 through 20. Link them with a Finish-to-Start relationship. Click the **Done** link.

15. **SAVE** the project plan.

   PAUSE. LEAVE Project and the project plan open to use in the next exercise.

➜ Project 2: Establishing Resources

You now need to establish the resources that will perform the work on the tasks in this project plan.

1. **SAVE** the project plan as *RFP Bank Software Resources*.

2. Activate the *Resources* pane of the Project Guide.

3. Click the **Specify people and equipment for the project** link.

4. Change the view to the Resource Sheet.

5. Click the **Enter resources manually** button.
6. Enter the following resource information on the Resource Sheet.

NAME	TYPE	INITIALS	GROUP	MAX UNITS	STD. RATE
Syed Abbas	Work	SA	CL Mgmt	100	2000/w
Eli Bowen	Work	EB	CL Mgmt	100	1850/w
Nicole Caron	Work	NC	IT Mgmt	100	2200/w
Aaron Con	Work	AC	IT Mgmt	100	2000/w
Andrew Dixon	Work	AD	IT	50	25/h
JoLynn Dobney	Work	JD	IT	100	1400/w
Mete Goktepe	Work	MG	IT	100	1250/w
Nicole Holliday	Work	NH	CwwL	50	20/h
Marc J. Ingle	Work	MJI	CL	100	1300/w
Kevin Kennedy	Work	KK	CL	100	1200/w
Dan Moyer	Work	DM	SR Mgmt	100	3000/w
Misty Shock	Work	MS	SR Mgmt	100	3500/w
Nate Sun	Work	NS	CL Ops	100	20/h
Tai Yee	Work	TY	CL Ops	100	19.50/h
Frank Miller	Work	FM	CL Ops	100	18/h
Jo Brown	Work	JB	CL Ops Mgmt	100	1850/w
Mike Tiano	Work	MT	CL Ops Mgmt	100	1900/w
CL Usergroup	Work	CLUG	CL	600	100/h
Digital Projector	Work	DP	Equip	200	0
Large Conference Room	Work	LCR	Location	100	0
Small Conference Room	Work	SCR	Location	400	0
Food/Catering	Cost	FOOD	Cost		
Travel	Cost	TRVL	Cost		

7. Click the **Done** link at the bottom of the *Specify Resource* pane.
8. **SAVE** the project plan.

   PAUSE. LEAVE Project and the project plan open to use in the next exercise.

⊙ Project 3: **Assigning Resources to Tasks**

Finally, you need to assign the resources to the tasks in your project plan.

1. **SAVE** the project plan as *RFP Bank Software Assignments*.
2. In the Resources pane of the Project Guide, click the **Assign people and equipment to tasks** link.
3. In the *Assign Resources* pane, click the **Assign resources** link.
4. Select the name of task 5, **Document software requirements**.

5. In the Assign Resources dialog box, select the following resources: **JoLynn Dobney, Nicole Holliday, CL Usergroup**. Click the **Assign** button.

6. Select the name of task 6, **Define evaluation criteria**.

7. In the Assign Resources dialog box, select the following resources: **Mete Goktepe, Syed Abbas, Nicole Caron, Mike Tiano**. Click the **Assign** button.

8. Using the same process that you used in steps 4–7, assign the following resources to the corresponding tasks.

TASK #	TASK NAME	RESOURCE NAMES TO ASSIGN
7	Identify evaluation team	Syed Abbas, Nicole Caron, Jo Brown
8	Draft RFP	Mete Goktepe, Kevin Kennedy
9	Review RFP with management . . .	Mete Goktepe, Kevin Kennedy, Eli Bowen, Large Conference Room
10	Refine RFP	Mete Goktepe, Kevin Kennedy
14	Identify software suppliers	Mete Goktepe, Kevin Kennedy
15	Determine deadline dates . . .	Eli Bowen, Mete Goktepe, Aaron Con
16	Finalize RFP with time frames . . .	Kevin Kennedy
17	Release RFP to target companies	Mete Goktepe, Kevin Kennedy
18	Conduct RFP briefing	Mete Goktepe, Kevin Kennedy, Nicole Caron, Small Conference Room

9. Select the name of task 5, **Document software requirements**.

10. In the Assign Resources dialog box, select the following resources: **Marc J. Ingle, Kevin Kennedy, Andrew Dixon**. Assign these resources to the task.

11. In the Smart Tag Actions button that appears in the Indicators column, select **Reduce the hours that resources work per day. Keep duration and work the same.**

12. Select the name of task 9, **Review RFP with management and commercial lending representatives**.

13. In the Assign Resources dialog box, select the following resources: **Marc J. Ingle, Nicole Holliday, Mike Tiano**. Assign these resources to the task.

14. In the Smart Tag Actions button that appears in the Indicators column, select **Increase total work because the task requires more person hours. Keep duration constant.**

15. Select the name of task 18, **Conduct RFP briefing**.

16. In the Assign Resources dialog box, select the following resources: **Eli Bowen, Jo Brown**. Assign these resources to the task.

17. In the Smart Tag Actions button that appears in the Indicators column, select **Reduce the hours that resources work per day. Keep duration and work the same.**

18. Click **Close** in the Assign Resources dialog box and click **Done** in the *Assign Resources* pane.

19. **SAVE** the project plan, and then **CLOSE** the project plan.

    CLOSE Microsoft Project.

Project Plan Formatting-Fundamentals

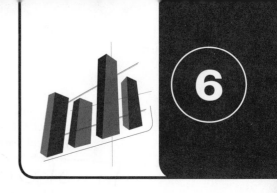

LESSON SKILL MATRIX

SKILLS	MATRIX SKILL
Gantt Chart Formatting	Modify the Gantt Chart using the Bar Styles dialog box
	Modify the Gantt Chart using the Gantt Chart Wizard
Drawing in a Gantt Chart	Add a text box to the Gantt Chart
Changing Text Appearance in a View	Change appearance of text in a view
Creating and Editing Tables	Create a custom table
Creating Custom Views	Create a custom view

KEY TERMS
chart
field
form
sheet
table
view

As a video production manager for Southridge Video and the project manager for the new Don Funk music video, you have the foundation of your project plan in place. However, a project manager doesn't usually look at all of the data in a project plan at once. In this lesson, you will learn to use some of the tools in Microsoft Office Project, such as views and reports, to look at the element or aspect of the project plan in which you are currently interested. With these tools, you can significantly impact how your data appears by the way in which you change the data format to meet your needs.

■ SOFTWARE ORIENTATION

Microsoft Project's Bar Styles Dialog Box

In Microsoft Project, you can use the Bar Styles dialog box to customize the appearance of items on the Gantt Chart.

Figure 6-1

Bar Styles dialog box

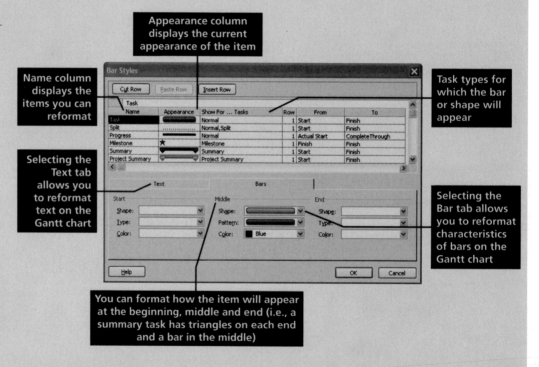

Appearance column displays the current appearance of the item

Name column displays the items you can reformat

Task types for which the bar or shape will appear

Selecting the Text tab allows you to reformat text on the Gantt chart

Selecting the Bar tab allows you to reformat characteristics of bars on the Gantt chart

You can format how the item will appear at the beginning, middle and end (i.e., a summary task has triangles on each end and a bar in the middle)

This dialog box enables you to change the appearance of items such as task bars, milestones, summary bars, and text that appear on the Gantt Chart. You can change characteristics such as bar types, patterns, colors, splits, and shapes.

■ Gantt Chart Formatting

THE BOTTOM LINE

The Gantt Chart view consists of two parts: a table on the left and a bar chart on the right. The default formatting of the Gantt Chart view is useful for onscreen project plan viewing and printing. However, you are able to change the formatting of almost any element on the Gantt Chart to suit your needs. In this exercise, you will learn to format Gantt Chart task bars. You can format whole categories of Gantt Chart task bars via the Bar Styles dialog box or the Gantt Chart Wizard, or you can format individual Gantt Chart task bars directly.

Modifying the Gantt Chart Using the Bar Styles Dialog Box

In this exercise, you will modify several items on the Gantt Chart using the Bar Styles dialog box.

⊕ MODIFY THE GANTT CHART USING THE BAR STYLES DIALOG BOX

The *Don Funk Music Video 6M* project plan is available on the companion CD-ROM.

GET READY. Before you begin these steps, launch Microsoft Project.

1. OPEN the *Don Funk Music Video 6M* project **plan** from the data files for this lesson.
2. SAVE the file as *Don Funk Music Video 6* in the solutions folder for this lesson as directed by your instructor.
3. On the menu bar click **Format**, and then click **Bar Styles**. The Bar Styles dialog box appears.
4. In the Name column, select **Milestone**. You want to change the shape of the milestones on the Gantt Chart.
5. In the bottom half of the dialog box under the Start label, locate the Shape box. Select the **star** shape from the dropdown list in the Shape box. Note that the star shape now appears in the Appearance column for Milestone. Your screen should look similar to Figure 6-2.

Figure 6-2

Bar Styles dialog box showing the star as the shape for the milestone appearance

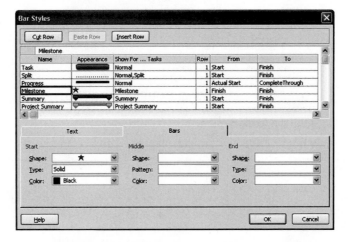

6. In the bottom half of the dialog box, click the **Text** tab. You want to make a change to display resource initials rather than full names next to the task bars.
7. In the Name column at the top of the dialog box, select **Task**.
8. In the Text tab, in the Right box, select **Resource Names**, click the down arrow, and then select **Resource Initials**. Your screen should look similar to Figure 6-3.

Figure 6-3

Bar Styles dialog box showing resource initials listed by task bar

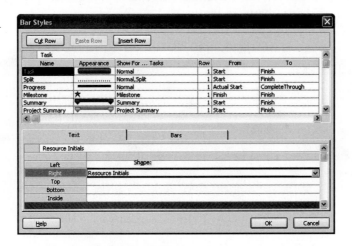

9. Click **OK** to close the Bar Styles dialog box. Microsoft Project applies the formatting changes you made to the Gantt Chart.

10. Select the name of Task 26, **Pre-Production complete**. On the Standard toolbar, click the **Scroll to Task** button. Microsoft Project scrolls the Gantt Chart bar view to task 26, where you can see the reformatted milestone and resource initials. Your screen should look similar to Figure 6-4.

Figure 6-4

Gantt Chart showing resource initials and new milestone indicator

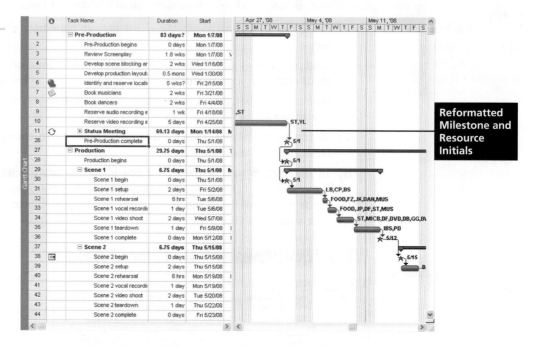

11. **SAVE** the project plan.

PAUSE. LEAVE the project plan open to use in the next exercise.

TAKE NOTE

With the Bar Styles dialog box, the formatting changes you make to a type of item (a milestone, for example) apply to all such items in the Gantt Chart.

You have just used the Bar Styles dialog box to make formatting changes to several items in the Gantt Chart view. The Gantt Chart is the primary way of viewing the data in a project plan. It became the standard for visualizing project plans in the early twentieth century when American engineer Henry Gantt developed a bar chart showing the use of resources over time. In Microsoft Project, the Gantt Chart view is the default view. A view is a window through which you can see various elements of your project plan. The three categories of views are charts, sheets, and forms.

THREE CATEGORIES OF VIEWS . . .

Charts (or graphs)	Present information graphically, such as the Network Diagram
Sheets	Present information in rows and columns, such as the Task Sheet
Forms	Present detailed information in a structured format about one task or resource at a time, such as the Task Form

Modifying the Gantt Chart Using the Gantt Chart Wizard

In this exercise, you will create a custom Gantt Chart and format it using the Gantt Chart Wizard.

➔ MODIFY THE GANTT CHART USING THE GANTT CHART WIZARD

USE the project plan you created in the previous exercise.

1. On the menu bar, click **Tools**, and then click **Options**.

2. In the Options dialog box, click the **View** tab, if necessary.

3. Under the *Outline options for 'Don Funk Music Video 6'* label, click the **Show project summary task** box, and then click **OK**. Microsoft Project displays the project summary task at the top of the Gantt Chart view. Now you will make a few adjustments to your screen so that all of the summary task information is visible.

4. Drag the vertical divider bar between the table and chart to the right until at least the Duration and Start columns are visible, if necessary.

5. Double-click the right edge of the Duration column, in the column heading, to expand the column so that you can see the entire value. Readjust the Start column, as necessary. Your screen should look similar to Figure 6-5.

ANOTHER WAY

You can also double-click the divider bar to snap the divider to the nearest column edge.

Figure 6-5

Gantt Chart showing summary task bar and widened Duration column

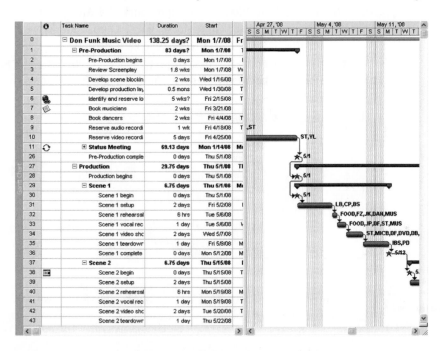

ANOTHER WAY

Double-clicking anywhere in a column heading will activate the Column Definition dialog box. In the dialog box, click the Best Fit button to automatically adjust the column width.

Before you make further formatting changes, you will make a copy of the Gantt Chart view so that you will not affect the original Gantt Chart view.

6. On the menu bar, click **View**, and then click **More Views**. The More Views dialog box appears with the Gantt Chart option highlighted.

7. Click the **Copy** button. The View definition dialog box appears. The Name field contains the proposed name of the new view (as it will appear in the More Views dialog box and, if you specify, on the View menu). Take note of the ampersand (&) in the Name field. This is a code that indicates the keyboard shortcut character of the new view name, if you wish to use one.

8. In the Name Field, key **My Custom Gantt Chart,** and then click **OK.** The View Definition dialog box closes. The More Views dialog box appears with My Custom Gantt Chart selected. Your screen should look similar to Figure 6-6.

Figure 6-6

More Views dialog box showing new view

9. In the More Views dialog box, click the **Apply** button. The My Custom Gantt Chart view is an exact copy of the Gantt Chart view; however, the new title is displayed on the left edge of the custom view.

10. On the menu bar, click **Format,** and then click **Gantt Chart Wizard.** The opening page of the Wizard appears. Your screen should look similar to Figure 6-7.

Figure 6-7

Opening screen of Gantt Chart Wizard

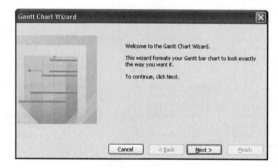

 **ANOTHER WAY** You can also start the Gantt Chart Wizard, as well as several other formatting features, by going to the *Reports* pane of the Project Guide.

11. Click the **Next** button to advance to the second screen of the Gantt Chart Wizard, and then click the **Other** button. In the dropdown list that is activated next to the Other option, click **Standard: Style 4.** Your screen should look similar to Figure 6-8.

Figure 6-8

Gantt Chart Wizard showing Standard: Style 4 selected

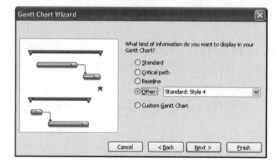

TAKE NOTE To see a preview of other built-in Gantt Chart formats available in the Wizard, click them in the Other box. Make sure that Standard: Style 4 is selected before you continue with this exercise.

12. Click the **Finish** button. The final page of the Gantt Chart Wizard appears.

13. Click the **Format It** button, and then click the **Exit Wizard** button. The Wizard applies the Standard: Style 4 formatting to the My Custom Gantt Chart view and then closes.

14. Click on the name of task 26, **Pre-Production complete**, and then click the **Scroll to Task** button on the Standard toolbar. Your screen should look similar to Figure 6-9.

Figure 6-9

My Custom Gantt Chart view with Standard: Style 4 applied

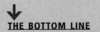

		Task Name	Duration	Start	Apr 27, '08	May 4, '08	May 11, '08
0		⊟ Don Funk Music Video	138.25 days?	Mon 1/7/08	Fr		
1		⊟ Pre-Production	83 days?	Mon 1/7/08	1		
2		Pre-Production begins	0 days	Mon 1/7/08	I		
3		Review Screenplay	1.8 wks	Mon 1/7/08	W		
4		Develop scene blockin	2 wks	Wed 1/16/08	T		
5		Develop production lay	0.5 mons	Wed 1/30/08	T		
6		Identify and reserve lo	5 wks?	Fri 2/15/08	T		
7		Book musicians	2 wks	Fri 3/21/08			
8		Book dancers	2 wks	Fri 4/4/08	T er[50%]		
9		Reserve audio recordi	1 wk	Fri 4/18/08	T ,Sound Technician		
10		Reserve video recordi	5 days	Fri 4/25/08	Sound Technician,Yan Li		
11		⊞ Status Meeting	69.13 days	Mon 1/14/08	M		
26		Pre-Production comple	0 days	Thu 5/1/08	5/1		
27		⊟ Production	29.75 days	Thu 5/1/08	Tl 5/1		
28		Production begins	0 days	Thu 5/1/08	5/1		
29		⊟ Scene 1	6.75 days	Thu 5/1/08	M		
30		Scene 1 begin	0 days	Thu 5/1/08	5/1		
31		Scene 1 setup	2 days	Fri 5/2/08	I Light Banks,Chris Preston,Brad S		
32		Scene 1 rehearsal	6 hrs	Tue 5/6/08	Food[$500.00],Frank Zhang[50%]		
33		Scene 1 vocal rec	1 day	Tue 5/6/08	V Food[$250.00],Jeff Pike,Don F		
34		Scene 1 video shc	2 days	Wed 5/7/08	Sound Technician,Mic		
35		Scene 1 teardowr	1 day	Fri 5/9/08	M Ido Ben-Sach		
36		Scene 1 complete	0 days	Mon 5/12/08	M 5/12		
37		⊟ Scene 2	6.75 days	Thu 5/15/08	I		
38		Scene 2 begin	0 days	Thu 5/15/08	T 5/15		
39		Scene 2 setup	2 days	Thu 5/15/08	T		
40		Scene 2 rehearsal	6 hrs	Mon 5/19/08	M		
41		Scene 2 vocal rec	1 day	Mon 5/19/08	T		
42		Scene 2 video shc	2 days	Tue 5/20/08	T		
43		Scene 2 teardowr	1 day	Thu 5/22/08			

15. **SAVE** the project plan.

   PAUSE. LEAVE the project plan open to use in the next exercise.

In this exercise, you made formatting changes to your project plan using the Gantt Chart Wizard. This is similar to making changes using the Bar Styles command; however, the Gantt Chart Wizard has fewer choices than the Bar Styles command. As you are reviewing the formatting changes in the My Custom Gantt Chart view, remember that none of the data in the project plan has changed—just the way it is formatted. These formatting changes affect only the My Custom Gantt Chart view; all other views in Microsoft Project are unaffected.

■ Drawing in a Gantt Chart

↓ THE BOTTOM LINE Included in Microsoft Project is a Drawing toolbar which enables you to draw objects or text directly onto a Gantt Chart. This feature allows you to call attention to a specific event or item. You can draw text boxes, arrows, and other items. In this exercise, you will add a text box to the Gantt Chart.

→ ADD A TEXT BOX TO THE GANTT CHART

USE the project plan you created in the previous exercise.

1. On the menu bar click **View,** and then click **More Views.** The More Views dialog box appears.

2. In the More Views box, select **Detail Gantt**, and then click **Apply**. The Detail Gantt view appears.

3. On the menu bar, click on **View**, point to **Toolbars**, and then click **Drawing**. The Drawing toolbar appears.

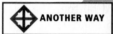

ANOTHER WAY You can also right-click on any toolbar to see the Toolbars shortcut menu. You can display or hide any toolbar listed on that menu.

4. On the Drawing toolbar, click the Text Box button, and then drag a small square anywhere on the chart portion of the Detail Gantt view.

5. In the box you just drew, key **CMT Music Awards May 31–June 1**.

6. On the menu bar, click **Format**, point to **Drawing**, and then click **Properties**. The Format Drawing dialog box appears.

7. Click the **Line and Fill** tab if it is not already selected.

8. Select **Lime** from the Color box under the Fill label.

9. Click the **Size and Position** tab.

10. Make sure that **Attach to Timescale** is selected. In the Date box, select or key **May 31, 2008**.

11. In the Vertical box, key **1**, and click **OK** to close the Format Drawing dialog box. Microsoft Project formats the text box with lime fill and positions it below the timescale on the date you specified.

12. If the text box is not visible on your screen, click **Edit** on the menu bar, and then click **Go To**.

13. In the Date box, select **May 31, 2008**, and click **OK**. Microsoft Project scrolls the view to display the date you specified. Your screen should look similar to Figure 6-10.

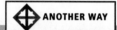

ANOTHER WAY

You can also double-click the border of the text box to view its properties.

Figure 6-10

Detail Gantt Chart view with text box attached to specific date

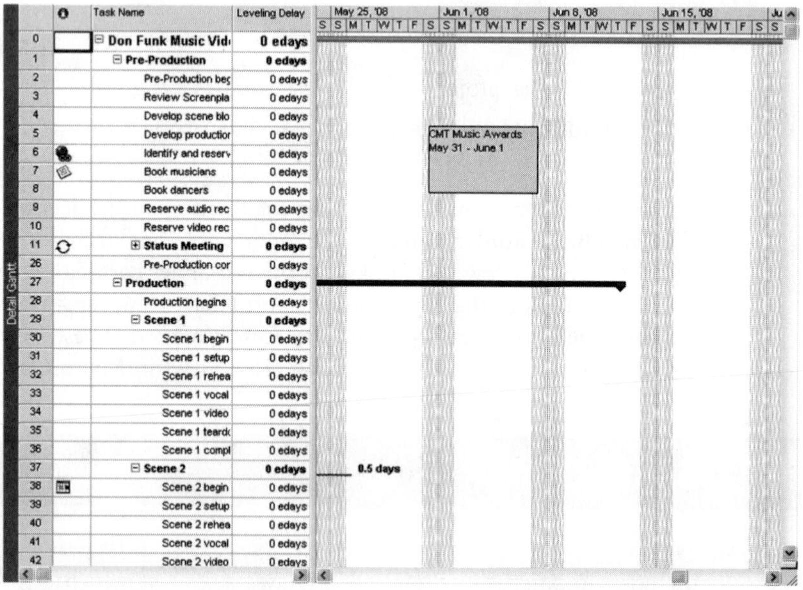

		Task Name	Leveling Delay	May 25, '08	Jun 1, '08	Jun 8, '08	Jun 15, '08	Ju
0		☐ Don Funk Music Vid	0 edays					
1		☐ Pre-Production	0 edays					
2		Pre-Production beg	0 edays					
3		Review Screenpla	0 edays					
4		Develop scene blo	0 edays					
5		Develop productior	0 edays		CMT Music Awards			
6	✎	Identify and reserv	0 edays		May 31 - June 1			
7		Book musicians	0 edays					
8		Book dancers	0 edays					
9		Reserve audio rec	0 edays					
10		Reserve video rec	0 edays					
11	↻	☐ Status Meeting	0 edays					
26		Pre-Production cor	0 edays					
27		☐ Production	0 edays					
28		Production begins	0 edays					
29		☐ Scene 1	0 edays					
30		Scene 1 begin	0 edays					
31		Scene 1 setup	0 edays					
32		Scene 1 rehea	0 edays					
33		Scene 1 vocal	0 edays					
34		Scene 1 video	0 edays					
35		Scene 1 teardc	0 edays					
36		Scene 1 compl	0 edays					
37		☐ Scene 2	0 edays	0.5 days				
38	🖽	Scene 2 begin	0 edays					
39		Scene 2 setup	0 edays					
40		Scene 2 rehea	0 edays					
41		Scene 2 vocal	0 edays					
42		Scene 2 video	0 edays					

14. On the menu bar, click **View**, point to **Toolbars**, and then click **Drawing**. Microsoft Project hides the Drawing toolbar.

15. SAVE the project plan.

PAUSE. LEAVE the project plan open to use in the next exercise.

In this exercise, you used the Drawing toolbar to add a text box to the Gantt Chart on your project plan. You also linked your text box to a date. When you are adding drawing objects and linking them to your project plan, there are two key considerations to remember.

- If an object you are adding is specific to a task, link the object to the Gantt bar. The object will move with the Gantt bar if it is rescheduled.
- If the object you are adding has information that is date specific, link the object to a date. The object will remain in the same position relative to the timescale, no matter what part of the timescale is in view.

TAKE NOTE ✱ If the Drawing toolbar does not have the type of item you would like to add to your Gantt Chart, you can use the Object command on the Insert menu to add bitmap images or documents.

■ Changing Text Appearance in a View

↓ **THE BOTTOM LINE** Since viewing a project plan is key to understanding the status of the project, changing the formatting of the text in the plan can help you to view the project plan information more quickly and easily. In this exercise, you will use text styles and direct formatting to change the appearance of text in a view.

→ **CHANGE APPEARANCE OF TEXT IN A VIEW**

USE the project plan you created in the previous exercise.

1. On the menu bar, click **View**, and then click **More Views**. The More Views dialog box appears. The current view (Detail Gantt) is selected.
2. Click **Task Sheet** in the Views box, and then click the **Apply** button. The Task Sheet view appears. This view has only a single table; there is no chart component.
3. On the menu bar, click **View**, point to **Table: Entry**, and then click **Summary**. The Summary table appears in the Task Sheet view. (You will be looking closely at the Cost field.) Your screen should look similar to Figure 6-11.

Figure 6-11

Task Sheet view showing Summary table

	Task Name	Duration	Start	Finish	% Comp.	Cost	Work
0	⊟ Don Funk Music Vid	8.25 days?	Mon 1/7/08	Fri 7/18/08	0%	$88,956.50	757.5 hrs
1	⊟ Pre-Production	83 days?	Mon 1/7/08	Thu 5/1/08	0%	$27,841.00	1,314 hrs
2	Pre-Production beg	0 days	Mon 1/7/08	Mon 1/7/08	0%	$0.00	0 hrs
3	Review Screenpla	1.8 wks	Mon 1/7/08	Wed 1/16/08	0%	$2,295.00	120 hrs
4	Develop scene blo	2 wks	Wed 1/16/08	Tue 1/29/08	0%	$1,560.00	80 hrs
5	Develop productio	0.5 mons	Wed 1/30/08	Thu 2/14/08	0%	$2,520.00	160 hrs
6	Identify and reserv	5 wks?	Fri 2/15/08	Thu 3/20/08	0%	$14,455.00	550 hrs
7	Book musicians	2 wks	Fri 3/21/08	Thu 4/3/08	0%	$1,360.00	80 hrs
8	Book dancers	2 wks	Fri 4/4/08	Thu 4/17/08	0%	$1,360.00	80 hrs
9	Reserve audio rec	1 wk	Fri 4/18/08	Thu 4/24/08	0%	$1,400.00	80 hrs
10	Reserve video rec	5 days	Fri 4/25/08	Thu 5/1/08	0%	$1,400.00	80 hrs
11	⊞ Status Meeting	69.13 days	Mon 1/14/08	Mon 4/21/08	0%	$1,491.00	84 hrs
26	Pre-Production cor	0 days	Thu 5/1/08	Thu 5/1/08	0%	$0.00	0 hrs
27	⊟ Production	29.75 days	Thu 5/1/08	Thu 6/12/08	0%	$23,369.50	709 hrs
28	Production begins	0 days	Thu 5/1/08	Thu 5/1/08	0%	$0.00	0 hrs
29	⊟ Scene 1	6.75 days	Thu 5/1/08	Mon 5/12/08	0%	$6,051.50	189 hrs
30	Scene 1 begin	0 days	Thu 5/1/08	Thu 5/1/08	0%	$0.00	0 hrs
31	Scene 1 setup	2 days	Fri 5/2/08	Mon 5/5/08	0%	$536.00	48 hrs
32	Scene 1 rehea	6 hrs	Tue 5/6/08	Tue 5/6/08	0%	$888.50	21 hrs
33	Scene 1 vocal	1 day	Tue 5/6/08	Wed 5/7/08	0%	$1,892.00	32 hrs
34	Scene 1 video	2 days	Wed 5/7/08	Fri 5/9/08	0%	$2,687.00	72 hrs
35	Scene 1 teardc	1 day	Fri 5/9/08	Mon 5/12/08	0%	$248.00	16 hrs
36	Scene 1 compl	0 days	Mon 5/12/08	Mon 5/12/08	0%	$0.00	0 hrs
37	⊟ Scene 2	6.75 days	Thu 5/15/08	Fri 5/23/08	0%	$6,923.00	226 hrs
38	Scene 2 begin	0 days	Thu 5/15/08	Thu 5/15/08	0%	$0.00	0 hrs
39	Scene 2 setup	2 days	Thu 5/15/08	Fri 5/16/08	0%	$1,066.00	64 hrs
40	Scene 2 rehea	6 hrs	Mon 5/19/08	Mon 5/19/08	0%	$824.00	18 hrs
41	Scene 2 vocal	1 day	Mon 5/19/08	Tue 5/20/08	0%	$1,440.00	32 hrs
42	Scene 2 video	2 days	Tue 5/20/08	Thu 5/22/08	0%	$3,345.00	96 hrs
43	Scene 2 teardc	1 day	Thu 5/22/08	Fri 5/23/08	0%	$248.00	16 hrs
44	Scene 2 compl	0 days	Fri 5/23/08	Fri 5/23/08	0%	$0.00	0 hrs

4. On the menu bar, click **Format,** and then click **Text Styles.** The Text Styles dialog box appears.

TAKE NOTE The text styles in Microsoft Project are similar to styles in Microsoft Word. The Item to Change list in the Text Styles dialog box displays all the types of information in a project plan you can consistently format.

5. In the Item to Change list, click **Summary Tasks.**

6. In the Size box, click **10.**

7. In the Color box, click **Green.** Your screen should look similar to Figure 6-12.

Figure 6-12

Text Styles dialog box

8. Click **OK.** Microsoft Project applies the new format settings to all summary tasks in the project. Note that the project summary task was listed separately in the *Item to Change* list, so it is not affected by the changes you just made. Also, any new summary tasks added to the project will appear with the new formatting.

9. If any columns display pound signs (###), double-click between the text in the column labels to widen columns as necessary. Your screen should look similar to Figure 6-13.

Figure 6-13

Summary table with reformatted summary tasks

	Task Name	Duration	Start	Finish	% Comp.	Cost	Work
0	⊟ Don Funk Music Vide	138.25 days?	Mon 1/7/08	Fri 7/18/08	0%	$88,956.50	,757.5 hrs
1	⊟ Pre-Production	83 days?	Mon 1/7/08	Thu 5/1/08	0%	$27,841.00	1,314 hrs
2	Pre-Production beg	0 days	Mon 1/7/08	Mon 1/7/08	0%	$0.00	0 hrs
3	Review Screenpla	1.8 wks	Mon 1/7/08	Wed 1/16/08	0%	$2,295.00	120 hrs
4	Develop scene blo	2 wks	Wed 1/16/08	Tue 1/29/08	0%	$1,560.00	80 hrs
5	Develop production	0.5 mons	Wed 1/30/08	Thu 2/14/08	0%	$2,520.00	160 hrs
6	Identify and reserv	5 wks?	Fri 2/15/08	Thu 3/20/08	0%	$14,455.00	550 hrs
7	Book musicians	2 wks	Fri 3/21/08	Thu 4/3/08	0%	$1,360.00	80 hrs
8	Book dancers	2 wks	Fri 4/4/08	Thu 4/17/08	0%	$1,360.00	80 hrs
9	Reserve audio rec	1 wk	Fri 4/18/08	Thu 4/24/08	0%	$1,400.00	80 hrs
10	Reserve video rec	5 days	Fri 4/25/08	Thu 5/1/08	0%	$1,400.00	80 hrs
11	⊞ Status Meeting	69.13 days	Mon 1/14/08	Mon 4/21/08	0%	$1,491.00	84 hrs
26	Pre-Production con	0 days	Thu 5/1/08	Thu 5/1/08	0%	$0.00	0 hrs
27	⊟ Production	29.75 days	Thu 5/1/08	Thu 6/12/08	0%	$23,369.50	709 hrs
28	Production begins	0 days	Thu 5/1/08	Thu 5/1/08	0%	$0.00	0 hrs
29	⊟ Scene 1	6.75 days	Thu 5/1/08	Mon 5/12/08	0%	$6,051.50	189 hrs
30	Scene 1 begin	0 days	Thu 5/1/08	Thu 5/1/08	0%	$0.00	0 hrs
31	Scene 1 setup	2 days	Fri 5/2/08	Mon 5/5/08	0%	$536.00	48 hrs
32	Scene 1 rehea	6 hrs	Tue 5/6/08	Tue 5/6/08	0%	$888.50	21 hrs
33	Scene 1 vocal	1 day	Tue 5/6/08	Wed 5/7/08	0%	$1,692.00	32 hrs
34	Scene 1 video	2 days	Wed 5/7/08	Fri 5/9/08	0%	$2,687.00	72 hrs
35	Scene 1 teardo	1 day	Fri 5/9/08	Mon 5/12/08	0%	$248.00	16 hrs
36	Scene 1 compl	0 days	Mon 5/12/08	Mon 5/12/08	0%	$0.00	0 hrs
37	⊟ Scene 2	6.75 days	Thu 5/15/08	Fri 5/23/08	0%	$6,923.00	226 hrs
38	Scene 2 begin	0 days	Thu 5/15/08	Thu 5/15/08	0%	$0.00	0 hrs
39	Scene 2 setup	2 days	Thu 5/15/08	Fri 5/16/08	0%	$1,066.00	64 hrs
40	Scene 2 rehea	6 hrs	Mon 5/19/08	Mon 5/19/08	0%	$824.00	18 hrs
41	Scene 2 vocal	1 day	Mon 5/19/08	Tue 5/20/08	0%	$1,440.00	32 hrs
42	Scene 2 video	2 days	Tue 5/20/08	Thu 5/22/08	0%	$3,345.00	96 hrs
43	Scene 2 teardo	1 day	Thu 5/22/08	Fri 5/23/08	0%	$248.00	16 hrs

10. In the Summary table, click the Cost field for task 27, the Production summary task. You will apply some direct formatting to this field.

11. On the menu bar, click **Format**, and then click **Font**. The Font dialog box appears. Although similar to the Text Styles dialog box, the options you choose here apply only to the selected text or cell.

12. In the Font Style box, click **Bold Italic**.

SHOOTING

You cannot use the Font command on the Format menu to affect the formatting of empty rows in a table (the Font command applies only to selections of text). To set the default formatting of rows, use the Text Styles command on the Format menu.

---

13. Click **OK**. Microsoft Project applies the bold italic formatting to the Cost field for task 27. Your screen should look similar to Figure 6-14.

Figure 6-14

Summary Task list showing specific formatting for Cost field of task 27

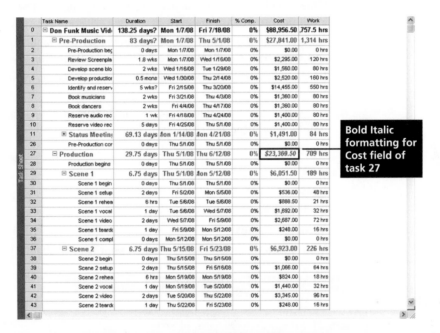

TAKE NOTE

To remove direct formatting that has been applied to text and restore it to the formatting defined by the Text Style dialog box, first select the cell containing the formatted text you wish to restore. Then, on the Edit menu, point to Clear, and click Formats.

---

14. **SAVE** the project plan.

PAUSE. LEAVE the project plan open to use in the next exercise.

In this exercise, you used text styles and direct formatting to customize the appearance of text in a view. Within a view, a *table* is a spreadsheet-like presentation of project data, organized in vertical columns and horizontal rows. Each column represents a field in Microsoft Project, and each row represents a single resource or task. The intersection of a row and a column is called a cell or a *field*, and represents the lowest-level information about a task, resource, or assignment.

When you format a category of text using the Text Styles dialog box, as you did when you formatted the summary tasks in this exercise, the formatting changes you make apply to all cases of that category (summary tasks, in this instance) in all the tables you can display in the active view. If you change the view, the format changes you made would not appear in the new view.

When you apply formatting to individual selections of text (such as the Cost field for task 27), the changes you make have no effect on other text in the view.

■ Creating and Editing Tables

<table>
<tr>
<td>
↓
THE BOTTOM LINE
</td>
<td>
Within Microsoft Project are a number of different tables that can be used in various views. These tables contain most of the commonly used data fields. However, you can create new tables that contain exactly the data you want, or you can modify any predefined table to meet your needs.
</td>
</tr>
</table>

⊕ CREATE A CUSTOM TABLE

USE the project plan you created in the previous exercise. Make sure that you are still in the Task Sheet view from the previous exercise.

1. On the menu bar, click **View**, point to **Table: Summary** and then click **More Tables**. The More Tables dialog box appears and displays all of the predefined tables available to you, depending on the type of view currently displayed (task or resource).

2. Confirm that the **Task** button is selected as the Tables option. Select **Entry**, and then click the **Copy** button. The Table Definition dialog box appears.

3. In the Name box, key **Music Video Schedule Table**. Now you will customize the table.

4. In the Field Name column, select the following field names and then click **Delete Row** after selecting each field name.

   Indicators

   Duration

   Finish

   Predecessors

   Resource Names

   After you have deleted these fields, your screen should look similar to Figure 6-15.

Figure 6-15

Table Definition dialog box

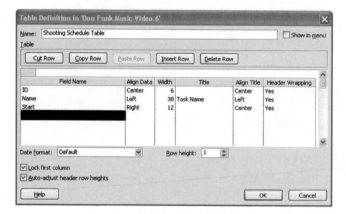

5. In the Field Name column, click the down arrow in the next empty cell below Start, and then select **Cast (Text1)** from the dropdown list.

6. In the Align Data column in the same row, select **Left**. In the Width column, key or select **30**.

7. In the Field Name column in the next empty row below Cast, select **Location (Text 2)** from the dropdown list.

8. In the Align Data column in the same row, select **Left** and then press ⏎Enter.

9. In the Field Name column, select **Start**, and then click the **Cut Row** button.

10. In the Field Name column, select **Name**, and then click the **Paste Row** button.

11. In the Date Format box, select **Mon 1/28/02 12:33 PM**. Your screen should look similar to Figure 6-16.

Figure 6-16

Customized Table Definition dialog box

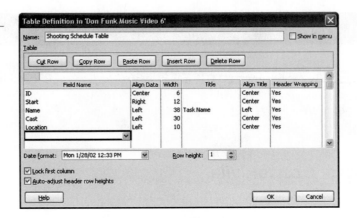

12. Click **OK** to close the Table Definition dialog box. The new table is highlighted in the More Tables dialog box.

13. Click **Apply**. Microsoft Project applies the new table to the Task Sheet view.

14. If the Start column displays pound signs (####), double-click the column heading's right edge to widen it. Your screen should look similar to Figure 6-17.

Figure 6-17

Task Sheet view showing custom table

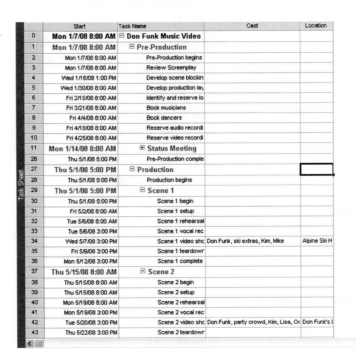

15. **SAVE** the project plan.

PAUSE. LEAVE the project plan open to use in the next exercise.

In this exercise, you created a custom table to display the information typically found on a video shooting schedule. You modified an existing table to include additional data that was important to your project plan. As you create future project plans, keep in mind that you that you have three options when setting up tables: you can create a new table, redefine an existing table, or copy an existing table and modify it as needed.

■ Creating Custom Views

THE BOTTOM LINE

Almost all of the work you perform in Microsoft Project is done in a view, which allows you to see your project plan in a useful way. Microsoft Project includes numerous pre-defined views. You can use these views, edit an existing view, or create your own view. In this exercise, you will create a custom view using the custom filter and custom table you created in earlier lessons.

→ CREATE A CUSTOM VIEW

USE the project plan you created in the previous exercise.

1. On the menu bar, click **View,** and then click **More Views.** The More Views dialog box appears, displaying all of the predefined views available to you.
2. Click the **New** button. The Define New View dialog box appears. Most views use only a single pane, but a view can consist of two separate panes.
3. Make sure **Single View** is selected, and then click **OK.** The View Definition dialog box appears.
4. In the Name box, key **Music Video Schedule View**.
5. In the Screen box, select **Task Sheet** from the dropdown list.
6. In the Table box, select **Music Video Schedule Table** from the dropdown list. The specific groups in the dropdown list depend on the type of view you selected in step 5 (task or resource).
7. In the Group box, select **No Group** from the dropdown list. The specific groups in the dropdown list again depend on the type of view you selected in step 5.
8. In the Filter box, select **Unfinished Shoots** from the dropdown list. The specific groups in the dropdown list depend on the type of view you selected in step 5. The View Definition dialog box shows all the elements that can make up a view. Your screen should look similar to Figure 6-18.

Figure 6-18

View Definition dialog box

> **View Definition in 'Don Funk Music Video 6'**
>
> Name: Music Video Schedule View
> Screen: Task Sheet
> Table: Music Video Schedule Table
> Group: No Group
> Filter: Unfinished Shoots
> ☐ Highlight filter
> ☑ Show in menu
> [Help]   [OK]   [Cancel]

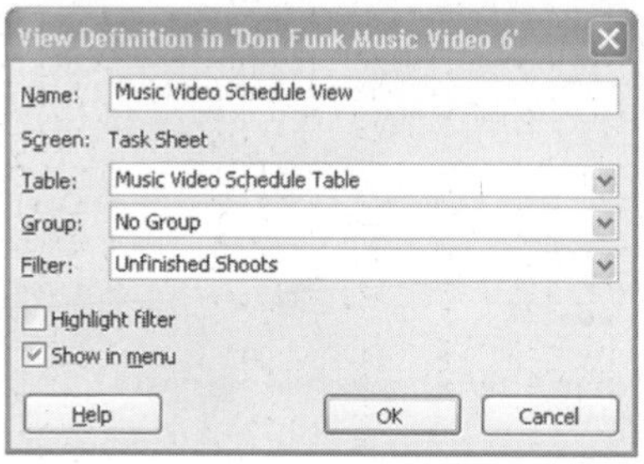

9. Select the **Show in Menu** check box, then click **OK** to close the View Definition dialog box. The new view appears and should be selected in the More Views dialog box.

TAKE NOTE

When you select the *Show in Menu* check box, Microsoft Project adds the new view to the View bar. This custom view will be saved with this Microsoft Project data file, and you can use it whenever you need it.

10. Click **Apply**. Microsoft Project applies the new view. Your screen should look similar to Figure 6-19.

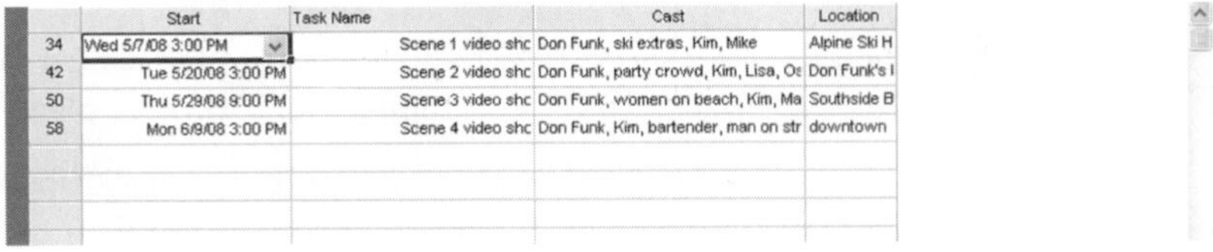

Figure 6-19

Custom view showing Music Video Schedule format

	Start	Task Name	Cast	Location
34	Wed 5/7/08 3:00 PM	Scene 1 video shc	Don Funk, ski extras, Kim, Mike	Alpine Ski H
42	Tue 5/20/08 3:00 PM	Scene 2 video shc	Don Funk, party crowd, Kim, Lisa, O:	Don Funk's l
50	Thu 5/29/08 9:00 PM	Scene 3 video shc	Don Funk, women on beach, Kim, Ma	Southside B
58	Mon 6/9/08 3:00 PM	Scene 4 video shc	Don Funk, Kim, bartender, man on str	downtown

11. **SAVE** the project plan. **CLOSE** the project plan.

PAUSE. If you are continuing to the next lesson, keep Project open. If you are not continuing to additional lessons, **CLOSE** Project.

In this exercise, you created a custom view that enabled you to look specifically at information that was of interest to you. Recall that a view is a window through which you can see the various elements of a project plan in a way that is helpful to the viewing audience. As you saw in this exercise, a view might contain elements such as tables, groups, or filters. You can combine these with other elements to create almost limitless custom views to suit any purpose.

SUMMARY SKILL MATRIX

IN THIS LESSON YOU LEARNED	MATRIX SKILL
To format the Gantt Chart	Modify the Gantt Chart using the Bar Styles dialog box Modify the Gantt Chart using the Gantt Chart Wizard
To draw in a Gantt Chart	Add a text box to the Gantt Chart
To change text appearance in a view	Change appearance of text in a view
To create and edit tables	Create a custom table
To create custom views	Create a custom view

■ Knowledge Assessment

Matching

Match the term in column 1 to its description in column 2.

Column 1	Column 2
1. field	**a.** a spreadsheet-like presentation of project data, organized in vertical columns and horizontal rows
2. Drawing	**b.** the default view in Microsoft Project
3. table	**c.** the right side of the Gantt Chart view
4. Gantt Chart Wizard	**d.** the intersection of a row and a column in a table
5. Bar Styles	**e.** a view that presents information in rows and columns
6. view	**f.** a guided series of dialog boxes in which you select formatting options for the most-used items on the Gantt Chart

7. Gantt Chart   **g.** another name for field

8. cell   **h.** the toolbar that enables you to add objects or text directly onto a Gantt Chart

9. bar chart   **i.** a window through which you can see the various elements of a project plan

10. sheet   **j.** the dialog box that can be used to format the graphical components of the Gantt Chart view

True / False

Circle T if the statement is true or F if the statement is false.

T | F   **1.** When you make a change to a milestone using the Bar Styles dialog box, the change applies to all milestones in the Gantt Chart.

T | F   **2.** The Drawing toolbar allows you to add text directly to Gantt Chart.

T | F   **3.** In Microsoft Project, you can edit predefined tables but you cannot create new custom tables to suit your needs.

T | F   **4.** The Gantt Chart view always consists of a table on the right and a bar chart on the left.

T | F   **5.** When you make formatting changes to your project plan, the data does not change, just the way it appears.

T | F   **6.** In addition to the drawing toolbar, you can use the Object command on the Insert menu to add bitmap images.

T | F   **7.** If you add an object to a Gantt Chart that is date specific, you should link it to the Gantt bar.

T | F   **8.** If you format data using the Format menu, the changes apply to only the data you have specifically selected.

T | F   **9.** The Gantt Chart Wizard has more formatting choices than the Bar Styles dialog box.

T | F   **10.** Changing the appearance of data in a view can make it easier to read and understand project data.

■ Competency Assessment

⊙ Project 6-1: Modifying the Don Funk Music Video Gantt Chart

You are reviewing your project plan with your team. Several team members make the suggestion that it would be nice to have the summary tasks stand out a little bit more on the project plan. You decide to format the summary tasks in purple with the task name listed on the right of the bar.

GET READY. Launch Microsoft Project if it is not already running.

The ***Don Funk Music Video 6-1*** project plan is available on the companion CD-ROM.

OPEN *Don Funk Music Video 6-1* from the data files for this lesson.

1. On the menu bar, click **Format**, and then click **Bar Styles**.
2. In the Name column, select **Summary**.
3. In the bottom half of the dialog box, make sure the Bars tab is selected. Under the Start, Middle, and End labels, select **Purple** from the dropdown list in the Color boxes.
4. Click on the **Text** tab.
5. Click the **Right** box. Click the down arrow, and select **Name** from the dropdown list.

6. Click **OK**.

7. Select the name of task 26, **Pre-Production complete**.

8. Click the **Scroll to Task** button.

9. **SAVE** the project plan as *Don Funk Music Video Purple Summary*, and then **CLOSE** the file.

   LEAVE Project open to use in the next exercise.

 Project 6-2: Interviewing Schedule Table

You have created a project plan for interviewing and hiring a new employee. Now you would like to create a table to display the information found on an internal interview schedule.

The *HR Interview and Hire Plan 6-2* project plan is available on the companion CD-ROM.

OPEN *HR Interview and Hire Plan 6-2* from the data files for this lesson.

1. On the menu bar, click **View**, and then click **More Views**.

2. Select **Task Sheet** from the More Views box, and then click **Apply**.

3. On the menu bar, click **View**, point to **Table: Entry** and then click **More Tables**.

4. Confirm that the **Task** button is selected as the Tables option. Select **Entry**, and then click the **Copy** button.

5. In the Name box, key **Interview Schedule**. Select the **Show in Menu** checkbox.

6. In the Field Name column, select each of the following names and then click **Delete Row** after selecting each field name.

   Indicators

   Finish

   Predecessors

   Resource Name

7. In the Date format box, select **1/28/02 12:33 PM**.

8. Click **OK**.

9. Make sure that **Interview Schedule** is selected in the More Tables dialog box, and then click **Apply**.

10. **SAVE** the project plan as *HR Interview Schedule*, and then **CLOSE** the file.

    LEAVE Project open to use in the next exercise.

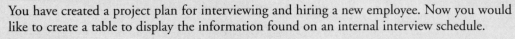

■ **Proficiency Assessment**

 Project 6-3: Office Remodel Contractor Tasks

You have developed a project plan for a kitchen/lunchroom remodel at your business. You are preparing to distribute the plan to some of the contractors who will work on the project. You would like to call attention to the summary tasks and the specific tasks that these contractors will be undertaking.

The *Office Remodel 6-3* project plan is available on the companion CD-ROM.

OPEN *Office Remodel 6-3* from the data files for this lesson.

1. Change the view to the Task Sheet.

2. Select **Text Styles** from the Format menu.

3. Select **Summary Tasks** as the item to change.

4. Select font size **10** and color **Blue**. Click **OK**.

5. Select tasks 9 through 14.

6. Select **Font** from the Format menu.

7. Select a Background color of **Yellow** and then click **OK**.

8. SAVE the project plan as *Office Remodel Contractor Tasks* and then CLOSE the file.

LEAVE Project open to use in the next exercise.

→ Project 6-4: Interviewing Schedule Custom View

The *HR Interview Plan 6-4* project plan is available on the companion CD-ROM.

You have created an interviewing schedule for hiring a new employee at your company. You want to create a custom view for this project plan that looks at only the summary tasks in the Interview Schedule format (which you created in Project 6-2).

OPEN *HR Interview Plan 6-4* from the data files for this lesson.

1. From the More Views dialog box, click **New** to create a new view.
2. Select **Single View**.
3. Name the new view **Summary Interview Schedule**.
4. Select **Task Sheet** from the Screen box.
5. Select **Interview Schedule** from the Table box.
6. Select **No Group** from the Group box.
7. Select **Summary Tasks** from the Filter box.
8. Select the **Show in Menu** check box.
9. Apply the new view.
10. SAVE the project plan as *HR Summary Interview Schedule*, and then CLOSE the file.

LEAVE Project open to use in the next exercise.

■ Mastery Assessment

→ Project 6-5: Don Funk Music Video

The *Don Funk Music Video 6-5* project plan is available on the companion CD-ROM.

You need to make some additional formatting changes to the Don Funk Music Video so that the critical path is more visible. You decide to make these changes using the Gantt Chart Wizard.

OPEN *Don Funk Music Video 6-5* from the data files for this lesson.

1. Make a copy of the Gantt Chart view.
2. Name the new view **Custom Gantt 6-5**.
3. Apply the custom view you have just created.
4. Activate the Gantt Chart Wizard.
5. Select **Critical Path: Style 3** as the type of information you want to display.
6. Complete the Gantt Chart Wizard.
7. SAVE the project plan as *Don Funk Critical Path Style 3*, and then CLOSE the file.

LEAVE Project open to use in the next exercise.

→ Project 6-6: Setting Up a Home Office–Attaching Task Info

The *Home Office Setup 6-6* project plan is available on the companion CD-ROM.

You need to add some information about new phone company billing to your Home Office project plan. You need to use the Drawing function in Project in order to attach your information to some specific dates.

OPEN *Home Office Setup 6-6* from the data files for this lesson.

1. Apply the Detail Gantt view.
2. Shift the view so that the bar chart for task 1 is visible.
3. Activate the Drawing toolbar.
4. Insert a small text box on the Gantt bar chart.
5. In the text box, key **Billing starts when phone line installed.**
6. Activate the Format Drawing dialog box.
7. Fill the text box using Yellow and attach it to task 10.
8. Next to the ID box, select the attachment point on the left side of the task bar.
9. Apply your changes.
10. Scroll to task 10 so that the text box is visible. Adjust the size of the box as necessary to read the text.
11. **SAVE** the project plan as *Home Office Task Info,* and then **CLOSE** the file. **CLOSE** Project.

INTERNET READY

In this lesson, you learned several ways to customize the format of your project plan. By changing the appearance of the data in your plan, you can make it easier for yourself and others to view and interpret your data.

Search the Internet for a detailed, complex project plan that is of some interest to you (a good place to start is the Templates page of Microsoft Office Online). Download the project plan or template to your computer. Using the skills you have learned in this lesson, modify the appearance of the plan so that it is easier to follow. Apply new bar styles and colors, milestone markers, critical path indicators, text formatting, and drawing objects as appropriate. You can also apply custom tables and views to draw attention to a specific part of the project plan. Save your modified project plan so that you can compare the old and new versions of the plan.

7

Project Information: Customizing and Printing

LESSON SKILL MATRIX

SKILLS	MATRIX SKILL
Customizing and Printing a View	Customize and print a Gantt Chart view
Customizing and Printing Reports	Customize and print a report

KEY TERMS
report
stakeholder
timescale

You are a video production manager for Southridge Video and the project manager for a new Don Funk music video. Your project plan has been assembled and activity is starting to occur. You know that one of the most important responsibilities for any project manager is communicating project information. It is time for you to begin formally sharing printed information with your project stakeholders. In this lesson, you will learn how to work with some of the many views and reports in Microsoft Office Project in order to print your project plan.

SOFTWARE ORIENTATION

Page Setup Dialog Box

The Page Setup dialog box provides options for customizing the appearance of views and reports when they are displayed via the Print Preview function or printed to paper.

Figure 7-1

Page Setup dialog box with Legend tab activated

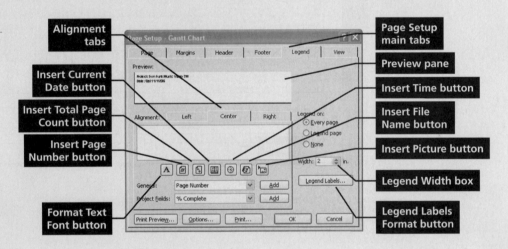

The Page Setup dialog box enables you to specify page options such as margins and paper orientation and size. You can also customize the information on and presentation of headers, footers, and the legend, and view formatting.

Customizing and Printing a View

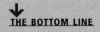 **THE BOTTOM LINE**

Using a view, you can see your project plan information on screen. You can change what you see by customizing the view. You can also apply these customized views to print the information on paper.

⊕ CUSTOMIZE AND PRINT A GANTT CHART VIEW

GET READY. Before you begin these steps, launch Microsoft Project.

OPEN the *Don Funk Music Video 7M* project plan from the data files for this lesson.

SAVE the file as *Don Funk Music Video 7* in the solutions folder for this lesson as directed by your instructor.

The Don *Funk Music Video 7M* project plan is available on the companion CD-ROM.

1. On the menu bar, click **File** and then click **Print Preview**. Microsoft Project displays the Gantt Chart view in the Print Preview window. Your screen should look like Figure 7-2.

Figure 7-2

Gantt Chart view in Print
Preview window

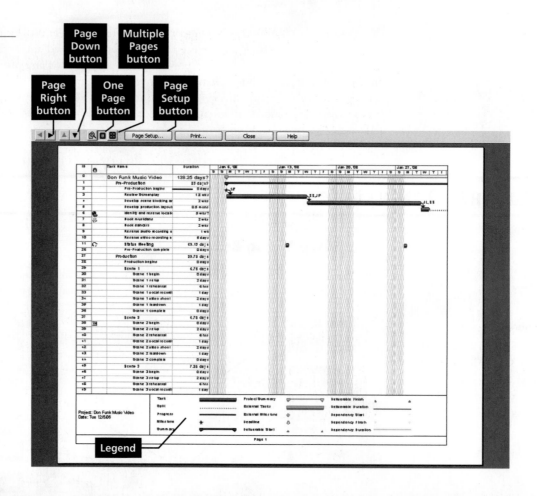

> **TAKE NOTE** ✳
>
> You may or may not see the Print Preview screens in color, depending upon the printer and print drivers you have installed.

▶ 2. On the Print Preview toolbar, click the **Page Right** button three times to display different pages.

▼ 3. On the Print Preview toolbar, click the **Page Down** button once.

▦ 4. On the Print Preview toolbar, click the **Multiple Pages** button. The entire Gantt Chart appears in the Print Preview window. When the multiple page Print Preview is active, the entire printed output is displayed on separate sheets (the paper size is determined by your printer settings). Your screen should look similar to Figure 7-3.

>
>
> You can also use the Project Guide to navigate through printing a view. On the Project Guide, click *Report*. In the *Report* pane, click the *Print current view as a report* link and then follow the Project Guide prompts to customize and print the view.

Figure 7-3

Print Preview window displaying entire Gantt Chart

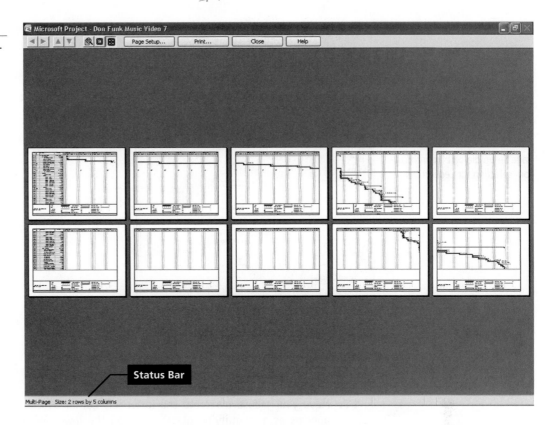

The status bar reads "2 rows by 5 columns." In the Print Preview window, this means there are two rows of pages by five columns of pages, for a total of ten pages. The status bar can help you quickly determine the total number of pages your printed view will be.

5. On the Print Preview toolbar, click the **One Page** button. The first page of the Gantt Chart is displayed.

6. Click the **Page Setup** button. The Page Setup dialog box appears. This is the same dialog box that would appear if you selected the Page Setup option on the File menu.

7. Click the **Header** tab. You want to add the company name to the header that prints on each page.

8. There are three Alignment tabs in the center section of the Header tab box. Select **Center** if it is not already selected. In the General box, click on **Company Name** and then click the **Add** button next to the General box. Microsoft Project places the &[Company] code into the header and displays a preview in the Preview window of the Page Setup dialog box. The company name comes from the Properties dialog box on the File menu.

9. Click the **Legend** tab. You want to change some of the content of the Gantt Chart view's legend.

10. There are three Alignment tabs in the center of the Legend tab box. Click the **Left** tab. Currently, Microsoft Project is formatted to print the project title and current date on the left side of the legend. You also want to print the start date and duration on the right side of the legend.

11. Click the **Right** Alignment tab. Click in the Right Alignment box and key **Start Date:** followed by a space.

12. In the General box, select **Project Start Date** from the dropdown list. Click the **Add** button next to the General box. Microsoft Project adds the label and code for the project start date to the legend.

13. Press **Enter** to add a second line to the legend and then key **Duration:** followed by a space.

14. In the Project Fields box, select **Duration** from the dropdown list. Click the **Add** button next to the Project Fields box. Microsoft Project adds the label and code for project duration to the legend.

15. In the Width box, key or click **3**. This increases the width of the box that appears on the left side of the legend. Your screen should look similar to Figure 7-4.

Figure 7-4

Page Setup dialog box with custom selection for Legend box

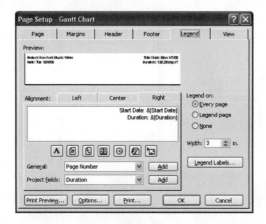

16. Click **OK** to close the Page Setup dialog box. Microsoft Project applies the custom changes to the legend.

17. Move your mouse cursor to the lower left corner of the page preview (your cursor appears as a magnifying glass). Click on the lower left corner of the page. Microsoft Project zooms in to show the legend. Your screen should look similar to Figure 7-5. The data you added to the legend will print on every page of the printed output.

Figure 7-5

Print Preview window zoomed to Legend box

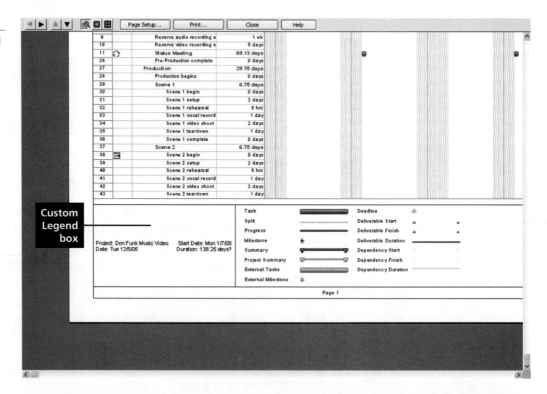

TAKE NOTE

At this point, you can print the project plan by clicking Print on the Print Preview toolbar (the print preview is adequate for purposes of this lesson). When printing in Microsoft Project, there are additional options in the Print dialog box (the Print command is accessed from the File menu). For example, you can print specific date or page ranges.

Close

The data you added to the legend will print on every page of the printed output.

18. Click **Close** on the Print Preview toolbar. The Gantt Chart view is restored. Take note that although you did not print, your changes to the header and the legend will be saved when you save the project file.

19. **SAVE** the project plan.

PAUSE. LEAVE Project open to use in the next exercise.

In this exercise, you customized a view to add information that you wanted to include when printing your project plan. Printing information from a project plan to share with stakeholders is a common activity for project managers. *Stakeholders* are all people or organizations that might be affected by project activities, from resources working on the project to customers receiving the end result of the project.

In a view, you can enter, read, edit, and print information. Printing a view allows you to provide, on paper, almost everything you see on your screen. You can print any view you see in Microsoft Project, with just a few exceptions.

X REF

For a review of the types of views, including form views, refer back to Lesson 6.

- You cannot print form views, such as the Relationship Diagram or the Task Form.
- If you have two views displayed in a combination view (one view in the top pane and the other view in the bottom pane), only the view in the active pane will print.

It is important to keep in mind that the part of the project plan you see on your screen is only a small part of the total project. For example, to print a six-month project with 75 tasks may require more than a dozen letter-sized pages. In general, Gantt Charts and Network Diagrams can use significant amounts of paper on large projects. Some experienced project managers who regularly use Microsoft Project print their projects on poster-sized paper using plotters (a type of printer that draws pictures or graphs using attached pens) or other specialized printing equipment.

Projects with several hundred tasks or long time frames will not print legibly on letter- or legal-sized paper. To reduce the number of required pages, you can print just summary tasks or filtered data. If you are interested in a specific timeframe, you can print just that portion of the timescale, which is the band across the top of the Gantt Chart grid that denotes units of time. A filter could be applied to display only the information that is of interest to a specific audience. In any case, it is a good idea to preview the views you want to print. By using the Page Setup dialog box along with the Print Preview window, you can control many features of the view to be printed. For example, you can set the number of pages on which the view will be printed, apply headers and footers, and determine content that appears in the legend of the Gantt Chart and some other views.

TAKE NOTE

When printing in views that contain a timescale, such as the Gantt Chart view, you can change the number of pages required by adjusting the timescale before printing. To adjust the timescale so that it shows the largest time span in the smallest number of pages, click View on the menu bar, then click Zoom. In the Zoom dialog box, click Entire Project.

Customizing and Printing Reports

THE BOTTOM LINE

In Microsoft Project, a report is a predefined format that is used to view or print project data. Microsoft Project includes several task, resource, and assignment reports you can edit to fit your needs.

CUSTOMIZE AND PRINT A REPORT

USE the project plan you created in the previous exercise.

1. On the Project Guide menu, click **Report**. The *Report* pane of the Project Guide appears.

2. Click the **Select a view or report** link. The *Views and Reports* pane opens.

3. Click the **Create a project report** button. Under *Select a report*, click the **Display Reports** link. The Reports dialog box appears.

4. Click **Custom**, and then click the **Select** button. The Custom Reports dialog box appears with a list of all predefined reports in Microsoft Project. Any custom reports that have been added will also be shown in this dialog box.

5. In the Custom Reports dialog box, select **Task**, and then click the **Preview** button. The Task report is displayed in the Print Preview window. Your screen should look similar to Figure 7-6.

    This report is a complete list of project tasks (summary tasks are not included) and is similar to what you would see in the Entry table of the Gantt Chart view.

Figure 7-6

Task report displayed in the Print Preview window

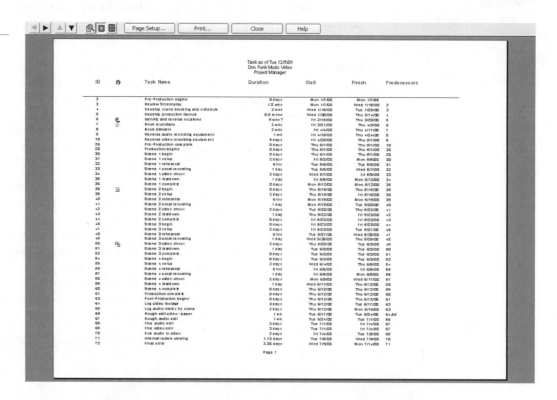

You want to present this data in a different way, so you will edit this report.

6. Click **Close** on the Print Preview toolbar. The Print Preview window closes and the Custom Reports dialog box reappears.

7. In the Custom Reports box, make sure that **Task** is still selected and then click the **Copy** button. The Task Report dialog box appears.

8. In the Name box, select the displayed text and then key **Custom Task Report**.

9. In the Period box, select **Months** from the dropdown list. Selecting Months at this point will group the tasks by the month in which they occur. Since the report now includes a time period element, the timescale options in the Print dialog box become available. This enables you to print data within a specific range if you choose.

10. In the Table box, select **Summary** from the dropdown list.

TAKE NOTE Notice that the tables listed in the Task Report dialog box are the same as those you can apply to a view. When you edit a report format, you can apply built-in or custom table and filters, select additional details to include in the report, and apply a sort order to the information—all by using the dialog box for the report you are currently editing.

11. Click **OK** to close the Task Report dialog box.

12. In the Custom Reports dialog box, select **Custom Task Report** (if it is not already selected) and then click the **Preview** button. Microsoft Project applies the custom report settings you selected, and the report is displayed in the Preview window. Your screen should look similar to Figure 7-7.

Figure 7-7

Print Preview window displaying Custom Task Report with tasks divided by month

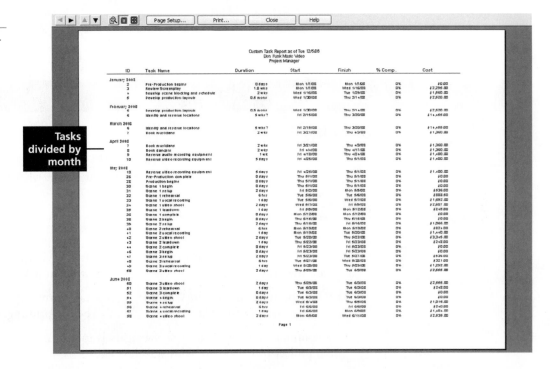

13. Click **Close** on the Print Preview toolbar. Click **Close** in the Custom Reports dialog box.

TAKE NOTE At this point, you can print the project plan by clicking Print on the Print Preview toolbar (the print preview is adequate for purposes of this lesson).

14. Click **Close** to close the Reports dialog box. The Gantt Chart view reappears. Click the **Done** link at the bottom of the *Views and Reports* pane.

15. **SAVE** and then **CLOSE** the project plan.

PAUSE. If you are continuing to the next lesson, keep Project open. If you are not continuing to additional lessons, **CLOSE** Project.

In this exercise, you learned to customize and print a report. A *report* is a predefined format intended for printing Microsoft Project data. Reports are intended only for printing or viewing in the Print Preview window. You cannot enter data or work within reports. Microsoft Project provides a variety of assignment, task, and resource reports that you can edit to fit your needs.

Keep in mind that although reports are different from views, some settings you specify for a view might affect certain reports.

- If subtasks are hidden under summary tasks in a view, reports that contain task lists will include only the summary tasks.
- If assignments are hidden under tasks or resources in a usage view, the usage reports will also hide the assignment details.

SUMMARY SKILL MATRIX

IN THIS LESSON YOU LEARNED	MATRIX SKILL
To customize and print a view	Customize and print a Gantt Chart view
To customize and print reports	Customize and print a report

■ Knowledge Assessment

Fill in the Blank

Complete the following sentences by writing the correct word or words in the blanks provided.

1. _____ enables you to see on your screen what will print on paper before you print it.

2. People or organizations that might be affected by project activities are _____

3. If you have two views displayed in a combination view and want to print the view, only the view in the _____ pane will print.

4. When printing in a Gantt Chart view, you can change the number of pages required by adjusting the _____ before printing.

5. A common activity for project managers is to _____ information from the project plan to share with stakeholders.

6. To add your company name so that it prints at the top of every page, use the _____ dialog box to add the company name to the header.

7. A _____ is a predefined format intended for printing Microsoft Project data.

8. To adapt a report to present the exact information you need, use the _____ dialog box to select and edit the desired report.

9. If subtasks are hidden in a view, reports that contain task lists will include only _____ tasks.

10. In a report, you can only _____ information.

Multiple Choice

Select the best response for the following statements.

1. In a view, you can _____ information.
   a. enter
   b. edit
   c. print
   d. All of the above are correct.

2. If assignments are hidden under tasks or resources in a usage view, what will the usage report show?

   a. tasks or resources with corresponding assignment details

   b. only the tasks or resources

   c. only overallocated assignment details

   d. it depends on how you set up the report

3. In the Print Preview window, the status bar shows "4 rows by 3 columns." How many pages will be printed?

   a. 7

   b. 4

   c. 12

   d. 3

4. To see all of the pages of a view while using Print Preview, you can click on which one of the following buttons?

   a. Multiple Pages

   b. Page Right

   c. One Page

   d. Page Setup

5. For large projects with several hundred tasks, you can condense the information that will print by

   a. printing just summary data.

   b. printing only the part of the timescale that is of interest.

   c. applying a filter to show only the information of interest.

   d. All of the above are correct.

6. If you wanted to print a list of tasks showing start dates, finish dates, and assigned resources, which view might you use?

   a. Tracking Gantt

   b. Task Sheet

   c. Resource Sheet

   d. Calendar

7. Which one of the following views cannot be printed in Microsoft Project?

   a. Tracking Gantt

   b. Calendar

   c. Task Form

   d. Resource Sheet

8. When printing a view with a timescale, you can adjust the timescale before printing to

   a. force the end date of the project.

   b. affect the number of pages required for printing.

   c. filter out unnecessary data.

   d. None of the above is correct.

9. To use the Project Guide to step you through adjusting print options for a view, which one of the following links in the Report pane should you select?

   a. Select a view or report

   b. Change the content or order of information in a view

   c. Print current view as a report

   d. Change the look or content of the Gantt Chart

10. The Custom Reports dialog box contains

    a. all predefined reports in Microsoft Project.

    b. any custom reports that have been added to Microsoft Project.

    c. complex reports that have beesn specifically designed for specific businesses and industries.

    d. all predefined reports plus any custom reports that have been added to Microsoft Project.

■ Competency Assessment

⊘ Project 7-1: Printing a Gantt Chart View

You are preparing to print and distribute a copy of your project plan to your team. You need to make several format changes to the printed version of the Gantt Chart view before you distribute it.

GET READY. Launch Microsoft Project if it is not already running.

OPEN *Don Funk Music Video 7-1* from the data files for this lesson.

The ***Don Funk Music Video 7-1*** project plan is available on the companion CD-ROM.

1. On the File menu, click **Print Preview**.
2. On the Print Preview toolbar, click **Page Setup**.
3. Click the **Header** tab, and then in the Alignment section click the **Center** tab.
4. In the Alignment box, click to position your cursor at the end of &[Company]. Press [Enter].
5. Key **2345 Main Street** and then press [Enter]. Key **New York, NY 45263**.
6. Click the **Footer** tab.
7. In the Alignment box, click to position your cursor at the end of &[Page].
8. Key **of** (note that there is a space before and after the word "of"). Click the **Insert Total Page Count** button.
9. Click the **Legend** tab, and then in the Alignment section, click the **Left** tab.
10. In the Alignment box, click to position your cursor at the end of &[Date]. Press [Enter].
11. Click the **Insert Current Time** button.
12. Click **OK**.
13. Click **Close** on the Print Preview toolbar.
14. **SAVE** the project plan as ***Don Funk Printing Gantt View*** and then **CLOSE** the file.

    LEAVE Project open to use in the next exercise.

Project 7-2: HR Interview Plan

For your HR Interview project plan, you want to set up a report that prints critical tasks and that also uses a custom table that you developed earlier. You will customize a report to meet your requirements.

The *HR Interview Plan 7-2* project plan is available on the companion CD-ROM.

OPEN *HR Interview Plan 7-2* from the data files for this lesson.

1. On the Project Guide, click **Report**.
2. Click the **Select a view or report** link.
3. Click the **Create a project report** button. Under the *Select a report* pane that appears, click the **Display Reports** link.
4. Click **Custom**, and then click the **Select** button.
5. In the Custom Reports dialog box, select **Critical Tasks** and then click the **Copy** button.
6. In the Name box of the Task Report dialog box, select the displayed text and then key **Custom Critical Task Report**.
7. In the Table box, select **Interview Schedule** from the dropdown list.
8. Click the **Text** button on the right side of the dialog box.
9. In the Text Styles dialog box, select **Critical Tasks** from the *Items to Change* dropdown list.
10. In the Color box, select **Red** from the dropdown list.
11. Click **OK** to close the Text Styles dialog box. Click **OK** again to close the Task Report dialog box.
12. Make sure that **Custom Critical Task Report** is selected in the Custom Reports dialog box, and then click **Preview** to view the custom report.
13. Click **Close** on the Print Preview toolbar. Click **Close** on the Custom Reports dialog box. Click **Close** on the Reports dialog box.
14. Click **Done** in the *Views and Reports* pane.
15. **SAVE** the project plan as *HR Interview Custom Critical Task Report* and then **CLOSE** the file.

   LEAVE Project open to use in the next exercise.

■ Proficiency Assessment

 Project 7-3: Reducing Insurance Claim Project Plan Printed Pages

You have a project plan for processing an insurance claim that you want to print. This plan has a large number of tasks. Because you are distributing this to a large number of people, you want to reduce the number of pages that will print by changing the timescale on the project.

The *Insurance Claim 7-3* project plan is available on the companion CD-ROM.

OPEN *Insurance Claim 7-3* from the data files for this lesson.

1. From the View menu, select **Zoom** and then select **Entire Project**.
2. On the Formatting menu, click **Show** and then select **Outline Level 1**.
3. Use Print Preview to view the report.
4. Click on **Page Setup** and then select the **Header** tab.
5. Key **Insurance Claim Processing** in the Center Alignment section.
6. Add the **Time** so that it will print under the date in the Left Alignment section of the Legend tab.
7. **Close** the Print Preview.

8. **SAVE** the file as *Insurance Claim Condensed* and then **CLOSE** the file.

   LEAVE Project open to use in the next exercise.

⊕ Project 7-4: Office Remodel Modified Resource View

You have developed a project plan for a kitchen and lunchroom remodel at your office. You want to distribute a list of tasks by resource so that everyone can see at a glance the tasks for which they are responsible. You will also customize this view to make it easier to read.

The *Office Remodel 7-4* project plan is available on the companion CD-ROM.

OPEN *Office Remodel 7-4* from the data files for this lesson.

1. Switch the view to the Resource Usage view.
2. Click **Print Preview**.
3. Open the Page Setup dialog box.
4. On the View tab, set up the view so that the first three columns print on all pages.
5. On the Footer tab, on the Left Alignment tab, insert the date. Under the date, insert the time.
6. On the Right Alignment tab, key **Start:** and then insert the Start field.
7. Preview your modified view.
8. Close the Print Preview.
9. **SAVE** the file as *Office Remodel Resource Usage* and then **CLOSE** the file.

   LEAVE Project open to use in the next exercise.

■ Mastery Assessment

⊕ Project 7-5: Don Funk Music Video Calendars

You would like to print a report to show the different calendars that are being used in the production of the Don Funk Music Video.

The *Don Funk Music Video 7-5* project plan is available on the companion CD-ROM.

OPEN *Don Funk Music Video 7-5* from the data files for this lesson.

1. Using the Reports dialog box, review the predefined reports that are available for this project. You would like to print a report that shows the different calendars that have been defined for this project so that you can quickly refer to them when needed. Identify the report that meets this need.
2. In a separate Word document, write a short paragraph detailing the steps you took to be able to preview this report.
3. Save the Word document as *Don Funk Music Video Calendars*. Save the Project file as *Don Funk Music Video Calendars*. Close both files.

   LEAVE Project open to use in the next exercise.

⊕ Project 7-6: HR Interview Custom Network Diagram

You want to view and print your HR Interview Plan as a Network Diagram, as well as customize some of the fields for printing.

The *HR Interview Plan 7-6* project plan is available on the companion CD-ROM.

OPEN *HR Interview Plan 7-6* from the data files for this lesson.

1. Change the view to the Network Diagram.
2. Activate the Page Setup dialog box.

3. In the Page Setup dialog box, make the following custom changes:
- increase the width of the Legend to 3in.
- add the time to the left side of the Legend, under the date
- key **Start:** and then insert the Start field on the right side of the Legend
- add the title "HR Interview Network Diagram" to the center of the header
- change the font of the title to Arial Bold 10pt. with color Blue
- add your name to the second line of the header, under the project title

4. Check your changes to make sure they appear correctly.

5. **SAVE** the file as *HR Interview Network Diagram* and then **CLOSE** the file. **CLOSE** Project.

INTERNET READY

As you learned in this chapter, one of the most important responsibilities for a project manager is communicating project information. How well a project manager organizes and presents project information may be a determining factor in the success (or failure) of a project.

There are a number of organizations and companies around the world that are focused on the training and support of project management professionals. Project Management Institute (PMI) is one such organization. Search the Internet for the Website of PMI. Explore the Website to find the purpose or goals of PMI. Give specific attention to project management training and certification programs. Also check to see if there is a PMI chapter in your area. Write a brief summary of your findings in a separate Word document.

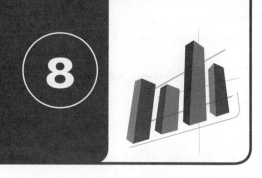

8

Project Plan Tracking— Fundamentals

LESSON SKILL MATRIX

SKILLS	MATRIX SKILL
Establishing a Project Baseline	Establish a project baseline
Tracking a Project as Scheduled	Track a project as scheduled
Entering the Completion Percentage for a Task	Enter the completion percentage for a task
Tasks and Assignments: Tracking Timephased Actual Work	Tasks and assignments: Track timephased actual work
Identifying Over Budget Tasks and Resources	Identify over budget tasks and resources
Identifying Time and Schedule Problems	Reschedule uncompleted work

You are a video production manager for Southridge Video and the project manager for the new Don Funk music video. Prior to work beginning, you focused on developing and communicating the project details. Now that work is starting, you are entering the next phase of project management: tracking progress. In order to properly manage your project, you need to know details such as who did what work, when the work was done, and the cost of the work. In this lesson, you will use Microsoft Office Project to apply some of the basic project tracking tools such as saving baselines, tracking actual work, entering completion percentages, and troubleshooting budget, time, and scheduling problems.

KEY TERMS
actual cost
actuals
baseline
baseline cost
current cost
planning
progress bar
remaining cost
sponsor
timephased fields
tracking
variance

146

SOFTWARE ORIENTATION

Task Usage View

The Task Usage view can be used to enter timephased actual work for both tasks and resources. The timephased grid makes it easier to locate and enter task and resource data.

Figure 8-1

Task Usage view timephased grid

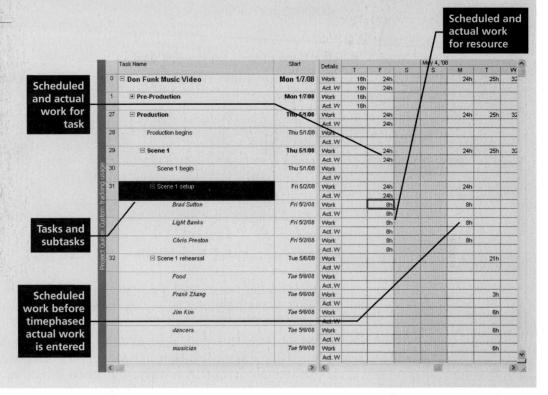

On the timephased grid in the Task Usage view, you enter actual work at the intersection of the desired date column and the actual work row for the desired task or resource.

Establishing a Project Baseline

THE BOTTOM LINE

In order to evaluate how well a project is progressing, it is important to review how well it was originally planned. The project baseline is the initial project plan that is saved and then referred to later to track project progress.

⊙ ESTABLISH A PROJECT BASELINE

GET READY. Before you begin these steps, launch Microsoft Project. **OPEN** the *Don Funk Music Video 8M* project plan from the data files for this lesson.
SAVE the file as *Don Funk Music Video 8* in the solutions folder for this lesson as directed by your instructor.

The *Don Funk Music Video 8M* project plan is available on the companion CD-ROM.

1. On the Project Guide toolbar, click the **Track** button. The *Track* pane appears.

2. In the *Track* pane, click the **Save a baseline plan to compare with later versions** link. The *Save Baseline* pane appears.

3. Click the **Save Baseline** button. Microsoft Project saves the baseline and adds a notation about when the baseline was saved in the *Save Baseline* pane. Although there is no indication in the Gantt Chart view that anything has changed, in the next few steps you will explore some of the changes caused by saving the baseline.

 **ANOTHER WAY**   You can also save the baseline by clicking Tools on the menu bar. Point to Tracking and then click Save Baseline.

4. Click **Done** in the *Save Baseline* pane.

5. Click the **Show/Hide Project Guide** button. The Project Guide closes.

TAKE NOTE   You can save up to eleven baselines in a single project plan. The baselines are named Baseline (the first baseline you would normally save) and Baseline 1 through Baseline 10. Saving multiple baselines is helpful if your project planning stage is especially long or if you have approved scope changes. You can save multiple baselines to record different sets of baseline values, and later compare these against each other and against actual values.

6. On the menu bar, click **View** and then click **More Views**. The More Views dialog box appears.

7. In the Views box, select **Task Sheet** and click **Apply**. There is more room to see the fields in the table because the Gantt Chart is not shown. Now you will switch to a different table in the Task Sheet view.

8. On the menu bar, click **View**, point to **Table: Summary** and then click **Variance**. The Variance table appears. This table includes both the Scheduled and Baseline columns so that you can compare them easily. Your screen should look similar to Figure 8-2.

Figure 8-2

Variance table displaying Scheduled and Baseline columns

	Task Name	Start	Finish	Baseline Start	Baseline Finish	Start Var.	Finish Var.
0	⊟ Don Funk Music	Mon 1/7/08	Fri 7/18/08	Mon 1/7/08	Fri 7/18/08	0 days	0 days
1	⊟ Pre-Production	Mon 1/7/08	Thu 5/1/08	Mon 1/7/08	Thu 5/1/08	0 days	0 days
2	Pre-Production	Mon 1/7/08	Mon 1/7/08	Mon 1/7/08	Mon 1/7/08	0 days	0 days
3	Review Scree	Mon 1/7/08	Wed 1/16/08	Mon 1/7/08	Wed 1/16/08	0 days	0 days
4	Develop scen	Wed 1/16/08	Tue 1/29/08	Wed 1/16/08	Tue 1/29/08	0 days	0 days
5	Develop prod	Wed 1/30/08	Thu 2/14/08	Wed 1/30/08	Thu 2/14/08	0 days	0 days
6	Identify and re	Fri 2/15/08	Thu 3/20/08	Fri 2/15/08	Thu 3/20/08	0 days	0 days
7	Book musician	Fri 3/21/08	Thu 4/3/08	Fri 3/21/08	Thu 4/3/08	0 days	0 days
8	Book dancers	Fri 4/4/08	Thu 4/17/08	Fri 4/4/08	Thu 4/17/08	0 days	0 days
9	Reserve audi	Fri 4/18/08	Thu 4/24/08	Fri 4/18/08	Thu 4/24/08	0 days	0 days
10	Reserve vide	Fri 4/25/08	Thu 5/1/08	Fri 4/25/08	Thu 5/1/08	0 days	0 days
11	⊞ Status Mee	Mon 1/14/08	Mon 4/21/08	Mon 1/14/08	Mon 4/21/08	0 days	0 days
26	Pre-Production	Thu 5/1/08	Thu 5/1/08	Thu 5/1/08	Thu 5/1/08	0 days	0 days
27	⊟ Production	Thu 5/1/08	Thu 6/12/08	Thu 5/1/08	Thu 6/12/08	0 days	0 days
28	Production be	Thu 5/1/08	Thu 5/1/08	Thu 5/1/08	Thu 5/1/08	0 days	0 days
29	⊟ Scene 1	Thu 5/1/08	Mon 5/12/08	Thu 5/1/08	Mon 5/12/08	0 days	0 days
30	Scene 1 b	Thu 5/1/08	Thu 5/1/08	Thu 5/1/08	Thu 5/1/08	0 days	0 days
31	Scene 1 s	Fri 5/2/08	Mon 5/5/08	Fri 5/2/08	Mon 5/5/08	0 days	0 days
32	Scene 1 r	Tue 5/6/08	Tue 5/6/08	Tue 5/6/08	Tue 5/6/08	0 days	0 days
33	Scene 1 v	Tue 5/6/08	Wed 5/7/08	Tue 5/6/08	Wed 5/7/08	0 days	0 days
34	Scene 1 v	Wed 5/7/08	Fri 5/9/08	Wed 5/7/08	Fri 5/9/08	0 days	0 days
35	Scene 1 t	Fri 5/9/08	Mon 5/12/08	Fri 5/9/08	Mon 5/12/08	0 days	0 days
36	Scene 1 c	Mon 5/12/08	Mon 5/12/08	Mon 5/12/08	Mon 5/12/08	0 days	0 days
37	⊟ Scene 2	Thu 5/15/08	Fri 5/23/08	Thu 5/15/08	Fri 5/23/08	0 days	0 days
38	Scene 2 b	Thu 5/15/08	Thu 5/15/08	Thu 5/15/08	Thu 5/15/08	0 days	0 days
39	Scene 2 s	Thu 5/15/08	Fri 5/16/08	Thu 5/15/08	Fri 5/16/08	0 days	0 days
40	Scene 2 r	Mon 5/19/08	Mon 5/19/08	Mon 5/19/08	Mon 5/19/08	0 days	0 days
41	Scene 2 v	Mon 5/19/08	Tue 5/20/08	Mon 5/19/08	Tue 5/20/08	0 days	0 days
42	Scene 2 v	Tue 5/20/08	Thu 5/22/08	Tue 5/20/08	Thu 5/22/08	0 days	0 days
43	Scene 2 t	Thu 5/22/08	Fri 5/23/08	Thu 5/22/08	Fri 5/23/08	0 days	0 days

"Scheduled" columns | "Baseline" columns | "Variancce" columns

SHOOTING If any column displays pound signs (####), double-click between the column titles to widen the column.

Note that at this point, the values in the Start and Baseline Start, as well as the values in the Finish and Baseline Finish, are identical. This is because no actual work has occurred and no changes to the scheduled work have been made. Once actual work has been recorded or schedule adjustments have been made, the scheduled values may differ from the baseline values. Any differences would be displayed in the Variance column.

9. **SAVE** the project plan.

   PAUSE. LEAVE Project open to use in the next exercise.

In this exercise, you learned how to save a baseline for your project plan. A *baseline* is a collection of key values in the project plan, such as the planned start dates, finish dates, and costs of the various tasks and assignments. A baseline allows you to begin the tracking phase of project management. The following table lists the specific values saved in the baseline, which include the task, resource, and assignment fields, as well as the *timephased fields*—task, resource, and assignment values distributed over time.

Task Fields	Start field
	Finish field
	Duration field
	Work and timephased Work fields
	Cost and timephased Cost fields
Resource Fields	Work and timephased Work fields
	Cost and timephased Cost fields
Assignment Fields	Start field
	Finish field
	Work and timephased Work fields
	Cost and timephased Cost fields

You should save a baseline when:

- You have developed the project plan as much as possible. (You can still add tasks, resources, or assignments after work has begun. This is usually not avoidable.)
- You have not started to enter actual values, such as a percentage of completion for the task.

The first phase of a project focuses on project *planning* – developing and communicating the details of a project before actual work begins. When work begins, so does your next phase of project management: tracking project progress. *Tracking* refers to all of the collecting, entering, and analyzing of actual project performance data, such as work on tasks, resource costs, and actual durations. These details are often called *actuals*, or project work completed and recorded in a Microsoft Project file. Accurately tracking project performance and comparing it against the original plan helps you to answer such questions as:

- Are tasks starting and finishing as planned? If not, what will be the impact on the finish date?
- Are resources requiring more or less than the scheduled amount of time to complete tasks?

• Are tasks being completed above or below scheduled cost?

There are several ways to track progress in Microsoft Project, depending on the level of detail or control required by you, the stakeholders, and the project *sponsor*—the individual or organization that provides financial support and supports the project team within the larger organization. Because tracking requires more work from you and possibly from the resources working on the project, you need to determine the level of detail you need. In this lesson, we will examine the following different levels of tracking:

• *Record project work as scheduled.* This works best if everything in the project occurs exactly as it was scheduled.

• *Record each task's percentage of completion.* You can do this at precise values or at increments such as 25%, 50%, 75%, and 100%.

• *Record the actuals.* The actual start, actual finish, actual work, and actual and remaining duration for each task or assignment are recorded.

• *Track assignment-level work by time period.* You record actual work values by day, week, or other time interval that you select. This is the most detailed level of tracking.

You can apply a combination of these approaches within a single project, as different parts of a project may have different tracking needs.

■ Tracking a Project as Scheduled

THE BOTTOM LINE

Once a baseline has been saved for a project plan, the work done on the project can be tracked against the baseline values. The simplest approach to tracking is to report that the actual work is proceeding as planned. You record project actuals by updating work to the current date.

⊕ TRACK A PROJECT AS SCHEDULED

USE the project plan you created in the previous exercise.

1. On the menu bar, click **View** and then click **Gantt Chart**. The Gantt Chart view appears.

2. On the menu bar, click **Tools**, point to **Tracking**, and then click **Update Project**. The Update Project dialog box appears.

3. Make sure the **Update work as complete through** option is selected. In the adjacent date box, key or select **February 11, 2008**, and then click **OK**. Microsoft Project records the actual work for the projects that were scheduled to start before February 11. It also draws progress bars in the Gantt bars for those tasks to show this progress visually.

4. Select the name of task 5, **Develop production layouts**. Click the **Scroll to Task** button on the Standard toolbar. Your screen should look similar to Figure 8-3.

5. **SAVE** the project plan.

   PAUSE. LEAVE the project plan open to use in the next exercise.

In this exercise, you updated the project to show that work had occurred as scheduled through a certain date. The *progress bar* in the Gantt Chart view shows how much of each task has been completed. A check mark appears in the Indicators column for tasks 2, 3, and 4 to indicate these tasks have been completed. In addition, a progress bar is drawn through the entire length of these tasks' Gantt bars. Because only a portion of task 5 has been completed by February 11, the progress bar for this task only extends to February 11 and no check mark appears in the Indicators column.

Figure 8-3

Progress bars for completed tasks in Gantt Chart view

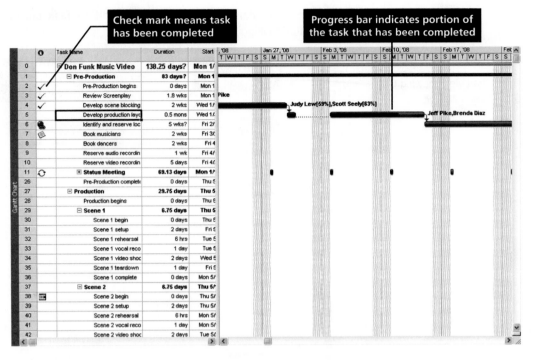

Also notice that because some of the recurring status meetings have been completed by February 11, progress bars appear in the summary Gantt bars for these tasks.

■ Entering the Completion Percentage for a Task

THE BOTTOM LINE

As you continue to make progress on your project, it is important to record the work that has been done on a task. There are many ways to record this work. One of the quickest ways is to record the completion percentage of the task.

➔ ENTER THE COMPLETION PERCENTAGE FOR A TASK

USE the project plan you created in the previous exercise.

1. Click the **Track** button on the Project Guide toolbar. The *Track* pane appears.

2. In the *Track* pane, click **Prepare to track the progress of your project** link. The *Setup Tracking* pane appears and the view changes to the *Project Guide: Custom tracking* table.

3. Slide the divider bar between the table and the Gantt bar chart so that more of the table columns are visible (notice the Work and % Work Complete columns).

4. In the *Setup Tracking* pane, select the **Always track by entering the Percent of Work Complete** button, and then click the **Done** link. You will enter task completion percentages in the % Work Complete column in the *Custom tracking* view.

5. In the *Track* pane, click the **Incorporate progress information into the project** link. The *Incorporate Progress* pane appears.

6. In the % Work Complete column for task 5, key or select 100, and then press **Enter**. Microsoft Project extends the progress bar through the length of the Gantt bar for task 5 and records the actual work for the task as scheduled.

TAKE NOTE

You can also use the Tracking toolbar to quickly update tasks that are 0%, 25%, 50%, 75%, and 100% complete. On the menu bar, click View, point to Toolbars, and then click Tracking. The Tracking toolbar will be activated. Select the task you want to update, and then click the appropriate percentage button on the Tracking toolbar.

7. On the Standard toolbar, click the **Scroll to Task** button. Your screen should look similar to Figure 8-4.

Figure 8-4

Gantt Chart view showing task 5 as 100% complete

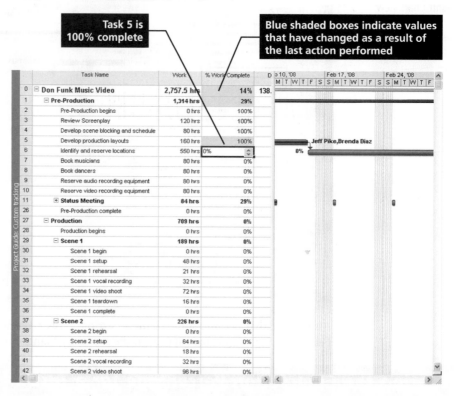

Task 5 is 100% complete

Blue shaded boxes indicate values that have changed as a result of the last action performed

8. In the % Work Complete field for task 6, key or select **50**, and then press **Enter**. Microsoft Project records the actual work for the task as scheduled, and then updates the progress line through 50 percent of the Gantt bar.

9. At the bottom of the *Incorporate Progress* pane, click the **Done** link.

10. SAVE the project plan.

11. CLOSE the project plan. In the next exercise, you will use an updated version of the Don Funk Music Video 8 project plan to simulate the passage of time.

PAUSE. LEAVE Microsoft Project open to use in the next exercise.

TAKE NOTE

You can view a task's completion percentage and other tracking information by pointing to a progress bar in a task's Gantt bar. A Screen Tip will appear.

In this exercise, you manually entered the completion percentage for a task. There are several ways you can quickly record task progress as a percentage:

• Use the Project Guide, as you did in this exercise.

• Use the Tracking toolbar (on the menu bar, click View, point to Toolbars, and then click Tracking). This toolbar has preset buttons for recording 0%, 25%, 50%, 75%, and 100% completion on a task.

• Use the Update Tasks dialog box (on the menu bar, click Tools, point to Tracking, and then click Update Tasks). Using this method, you can enter any percentage you want.

When you use any of these methods to enter a percentage other than 0% complete, Microsoft Project changes the task's actual start date to match its scheduled start date. It also calculates actual duration, remaining duration, actual costs, and other values, based on the percentage you enter.

■ Tasks and Assignments: Tracking Timephased Actual Work

THE BOTTOM LINE

Using timephased values is the most detailed method for tracking actual work on a project. More effort is required to track this way, but the detailed information is often very useful.

 TASKS AND ASSIGNMENTS: TRACK TIMEPHASED ACTUAL WORK

The *Don Funk Music Video 8MA* project plan is available on the companion CD-ROM.

OPEN the *Don Funk Music Video 8MA* project plan from the data files for this lesson.

SAVE the file as *Don Funk Music Video 8A* in the solutions folder for this lesson as directed by your instructor.

1. On the menu bar click **View,** and then click **Task Usage.** The Task Usage view appears.

2. In the *Track* pane, click **Prepare to track the progress of your project** link. The *Setup Tracking* pane appears and the view changes to the *Project Guide: Custom tracking* table.

3. In the *Setup Tracking* pane, select the **Always track by entering the hours of work done per time period** button, and then click the **Done** link.

4. Collapse the Pre-Production phase of the project by clicking the minus sign (−) next to the name of task 1, Pre-Production. This phase of the project is complete, so hiding these tasks simplifies your view.

5. Select the name of task 31, Scene 1 setup. On the Standard toolbar, click the **Scroll to Task** button. Microsoft Project scrolls the timescaled grid to show the first scheduled work values of the Production phase. Your screen should look similar to Figure 8-5.

Figure 8-5

Task Usage view showing work values for task 31 in the Production phase

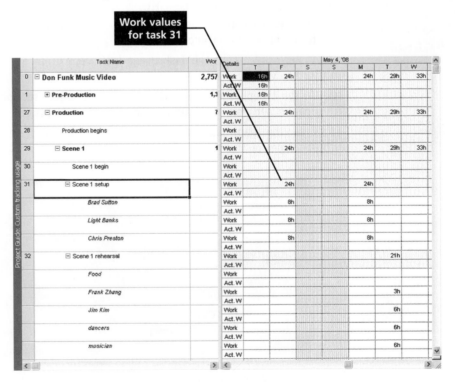

6. On the timephased grid, click the yellow cell at the intersection of the Friday, May 2 column and the task 31 Actual Work (Act. Work) row.

7. Key **24h** and press Enter. Microsoft Project distributes the actual work among assigned resources and rolls up the values to the summary tasks. Your screen should look similar to Figure 8-6.

Figure 8-6

Task Usage view showing time-phased actual work entered for task 31

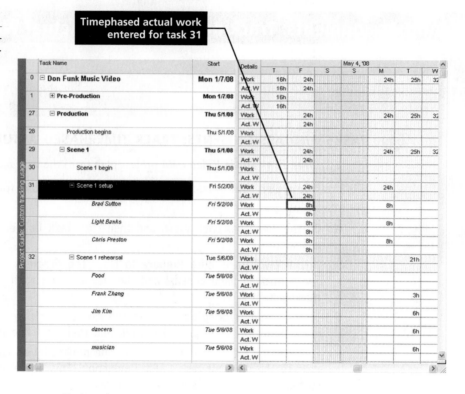

Timephased actual work entered for task 31

Notice that as soon as you entered the actual value for this task, the scheduled work value changed to match it. Both work and actual values rolled up to the task and summary task levels. In addition, the work was distributed among the specific assignments on the task.

8. In the Monday, May 5 Actual Work cell for task 31, key **24h** and press Enter. You are finished entering actual work for this task. You will enter actual work values for assignments on another task.

9. If necessary, scroll the Task Usage view up so that all of the assignments for task 33 are visible.

10. In the timephased grid, click the cell at the intersection of the Tuesday, May 6 column and Jeff Pike's Actual Work row for his assignment on task 33.

11. Enter the following actual work values in the timescale grid (make sure to check the order of the names):

Resource Name	Tuesday's Actual Work	Wednesday's Actual Work
Jeff Pike	1h	7h
Sound Technician	1h	7h
Don Funk	1h	7h
musician	1h	7h

After you have entered these values, your screen should look similar to Figure 8-7. As before, the individual resources' actual work values were rolled up to the task's actual work values. The original work values are saved in the baseline, in case you need to refer to them later.

TAKE NOTE

Microsoft Project may list your tasks in a different order than is shown in the exercise. Make sure that you click on the correct task name.

Figure 8-7

Task Usage view showing
actual work entered

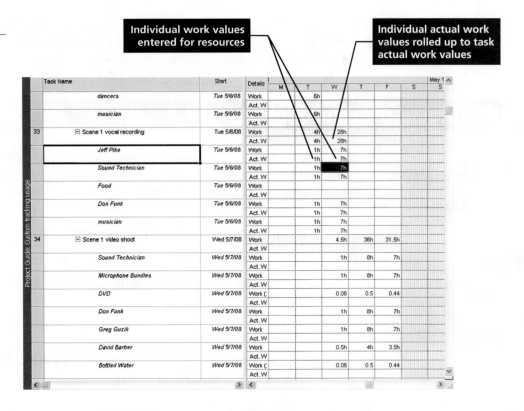

12. **SAVE** the project plan.

13. **CLOSE** the project plan. In the next exercise, you will use an updated version of the Don Funk Music Video 8 project plan to simulate the passage of time.

PAUSE. LEAVE Microsoft Project open to use in the next exercise.

In this exercise, you entered timephased values in the Task Usage view to track actual work on a project. Both the Task Usage and Resource Usage views enable you to track work at the most detailed level possible. In either view, you can enter actual work values for individual assignments as frequently as you wish.

Entering timephased values means more work on the part of the project manager and it may mean more work from individual resources as well (to inform the project manager of their daily actuals). Even so, this method gives you much greater detail than the other methods you have learned about in this lesson. Entering timephased values may be the best method to use if you have tasks or projects that have any of the following characteristics:

- High-risk tasks
- Tasks that require hourly billing for labor
- Tasks in which stakeholders have a very strong interest
- Short-duration tasks for which a ***variance***—a deviation from the schedule or budget established—of even an hour or two could put the overall project at risk

You may have noticed that the information you entered in this lesson is similar to the information found on a time sheet. To enter assignment-level actual work values, you need a time card of sorts–whether it is paper or electronic. Your actual solution for collecting actuals will depend upon your organization's existing policies, practices, and existing systems for collection information. You may be able to use one or more of the following:

- Collecting the actuals yourself. This will only work if you are in contact with a small group of resources on a frequent basis. This also gives you the opportunity to talk to the resources about their participation in the project.

- Collecting the actuals through a formal reporting system. This may be a system that already exists in your organization or one that you develop specifically for your project.
- Use Microsoft Project's e-mail-based collaboration features to collect assignment status data.

■ Identifying Over Budget Tasks and Resources

↓
THE BOTTOM LINE

So far, you have focused on a project's schedule as a key part of the overall success of the plan. However, another critical piece of information is the cost variance, or how the actual costs compare to the projected costs.

IDENTIFY OVER BUDGET TASKS AND RESOURCES

The ***Don Funk Music Video 8MB*** project plan is available on the companion CD-ROM.

OPEN the ***Don Funk Music Video 8MB*** project plan from the data files for this lesson.

SAVE the file as ***Don Funk Music Video 8B*** in the solutions folder for this lesson as directed by your instructor.

1. On the menu bar, click **Project**, and then click **Project Information**. The Project Information Dialog box appears.
2. Click the **Statistics** button. The Project Statistics dialog box appears. Your screen should look similar to Figure 8-8.

Figure 8-8

Project Statistics dialog box

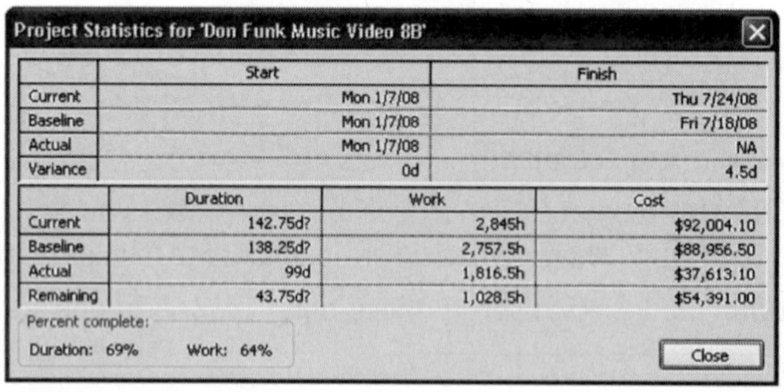

Project Statistics for 'Don Funk Music Video 8B'

	Start		Finish
Current		Mon 1/7/08		Thu 7/24/08
Baseline		Mon 1/7/08		Fri 7/18/08
Actual		Mon 1/7/08		NA
Variance		0d		4.5d

	Duration	Work	Cost
Current	142.75d?	2,845h	$92,004.10
Baseline	138.25d?	2,757.5h	$88,956.50
Actual	99d	1,816.5h	$37,613.10
Remaining	43.75d?	1,028.5h	$54,391.00

Percent complete:
Duration: 69% Work: 64%

The Cost column displays the current, baseline, actual, and remaining cost values for the entire project.

- The ***current cost*** is the sum of the actual and remaining cost values.
- The ***baseline cost*** is the total planned cost of the project when the baseline was saved.
- The ***actual cost*** is the cost that has been incurred so far (after the indicated total work has been completed).
- The ***remaining cost*** is the difference between the current cost and actual cost.

ANOTHER WAY

To change the table, you can also right-click on the upper left corner of the active table, and click Cost in the shortcut menu that appears.

It is obvious that some cost variance has occurred, but it is not possible to tell from the Project Statistics dialog box when or where the variance occurred.

3. Click the **Close** button. The Project Statistics dialog box closes.
4. On the menu bar, click **View**. Point to **Table: Variance**, and then click **Cost**. The Cost table appears in the Task Sheet view. Take a moment to review the columns in the Cost table. Note that although costs are not scheduled in the same sense that work is scheduled, costs (except fixed costs) are derived from the scheduled work.
5. Click the Task Name column heading.
6. Click the **Hide Subtasks** button on the Formatting toolbar. Microsoft Project collapses the task list to display on the top summary tasks (which in this case correspond to the major phases of the project).

7. Click the plus sign (+) next to task 27, Production. Microsoft Project expands the Production summary task to show the summary tasks for the individual scenes. Your screen should look similar to Figure 8-9.

Figure 8-9

Production subtasks expanded in the Cost table in the Task Sheet view

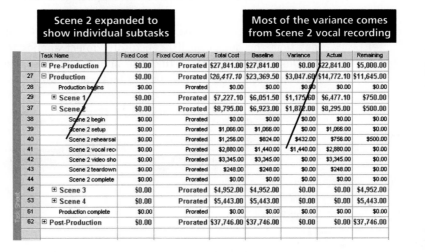

	Task Name	Fixed Cost	Fixed Cost Accrual	Total Cost	Baseline	Variance	Actual	Remaining
1	⊞ Pre-Production	$0.00	Prorated	$27,841.00	$27,841.00	$0.00	$22,841.00	$5,000.00
27	⊟ Production	$0.00	Prorated	$26,417.10	$23,369.50	$3,047.60	$14,772.10	$11,645.00
28	Production begins	$0.00	Prorated	$0.00	$0.00	$0.00	$0.00	$0.00
29	⊞ Scene 1	$0.00	Prorated	$7,227.10	$6,051.50	$1,175.60	$6,477.10	$750.00
37	⊞ Scene 2	$0.00	Prorated	$8,795.00	$6,923.00	$1,872.00	$8,295.00	$500.00
45	⊞ Scene 3	$0.00	Prorated	$4,952.00	$4,952.00	$0.00	$0.00	$4,952.00
53	⊞ Scene 4	$0.00	Prorated	$5,443.00	$5,443.00	$0.00	$0.00	$5,443.00
61	Production complete	$0.00	Prorated	$0.00	$0.00	$0.00	$0.00	$0.00
62	⊞ Post-Production	$0.00	Prorated	$37,746.00	$37,746.00	$0.00	$0.00	$37,746.00

Scene 2 has greatest variance

Although Scenes 1 and 2 both had some variance, Scene 2 had the greater variance, so you will focus on that scene.

8. Click the plus sign (+) next to summary task 37, Scene 2. Microsoft Project expands the Scene 2 summary task to show all of the subtasks. Your screen should look similar to Figure 8-10.

Figure 8-10

Scene 2 individual tasks in the Cost table in the Task Sheet view

Scene 2 expanded to show individual subtasks

Most of the variance comes from Scene 2 vocal recording

	Task Name	Fixed Cost	Fixed Cost Accrual	Total Cost	Baseline	Variance	Actual	Remaining
1	⊞ Pre-Production	$0.00	Prorated	$27,841.00	$27,841.00	$0.00	$22,841.00	$5,000.00
27	⊟ Production	$0.00	Prorated	$26,417.10	$23,369.50	$3,047.60	$14,772.10	$11,645.00
28	Production begins	$0.00	Prorated	$0.00	$0.00	$0.00	$0.00	$0.00
29	⊞ Scene 1	$0.00	Prorated	$7,227.10	$6,051.50	$1,175.60	$6,477.10	$750.00
37	⊟ Scene 2	$0.00	Prorated	$8,795.00	$6,923.00	$1,872.00	$8,295.00	$500.00
38	Scene 2 begin	$0.00	Prorated	$0.00	$0.00	$0.00	$0.00	$0.00
39	Scene 2 setup	$0.00	Prorated	$1,066.00	$1,066.00	$0.00	$1,066.00	$0.00
40	Scene 2 rehearsal	$0.00	Prorated	$1,256.00	$824.00	$432.00	$756.00	$500.00
41	Scene 2 vocal rec	$0.00	Prorated	$2,880.00	$1,440.00	$1,440.00	$2,880.00	$0.00
42	Scene 2 video sho	$0.00	Prorated	$3,345.00	$3,345.00	$0.00	$3,345.00	$0.00
43	Scene 2 teardown	$0.00	Prorated	$248.00	$248.00	$0.00	$248.00	$0.00
44	Scene 2 complete	$0.00	Prorated	$0.00	$0.00	$0.00	$0.00	$0.00
45	⊞ Scene 3	$0.00	Prorated	$4,952.00	$4,952.00	$0.00	$0.00	$4,952.00
53	⊞ Scene 4	$0.00	Prorated	$5,443.00	$5,443.00	$0.00	$0.00	$5,443.00
61	Production complete	$0.00	Prorated	$0.00	$0.00	$0.00	$0.00	$0.00
62	⊞ Post-Production	$0.00	Prorated	$37,746.00	$37,746.00	$0.00	$0.00	$37,746.00

Take note of the variance column. It shows that most of the Scene 2 variance can be tracked to the Scene 2 vocal recording.

9. Click the Task Name column heading.

10. Click the **Show Subtasks** button on the Formatting toolbar. Microsoft Project expands all of the summary tasks to show all of the tasks in the project.

11. Click the **Report** button on the Project Guide toolbar.

12. In the *Reports* pane, click the **See project costs** link. The Project Guide: Analyze Costs view appears. In the *Project Costs* pane, you have access to the filters that are most closely related to project costs. Your screen should look similar to Figure 8-11.

Figure 8-11

Project Guide: Analyze Costs
view

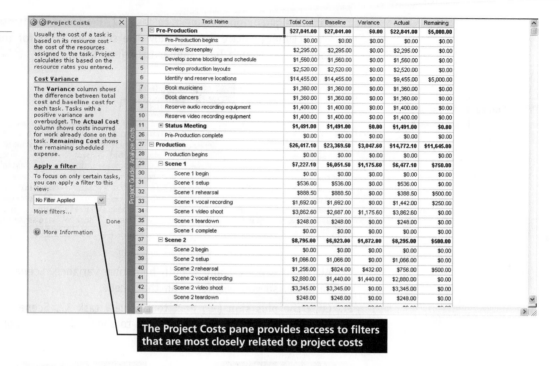

The Project Costs pane provides access to filters
that are most closely related to project costs

13. In the *Project Costs* pane, under the *Apply a filter* heading, select **Cost Overbudget** from the dropdown list. Microsoft Project applies the filter to the task list to show only those tasks that had actual and scheduled costs greater than their baseline costs. Your screen should look similar to Figure 8-12.

Figure 8-12

Analyze Costs view with Costs
Overbudget filter applied

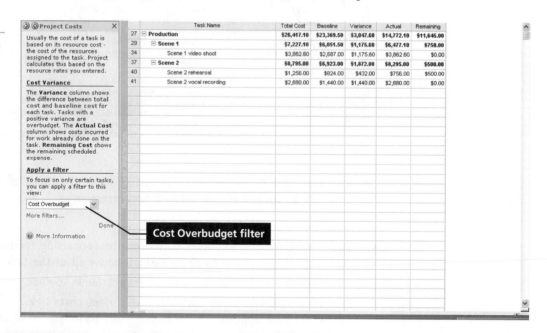

Cost Overbudget filter

Since this project's costs are almost entirely derived from work performed by resources, by reviewing the filtered Analyze Costs table, you can conclude that more work than was scheduled has been needed to complete the tasks up to this point.

14. Click **Done** in the *Project Costs* pane.

15. **SAVE** the project plan.

16. **CLOSE** the project plan. In the next exercise, you will use an updated version of the Don Funk Music Video 8 to simulate the passage of time.

PAUSE. LEAVE Microsoft Project open to use in the next exercise.

In this exercise, you used several different views and tables to identify tasks and resources that were over budget. Project managers and stakeholders often focus on the project schedule (Did tasks start and finish on time?). For projects such as this one that include cost information, cost variance is another critical indicator of overall project health. In Microsoft Project, evaluating cost variance enables you to make incremental budget adjustments for individual tasks to avoid exceeding your project's overall budget.

■ Identifying Time and Schedule Problems

<table>
<tr>
<td>↓
THE BOTTOM LINE</td>
<td>In complex projects, it is very likely that there will be some schedule variance. The project manager must control the project by identifying the problem, understanding the problem, and correcting the problem.</td>
</tr>
</table>

→ **RESCHEDULE UNCOMPLETED WORK**

The ***Don Funk Music Video 8MC*** project plan is available on the companion CD-ROM.

OPEN the ***Don Funk Music Video 8MC*** project plan from the data files for this lesson.
SAVE the file as ***Don Funk Music Video 8C*** in the solutions folder for this lesson as directed by your instructor.

1. On the menu bar, click **Edit**, and then click **Go To**.

2. Key **47** in the ID box, and then click **OK**. The Gantt Chart view scrolls to display the Gantt bar for task 47, Scene 3 setup. At this point in the project, the first two scheduled scenes have been completed. This task has one day of actual work completed and one day of scheduled work remaining.

3. Scroll the Gantt Chart view so that the Scene 3 summary task appears near the top of the view. Your screen should look similar to Figure 8-13.

Figure 8-13

Gantt Chart view showing Scene 3 summary task and subtasks

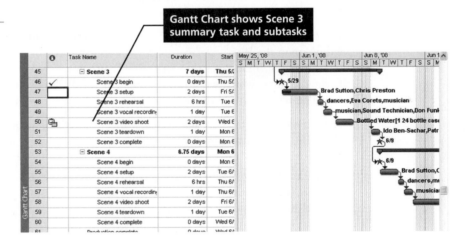

You have just been informed that on the afternoon of June 1, a lightning strike caused a nearby electrical transformer to short-circuit, and that repairs will not be completed until Thursday, June 5. You will not be able to resume work in the studio until Friday, June 6.

4. On the menu bar, click **Tools**, point to **Tracking**, and then click **Update Project**. The Update Project dialog box appears.

5. Select the **Reschedule uncompleted work to start after** option, and in the date box key or select **06/05/08**.

6. Click **OK** to close the Update Project dialog box. Microsoft Project splits task 47 so that the incomplete portion is delayed until Friday, June 6. Your screen should look similar to Figure 8-14.

Figure 8-14

Gantt Chart view showing task
47 split and rescheduled

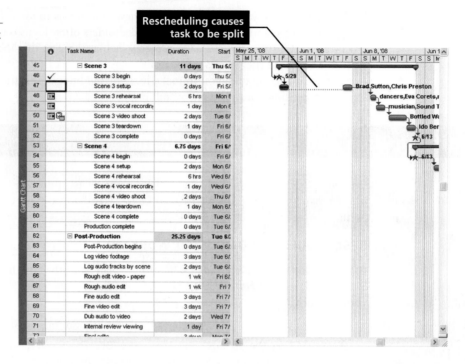

Note that although the duration of task 47 remains at two days, its finish and subsequent start dates for successor tasks have been pushed out.

7. **SAVE** the project plan. **CLOSE** the project plan.

   PAUSE. If you are continuing to the next lesson, keep Project open. If you are not continuing to additional lessons, **CLOSE** Project.

In this exercise, you rescheduled an incomplete task due to an uncontrollable delay. Depending upon the length and complexity of your project, as a project manager you may see one or many of these types of interruptions. When you reschedule incomplete work, you specify the date after which work can resume. Microsoft Project handles tasks in relation to the scheduled restart date in the following ways:

- If the task does not have any actual work recorded for it prior to the rescheduled date, and there is no constraint in place, the entire task is rescheduled to begin after that date.

- If the task has some actual work recorded prior to but not after the rescheduled date, the task is split so that all remaining work starts after the rescheduled date. The actual work is not affected.

- If the task has some actual work recorded for it prior to as well as after the rescheduled date, the task is not affected.

Keep in mind that when you address a given problem by rescheduling a task, you may create other issues or problems in the remainder of the project. This is why project management is an iterative process: a change in one part of the schedule–be it a time, cost, or scope change–can, and usually does affect the schedule elsewhere.

SUMMARY SKILL MATRIX

IN THIS LESSON YOU LEARNED	MATRIX SKILL
To establish a project baseline	Establish a project baseline
To track a project as scheduled	Track a project as scheduled
To enter the completion percentage for a task	Enter the completion percentage for a task
To track timephased actual work	Tasks and assignments: Track timephased actual work
To identify over budget tasks and resources	Identify over budget tasks and resources
To identify time and schedule problems	Reschedule uncompleted work

■ Knowledge Assessment

Matching

Match the term in column 1 to its description in column 2.

Column 1	Column 2
1. actual cost	**a.** the collecting, entering, and analyzing of actual project performance data
2. baseline	**b.** the individual or organization that provides financial support and supports the project team
3. sponsor	**c.** the cost that has been incurred so far
4. variance	**d.** in the Gantt Chart view, shows how much of the task has been completed
5. timephased fields	**e.** the total planned cost of the project when the baseline was saved
6. current cost	**f.** project work completed and recorded in a Microsoft Project file
7. actuals	**g.** a collection of key values in the project plan
8. progress bar	**h.** task, resource, and assignment values distributed over time
9. tracking	**i.** the sum of the actual and remaining cost values
10. baseline cost	**j.** a deviation from the schedule or budget established

True / False

Circle T if the statement is true or F if the statement is false.

T F **1.** You can save up to 11 different baselines for a single project plan.

T F **2.** Time-sensitive fields show task, resource, and assignment values distributed over time.

T F **3.** A check mark in the Indicators column for a task means that the task is on schedule.

T F **4.** You should save a project baseline when you have developed the project plan as fully as possible.

T F **5.** Planning refers to the collecting, entering, and analyzing of actual project performance data.

T F **6.** If you reschedule a task, the delay is shown as a split on the Gantt Chart.

T F **7.** The only true indicator of project health is whether or not the project is on schedule.

T F **8.** The Project Statistics dialog box pinpoints the point of cost variance in a project plan.

T F **9.** You can only enter completion percentages for a task in multiples of 10.

T F **10.** The remaining cost is the difference between the current cost and the actual cost.

■ Competency Assessment

→ Project 8-1: Insurance Claim Processing Baseline

You are ready to begin entering actuals on your Insurance Claim Processing plan. Before you do this, you need to save a baseline for your plan.

GET READY. Launch Microsoft Project if it is not already running.

OPEN *Insurance Claim Processing 8-1* from the data files for this lesson.

The *Insurance Claim Processing 8-1* project plan is available on the companion CD-ROM.

1. On the Project Guide toolbar, click the **Track** button.
2. In the *Track* pane, click the **Save a baseline plan to compare with later versions** link.
3. Click the **Save Baseline** button.
4. Click **Done**.
5. Click the **Show/Hide Project Guide** button.
6. **SAVE** the project plan as *Insurance Plan Processing Baseline*, and then **CLOSE** the file.

   LEAVE Project open to use in the next exercise.

→ Project 8-2: Tracking Timephased Actual Work for Don Funk Music Video

Several of the resources on the Don Funk Music Video have reported their daily actuals to you. You now need to enter them into your project plan.

OPEN *Don Funk Music Video 8-2* from the data files for this lesson.

The *Don Funk Music Video 8-2* project plan is available on the companion CD-ROM.

1. On the menu bar click **View**, then click **Task Usage**.
2. Click the **Track** button on the Project Guide toolbar. In the *Track* pane, click **Prepare to track the progress of your project** link.
3. In the *Setup Tracking* pane, select the **Always track by entering the hours of work done per time period** button, and then click the **Done** link.

4. On the menu bar, click **Edit**, then click **Go To**. In the ID box, key **47** and then click **OK**.

5. Scroll the timephased grid to the right until Friday, June 6, 2008 and Monday, June 9, 2008 are visible.

6. On the timephased grid, click the cell at the intersection of the Friday, June 6 column and Brad Sutton's Actual Work row.

7. Key **8h** and press Enter. Press the down arrow once, key **8h**, and then press Enter.

8. Enter the following actual work values in the timephased grid for the specified tasks on Monday, June 9.

TASK NAME	RESOURCE NAME	ACTUAL WORK
Scene 3 rehearsal	Eva Corets	6h
	dancers	6h
	musician	6h
Scene 3 vocal recording	Sound Technician	2h
	Don Funk	2h
	musician	2h

9. **SAVE** the project plan as *Don Funk Actual Work*, and then **CLOSE** the file.

LEAVE Project open to use in the next exercise.

■ Proficiency Assessment

Project 8-3: **Completion Percentages for HR Interview Plan**

Now that portions of your HR Interview project have been completed, you need to record the completion percentages of tasks.

OPEN *HR Interview Plan 8-3* from the data files for this lesson.

1. Activate the *Track* pane of the Project Guide toolbar, if it is not already active.

2. Click the **Prepare to track the progress of your project** link.

3. Select the option that enables you to track the percentage of work complete.

4. In the *Track* pane, select the option that enables you to begin to add progress information into the project.

5. Adjust the Custom Tracking Sheet and Gantt Chart so that the Work and % Work Complete columns are visible.

6. Enter percentages to show that the project is 100% complete through task 10, and that task 11 is 25% complete. (HINT: Remember to make entries for the subtasks, not the summary tasks.)

7. Click **Done** at the bottom of the *Incorporate Progress* pane.

8. **SAVE** the project plan as *HR Interview Plan Percentages*, and then **CLOSE** the file.

LEAVE Project open to use in the next exercise.

Project 8-4: **Don Funk Music Video Over Budget Tasks**

Even more progress has been made on the Don Funk Music Video, with tasks being complete through the Production phase. You need to analyze the project to determine the over budget tasks.

The *Don Funk Music Video 8-4* project plan is available on the companion CD-ROM.

OPEN *Don Funk Music Video 8-4* from the data files for this lesson.

1. Click the **Show/Hide Project Guide** button to activate the Project Guide, if it is not already active.
2. Activate the *Report* pane of the Project Guide.
3. Click on the link to view project costs.
4. Filter the tasks to show only the tasks that are over budget.
5. Collapse all summary tasks (hide subtasks) except for the summary task with the greatest cost variance.
6. **SAVE** the project plan as *Don Funk Over Budget*, and then **CLOSE** the file.

LEAVE Project open to use in the next exercise.

■ Mastery Assessment

⊙ Project 8-5: Office Remodel Task Delay

You have just been informed that while the plumber was re-running the pipes for the office lunchroom remodel, a pipe burst and the floor was flooded with several inches of water. It will take a week to clean and dry the water damage. You need to reschedule the remaining work on uncomplete tasks to restart when the cleanup is complete.

The *Office Remodel 8-5* project plan is available on the companion CD-ROM.

OPEN the *Office Remodel 8-5* project plan from the data files for this lesson.

1. Go to task 11.
2. Activate the Update Project dialog box.
3. Reschedule uncompleted work to start after Thursday, November 8, 2007.
4. **SAVE** the project plan as *Office Remodel Reschedule*, and then **CLOSE** the file.

LEAVE Project open to use in the next exercise.

⊙ Project 8-6: Tracking the Don Funk Music Video as Scheduled

The last phase of the Don Funk Music Video, Post-Production, is going well. Tasks are being completed on schedule. You want to update the project to show that the tasks are complete through a specified current date.

The *Don Funk Music Video 8-6* project plan is available on the companion CD-ROM.

OPEN the *Don Funk Music Video 8-6* project plan from the data files for this lesson.

1. Activate the Update Project dialog box.
2. Update the project as complete through July 14, 2008.
3. Scroll the Gantt Chart bars so that the task and progress bars on July 14, 2008 are visible.
4. **SAVE** the project plan as *Don Funk On Schedule*, and then **CLOSE** the file.

CLOSE Project.

INTERNET READY

Recall what you have learned in this lesson about tracking work, identifying time and schedule problems, and identifying over budget tasks and resources. Now, search the Internet for information on a current project of a Fortune 500 company or a company that is in the same line of business as you are. Gather as much information as possible. Using the information you have gathered, comment on this company's process for project tracking and identifying problems (or potential problems). Use actual process information, if possible, or suggest possible processes based on your research. Include your thoughts on how the company may have better identified time and schedule problems or over budget tasks and resources. Summarize your thoughts in a Word document.

Managing Multiple Projects

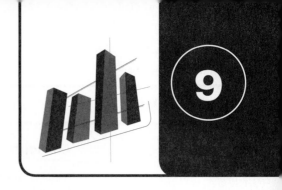

9

LESSON SKILL MATRIX

SKILLS	MATRIX SKILL
Managing Consolidated Projects	Create a consolidated project plan
Creating Dependencies Between Projects	Link tasks from two different project plans

As a project manager for Southridge video, you are responsible for managing several other projects in addition to the Don Funk Music Video. Now that progress is occurring on some of your projects, you would like to find an easier way to work with multiple project files. In this lesson, you will learn to use some of the features that Microsoft Office Project provides to enable you to consolidate multiple project files and create cross-project links.

KEY TERMS
consolidated project
ghost task
inserted project
master project
subproject

SOFTWARE ORIENTATION

Consolidated Project Gantt Chart View

The Gantt Chart view of a consolidated project allows you to see multiple projects collected in one project plan, so that you can filter, sort, and group the data, as well as see relationships (dependencies) between projects.

Figure 9-1

Gantt Chart view of a consolidated project file

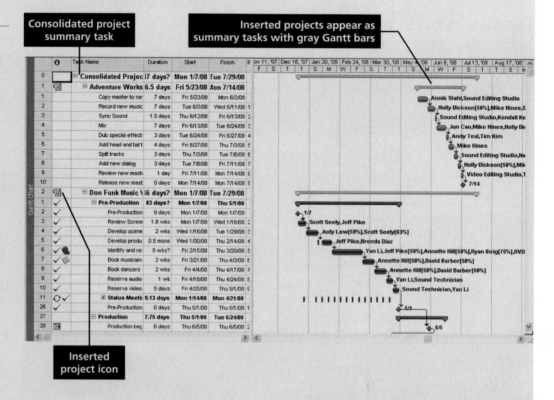

In the Gantt Chart view of a consolidated project, the inserted projects appear as summary tasks with gray Gantt bars. Also, an inserted project icon appears in the Indicators column.

Managing Consolidated Projects

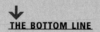
THE BOTTOM LINE

In Microsoft Project, a consolidated project enables a project manager to link and manage multiple projects within one master project file.

CD

The *Don Funk Music Video 9M* project plans are available on the companion CD-ROM.

GET READY. Before you begin these steps, launch Microsoft Project. **OPEN** the *Don Funk Music Video 9M* and *Adventure Works Promo 9M* project plans from the data files for this lesson.

SAVE the files as *Don Funk Music Video 9* and *Adventure Works Promo 9* in the solutions folder for this lesson as directed by your instructor. Make sure the *Don Funk Music Video 9* project plan is in the active window.

⊕ **CREATE A CONSOLIDATED PROJECT PLAN**

1. On the menu bar, click **Window** and then click **New Window**. The New Window dialog box appears.

2. In the Projects list, select the names of both open projects either by holding down the Ctrl key while clicking, or clicking and dragging to select both names. After you have selected both project plans, click the **OK** button.

3. Click the **Show/Hide Project Guide** button on the Project Guide toolbar. The Project Guide closes.

4. On the menu bar, click **View** and then click **Zoom**. The Zoom dialog box appears.

5. In the Zoom dialog box, click **Entire Project**, and then click the **OK** button. Microsoft Project adjusts the timescale in the Gantt Chart so that the full duration of both projects is visible. Make sure that the Duration, Start, and Finish columns are visible on your screen. If necessary, double click the right edge of any columns that display pound signs (###).Your screen should look similar to Figure 9-2.

Figure 9-2

Gantt Chart displaying both inserted project plans

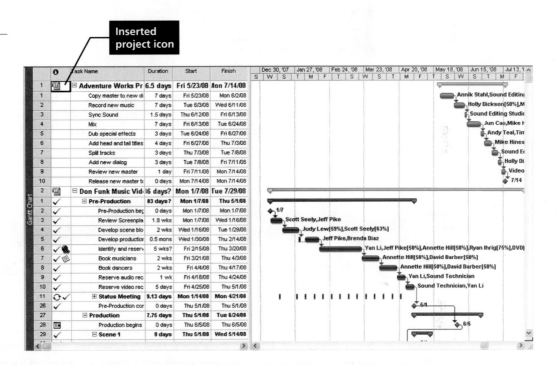

> **TAKE NOTE** When you point to the Inserted Project icon in the Indicators column, Microsoft Project displays the full path to the inserted project file.

6. **SAVE** the consolidated project plan as *Consolidated Project 9*. If you are prompted to save changes to the inserted projects, click the **Yes to All** button.

7. On the menu bar, click **Tools**, and then click **Options**. The Options dialog box appears.

8. On the View tab, under the *Outline options* section, select **Show project summary task**, and then click **OK**. Microsoft Project displays the Consolidated Project 9 summary task. Your screen should look similar to Figure 9-3.

Figure 9-3

Gantt Chart view with
Consolidated Project 9
summary task

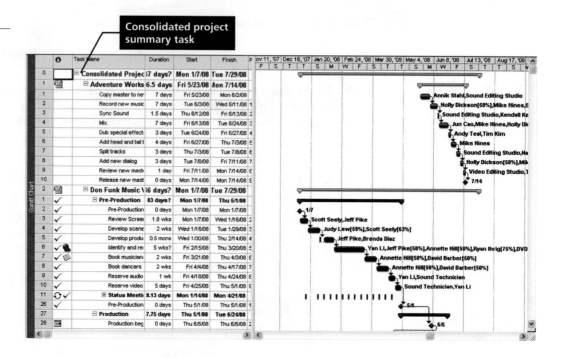

The values of the consolidated project summary task, such as duration and work, represent the rolled-up (or combined) values of both inserted projects. As Southridge Video acquires contracts for more projects, inserting them into the consolidated project plan in this way provides a single location in which to view all the activities of the company.

TAKE NOTE *If you want to add more project plans to a consolidated project, click Insert on the menu bar, and then click Project.*

9. **SAVE** the consolidated project plan, as well as the individual project plans.
PAUSE. LEAVE Project open to use in the next exercise.

In real life, it is rare that a project manager would manage only a single, small project from beginning to end. Usually, there are several complex projects that involve several people working on different tasks at different times and locations, and often for different supervisors.

As you saw in this exercise, Microsoft Project enables you to combine two projects to form a consolidated project. A **consolidated project** is a Microsoft Project file that contains other Microsoft Project files, called inserted projects. An **inserted project** is the Microsoft Project file that is inserted into another Microsoft Project file. Consolidated projects are also known as **master projects**, and inserted projects are also known as **subprojects**. The inserted projects do not really reside within the consolidated project. They are linked to it in such a way that they can be viewed and edited from the consolidated project. If an inserted project is edited outside the consolidated project, the updated information appears in the consolidated project the next time it is opened. When you save a consolidated project, any changes you have made to inserted projects are saved in the source file as well.

Using a consolidated project gives you the capability to do such things as:

- see all of your organization's project plans in a single view
- "roll up" project information to higher management levels. For example, one group's project may be an inserted project for the department's consolidated project, which then may be an inserted project for the company's consolidated project.

- divide your project plan into separate project plans to match the nature of your project. For example, you could divide your project plan into separate plans by phase, component, or location. You can then group the information back together in a consolidated project plan for a view of the complete project.

- see all of the information for your projects in one location, so you can filter, sort, and group the data as needed.

Consolidated projects use the standard Microsoft Project outlining features. For a consolidated project, the Gantt bar for an inserted project is gray and an inserted project icon appears in the Indicators column. Also, when you save a consolidated project, any changes you have made to inserted projects are saved in the source file as well. It is possible to add an unlimited number of project plans to a consolidated project file (although in real life, you are limited by time and space constraints).

■ Creating Dependencies Between Projects

↓
THE BOTTOM LINE
Sometimes, tasks or phases in one project may depend on tasks or phases in other projects. Microsoft Project enables you to show dependencies by linking tasks between projects.

USE the project plans you created in the previous exercise.

⊕ LINK TASKS FROM TWO DIFFERENT PROJECT PLANS

1. On the menu bar, click **Window**, and then click **Adventure Works Promo 9**. The *Adventure Works Promo 9* project plan is visible in the active window.

2. In the Task Name column, click the name of task 9, **Review new master**.

3. On the Standard toolbar, click the **Scroll to Task** button. On the right of the task's Gantt bar, note that one of the resources assigned to this task is Video Editing Studio. You want to use this video studio for work on the *Don Funk Music Video 9* project after this task is completed, so you need to link task 9 to a task in the *Don Funk Music Video 9*.

4. On the menu bar, click **Window**, and then click **Don Funk Music Video 9**.

5. On the menu bar, click **Edit**, and then click **Go To**. In the ID box, key 69, and then click **OK**.

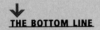 6. On the Standard toolbar, click the **Task Information** button. The Task Information dialog box appears.

   In the next two steps, you will enter the file name and task ID of the predecessor task in this format: File Name\Task ID.

7. In the Task Information dialog box, click the **Predecessors** tab.

8. In the ID column, click the next empty cell below task 67, and key **Adventure Works Promo 9\9**. (Make sure you are in the ID column when you perform this step.) The Task Information dialog box should look similar to Figure 9-4.

Figure 9-4

Task Information dialog box
with predecessor task entered

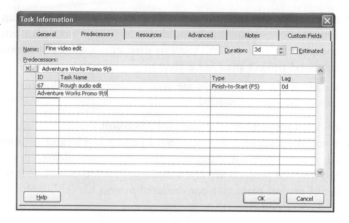

9. Press **Enter**. Notice that *External Task* appears in the remaining columns. Click **OK** to close the Task Information dialog box. Microsoft Project inserts the ghost task named *Review new master* into the project. The ghost task represents task 9 from the ***Adventure Works Promo 9*** project. Your screen should look similar to Figure 9-5.

Figure 9-5

Gantt Chart view with
Adventure Works Promo ghost
task added

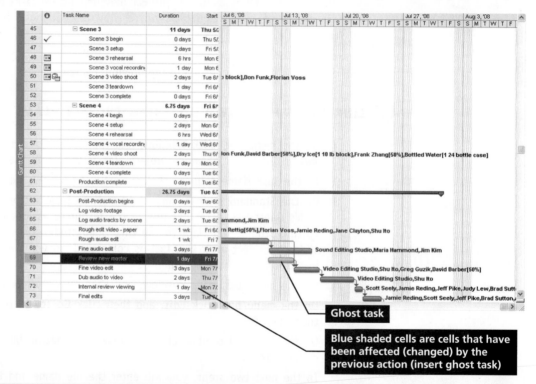

Ghost task

Blue shaded cells are cells that have
been affected (changed) by the
previous action (insert ghost task)

TAKE NOTE If you point to the Gantt bar for the ghost task, Microsoft Project will display a Screen-Tip that contains details about the ghost task, including the full path to the external project where the ghost task (the external predecessor) resides.

Now you will switch views to look at the ghost task in the ***Adventure Works Promo 9*** project plan.

10. On the menu bar, click **Window**, and then click **Adventure Works Promo 9**. You can see that the ghost task 10, *Fine video edit*, is a successor for task 9, *Review new master*. Because task 10 is a successor task with no other links to this project, it has no effect on other tasks here. The link between these two project plans will remain until you break it. When you delete a task in the source plan or the ghost task in the destination plan, Microsoft Project also deletes the corresponding task or ghost task in the other plan.

11. On the menu bar, click **Window**, and then click **Consolidated Project 9**. You can see the link between the task *Review new master* (task 9) in the first inserted project and the task *Fine video edit* (task 70) in the second inserted project. The cross-project link does not appear as a ghost task because you are looking at the consolidated project file. Your screen should look similar to Figure 9-6 (note that you may need to scroll your screen to see the entire link).

Figure 9-6

Consolidated files Gantt Chart showing link between Adventure Works task 9....

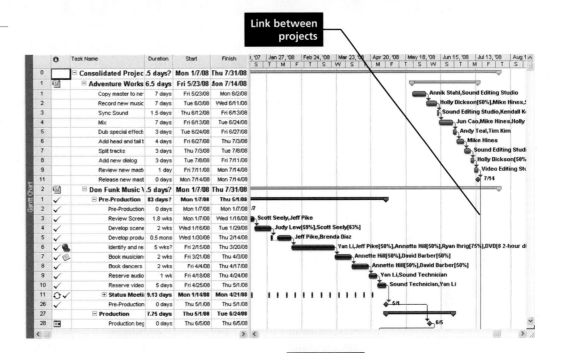

...and Don Funk task 70

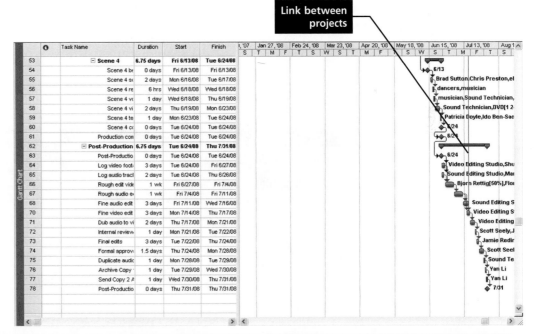

TAKE NOTE

If you do not want to see cross-project links, click Tools on the menu bar, and then click Options. On the View tab, clear the Show external successors or Show external predecessors check box.

ANOTHER WAY

When viewing a consolidated project, you can quickly create cross-project links by clicking the Link Tasks button on the Standard toolbar. Dragging the mouse between two task bars will also perform this action.

> **TAKE NOTE**
>
> Whenever you open a project plan with cross-project links, Microsoft Project will prompt you to update these cross-project links. You can suppress this prompt if you prefer not to be reminded. You can also tell Microsoft Project to automatically accept updated data from the linked project file. Click Tools on the menu bar, then click Options, and then click the View tab. Under *Cross-Project linking options for <file name>*, select the options you want.

12. **SAVE** the all of the project plans, and then **CLOSE** all files.

PAUSE. If you are continuing to the next lesson, keep Project open. If you are not continuing to additional lessons, **CLOSE** Project.

In this exercise, you linked a task in one project to a task in another project to show a dependency. Most projects are like this—they do not exist in a vacuum. There are various reasons you might need to create dependencies between projects. Some of the more common reasons are:

- The completion of a task in one project might enable the start of a task in another project. For example, one project manager may need to complete a geological study before a second project manager can begin to construct a building. These two tasks may be managed in separate project files (perhaps because they are being completed by different departments of the same company, or even two different companies), but they still have a logical dependency on each other.

- A person or piece of equipment may be assigned to a task in one project, and you need to delay the start of a task in another project until that resource completes the first task. The only commonality between the two tasks is that the same resource is required for both.

Task relationships between project files are similar to links between tasks within a project file, except that external predecessor and successor tasks have gray task names and Gantt bars. Sometimes these tasks are called ***ghost tasks*** because they are not linked to tasks within the project file, only to tasks in other project files.

SUMMARY SKILL MATRIX

IN THIS LESSON YOU LEARNED	MATRIX SKILL
To manage consolidated projects	Create a consolidated project plan
To create dependencies between projects	Link tasks from two different project plans

■ Knowledge Assessment

Fill in the Blank

Complete the following sentences by writing the correct word or words in the blanks provided.

1. For a consolidated project, the Gantt bar is _____.

2. A(n) _____ is the Microsoft Project file that is put into another Microsoft Project file.

3. If you point to the Gantt bar for a ghost task, Microsoft Project displays a(n) _____ that contains the details about the ghost task.

4. Another name for an inserted project is a(n) _____.

5. To initially select the projects that you want to insert into a consolidated project, use the _____ dialog box.

6. A(n) _____ is a Microsoft Project file that contains other Microsoft Project files.

7. The values of a consolidated project _____, such as duration and work, represent the rolled-up values of the inserted projects.

8. Another name for a consolidated project is a(n) _____ project.

9. You can create a(n) _____ between projects if the completion of a task in one project will enable the start of a task in another project.

10. A(n) _____ is not linked to a task within the consolidated project file, only to tasks in another project file.

Multiple Choice

Select the best response for the following statements.

1. How many project plans can you add to a consolidated project file?
   a. two
   b. three
   c. ten
   d. unlimited

2. When you save a consolidated project,
   a. only the consolidated project is saved.
   b. only changes to the inserted project source files are saved.
   c. changes to both the consolidated project and the inserted project source files are saved.
   d. the consolidated project is saved within the first inserted project.

3. When you insert a project in a consolidated project, an inserted project icon appears
   a. in the Task Information dialog box.
   b. in the Indicators column.
   c. in the Task Name column.
   d. in the Project Information dialog box.

4. In a consolidated project, inserted projects
   a. do not really reside within the consolidated project.
   b. can only be edited outside the consolidated project.
   c. reside within the consolidated project.
   d. none of the above

5. What is a reason to use a consolidated project plan?

   a. to see all of your company's project plans in a single view

   b. to see all of your projects' information in a single view, so you can filter, group, and sort data

   c. to "roll up" project information to higher levels of management

   d. all of the above

6. A cross project link is called a(n)

   a. dependency.

   b. subproject.

   c. integrated project.

   d. co-dependency.

7. The external predecessor and successor tasks in the task relationships between project files are sometimes called

   a. inserted tasks.

   b. phantom tasks.

   c. ghost tasks.

   d. subtasks.

8. To add plans to a consolidated project,

   a. on the Window menu, click Add Project.

   b. on the Edit menu, click Insert.

   c. on the File menu, click Insert Project.

   d. on the Insert menu, click Project.

9. Another name for a consolidated project is a(n)

   a. inserted project.

   b. subproject.

   c. master project.

   d. summary project.

10. When you create a task dependency between projects, what do you key in the ID column of the Predecessors tab of the Task Information dialog box?

   a. File Name\Task ID

   b. File Name, Task ID

   c. File Name/Task ID

   d. File Name—Task ID

■ Competency Assessment

⊙ Project 9-1: Southridge Video Consolidated Project Plan

The director of Southridge Video would like to see a consolidated project plan for all of the projects on which Southridge Video is currently working, both internal and external. You are beginning to assemble the consolidated plan.

GET READY. Launch Microsoft Project if it is not already running.

OPEN the *Don Funk Music Video 9-1* and *Gregory Weber Biography 9-1* project plans from the data files for this lesson. **SAVE** the files as *Don Funk Consolidated and Gregory Weber Consolidated*.

1. On the menu bar, click **Window** and then click **New Window**.

The *Don Funk Music Video 9-1* and *Gregory Weber Biography 9-1* project plans are available on the companion CD-ROM.

2. In the Projects list, select the names of both open projects. After you have selected both project plans, click the **OK** button.

3. Click the **Show/Hide Project Guide** button on the Project Guide toolbar to close the Project Guide.

4. On the menu bar, click **View** and then click **Zoom**.

5. In the Zoom dialog box, click **Entire Project**, and then click the **OK** button.

6. **SAVE** the consolidated project plan as *Southridge Video Consolidated*. If you are prompted to save changes to the inserted projects, click the **Yes to All** button.

7. On the menu bar, click **Tools**, and then click **Options**.

8. Under the *Outline options* section, select **Show project summary task**, and then click **OK**.

9. **SAVE** the consolidated project plan, as well as the individual project plans. **DO NOT close** the files.

   LEAVE Project and the three files open to use in the next exercise.

⊙ Project 9-2: Don Funk–Gregory Weber Dependency

Now that you have created a consolidated file for the Don Funk and Gregory Weber projects, you need to link the inserted plans to show a dependency between them. Due to resource constraints, one of the tasks (task 3) in the Gregory Weber project cannot begin until another task (task 65) in the Don Funk project is complete.

USE the project plans you created in the previous exercise.

1. On the menu bar, click **Window**, and then click *Gregory Weber Consolidated*.

2. In the task name column, click on the name of task 3, **Review Screenplay**.

3. On the Standard toolbar, click the **Task Information** button.

4. In the Task Information dialog box, click the **Predecessors** tab.

5. In the ID column, click the next empty cell below task 2, and key **Don Funk Consolidated\65**.

6. Press ⏎ Enter, and then click **OK** to close the Task Information dialog box.

7. On the menu bar, click **Window**, and then click *Southridge Video Consolidated*.

8. **SAVE** the consolidated file as *Southridge Video Consolidated 2*. If you are prompted to save changes to the inserted projects, click the **Yes to All** button. **CLOSE** all files.

   LEAVE Project open to use in the next exercise.

■ Proficiency Assessment

⊙ Project 9-3: Gregory Weber Biography Inserted Project

You are the project manager on a new project for Southridge Video, a biography of Gregory Weber. An interview with Gregory Weber is a part of the production phase of the overall project. Make the Gregory Weber Interview an inserted project of the Gregory Weber Biography project plan, inserted below the Production task.

OPEN *Gregory Weber Biography 9-3* from the data files for this lesson.

1. Click on the name of task 11, **Post-Production**.

2. On the menu bar, click **Insert**, and then click **Project**.

3. Using the Insert Project dialog box, find and select the *Gregory Weber Interview 9-3* file, and then click **Insert**.

The *Gregory Weber Biography 9-3* project plan is available on the companion CD-ROM.

The *Gregory Weber Interview 9-3* project plan is available on the companion CD-ROM.

4. On the Formatting toolbar, click the **Indent** button (green arrow).

5. Click the plus sign (+) next to the Gregory Weber Interview task name. (If necessary, identify the location of the file.)

6. **SAVE** the project plan as *Gregory Weber Biography Consolidated*. If you are prompted to save changes to the inserted project, click the **Yes to All** button. **CLOSE** the file.

PAUSE. LEAVE Project open to use in the next exercise.

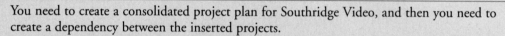

Project 9-4: Southridge Video Consolidated Dependencies

You need to create a consolidated project plan for Southridge Video, and then you need to create a dependency between the inserted projects.

OPEN *Don Funk Music Video 9-4* and *Gregory Weber Interview 9-4* from the data files for this lesson.

SAVE the files as *Don Funk Dependency* and *Gregory Weber Dependency*.

The *Don Funk Music Video 9-4* and *Gregory Weber Interview 9-4* project plans are available on the companion CD-ROM.

1. On the menu bar, click **Window** and then click **New Window**.

2. In the Projects list, select the names of both open projects. After you have selected both project plans, click the **OK** button.

3. **SAVE** the consolidated project plan as *Southridge Video Dependency*. If you are prompted to save changes to the inserted projects, click the **Yes to All** button.

4. Make sure the *Gregory Weber Dependency* project plan is visible in the active window.

5. Hide the Project Guide.

6. Click on the name of task 5, **Set up for interview**.

7. Activate the Task Information dialog box, and click on the **Predecessors** tab, if it is not already selected.

8. Click on the first empty cell in the ID column. Enter the following: **Don Funk Dependency\74**, and then press Enter. Close the dialog box.

9. Make *Southridge Video Dependency* visible in the active window.

10. Click on the name of task 74 of the *Don Funk Dependency* inserted project, and then scroll the Gantt Chart so the Gantt bar for this task is visible.

11. **SAVE** all project plans and then **CLOSE** all files.

PAUSE. LEAVE Project open to use in the next exercise.

■ Mastery Assessment

Project 9-5: Triple Consolidated Project

In addition to two Human Resource-based projects you manage, you have also just been asked to oversee the remodel of the lunchroom at your office. You have decided to put all three projects in a consolidated project so that you can see all of your responsibilities in one place.

The *HR Interview Schedule 9-5*, *Office Remodel 9-5*, and *New Employee Orientation 9-5* project plans are available on the companion CD-ROM.

OPEN *HR Interview Schedule 9-5*, *Office Remodel 9-5*, and *New Employee Orientation 9-5* from the data files for this lesson.

SAVE the files as *HR Interview 3Consolidated*, *Office Remodel 3Consolidated* and *New Employee 3Consolidated*.

1. Insert all three project plans into a new project plan.

2. **SAVE** the new project plan as *Triple Consolidated*. If you are prompted to save changes to the inserted projects, click the **Yes to All** button.

3. Activate the summary task for this project plan.

4. Hide the Project Guide.

5. Zoom the Gantt Chart to show the entire project.

6. **SAVE** all the project plans.

LEAVE Project and the project plans open to use in the next exercise.

Project 9-6: Establishing Dependencies in Triple Consolidated Plan

Now that you have created a consolidated plan for the projects for which you are responsible, you also need to establish some dependencies across inserted projects.

USE the *Triple Consolidated*, *HR Interview 3Consolidated*, and *New Employee 3Consolidated* project plans you created in the previous exercise.

1. Link task 31 of *HR Interview 3Consolidated* with task 3 of *New Employee 3Consolidated* by making task 31 a predecessor of task 3. (HINT: Make sure that New Employee 3Consolidated is in the active window, and use the Predecessors tab of the Task Information dialog box to make task 31 of HR Interview 3Consolidated a predecessor of New Employee 3Consolidated.)

2. Change the active window to Triple Consolidated, and review the link you just created.

3. **SAVE** the project plan as *Triple Consolidated Dependency*. If you are prompted to save changes to the inserted projects, click the **Yes to All** button.

4. **CLOSE** all open files.

CLOSE Project.

INTERNET READY

In this lesson, you learned how to create a consolidated project file, and how to link tasks between inserted project files. These skills are important because in real life, it is rare that anyone manages only a single project at a time. In fact, taking on new projects and multitasking seems to be the trend in today's business (and personal) world. By multitasking, you can accomplish more, but at the same time, not everyone is born with the knack for managing multiple projects. It is a skill you need to practice and fine-tune.

Search the Internet for information on Managing Multiple Projects. Look for information that will help you fine-tune your project management skills. You might find Websites, white papers, user groups, or other information that provide helpful information. Take note on what you find from these multiple sources. Develop a bulleted list or write a few paragraphs that highlight practical suggestions that will help you to better manage multiple projects.

Integrating Microsoft Project with Other Programs

LESSON SKILL MATRIX

Skills	Matrix Skill
Using a GIF Image to Display Project Information	Use a GIF image to display project information
Copying and Pasting with Microsoft Project	Copy an image from Project and paste it into another document
Using Other File Formats in Microsoft Project	Use a different file format in Microsoft Project

As a project manager for Southridge Video, communicating project information is a critical part of your role. You know that although printing project information is a common way to share details with shareholders, it has some limitations. Sometimes, project details are out of date by the time you print them. In addition, you must spend the time and financial resources to copy and distribute your information. On the other hand, publishing information online allows you provide updates in "real time" and more easily share details with a large audience of online viewers. In this lesson, you will learn various ways of getting information in and out of Microsoft Office Project by importing and exporting data between Microsoft Project and other applications.

KEY TERMS
Copy Picture
data map
export map
GIF
import map
OLE

■ SOFTWARE ORIENTATION

Microsoft Project's Copy Picture Dialog Box

The Copy Picture feature enables you to copy images and create snapshots of a view.

Figure 10-1

Copy Picture dialog box

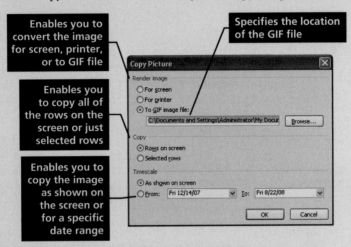

In the Copy Picture dialog box, you can render the image for screen, printer, or to a GIF file. You can also copy the entire view visible on the screen or just selected rows of a table, as well as a specified range of time.

■ Using a GIF Image to Display Project Information

 THE BOTTOM LINE   It is often useful to copy project information from Microsoft Project into other programs and formats in order to communicate project details to stakeholders.

GET READY. Before you begin these steps, launch Microsoft Project.

OPEN the *Don Funk Music Video 10M* project plan from the data files for this lesson.
SAVE the file as *Don Funk Music Video 10* in the solutions folder for this lesson as directed by your instructor.

The *Don Funk Music Video 10M* project plan is available on the companion CD-ROM.

➔ USE A GIF IMAGE TO DISPLAY PROJECT INFORMATION

1. On the menu bar, click **Project**. Point to **Filtered for: All Tasks**, and then click **Summary Tasks**. Microsoft Project filters the Gantt Chart to show only summary tasks.

2. On the menu bar, click **View**, and then click **Zoom**. The Zoom dialog box appears.

3. Click **Entire Project**, and then click **OK**. Microsoft Project adjusts the Gantt Chart timescale so that the entire project's duration is visible in the window. Your screen should look similar to Figure 10-2.

Figure 10-2

Gantt Chart view with full
project duration visible

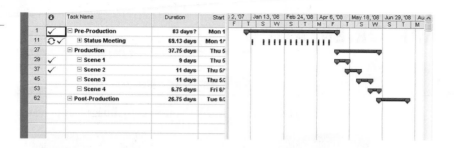

4. On the Standard toolbar, click the **Copy Picture** button. (If the Copy Picture
button is not visible, click the on the **Toolbar Options** button at the right side of
the Standard Toolbar and click **Copy Picture.** Or, click the Toolbar Options button,
point to **Add or Remove Buttons**, point to **Standard,** and then click on
Copy Picture.) The Copy Picture dialog box appears.

ANOTHER WAY You can also copy the picture by clicking Report on the menu bar, and then clicking
Copy Picture.

5. In the Copy Picture dialog box, under the *Render image* label, click **To GIF image
file.** The Microsoft Project default suggests that you save the file in the same
location as the practice file and with the same name, except with a .gif extension.
(Save your file as Don Funk Music Video 10 in the location specified by your
instructor.) Your screen should look similar to Figure 10-3.

Figure 10-3

Copy Picture dialog box

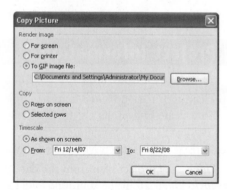

TAKE NOTE When you take a snapshot of a view, the Copy Picture dialog box enables you to select
how you want to render the image. The first two options, *For screen* and *For printer,*
copy the image to the Windows clipboard. The *To GIF image file* option enables you to
save the image as a GIF file.

6. Click **OK** to close the Copy Picture dialog box. The GIF image is saved.

7. On the menu bar, click **View,** point to **Toolbars,** and then click **Web.** The Web
toolbar appears.

ANOTHER WAY You can also right-click any toolbar to display the Toolbar shortcut menu, and then hide
or display a toolbar listed on the menu.

8. On the Web toolbar, click **Go,** and then click **Open Hyperlink.** The Open Internet
Address dialog box appears.

9. Click **Browse.** The Browse dialog box appears.

10. In the *Files of type* box, select **GIF Files** from the dropdown list.

11. Locate the GIF image named **Don Funk Music Video 10** in the location where your instructor directed you to save it earlier in this lesson. Select the GIF image, and then click **Open**.

12. In the Open Internet Address dialog box, click **OK**. Microsoft Project opens the GIF image. If you have Microsoft Internet Explorer as your default program for viewing GIF files, your screen should look similar to Figure 10-4.

Figure 10-4

Don Funk Music Video 10 displayed as a GIF file

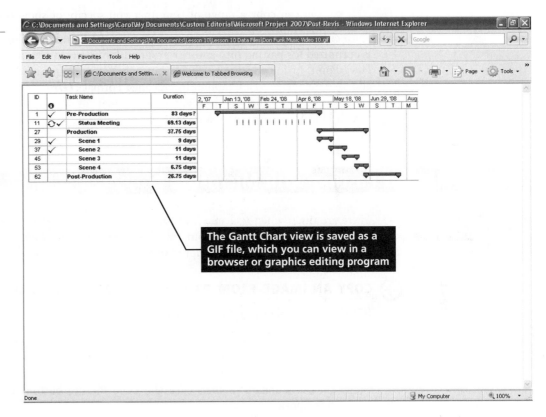

As noted above, you are looking at a graphic image of the Gantt Chart view. The GIF image shows the view you displayed in Microsoft Project almost the same as you had it set up.

TROUBLESHOOTING The Copy Picture feature is unavailable when a form view, such as the Task Form or Relationship Diagram view, is displayed.

13. **CLOSE** the program you used to display the GIF file. If the view does not automatically return to Microsoft Project, select Don Funk Music Video 10 from the Taskbar on your screen.

TAKE NOTE In addition to saving GIF images of views in Microsoft Project, you can also save Microsoft Project data as an XML file for publishing to the Web or to an intranet site.

14. **SAVE** the project plan.

PAUSE. LEAVE Project open to use in the next exercise.

In this exercise, you made a copy of a view in Microsoft Project to display in another program. As you learned in previous lessons, communicating project details to resources, managers, and other stakeholders is a very important part of being a successful project manager. Making a copy of parts of your project to share with stakeholders is one way to effectively communicate your progress.

Microsoft Project supports the standard copy and paste functionality of most Microsoft Windows programs. As you saw in this exercise, it also has an additional feature, called *Copy Picture,* which enables you to take a snapshot of a view. With Copy Picture, you have several options when taking snapshots of the active view:

- You can copy the entire view that is visible on the screen, or just selected rows of a table in a view.
- You can copy a range of time that you specify or show on the screen.

With either of these options, you can copy onto the Windows Clipboard an image that is optimized for pasting into another program for onscreen viewing (such as in Microsoft PowerPoint) or for printing (such as Microsoft Word). As you did in this exercise, you can also save the image to a Graphics Interchange Format (*GIF*) file. Once you save the image to a GIF file, you can then use it in any program that supports the GIF format. You can also use it with HTML content on a Web page.

■ Copying and Pasting with Microsoft Project

THE BOTTOM LINE

There are times when you may need to copy data to and from a project plan in order to communicate information to your stakeholders. There are several methods and options available to transfer text and graphic images.

⊙ COPY AN IMAGE FROM PROJECT AND PASTE IT INTO ANOTHER DOCUMENT

USE the project plan you created in the previous exercise.

1. Make sure that your view still shows just the project summary tasks, zoomed to show the entire project. (If it doesn't, repeat the first two steps of the previous exercise.)
2. On the Standard toolbar, click the **Copy Picture** button. The Copy Picture dialog box appears.
3. Under the *Render image* label, select **For screen**, and then click **OK**. Microsoft copies a snapshot of the Gantt Chart view to the Windows Clipboard.
4. Do one of the following:
   - If you have Microsoft Word installed, start it.
   - If you do not have Microsoft Word installed, click the **Windows Start** button, point to **All Programs**, point to **Accessories**, and then click **WordPad**.
5. In WordPad or in Microsoft Word, locate and **OPEN** the document named *Letter to Agent* in your Lesson 10 folder. (If you use WordPad, in the *Files of type* box, select **Word for Windows**.)
6. Highlight the phrase "(Insert summary Gantt Chart here.)"
7. In WordPad or in Microsoft Word, click the **Paste** button to paste the snapshot into the *Letter to Agent*. Microsoft Project pastes the snapshot of the Gantt Chart view from the Windows Clipboard into the document. The Gantt Chart cannot be edited in this format except as a graphic image. Your screen should look similar to Figure 10-5.

The *Letter to Agent* document file is available on the companion CD-ROM.

Figure 10-5

Letter to Agent document containing snapshot of Gantt Chart view

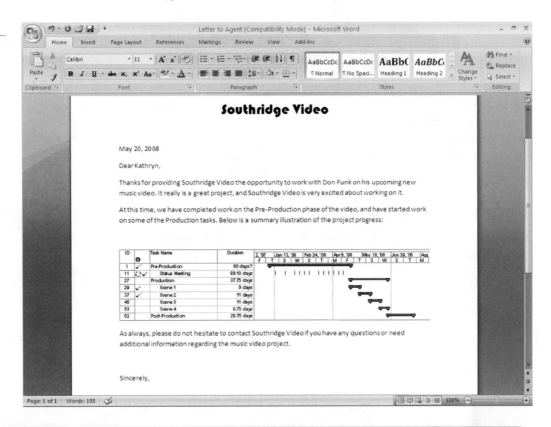

TAKE NOTE

You can also paste the image into an e-mail message or a variety of other types of documents.

8. CLOSE WordPad or Word. If prompted to save the document, click **No**.

9. SAVE the project plan.

PAUSE. LEAVE Project open to use in the next exercise.

In this exercise, you made a snapshot of a Gantt Chart and pasted the image into a letter you had prepared for Don Funk's agent. In general, you can copy and paste data to and from Microsoft Project using the various copy and paste commands in Microsoft Project (Copy, Copy Picture, Copy Cell, Paste, Paste Special, etc.). When you *copy data from* Microsoft Project, you can choose one of two options to achieve your desired results:

- You can copy text (such as task names or dates) from a table and paste it as text into the destination program. Using a Copy command enables you to edit data in the destination program.

- You can copy a graphic image of a view from Microsoft Project and paste it as a graphic image in the destination program (as you did in this exercise). You can create a graphic image of a view or part of a view using the Copy Picture command on the Report menu. Using the Copy Picture command results in an image that can only be edited with a graphics editing program (such as Microsoft Paint).

When you *paste data into* Microsoft Project from other programs, you also have two options to achieve your desired results:

- You can paste text (such as a task list) into a table in Microsoft Project. For example, you could paste a series of resource names that are organized in a vertical column from Microsoft Excel to the Resource Name column in Microsoft Project.

- You can paste a graphic image or an OLE object from another program into a graphical portion of a Gantt Chart view; to a task, resource, or assignment note; to a form view, such as the Task form view; or even to the header, footer, or legend of a view or report.

TAKE NOTE *OLE* is a protocol that allows you to transfer information, such as a chart or text (as an OLE object), to documents in different programs.

 REF

For more information about printing views and reports, go back to Lesson 7.

Be careful when pasting text as multiple columns. First, make sure that the order of the information in the source program matches the order of columns in the Microsoft Project table. (You can rearrange the order of the columns in the source program to match the order of the columns in Microsoft Project or vice versa.) Second, make sure that the columns in the source program support the same type of data as do the columns in Microsoft Project (text, currency, numbers, etc.).

■ Using Other File Formats in Microsoft Project

↓ **THE BOTTOM LINE** You can add information directly to your project plan from sources outside Microsoft Project by using import/export maps to specify how the data will be used within Microsoft Project.

GET READY. Microsoft Project has a security setting that may prevent you from opening legacy or non-default file formats. Depending on the default settings in your version of Microsoft Project, you may see a Microsoft Office Project dialog box with the following message when you try to open a file:

"You are trying to open a file saved in an older file format. Your settings do not allow you to open files saved in older file formats. To change your settings, navigate to the 'Security' tab in the Options dialog box."

In order to change your settings, on the menu bar in Microsoft Project, click **Tools**, and then click **Options**. In the Options dialog box, click the **Security** tab. Under Legacy Formats, select **Prompt when loading files with legacy or non default file format** and click **OK**.

 CD

The *Sample Task List* workbook file is available on the companion CD-ROM.

GET READY. If you have Microsoft Excel installed on your computer, open the file named *Sample Task List* from the data files for this lesson.

Review the workbook file, paying special attention to the names and order of the columns, the header row, and the actual data that is in the worksheet named *Task List*. After reviewing the workbook file, **CLOSE** the file without saving changes.

■ Use a Different File Format in Microsoft Project

1. In Microsoft Project, on the menu bar, click on **File**, and then click **Open**. The Open dialog box appears.
2. In the *Files of type* box, select **Microsoft Excel Workbooks**.
3. Locate the folder where the *Sample Task List* workbook file is saved.

TROUBLESHOOTING If you are working independently (outside of this lesson) and are trying to import an Excel file, but you are unable to view saved Microsoft Excel 2007 files from the Microsoft Project Open dialog box, you may need to save your files as Microsoft Excel 97-2003 Worksheets rather than Microsoft Excel 2007 worksheets.

4. Double-click the *Sample Task List* file. The Import Wizard appears. The Import Wizard helps you import data from a different format into Microsoft Project.
5. Click the **Next** button. The Import Wizard–Map page appears. The Import Wizard uses maps to organize the way that structured data is brought into Microsoft Project.
6. Make sure that **New map** is selected, and then click the **Next** button. The Import Wizard–Import Mode page appears.

7. Make sure that **As a new project** is selected, and then click the **Next** button. The Import Wizard–Map Options page appears.

8. Select the **Tasks** checkbox. Make sure that the **Import includes headers** checkbox is also selected. (Headers means column headings, in this case.)

9. Click the **Next** button. The Import Wizard–Task Mapping page appears. This is where you select the source worksheet and specify how you want to map the data from the source worksheet to the fields in Microsoft Project.

10. In the *Source worksheet name* list, select **Task List**. Microsoft Project analyzes the header row names from the worksheet, and then suggests the Microsoft Project field names that are likely matches. Review the fields on this screen. Your screen should look similar to Figure 10-6.

Figure 10-6

Import Wizard–Task Mapping page

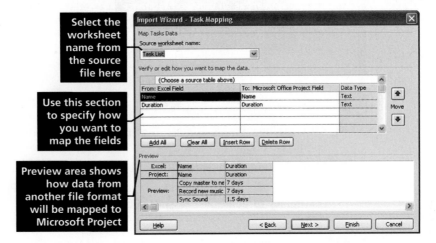

11. Click the **Next** button. The Import Wizard–End of Map Definition page appears. On this screen, you have the opportunity to save the settings for the new import map, if you desire. This is useful when you anticipate importing similar data into Microsoft Project in the future. For now, you will skip this step.

12. Click the **Finish** button. A Microsoft Office Project dialog box appears to inform you that you may be opening a file that was saved in a version of Microsoft Excel earlier than 2007. Your screen should look similar to Figure 10-7.

Figure 10-7

Microsoft Office Project dialog box

13. Click **Yes**. Microsoft Project imports the Excel data into a new Microsoft Project file. The dates you see on the timescale will differ from those shown because Microsoft Project uses the current date as the project start date in the new file. Your screen should look similar to Figure 10-8.

Figure 10-8

New Sample Task List project
plan containing tasks imported
from Excel file

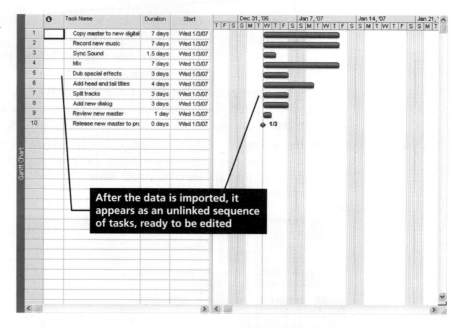

After the data is imported, it
appears as an unlinked sequence
of tasks, ready to be edited

14. **SAVE** the new file as *Sample Task List* in the solutions folder as directed by your
    instructor. **CLOSE** the new file.

15. **SAVE** the **Don Funk Music Video 10** project plan, and then **CLOSE** this file.

    PAUSE. If you are continuing to the next lesson, keep Project open. If you are not
    continuing to additional lessons, **CLOSE** Project.

In this exercise, you opened an Excel workbook in Microsoft Project, and then set up an
import/export map to control how the Excel data is imported into Microsoft Project. As you
gain experience as a project manager, you may need to incorporate data into a Microsoft
Project project plan from a variety of sources. As you saw in this exercise, you imported a task
list from a spreadsheet. You could also import resource costs from a database or a resource list
from a document.

Microsoft Project uses export maps when saving data to other files formats. An ***export map***
specifies the exact data to export and how to structure it. Similarly, Microsoft Project uses
import maps when opening data from another file format in Microsoft Project, as you saw
in this lesson. The ***import map*** specifies the exact data to import and how to structure it. In
fact, the same maps are used for both opening and saving data, so they are often referred to as
import/export maps, or ***data maps***. Data maps allow you to specify how you want individual
fields in the source program's file to correspond to individual fields in the destination program. Once you set up an import/export map, you can use it over and over again.

SUMMARY SKILL MATRIX

IN THIS LESSON YOU LEARNED	MATRIX SKILL
To use a GIF image to display project information	Use a GIF image to display project information
To copy and paste with Microsoft Project	Copy an image from Project and paste it into another document
To use other file formats in Microsoft Project	Use a different file format in Microsoft Project

■ Knowledge Assessment

Matching

Match the term in column 1 to its description in column 2.

	Column 1		Column 2
1.	Copy Picture	**a.**	a set of specifications for moving specific data to Microsoft Project fields
2.	import map	**b.**	a set of step-by-step prompts that walks you through opening a different file format in Microsoft Project
3.	OLE	**c.**	a set of specifications for moving specific data from Microsoft Project fields
4.	export map	**d.**	a function used to copy portions of a table rather than copying a graphic image
5.	GIF	**e.**	a feature that allows you to copy images and create snapshots of a view
6.	Import Wizard	**f.**	a protocol that enables you to transfer information to documents in different programs
7.	Copy	**g.**	also known as an import/export map
8.	Copy Cell	**h.**	a file type that enables you to publish Microsoft Project data to the Web or an intranet site
9.	data map	**i.**	Graphics Interchange Format, a file format that enables you to save an image for use in other programs
10.	XML	**j.**	a function that allows you to copy data from Microsoft Project and edit it in the destination program

True / False

Circle T if the statement is true or F if the statement is false.

T F 1. When saving a snapshot as a GIF file, the default location and name recommended by Microsoft Project for saving is the same name and location as the file being copied, except with a .gif extension.

T F 2. When moving data from another program into Microsoft Project, Microsoft Project is referred to as the source program.

T F 3. It is possible to import data from many different sources for use in Microsoft Project.

T F 4. The Copy Picture function is unavailable when a form view is displayed.

T F 5. Microsoft Project uses a GIF map to specify the exact data to export and how to structure it.

T F 6. When you create a data map, it can only be used once.

T F 7. When you import an Excel file into Project, Microsoft Project analyzes the header rows on the worksheet, and suggests the Project field names that are possible matches.

T F 8. When importing or exporting data, Microsoft Project is always the destination program.

T F 9. You can use the Paste function in Microsoft Project to paste a graphic image from another program into the graphical portion of a Gantt Chart view.

T F 10. When you use the Copy Picture function in Microsoft Project, you can specify the range of time that you want to copy.

■ Competency Assessment

➜ Project 10-1: Displaying Project Information

Several stakeholders of the Don Funk Music Video have asked for an update on the status and schedule for Scenes 3 and 4 of the music video. You need to take a snapshot of the current state of the project for these scenes so that you can send it to them for review.

GET READY. Launch Microsoft Project if it is not already running.

OPEN the *Don Funk Music Video 10-1* project plan from the data files for this lesson.

The *Don Funk Music Video 10-1* project plan is available on the companion CD-ROM.

1. Click the **Show/Hide Project Guide** button to close the Project Guide.
2. On the menu bar, click **Edit**, and then click **Go to**. In the ID box, key **45**, and then click **OK**.
3. Click the **Copy Picture** button.
4. In the Copy Picture dialog box, under the *Render image* label, click **To GIF image file**. Name the file *Don Funk GIF*, using the folder hierarchy as directed by your instructor. Click **OK**.
5. Activate the Web toolbar, if necessary. (On the menu bar, click **View**, point to **Toolbars**, and then click **Web**.) On the menu bar, click **View**, point to **Toolbars**, and then click **Web**.)
6. On the Web toolbar, click **Go**, and then click **Open Hyperlink**.
7. Click **Browse**.
8. In the *Files of type* box, select **GIF Files**.
9. Locate the *Don Funk GIF* file that you saved earlier in this exercise. Select the image, and then click **Open**.
10. In the Open Internet Address dialog box, click **OK**. View the image in your default program for viewing .gif files.
11. **CLOSE** the program you used to display the .gif file.
12. **SAVE** the project plan as *Don Funk GIF* and then **CLOSE** the file.

    PAUSE. LEAVE Project open to use in the next exercise.

➜ Project 10-2: HR Interview Critical Task Letter

Your manager is traveling on business, but has asked for an update on the critical tasks of the HR Interview Plan. You need to copy an image from your Project plan and paste it into a memo to send to your manager.

GET READY. OPEN the *HR Interview Plan 10-2* project plan from the data files for this lesson. **START** Microsoft Word or WordPad, and then locate and **OPEN** the document named *Memo to Manager 10-2* from the data files for this lesson.

The *HR Interview Plan 10-2* and Memo to Manager 10-2 project plans are available on the companion CD-ROM.

1. Make sure Microsoft Project is in the active view. On the menu bar, click **Project**. Point to **Filtered for: All Tasks**, and then click **Critical**.
2. On the menu bar, click **View**, and then click **Zoom**.
3. Click **Entire Project**, and then click **OK**.
4. Click the **Copy Picture** button.
5. Under the *Render image* label, select **For screen**, and then click **OK**.
6. Switch the view to Microsoft Word or WordPad.
7. In the *Memo to Manager 10-2*, highlight the phrase "(Insert image here.)"
8. **PASTE** the snapshot into the *Memo to Manager 10-2*. If you are using WordPad, you may need re-size the image (by dragging the handles on the image sides and/or corners) so that it will fit within the memo area.
9. **SAVE** the document as *Memo to Manager*. **CLOSE** the document.

10. **SAVE** the project plan as *HR Interview Critical*, and then **CLOSE** the file.

PAUSE. LEAVE Project open to use in the next exercise.

■ Proficiency Assessment

Project 10-3: Building a Audit Preparation Project Plan

You have been asked to prepare an audit preparation plan for your company's end-of-year audit. You have worked with several co-workers to develop a general task list, which you have entered into Microsoft Excel. Now you need to import this list into Microsoft Project so that you can build the project plan.

GET READY. START Microsoft Excel. **OPEN** the *Audit Prep Task List 10-3* Microsoft Excel file from the data files for this lesson. Review the layout and the data in this file. When you are finished, **CLOSE** the file and **CLOSE** Microsoft Excel.

The *Audit Prep Task List 10-3* file is available on the companion CD-ROM.

1. Make sure Microsoft Project is in the active window. Click **File**, and then click **Open**.
2. Set the file type to be **Microsoft Excel Workbook**.
3. Locate the folder containing the data files for this lesson.
4. Open the file named *Audit Prep Task List 10-3*.
5. Using the Import Wizard, select the following:

   Map: map

   Import Mode: new project

   Map Options: Tasks, including headers
6. On the Task Mapping screen, select the **Audit Task List** source worksheet name.
7. Under *Verify how you want to map the data*, in the To column, click on **(not mapped)**.
8. Select **Name** from the dropdown list, and then press Enter.
9. Finish the Import Wizard. If you receive a Microsoft Office Project message regarding older file formats, click **Yes**.
10. **SAVE** the new project plan as **Audit Prep Plan**, and then **CLOSE** the file.

    PAUSE. LEAVE Project open to use in the next exercise.

Project 10-4: Internship Report

An intern who has been working with you on the Don Funk Music Video is writing a report to turn in to the Internship office at her university. She has asked if you could provide a snapshot of Scenes 1 and 2 of the project plan to use as an illustration in her report.

OPEN the *Don Funk Music Video 10-4* project plan from the data files for this lesson. **OPEN** a blank document in Microsoft Word or WordPad.

The *Don Funk Music Video 10-4* project plan is available on the companion CD-ROM.

1. Make sure that Microsoft Project is in the active window.
2. Zoom the view to show the entire project.
3. Click on the name of task 29, **Scene 1**. Scroll the view so that task 29 is the first task below the Task Name column heading. Scroll the bar chart to this task.
4. Click and drag your cursor to select tasks 29 through 44.
5. Copy the picture using these options:

   • For screen

   • Selected rows

   • As shown on screen
6. Switch your view to Microsoft Word or WordPad.

7. **PASTE** the image into the open blank document.

8. **SAVE** the document as *Don Funk Scene 1-2*, and then **CLOSE** Word or WordPad.

9. **CLOSE** the *Don Funk Music Video 10-4* project plan without saving.

   PAUSE. LEAVE Project open to use in the next exercise.

■ Mastery Assessment

➔ Project 10-5: Building a Resource List

You are assembling a resource list for several upcoming projects at Southridge Video. Because there are several people who will use this resource list for different purposes, you want to build this list in an Excel file for ease of use by everyone.

GET READY. START Microsoft Excel and **OPEN** a new workbook, if necessary.

1. Enter the following data into the Microsoft Excel worksheet, using column names. You may use the column names provided, or substitute a column name that you think more closely corresponds with the column names in Microsoft Project.

Name	Initials	Rate
Mary Baker	MB	18.50/hr
Ryan Calafato	RC	20.00/hr
John Frum	JF	1000/wk
Arlene Huff	AH	25.00/hr
Linda Martin	LM	2000/wk
Merav Netz	MN	18.50/hr
John Peoples	JP	20.00/hr
Ivo Salmre	IS	1500/wk
Tony Wang	TW	19.00/hr

2. Name the worksheet *Resources* (on the tab at the lower left corner of the workbook).

3. **SAVE** the file as *General Resources List*. If you are using Excel 2007, set the file type as Microsoft Excel 97-2003 Workbook.

4. **CLOSE** the file, and then **CLOSE** Microsoft Excel.

   PAUSE. Continue to the next exercise.

➔ Project 10-6: General Resource Project Plan

Now that you have developed and distributed a general resource list, you would like to import it into Microsoft Project so that you can begin to use it on your own projects.

GET READY. START Microsoft Project if it is not already running.

1. Locate and open the *General Resources List* Microsoft Excel workbook you created in the previous exercise.

2. Using the Import Wizard, create a new map as a new project to map resource information.

3. Map the data using the sheet named Resources, and then verify or edit the mapping that Microsoft Project suggests.

4. Finish the mapping without saving the map.

5. If you receive a Microsoft Office Project message regarding older file formats, click **Yes**.

6. In the new project plan that is generated, change the view to the Resource Sheet.

7. **SAVE** the project plan as *General Resources List*, and then **CLOSE** the file. **CLOSE** Project.

INTERNET READY

As you learned in this lesson, it is possible to import data from a variety of sources for use in Microsoft Project. One of the most useful functions for beginning project managers is the ability to import a task or resource list from Microsoft Excel or Word into Microsoft Project.

Search the Internet for a Microsoft Word or Excel template or file that provides a list of data that could be tracked in greater detail using Microsoft Project. Some examples might be a marketing research plan, a task list for planning a wedding or building a house, activities for searching for new employment, or possibly planning an office move. Review in detail the file that you select. (If possible, download the file or template.) Write several paragraphs explaining the layout of the file you have selected and the information it contains, and then explain how the data could be better managed in Microsoft Project. Include ideas on tasks, resources, timelines, critical path, and costs.

⟳ Circling Back

Mete Goktepe is a project management specialist at Woodgrove Bank. He has put together the initial components of a project plan for a Request for Proposal (RFP) process to evaluate and select new commercial lending software. This process entails determining needs, identifying vendors, requesting proposals, reviewing proposals, and selecting the software.

Now that Mete has established the foundation of the project plan, he will begin to put the plan into action.

⊙ Project 1: FORMATTING AND PRINTING THE PROJECT PLAN

Acting as Mete, you need to change the appearance of some of your data before sharing it with stakeholders. You then need to prepare to print the project plan for distribution.

GET READY. Launch Microsoft Project if it is not already running.

OPEN the *RFP Bank Software Plan* project plan from the data files for this lesson.

The *RFP Bank Software Plan* project plan is available on the companion CD-ROM.

1. On the menu bar, click **Tools**, and then click **Options**.
2. In the Options dialog box, click the **View** tab, click the **Show project summary task** check box, and click **OK**.
3. Adjust your screen so that the Duration and Start columns are fully visible and expanded to show entire values.
4. On the menu bar, click **View**, and then click **More Views**.
5. Make sure that the Gantt Chart option is highlighted, and then click the **Copy** button.
6. In the Name field, key **Custom Gantt Chart**, and then click **OK**.
7. Make sure that the Custom Gantt Chart option is highlighted, and then click the **Apply** button.
8. On the menu bar, click **Format**, and then click **Gantt Chart Wizard**.
9. Click the **Next** button, and then click the **Other** button. Select **Standard Style: 2** from the drop-down list next to the Other button.
10. Click the **Finish** button. Click the **Format It** button, and then click the **Exit Wizard** button.
11. **SAVE** the project plan as *RFP Bank Software Plan 1* in the solutions folder for this lesson as directed by your instructor.
12. On the Standard toolbar, click the **Print Preview** button.
13. On the Print Preview toolbar, click the **Page Setup** button.
14. Click the **Header** tab. Select the **Center** alignment tab.
15. In the General box, click on **Company Name** and then click the **Add** button.
16. Click the **Legend** tab. Select the **Left** alignment tab.
17. In the Alignment box, position your cursor after &[Date] and then press ⏎Enter.
18. Key **Start Date:** followed by a space. In the General box, select **Project Start Date** from the drop-down list, and then click **Add**.
19. Click **OK**.
20. On the Print Preview toolbar, click **Close**.
21. **SAVE** the project plan.

    PAUSE. LEAVE Project and the project plan open to use in the next exercise.

➔ Project 2: Tracking the Project Plan

Now that work is starting on your project, it is time to begin tracking progress. You need to save a baseline, track actual work, and enter completion percentages.

GET READY. SAVE the open project plan as *RFP Bank Software Plan 2*. If necessary, activate the Project Guide.

1. On the Project Guide toolbar, click the **Track** button.
2. In the *Track* pane, click the **Save a baseline plan to compare with later versions** link. Click the **Save baseline** button.
3. Click **Done**.
4. Click and drag your cursor to select tasks 5 and 6.
5. On the menu bar, click **Tools**, point to **Tracking**, and then click **Update Project**.
6. Make sure the **Update work as complete through** option is selected. In the adjacent date box, key or select **6/1/08**. Next to *For*, click **Selected tasks**, and then click **OK**.
7. In the *Track* pane, click the **Prepare to track the progress of your project** link. Select the **Always track by entering the Percent of Work Complete** button, and then click the **Done** link.
8. In the *Track* pane, click the **Incorporate progress information into the project** link. Slide the divider bar between the table and Gantt bar chart so that the % Work Complete column is visible.
9. In the % Work Complete column for task 7, key or select **100**, and then press Enter.
10. At the bottom of the *Incorporate Progress* pane, click the **Done** link.
11. In the *Track* pane, click the **Prepare to track the progress of your project** link. Select the **Always track by entering the hours of work done per time period** button, and then click the **Done** link.
12. Click on the name of task 8, **Draft RFP**. Click the **Scroll to Task** button.
13. On the timephased grid, click the yellow cell at the intersection of the Tuesday, May 20 column and the task 8 Actual Work (Act. Work) row. Key **16h** and press Enter.
14. Repeat this step for Wednesday through the following Monday, entering **16h** for each workday.
15. Click on the name of task 9, **Review RFP with management and commercial lending representatives**. Click the **Scroll to Task** button.
16. In the timephased grid, click the cell at the intersection of the Tuesday, May 27 column and Eli Bowen's Actual Work row for his assignment on task 9.
17. Enter the following actual work values in the timescale grid:

RESOURCE NAME	TUESDAY'S ACTUAL WORK
Eli Bowen	8h
Mete Goktepe	8h
Nicole Holiday	4h
Marc J. Ingle	8h
Kevin Kennedy	8h
Mike Tiano	8h
Large Conference Room	8h

18. SAVE the project plan.

    PAUSE. LEAVE Project and the project plan open to use in the next exercise.

⊕ Project 3: **Importing Data into the Project Plan**

Next, you need to prepare some of your data to share with your stakeholders. Finally, you will import some additional tasks to add to your project plan.

GET READY. SAVE the open project plan as *RFP Bank Software Plan 3*.

1. Switch the view to the Gantt Chart view.
2. Adjust the table and bar chart so that only the Task Name and Duration columns are visible in the table.
3. On the menu bar, click View, and then click Zoom. Click Entire Project, and then click OK.
4. On the Standard toolbar, click the Copy Picture button. Under the *Render image* label, select For screen, and then click OK.
5. Launch either Microsoft Word or WordPad.
6. PASTE the snapshot into a new blank document to send to your stakeholders. You will finish the memo to the stakeholders later.
7. SAVE the document as *RFP Bank Software Memo*, and then CLOSE the document.
8. SAVE the project plan.
9. On the menu bar, click on File, and then click Open.
10. In the *Files of type* box, select Microsoft Excel Workbooks.
11. Locate the *RFP Additional Tasks* Microsoft Excel workbook in the data files for this exercise. Double-click the *RFP Additional Tasks* file.
12. In the Import Wizard, select the following options:

    Map: New map

    Import Mode: Append the data to the active project

    Map Options: Tasks, including headers
13. On the Task Mapping page of the Import Wizard, select More Tasks from the *Source worksheet name* list.
14. Click Next. Click Finish. Click Yes.
15. SAVE the project plan, and then CLOSE the file.

    CLOSE Microsoft Project.

The *RFP Additional Tasks* workbook is available on the companion CD-ROM.

Fine-Tuning Tasks

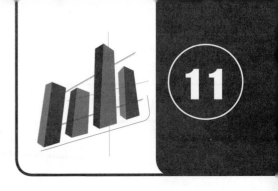

LESSON SKILL MATRIX

SKILLS	MATRIX SKILL
Managing Task Constraints and Dependencies	Explore the effects of constraints and dependencies on task scheduling
Setting Deadline Dates	Set a deadline date for a task
Establishing Task Priorities	Establish task priorities

You are a video project manager for Southridge Video, and one of your primary responsibilities recently has been to manage the new Don Funk Music Video project. You have learned most of the basics for building a project plan, communicating project data to shareholders, and tracking work. In this lesson, you will learn some of the more advanced features of Microsoft Office Project that focus on fine-tuning details in a project plan *prior* to saving a baseline and commencing project work.

KEY TERMS
deadline
resource leveling
task priority

SOFTWARE ORIENTATION

Microsoft Project's Task Information Dialog Box—General Tab

The General tab of the Task Information dialog box provides general information about the selected task, and allows you to make changes and updates to the task.

Figure 11-1

The General tab of the Task Information dialog box

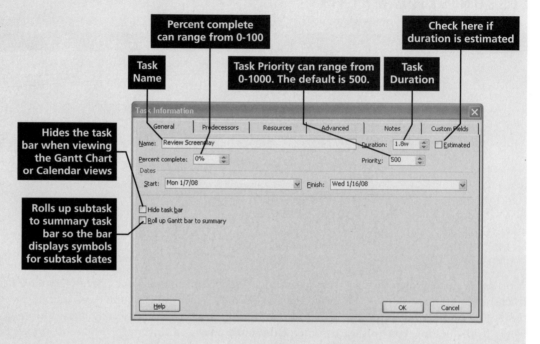

On the General tab, you can edit the task name, update the duration and the percent complete, change the priority, and modify the start and finish dates.

■ Managing Task Constraints and Dependencies

THE BOTTOM LINE As you are building a project plan, you will usually use both task dependencies and constraints within the plan. You can control how Microsoft Project schedules these elements.

⊙ EXPLORE THE EFFECTS OF CONSTRAINTS AND DEPENDENCIES ON TASK SCHEDULING

The **Don Funk Music Video 11M** project plan is available on the companion CD-ROM.

GET READY. Before you begin these steps, launch Microsoft Project.

OPEN the **Don Funk Music Video 11M** project plan from the data files for this lesson.

SAVE the file as **Don Funk Music Video 11** in the solutions folder for this lesson as directed by your instructor.

1. Make sure the view is the Gantt Chart view. Review the start-to-finish dependency between tasks 3 and 4. Your screen should look similar to Figure 11-2.

Figure 11-2

Gantt Chart view with start-to-finish dependency between tasks 3 and 4

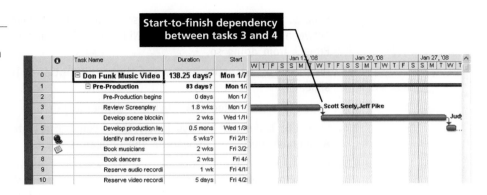

Start-to-finish dependency between tasks 3 and 4

Assume you have just been told that task 4, Develop scene blocking and schedule, must begin no later than Thursday, January 10, 2008.

2. In the Task Name column, select the name of task 4, **Develop scene blocking and schedule**.

3. On the Standard toolbar, click the **Task Information** button. The Task Information dialog box appears.

4. Click the **Advanced** tab.

5. In the *Constraint type* box, select **Start No Later Than**. In the *Constraint date* box, key or select **January 10, 2008**.

6. Click **OK** to close the dialog box. The Planning Wizard appears, notifying you of a scheduling conflict between the constraint you just applied to task 4, and the existing task dependency between tasks 3 and 4. Your screen should look similar to Figure 11-3.

Figure 11-3

Planning Wizard dialog box

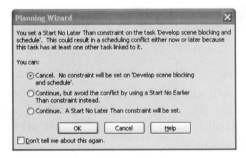

7. Under *You can:*, click **Continue**. A Start No Later Than constraint will be set.

8. Click **OK**.

9. A second alert appears. Click **Continue. Allow the scheduling conflict**, and then click **OK**. Microsoft Project applies the SNLT constraint to task 4 and reschedules it to start on Thursday. Your screen should look similar to Figure 11-4.

Figure 11-4

Gantt Chart view showing tasks 3 and 4 with new constraints

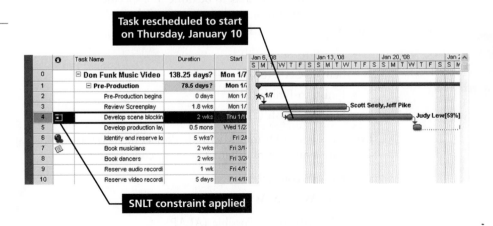

Task rescheduled to start on Thursday, January 10

SNLT constraint applied

Usually, Microsoft Project would reschedule task 4 to avoid the negative slack between tasks 3 and 4, but the SNLT constraint you applied prevents Microsoft Project from doing so.

10. On the menu bar, click **Tools**, and then click **Options**. The Options dialog box appears.

11. In the Options dialog box, click the **Schedule** tab.

12. Clear the **Tasks will always honor their constraint dates** box, and then click **OK**. A calendar alert icon appears in the indicators column for task 4.

13. Rest the mouse pointer on the calendar alert icon in the indicators column. A ScreenTip appears. Now Microsoft Project honors the task relationship over the constraint. Microsoft Project preserves the constraint information, but does not honor the constraint. If the scheduling conflict is removed (by a change in task duration, for example), Microsoft Project would then honor the constraint. Your screen should look similar to Figure 11-5.

Figure 11-5

Calendar alert icon ScreenTip

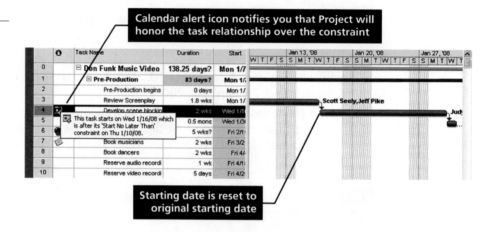

14. On the menu bar, click **Tools**, and then click **Options**.

15. Click the **Tasks will always honor their constraint dates** box on the Schedule tab, and then click **OK**. This restores the default behavior to Microsoft Project, and task 3 is rescheduled to honor its constraint date.

16. SAVE the project plan.

   PAUSE. LEAVE Project open to use in the next exercise.

In this exercise, you reviewed two of the basic elements of scheduling: constraints and task relationships, and how you can control the actions of Microsoft Project when there is a conflict between a constraint and a task relationship.

Projects require some tasks to be done in a specific order. Recall from Lesson 1 that when you link the tasks in a project plan, you establish a *relationship* between the tasks. The four possible types of task relationships are:

X REF

For a review of task relationships, refer back to Lesson 1.

- Finish-to-Start (FS)
- Start-to-Start (SS)
- Finish-to-Finish (FF)
- Start-to-Finish (SF)

Every task you enter into Microsoft Project has some type of constraint applied to it. There are a number of different types of constraints:

- Flexible constraints
  a. As Soon As Possible (ASAP)
  b. As Late As Possible (ALAP)

- Semi-flexible constraints
    a. Start No Earlier Than (SNET)
    b. Start No Later Than (SNLT)
    c. Finish No Earlier Than (FNET)
    d. Finish No Later Than (FNLT)

- Inflexible constraints
    a. Must Start On (MSO)
    b. Must Finish On (MFO)

 REF For a review of task constraints, refer back to Lesson 4.

Within the same project, you usually use both constraints and task dependencies. Whenever possible, you should use task dependencies and avoid semi-flexible or inflexible constraints. For tasks that have both dependencies and semi-flexible or inflexible constraints, you can control how Microsoft Project should schedule them. As you saw in this exercise, Microsoft Project always honors constraint dates over task dependencies by default, even if this causes negative slack.

 REF For a review of negative slack, refer back to Lesson 4.

It is a good idea to develop a consistent strategy for using constraints and dependencies in your projects. We recommend using the default behavior of honoring constraint dates. As you learned in previous lessons, you should always set task relationships in your projects, and then apply semi-flexible or inflexible constraints only when truly necessary. Recall that Microsoft Project alerts you to conflicts between relationships and constraints, so that you can maintain control over the rules that Microsoft Project follows. It is important to make sure that you understand the effects of the constraints you apply on the overall project schedule–not just on the task to which you have applied the constraint.

■ Setting Deadline Dates

 THE BOTTOM LINE Assigning a deadline date to a task, rather than a semi-flexible or inflexible constraint, allows the most flexibility in scheduling tasks.

⊙ SET A DEADLINE DATE FOR A TASK

USE the project plan you created in the previous exercise.

1. On the menu bar, click **Edit**, and then click **Go To**.
2. In the ID box, key **26** and then click **OK**. Microsoft Project displays task 26. You want to make sure that the pre-production tasks conclude by April 30, 2008, so you will enter a deadline date for this milestone.
3. If the *Tasks* pane is not already displayed, on the Project Guide, click **Tasks**. The *Tasks* pane appears.
4. In the *Tasks* pane, click the **Set deadlines and constrain tasks** link. The *Deadlines and Constraints* pane appears.
5. In the dropdown date box under *Set a deadline*, key or select **4/30/08**, and then press the Tab key. Microsoft Project inserts a deadline marker in the chart portion of the Gantt Chart view. Your screen should look similar to Figure 11-6.

Figure 11-6

Gantt Chart with deadline
marker assigned to task 26

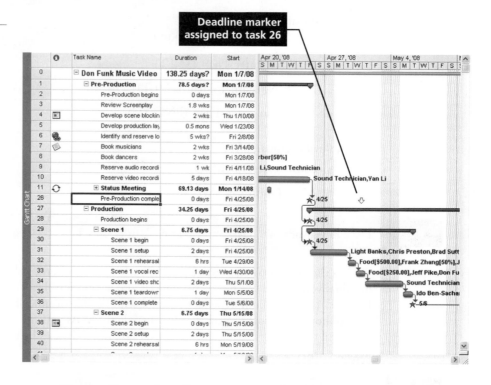

The deadline marker allows you to monitor how close the pre-production phase is
to missing its deadline. If the scheduled completion of the pre-production phase
moves past 4/30/08, Microsoft Project will display a missed deadline indicator in
the Indicators column.

 **ANOTHER WAY**

> You can also enter a deadline date for a selected task via the Task Information dialog
> box. Click the Advanced tab and enter a date in the Deadline box.

6. Select the name of task 27, **Production**.

7. In the dropdown date box under *Set a deadline*, key or select **6/23/08**, and then
press the [Tab] key. Microsoft Project inserts a deadline date marker for the summary task. Scroll the chart portion of the Gantt Chart view to the right to view the
marker.

TAKE NOTE

> To remove a deadline from a task, clear the date field in the *Deadlines and Constraints*
> pane of the Project Guide, or clear the Deadline field on the Advanced tab of the Task
> Information dialog box.

8. In the *Deadlines and Constraints* pane, click the **Done** link.

TAKE NOTE

> Entering a deadline date has no effect on the scheduling of a summary or subtask,
> except for one situation. A deadline date will cause Microsoft Project to notify you if
> the scheduled completion of a task exceeds its deadline date. The one instance in which
> the deadline date can affect the scheduling of a summary task (or any task) involves
> slack. When a task is assigned a deadline date, its slack does not extend beyond the
> deadline date.

9. SAVE the project plan.

PAUSE. LEAVE Project open to use in the next exercise.

In this exercise, you entered a deadline date for a task rather than entering a constraint. It is a common mistake of new Microsoft Project users to place semi-flexible or inflexible constraints on too many tasks in their projects. As you saw in the previous exercise, such constraints greatly limit your scheduling flexibility.

Rather than using semi-flexible or inflexible constraints, a better approach to scheduling is to use the default As Soon As Possible (ASAP) constraint and then enter a deadline for the task. A ***deadline*** is a date value you enter for a task that indicates the latest date by which you want the task to be completed, but the deadline date itself does not constrain the task. When you enter a deadline date, Microsoft Project displays a deadline marker on the Gantt Chart and alerts you if the task's finish date moves beyond the deadline.

■ Establishing Task Priorities

 THE BOTTOM LINE   Microsoft Project uses task priorities to determine which tasks can be delayed in order to resolve periods of resource overallocation. The default task priority Microsoft Project assigns is 500.

⊕ ESTABLISH TASK PRIORITIES

USE the project plan you created in the previous exercise.

1. In the Task Name column, select the name of task 6, **Identify and reserve locations**.
2. On the Standard toolbar, click the **Task Information** button. The Task Information dialog box appears.
3. Click the **General** tab.
4. In the Priority box, key or select **1000**. Your screen should look similar to Figure 11-7.

Figure 11-7

Task Information dialog box with 1000 priority for task 6

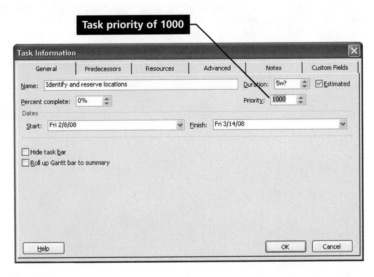

5. Click **OK** to close the dialog box. Microsoft Project adjusts the task's priority. Note that there is no visual indicator for the adjusted priority, and the effect of the new task's priority is only apparent after resource leveling.

 **ANOTHER WAY**   To simultaneously adjust the priority of multiple tasks, select the desired tasks by clicking and holding the Ctrl key. Click the Task Information button, click the General tab, and enter the desired priority in the priority box. Note that because you have selected multiple tasks, this dialog box is now labeled "Multiple Task Information."

6. SAVE the project plan, and then close the file.

PAUSE. If you are continuing to the next lesson, keep Project open. If you are not continuing to additional lessons, **CLOSE** Project.

In this exercise, you set the priority for a task, giving it the highest priority possible in Microsoft Project (1000). A task with a priority of 1000 is never delayed by leveling. ***Resource leveling*** is the process of delaying a resource's work on a task to resolve an overallocation. Depending on the options you choose, resource leveling might delay the start date of an assignment or an entire task, or split up the work on a task. Resource leveling evaluates several factors to determine how to resolve resource overallocation.

LOOKING AHEAD You can find more information about resource leveling in Lesson 12.

One of the factors evaluated during resource leveling is task priorities. ***Task priority*** is a numeric ranking between 0 and 1000 of a task's importance and appropriateness for leveling. When you level resources, Microsoft Project will delay a task with a lower priority before delaying a task with a higher priority in order to resolve a resource overallocation:

- Tasks with priority 0 are leveled first, so they are likely to be delayed by leveling.
- Tasks with priority 1000 are never delayed by leveling. Assign this task priority carefully, as it limits Microsoft Project's capabilities to resolve resource overallocations.

TAKE NOTE To remove a deadline from a task, clear the date field in the *Deadlines and Constraints* pane of the Project Guide, or clear the Deadline field on the Advanced tab of the Task Information dialog box.

SUMMARY SKILL MATRIX

IN THIS LESSON YOU LEARNED	MATRIX SKILL
To manage task constraints and dependencies	Explore the effects of constraints and dependencies on task scheduling
To set deadline dates	Set a deadline date for a task
To establish task priorities	Establish task priorities

■ Knowledge Assessment

Fill in the Blank

Complete the following sentences by writing the correct word or words in the blanks provided.

1. A numeric ranking of a task's importance and appropriateness for leveling is called _____.

2. A better approach to scheduling tasks is to use a deadline date rather than a(n) _____.

3. When you link the tasks in a project plan, you establish a(n) _____ between the tasks.

4. _____ is the process of delaying a resource's work on a task to resolve an overallocation.

5. Microsoft Project honors constraint dates over task dependencies, even if this causes _____.

6. Tasks with a priority of _____ are leveled first.

7. When you enter a deadline date, Microsoft Project alerts you if the task's _____ moves beyond the deadline.

8. A(n) _____ is a value you enter for a task that indicates the latest date by which you want the task to be completed.

9. The default task priority value for all tasks is _____.

10. Tasks with a priority of _____ are never delayed by leveling.

Multiple Choice

Select the best response for the following statements.

1. Microsoft Project uses _____ to determine which tasks can be delayed in order to resolve periods of resource overallocation.

   a. load balancing

   b. random selection

   c. task priorities

   d. task deadlines

2. The numeric ranking range for task priority is

   a. 1 to 100.

   b. 0 to 100.

   c. 1 to 500.

   d. 0 to 1000.

3. Entering a deadline date has no effect on the scheduling of a summary or subtask, except when the task involves

   a. slack.

   b. the critical path.

   c. dependencies.

   d. a priority equal to 0.

4. Which of the following is NOT a semi-flexible constraint?

   a. Start No Earlier Than

   b. Must Start On

   c. Finish No Earlier Than

   d. Start No Later Than

5. Depending on options you choose, resource leveling might

   a. delay the start date of an assignment.

   b. delay the start date of an entire task.

   c. split up the work on a task.

   d. all of the above.

6. What must be done to remove a deadline from a task?

   a. Delete the deadline indicator from the bar chart portion of the Gantt Chart.

   b. Slide the deadline indicator off of the active portion of the Gantt Chart.

   c. Clear the Deadline field on the Advanced tab of the Project Information dialog box.

   d. Change the deadline date to 00/00/00.

7. Which of the following is NOT a type of task relationship?

   a. Finish-to Start

   b. Start-to-Finish

   c. Start-to Start

   d. Start-No-Earlier-Than

8. A deadline date

   a. is the due date of the project.

   b. does not constrain a task.

   c. is not indicated on the Gantt Chart.

   d. is a semi-flexible constraint.

9. Which of the following allows the most flexibility in scheduling a task?

   a. semi-flexible constraint

   b. deadline date

   c. inflexible constraint

   d. none of the above

10. By default, Microsoft Project honors

   a. constraint dates over dependencies.

   b. deadline dates over dependencies.

   c. dependencies over constraint dates.

   d. negative slack over dependencies.

■ Competency Assessment

➔ Project 11-1: Setting a Constraint for Insurance Claim Processing

You are managing an insurance claim processing process, and have just been informed that the repairer, Chris Gray, will not be available for work after June 10, 2008, for several days. You need to set a constraint on one of his tasks to reflect this information, even if it causes a conflict with existing task relationships.

GET READY. Launch Microsoft Project if it is not already running. **OPEN** *Insurance Claim Processing 11-1* from the data files for this lesson.

The *Insurance Claim Processing 11-1* project plan is available on the companion CD-ROM.

1. Click on the name of task 16, **Repairer notifies adjuster.**
2. On the Standard toolbar, click the **Task Information** button. Click the **Advanced** tab.
3. In the *Constraint type* box, select **Start No Later Than.** In the *Constraint date* box, key or select **6/10/08.** Click **OK.**
4. In the Planning Wizard dialog box that appears, select the **Continue. A Start No Later Than constraint will be set.** option. Click **OK.**
5. In the next Planning Wizard dialog box that appears, select the **Continue. Allow the scheduling conflict.** option, and then click **OK.**
6. **SAVE** the project plan as *Insurance Claim Processing Constraint*, and then **CLOSE** the file.

   PAUSE. LEAVE Project open to use in the next exercise.

➔ Project 11-2: Don Funk Music Video Deadlines

You have just received additional information about scheduling on the Don Funk Music Video, and need to add some deadline dates to your project plan.

OPEN *Don Funk Music Video 11-2* from the data files for this lesson.

The *Don Funk Music Video 11-2* project plan is available on the companion CD-ROM.

1. Select the name of task 9, **Reserve audio recording equipment.**
2. On the Standard toolbar, click the **Scroll to Task** button.
3. If the *Tasks* pane is not displayed, click **Tasks** on the Project Guide.
4. In the *Tasks* pane, click the **Set deadlines and constrain tasks** link.
5. In the date box under *Set a deadline*, key or select **5/1/08**, and then press Tab.
6. Select the name of task 61, **Production complete.**
7. On the Standard toolbar, click the **Scroll to Task** button.
8. In the date box, key or select **6/20/08**, and then press Tab.
9. In the Deadlines and Constraints pane, click **Done.**
10. **SAVE** the project plan as *Don Funk Deadlines*, and then **CLOSE** the file.

    PAUSE. LEAVE Project open to use in the next exercise.

■ Proficiency Assessment

➔ Project 11-3: Task Priorities for HR Interview Plan

You are making some changes and adjustment to your HR Interview project plan, and have decided to establish task priorities for some tasks in case there are resource allocation issues later. Make the indicated priority assignments.

The *HR Interview 11-3* project plan is available on the companion CD-ROM.

OPEN *HR Interview 11-3* from the data files for this lesson.

1. Select the name of task 21.
2. Open the Task Information dialog box. Select the **General** tab.
3. Key or select a priority of **800**. Click **OK**.
4. Select the names of tasks 13 and 14.
5. Open the Task Information dialog box and select the **General** tab.
6. Key or select a priority of **400** for these two tasks. Click **OK**.
7. **SAVE** the project plan as *HR Interview Priorities*, and then **CLOSE** the file.

   PAUSE. LEAVE Project open to use in the next exercise.

→ Project 11-4: Deadline Dates for Office Remodel

You would like to keep a closer eye on some of the tasks for the lunchroom office remodel project you are managing. You decide it is a good idea to add some deadline dates to several tasks. You know that Microsoft Project will alert you if a task's finish date moves beyond the deadline.

The *Office Remodel 11-4* project plan is available on the companion CD-ROM.

OPEN *Office Remodel 11-4* from the data files for this lesson.

1. Select the name of task 7.
2. Activate the *Deadlines and Constraints* pane from the *Tasks* pane of the Project Guide.
3. Set a deadline date of 11/2/07.
4. Select the name of task 14.
5. Set a deadline date of 11/23/07.
6. Close the *Deadlines and Constraints* pane.
7. **SAVE** the project plan as *Office Remodel Deadlines*, and then **CLOSE** the file.

   PAUSE. LEAVE Project open to use in the next exercise.

■ Mastery Assessment

→ Project 11-5: Changing Default Handling for Task Relationships/ Constraints on Insurance Claim Processing

After a meeting with your project team, a decision has been made to honor task relationships over constraints for the Insurance Claim plan from Project 11-1. Another repairer has agreed to fill in for Chris Gray if necessary. You need to revise your project plan to change the default method by which Microsoft Project handles dependencies and constraints.

The *Insurance Claim Processing 11-5* project plan is available on the companion CD-ROM.

OPEN *Insurance Claim Processing 11-5* from the data files for this lesson.

1. Review the task list.
2. Open the Options dialog box from the Tools menu.
3. Select the **Schedule** tab, if necessary.
4. Clear the checkbox so that tasks do not always honor their constraint dates.
5. Close the dialog box.
6. Review the task list and locate the task that has been affected by this change. In a separate Microsoft Word document, state the information that is contained in the calendar alert icon for this task, and briefly explain how your change has affected the task.
7. **SAVE** the project plan as *Insurance Claim No Default*. **SAVE** the Word document as *Insurance Claim No Default*. **CLOSE** the files.

   PAUSE. LEAVE Project open to use in the next exercise.

The Don Funk Music Video 11-6 project plan is available on the companion CD-ROM.

Project 11-6: Removing, Adding, and Changing Deadlines

You have just finished reviewing the Don Funk Music Video project plan, and have decided to make some changes and additions to the deadlines on this project.

OPEN *Don Funk Music Video 11-6* from the data files for this lesson.

1. Remove the deadline for task 9.
2. Change the deadline for task 61 to June 25, 2008.
3. Add a deadline of May 21, 2008 for task 36.
4. **SAVE** the project plan as *Don Funk Revised Deadlines*, and then **CLOSE** the file. **CLOSE** Project.

INTERNET READY

Establishing priorities is something you do every day of your life, whether you realize it or not: Do I buy gas for the car on my way to work or on my way home? Do I buy this new pair of shoes or go to a concert? Do I finish the inventory report before lunch or after? Do I remodel the basement or go on vacation?

Search the Internet for suggestions on establishing and managing priorities. Review several sources—they can be personal or business related. From the information you review, put together a summary list of suggestions that you think will help you set priorities, personally and/or professionally. Select a project plan on which you are currently working (or use a template from Microsoft Project) and try to apply some of these suggestions to prioritize tasks in the project.

Fine-Tuning Resources

LESSON SKILL MATRIX

SKILLS	MATRIX SKILL
Entering Material Resource Consumption Rates	Enter a variable consumption rate for a material resource
Entering Costs Per Use for Resources	Enter a cost per use for a resource
Assigning Multiple Pay Rates for a Resource	Assign multiple pay rates for a resource
Applying Different Cost Rates to Assignments	Apply a different cost rate to an assignment
Specifying Resource Availability at Different Times	Specify a resource's availability over time
Resolving Resource Overallocations Manually	Manually resolve a resource overallocation
Leveling Overallocated Resources	Use resource leveling to resolve an overallocation

KEY TERMS
cost rate table
fixed consumption rate
variable consumption rate

You are a video project manager for Southridge Video, and one of your primary responsibilities recently has been to manage the new Don Funk Music Video project. You have just finished applying some of the more advanced features of Microsoft Office Project that focus on fine-tuning task details in a project plan *prior* to saving a baseline and commencing project work. Another important part of project management is to understand how to make the best use of resources' time, as people and equipment resources are often the most costly and limited part of a project. In this lesson, you will continue the fine-tuning activities on which you have been working, this time focusing on resources.

■ Entering Material Resource Consumption Rates

THE BOTTOM LINE   In order to accurately calculate the cost of a material resource, you also need to know its consumption rate, or how quickly it is used up.

The ***Don Funk Music Video 12M*** project plan is available on the companion CD-ROM.

GET READY. Before you begin these steps, launch Microsoft Project. OPEN the Don Funk Music Video 12M project plan from the data files for this lesson.

SAVE the file as **Don Funk Music Video 12** in the solutions folder for this lesson as directed by your instructor.

⊕ ENTER A VARIABLE CONSUMPTION RATE FOR A MATERIAL RESOURCE

1. On the menu bar, click **Edit**, and then click **Go To**. Key **34** in the ID box, and then click **OK**. Microsoft Project displays task 34, Scene 1 video shoot.

   This is the first of several scenes that requires DVDs to be recorded. You have determined that the initial estimates for DVD consumption were incorrect. Because for each hour of work you will only be recording for 30 minutes, you have determined that the correct consumption rate for the DVD resource is 0.25 DVD/hour (the DVDs record 2 hours of filming).

2. On the Standard toolbar, click the **Assign Resources** button. The Assign Resources dialog box appears.

3. In the Assign Resources dialog box, click the Units field for DVD. Key **0.25/h** and then press **Enter**. Microsoft Project changes the consumption rate of DVDs for this task to 0.25 per hour.

4. Double-click the column divider between the Units and Cost columns to expand the Units column. The Assign Resources dialog box should look similar to Figure 12-1.

Figure 12-1

Assign Resources dialog box displaying new DVD consumption rate.

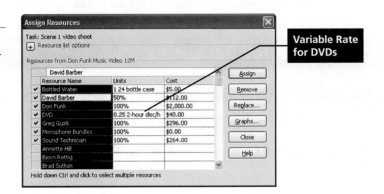

5. Click the **Close** button in the Assign Resources dialog box.

   You will now verify the cost and work values of the DVD assignment to task 34.

6. On the menu bar, click **View**, and then click **Task Usage**.

7. Click the **DVD** assignment under task 34, Scene 1 video shoot.

8. On the Standard toolbar, click the **Assignment Information** button. The Assignment Information dialog box appears.

9. Select the **General** tab, if it is not already selected. Note the Work, Units, and Cost fields. The Assignment Information box should look similar to Figure 12-2.

Figure 12-2

Assignment Information dialog box showing DVD assignment details

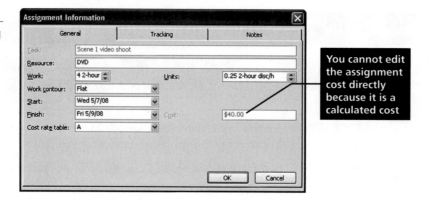

You cannot edit the assignment cost directly because it is a calculated cost

10. Click **OK** to close the Assignment Information dialog box.

11. **SAVE** the project plan.

    PAUSE. LEAVE Project open to use in the next exercise.

In this exercise, you have just assigned a variable consumption rate to a material resource. As you have seen, in Microsoft Project, you can assign two types of consumption rates:

- A fixed consumption rate means that an absolute quantity of the resources will be used, no matter the duration of the task to which the material is assigned. For example, filling a swimming pool requires a fixed amount of water to be used.

- A variable consumption rate means that the amount of the material resource consumed is dependent upon the duration of the task. When shooting DVDs, as in this exercise, you will use more DVDs in six hours than in four. After you enter a variable consumption rate for a material resource's assignment, Microsoft Project calculated the total quantity and cost of the material resource consumed, based on the task's duration. An advantage of using a variable rate of consumption is that as the duration of the task changes, so do the calculated amount and cost of the material resource, since the rate is tied to the task's duration.

■ Entering Costs Per Use for Resources

 THE BOTTOM LINE

In addition to its pay or consumption rate, a resource can also have a cost associated with each use.

➔ ENTER A COST PER USE FOR A RESOURCE

USE the project plan you created in the previous exercise.

1. On the Project Guide toolbar, click **Resources**.

2. In the *Resources* pane, click the **Specify people and equipment for the project** link. The *Specify Resources* pane appears, and the Project Guide: Simple Resource Sheet view is activated.

3. On the Simple Resource Sheet, select resource 11, **Digital Truck-Mounted Video Camera**.

4. On the Standard toolbar, click the **Resource Information** button. The Resource Information dialog box appears.

5. Select the **Costs** tab, if it is not already selected.

6. Under *Cost rate tables*, select the **A(default)** tab if it is not already selected.

   The Digital Truck-Mounted Video Camera has a $100 maintenance fee for every time you use it.

7. In the first row under the Per Use Cost column, key **100**, and then press Enter.

8. Select **End** from the *Cost accrual* dropdown box, and then press Tab. Your screen should look similar to Figure 12-3.

Figure 12-3

Resource Information dialog box displaying per use cost for Digital Truck-Mounted Video Camera

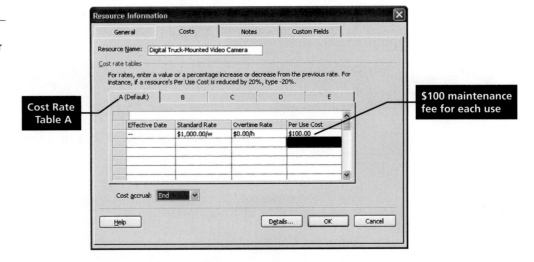

9. Click **OK** to close the Resource Information dialog box.

10. Click **Done** in the *Specify Resources* pane.

11. **SAVE** the project plan.

    PAUSE. LEAVE Project open to use in the next exercise.

In this exercise, you entered a per-use cost for a material resource. Any resource can have a cost per use, in place of or in addition to the costs derived from their pay rates (work resources) or consumption rates (material resources). You can also specify whether the per-use cost should accrue at the beginning or end of the task to which it is assigned.

■ Assigning Multiple Pay Rates for a Resource

THE BOTTOM LINE   Sometimes, the same work resource may perform different tasks with different pay rates. Microsoft Project enables you to enter multiple pay rates for a single resource.

➔ ASSIGN MULTIPLE PAY RATES FOR A RESOURCE

USE the project plan you created in the previous exercise.

1. On the menu bar, click **View** and then click **Resource Sheet**. The Resource Sheet view is activated.

2. In the Resource Sheet view, click the name of resource 9, **Yan Li**.

Because Yan Li's rate differs depending on whether he is working on sound production tasks or administrative tasks, you need to enter a second rate for him.

3. On the Standard toolbar, click the **Resource Information** button. The Resource Information dialog box appears.

ANOTHER WAY You can also double-click the Resource Name field to activate the Resource Information dialog box.

4. Click the **Costs** tab, if it is not already selected. Each tab of the Cost Rate table corresponds to one of the five pay rates a resource can have.

5. Under Cost rate tables, click the **B** tab.

6. Select the default entry of **$0.00/h** in the field directly below the Standard Rate column heading, key **15/h**, and then press **Enter**.

TAKE NOTE When you enter a pay rate, if you do not key in the currency symbol, Microsoft Project will supply it for you.

7. In the Overtime Rate field, key **22.50/h**, and then press **Enter**. Your screen should look similar to Figure 12-4.

Figure 12-4

Resource Information dialog box showing second rate table for Yan Li

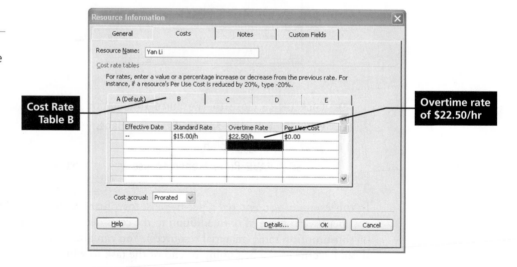

8. Click **OK** to close the Resource Information dialog box. Note that on the Resource Sheet, Yan Li's standard pay rate is still $18.50 per hour. This was the value in Rate Table A, the default rate table. This value will be used for all of Yan Li's task assignments unless you specify a different rate table.

9. **SAVE** the project plan.

PAUSE. LEAVE Project open to use in the next exercise.

In this exercise, you entered a second cost rate table for a resource. A cost rate table is resource pay rates that are stored on the Costs tab of the Resource Information dialog box. For a given resource you can enter up to five cost rate tables for a resource. After you assign a resource to a task, you can specify which rate table should apply.

■ Applying Different Cost Rates to Assignments

Microsoft Project enables you to enter as many as five different pay rates for a resource. These pay rates may be applied to different assignments as necessary.

➔ APPLY A DIFFERENT COST RATE TO AN ASSIGNMENT

USE the project plan you created in the previous exercise.

1. On the menu bar, click **View** and then click **Task Usage**.
2. On the menu bar, click **Edit**, click **Go To**, key **6** in the ID box, and then click **OK**.
3. On the menu bar, click **View**, point to **Table: Usage**, and then click **Cost**.
4. Under task 6, click the row heading directly to the left of Yan Li so that Yan Li's entire assignment is selected.
5. Scroll the table portion (on the left) of the Task Usage view to the right until the Total Cost column is visible. You can see that the total cost of Yan's assignment to this task is $3,700. You can also see other assignment cost values, such as variance and actual cost, by dragging the vertical divider bar or scrolling the table to the right. Your screen should look similar to Figure 12-5.

Figure 12-5

Task Usage view showing total cost for Yan Li's assignment using Cost Table A

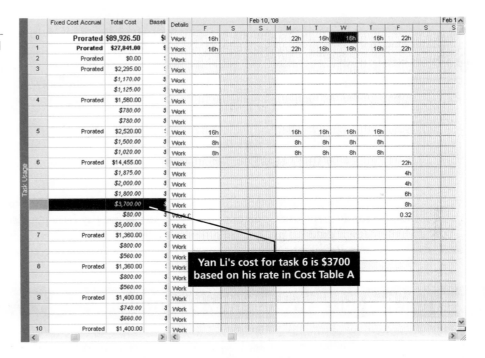

6. Click the **Assignment Information** button on the Standard toolbar. The Assignment Information dialog box appears.
7. Click the **General** tab, if it is not already selected.
8. In the *Cost rate table* box, key or select **B**, and then click **OK**. Microsoft Project applies Yan Li's Cost Rate Table B to the assignment. The new cost of the assignment, $3,000, is reflected in the total cost column. Your screen should look similar to Figure 12-6.

Figure 12-6

Task Usage view showing total cost for Yan Li's assignment using Cost Table B

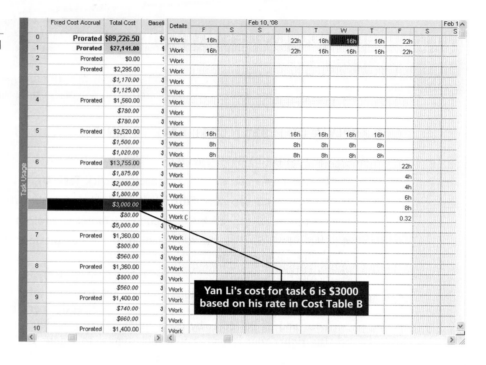

Yan Li's cost for task 6 is $3000 based on his rate in Cost Table B

 ANOTHER WAY

If you find that you are changing cost rate tables frequently, it is quicker to display the Cost Rate Table field directly in the Resource Usage or Task Usage view. To add the Cost Rate Table Field, select a column heading, and then click Column on the Insert menu. In the Field name box, select Cost Rate Table from the dropdown list, and then click OK.

9. SAVE the project plan.

PAUSE. LEAVE Project open to use in the next exercise.

In this exercise, you applied an alternate rate table for a resource to reflect a different pay rate for different work. You can set up as many as five pay rates per resource. This enables you to assign different pay rates to different assignments for a resource. By default, Microsoft Project uses Rate Table A, but you can specify any time another rate table should be used.

▪ Specifying Resource Availability at Different Times

↓ THE BOTTOM LINE

Sometimes, as you are working on a project plan, you will find that a resource will have varying availability. To control this availability, Microsoft Project uses Max. Units, or the maximum capacity of a resource to accomplish tasks.

⊙ SPECIFY A RESOURCE'S AVAILABILITY OVER TIME

USE the project plan you created in the previous exercise.

1. On the menu bar, click **View**, and then click **Resource Sheet**.
2. In the Resource Name column, click the name of resource 38, **electrician**.
3. On the Standard toolbar, click the **Resource Information** button.
4. Click the **General** tab, if it is not already selected.

   You originally planned that there would be three electricians available for the entire video production, but you have just determined that there will only be two electricians available from May 1–May 20, 2008.

5. Under Resource Availability, in the first row of the Available From column, leave NA (for Not Applicable).

6. In the Available To cell in the first row, key or select **4/30/08**.

7. In the Available From cell in the second row, key or select **5/1/08**.

8. In the Available To cell in the second row, key or select **5/20/08**.

9. In the Units cell in the second row, key or select **200%**.

10. In the Available From cell in the third row, key or select **5/21/08**.

11. Leave the Available To cell in the third row blank. Microsoft Project will fill this with NA.

12. In the Units cell in the third row, key or select **300%**, and then press [Enter]. Your screen should look similar to Figure 12-7.

Figure 12-7

Resource Information dialog box showing custom resource availability dates

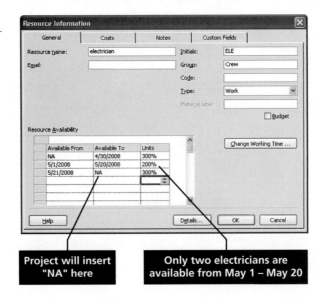

13. Click **OK** to close the Resource Information dialog box.

TAKE NOTE Microsoft Project will display 200% in the Max. Units field only when the current date (based on your computer's system clock) is within the May 1–May 20 range. At other times it will display 300%.

14. **SAVE** the project plan.

PAUSE. LEAVE Project open to use in the next exercise.

In this exercise, you set resource availability over time using the Resource Availability grid on the General tab of the Resource Information dialog box. Recall from Lessons 3 and 4 that a resource's capacity to work is measured in *units*. The *Max. Units* value stored in Microsoft Project is the maximum capacity of a resource to accomplish tasks. A resource's calendar determines when a resource is available to work. However, the resource's capacity to work (measured in units and limited by their Max. Units value) determines how much that resource can work within those hours without becoming overallocated.

You can set different Max. Units values to be applied over different time periods for any resource. Setting a resource's availability over time enables you to control exactly what a resource's Max. Units value is at any time.

■ Resolving Resource Overallocations Manually

THE BOTTOM LINE — A resource is overallocated when it is scheduled for work that exceeds its maximum capacity to work. You can manually resolve this situation within the project plan.

⊕ MANUALLY RESOLVE A RESOURCE OVERALLOCATION

USE the project plan you created in the previous exercise.

1. Click the **Show/Hide Project Guide** button on the Project Guide toolbar. The Project Guide closes.

2. On the menu bar, click **View**, click **More Views**, select **Resource Allocation**, and then click the **Apply** button. Microsoft Project switches to the Resource Allocation view. This is a split view that displays the Resource Usage view in the top pane and the Leveling Gantt view in the bottom pane. Your screen should look similar to Figure 12-8.

Figure 12-8

Resource Allocation view

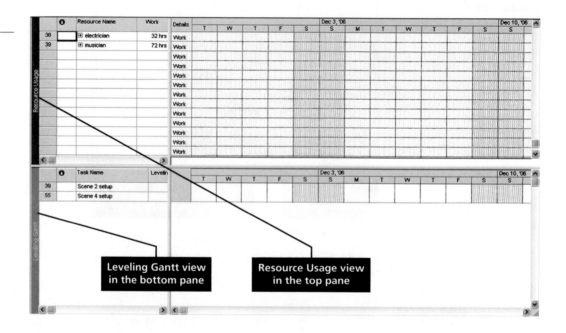

3. In the Resource Usage view, click on the Resource Name column heading, and then click the **Hide Subtasks** button on the Formatting toolbar. (The column appears to go blank, but actually the resources have just shifted up in the list because the tasks under the resource names have been hidden.)

4. In the Resource Usage view, scroll up vertically through the Resource Name column so that you can see the names. The names that you see that are formatted in red are overallocated resources.

5. In the Resource Name column, select the name of resource 27, **Greg Guzik**.

6. Click the plus sign (+) next to Greg Guzik's name to display his assignments. Scroll down to see the assignments, if necessary.

7. On the menu bar, click **Edit**, click **Go To**, key **6/29/08** in the Date box, and then click **OK**. The *Leveling Gant* pane shows the task bars for two of Greg Guzik's assignments. Your screen should look similar to Figure 12-9.

Figure 12-9

Resource Allocation view showing overallocations for Greg Guzik

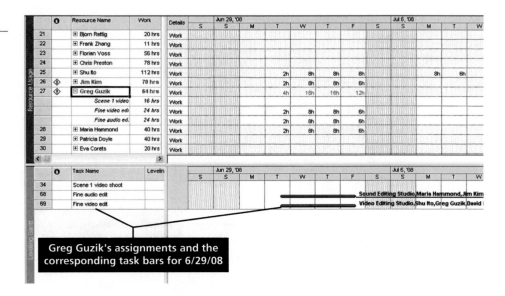

Greg Guzik's assignments and the corresponding task bars for 6/29/08

In the upper pane, you see that Greg is assigned full-time to two tasks that both start on Tuesday, July 1. He is overallocated for the duration of both tasks. In the lower pane, you can see the Gantt bars for the two tasks that have caused Greg to be overallocated during this time. For tasks 68 and 69, Greg is assigned eight hours of work on both Wednesday and Thursday, and six hours of work on Friday. This results in 16 hours of work on two days, and 12 hours of work on another—beyond Greg's capacity to work. In addition, Greg is assigned to only four hours of work on Tuesday, but this assignment is also shown in red. This is because the two tasks to which he is assigned are scheduled to start at the same time on Tuesday. These two assignments in parallel are also an overallocation.

8. In the Resource Name column, click Greg's second assignment, **Fine video edit**.

9. On the Standard toolbar, click the **Assignment Information** button. The Assignment Information dialog box appears.

10. Click the **General** tab, if it is not already selected.

11. In the Units box, key or select **50%**, and then click **OK** to close the Assignment Information dialog box.

   Note that Greg's daily work assignments on this task are reduced, but the task duration is increased. You want to reduce the work, but not increase the duration of the task. Also note the SmartTag indicator that has been activated next to the name of the assignment.

12. Click the **SmartTag Actions** button. Review the options in the list that appears. Your screen should look similar to Figure 12-10.

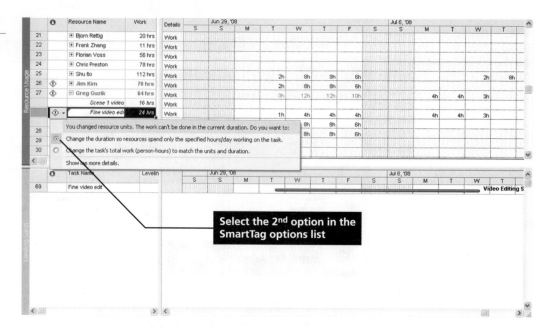

13. Click **Change the task's total work (person-hours) to match the units and
duration** in the SmartTag Actions list. Microsoft Project reduces Greg's work
assignments on the task and restores the task to its original duration. Your screen
should look similar to Figure 12-11.

Figure 12-11

Resource Allocation view

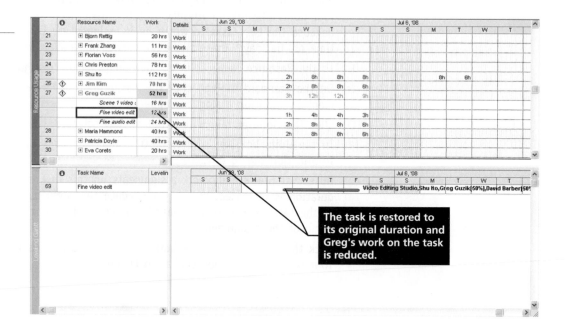

Notice that Greg is still overallocated, so now you will reduce the assignment
units on his second task.

14. In the Resource Name column, click Greg's third assignment, **Fine audio edit**.

15. On the Standard toolbar, click the **Assignment Information** button. The Assignment Information dialog box appears.

16. Click the **General** tab if it is not already visible.

17. In the Units box, key or select **50%**, and then click **OK** to close the Assignment
Information dialog box.

18. Click the **SmartTag Actions** button. Click **Change the task's total work (person-
hours) to match the units and duration** in the SmartTag Actions list. Greg's

assignments on Wednesday and Thursday are now reduced to eight hours each day. You have manually changed Greg's assignments to reduce his work and resolve his overallocation. He is now fully allocated on these days. Your screen should look similar to Figure 12-12.

Figure 12-12

Resource Allocation view showing Greg's resolved over-allocation

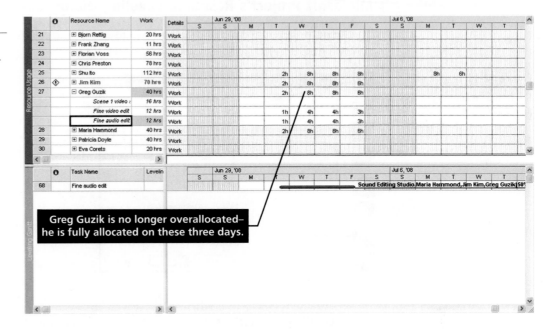

19. SAVE the project plan.

PAUSE. LEAVE Project open to use in the next exercise.

In this exercise, you have manually resolved a resource overallocation. Recall from Lesson 4 that a resource's capacity to work is called *allocation*, and a resource is said to be in one of three states:

- *Underallocated*: the work assigned to the resource is less than the resource's maximum capacity
- *Fully allocated*: the total work of a resource's task assignments is exactly equal to that resource's work capacity
- *Overallocated*: a resource is assigned to do more work than can be done within the normal work capacity of the resource

Manually-editing an assignment is one way to resolve a resource overallocation, but there are several other options.

- You can replace the overallocated resource with another resource using the Replace button in the Assign Resources dialog box.
- You can reduce the value in the Units field in the Assignment Information or Assign Resources dialog box.
- If the overallocation is not extreme (for instance, 9 hours of work assigned in a normal 8-hour workday), you can just allow the overallocation to remain in the schedule.

■ SOFTWARE ORIENTATION

Microsoft Project's Resource Leveling Dialog Box

The Resource Leveling dialog box allows you to specify the rules and options that control how Microsoft Project performs resource leveling.

Figure 12-13

The Resource Leveling dialog box

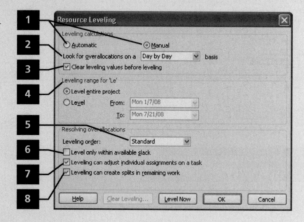

The options in the Resource Leveling Dialog box are:

1. **Leveling calculations**–These selections determine whether Microsoft Project levels resources constantly (Automatic) or only when you tell it to do so (Manual). Automatic leveling occurs as soon as a resource becomes overallocated.

2. **Look for overallocations on a .....basis**–This selection determines the timeframe in which Microsoft Project will look for overallocations. If a resource is at all overallocated, its name will be formatted in red. If it is overallocated at the level you choose here, the Overallocated indicator will be shown next to its name.

3. **Clear leveling values before leveling**–There are times where you may have to level resources repeatedly to get the results you want. (You might first try to level day by day, and then switch to hour by hour, for example.) If the *Clear leveling values before leveling* check box is selected, Microsoft Project removes any existing delays from all tasks before leveling. In most cases, you would clear this option only if you have delayed tasks manually and you want to keep these delays.

4. **Leveling range for...**–This selection determines whether you level the entire project or only those assignments that fall within a date range you specify. Leveling within a date range is advantageous when you have started tracking actual work and you want to level only the remaining assignments in a project.

5. **Leveling order**–This setting allows you to control the priority Microsoft Project uses to determine which tasks it should delay to resolve a resource conflict. There are three options: ID Only, Standard, and Priority, Standard. The ID Only option delays tasks according to their ID numbers only. Use this option when your project plan has no task relationships or constraints. The Standard option delays tasks according to their predecessor relationships, start dates, task constraints, slack, priority, and IDs. The Priority, Standard option looks at the task's priority value before other standard criteria.

6. **Level only within available slack**–Clearing this setting allows Microsoft Project to extend the project's finish date, if necessary, to resolve resource overallocations. Selecting this setting would prevent Microsoft Project from extending the project's finish date in order to resolve resource overallocations. Instead, Project would only use the free slack of tasks, which may or may not be adequate to fully resolve resource overallocations.

7. **Leveling can adjust individual assignments to work on a task**–This setting allows Microsoft Project to add leveling delay (or, if *Leveling can create splits in remaining work* is selected, to split work on assignments) independently of any other resources assigned to the same task. This could cause resources to start and finish work on a task at different times.

8. **Leveling can create splits in remaining work**–This setting allows Microsoft Project to split work on a task in order to resolve an overallocation.

■ Leveling Overallocated Resources

THE BOTTOM LINE   To avoid an overallocation situation, you can cause a resource's work on a specific task to be delayed through a process known as resource leveling.

→ USE RESOURCE LEVELING TO RESOLVE AN OVERALLOCATION

USE the project plan you created in the previous exercise.

1. On the menu bar, click **Window**, and then click **Remove Split**.
2. On the menu bar, click **View**, and then click **Resource Sheet**. The Resource Sheet view appears. Take note of the resource names that appear in red and have the Overallocated icon in the Indicators column.
3. On the menu bar, click **Tools**, and then click **Level Resources**. The Resource Leveling dialog box appears.

TAKE NOTE* Depending on previous uses of the Resource Leveling dialog box in Microsoft Project, the options you are selecting in steps 4 through 11 may already be selected for you.

4. In the Resource Leveling dialog box, under *Leveling calculations*, select **Manual**, if it is not already selected.

TAKE NOTE* All of the settings in the Resource Leveling dialog box apply to all project plans with which you work in Microsoft Project–NOT just the active project plan. It might sound easier to use automatic leveling, but it will make frequent adjustments to project plans whether you want them to occur or not. Because of this, it is recommended that you select the Manual Leveling calculations setting.

5. In the *Look for overallocations on a ..... basis* box, select **Day by Day**.

SHOOTING In most projects, leveling in detail more precise than Day by Day can result in unrealistically precise adjustments to assignments.

6. Select the **Clear leveling values before leveling** box.
7. Under *Leveling range for*, select **Level entire project**.
8. Under *Resolving overallocations*, in the *Leveling order* box, select **Standard**.
9. Clear the **Level only within available slack** check box.

10. Select the **Leveling can adjust individual assignments on a task** check box.

11. Select the **Leveling can create splits in remaining work** check box. Your screen should look similar to Figure 12-14.

Figure 12-14

Resource Leveling dialog box

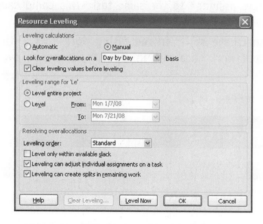

12. Click the **Level Now** button.

13. Microsoft Project asks whether you want to level the entire pool or only selected resources. Select **Entire pool**, if it is not already selected, and then click **OK**. Microsoft Project levels the overallocated resources. Some resources may still be formatted in red, meaning that these resources are still overallocated hour by hour (or even minute by minute), but not day by day. Your screen should look similar to Figure 12-15.

Figure 12-15

Resource list after leveling

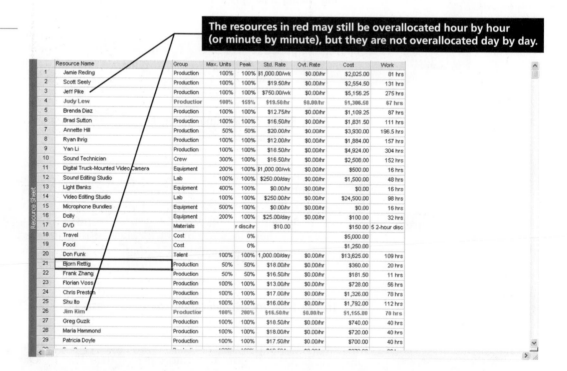

14. On the menu bar, click **View**, click **More Views**, select **Leveling Gantt**, and then click the **Apply** button. Microsoft Project switches to the Leveling Gantt view.

15. Scroll down and select the name of task 66, **Rough edit video–paper**, and then click the **Scroll to Task** button on the Standard toolbar. Your screen should look similar to Figure 12-16.

Figure 12-16

Leveling Gantt view showing resources leveled

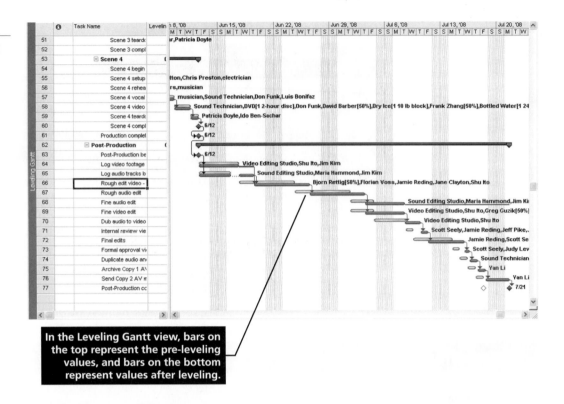

In the Leveling Gantt view, bars on the top represent the pre-leveling values, and bars on the bottom represent values after leveling.

Notice that each task now has two bars. The green bar on the top represents the preleveled task. The blue bar on the bottom represents the leveled task. For this particular project, the effect leveling had on the project finish date was to extend it by about three days. You can see all of the preleveled start, duration, and finish values for any task by pointing to the desired green bar.

16. **SAVE** the project plan, and then **CLOSE** the file.

PAUSE. If you are continuing to the next lesson, keep Project open. If you are not continuing to additional lessons, **CLOSE** Project.

In this exercise, you used resource leveling to resolve overallocations. Recall that *resource leveling* is the process of delaying or splitting a resource's work on a task to resolve an overallocation. The options in the Resource Leveling dialog box enable you to set parameters about how you want Microsoft Project to resolve resource overallocations. Depending on the options you choose, Microsoft Project might try to level resources by delaying the start date of an assignment or task, or splitting the work on the task.

TAKE NOTE

Even though the effects of resource leveling might sometimes be significant, resource leveling never changes who is assigned to tasks, or the total work or assignment unit values of those assignments.

Resource leveling is a powerful tool, but it has limits. It can only do a few things: it adds delays to tasks, it splits tasks, and it adjusts resource assignments. It does this by following a complex set of rules and options that you specify in the Resource Leveling dialog box. Although resource leveling is very useful for fine tuning, it can't replace the judgment of a good project manager about task durations, relationships, and constraints, or about resource availability. Resource leveling will work with all of this information as it exists in your project plan, but it still might not be possible to completely resolve all resource overallocations within the timeframe you want without changing more basic task and resource information.

SUMMARY SKILL MATRIX

In this lesson you learned	Matrix Skill
To enter material resource consumption rates	Enter a variable consumption rate for a material resource
To enter costs per use for resources	Enter a cost per use for a resource
To assign multiple pay rates for a resource	Assign multiple pay rates for a resource
To apply different cost rates to assignments	Apply a different cost rate to an assignment
To specify resource availability at different times	Specify a resource's availability over time
To resolve resource overallocations manually	Manually resolve a resource overallocation
To level overallocated resources	Use resource leveling to resolve an overallocation

■ Knowledge Assessment

Matching

Match the term in column 1 to its description in column 2.

Column 1

1. cost rate table
2. underallocated
3. variable consumption rate
4. units
5. allocation
6. fixed consumption rate
7. overallocated
8. resource leveling
9. fully allocated
10. Max. Units

Column 2

a. an absolute quantity of resources will be used, no matter the duration of the task to which the material is assigned

b. the total work of a resource's task assignments is exactly equal to that resource's work capacity

c. a resource is assigned to do more work than can be done within the normal capacity of the resource

d. the amount of the material resource consumed is dependent upon the duration of the task

e. the work assigned to a resource is less than the resource's maximum capacity

f. the process of delaying or splitting a resource's work on a task to resolve an overallocation

g. the maximum capacity of a resource to accomplish tasks

h. resource pay rates that are stored on the Costs tab of the Resource Information dialog box

i. the portion of a resource's capacity devoted to work on a specific task

j. the measurement of a resource's capacity to work

True / False

Circle T if the statement is true or F if the statement is false.

T | F 1. Resource leveling cannot always resolve all resource overallocations.

T | F 2. A resource cannot have both a cost per use and a cost derived from its pay rate.

T | F 3. Resource leveling never changes who is assigned to tasks, or the total work value of those assignments.

T | F 4. You can resolve a resource overallocation by replacing the overallocated resource with another resource.

T | F 5. You can assign two types of consumption rates in Microsoft Project.

T | F 6. The settings in the Resource Leveling dialog box apply to all of the project plans you work with in Microsoft Project.

T | F 7. You can have up to six cost rate tables for a resource.

T | F 8. It is not acceptable to allow a minor overallocation to remain in a schedule.

T | F 9. The default rate table in Microsoft Project is Rate Table 1.

T | F 10. When a variable consumption rate is assigned to a material resource, and the duration of the task to which it is assigned changes, so do the calculated amount and cost of the material resource.

■ Competency Assessment

⊕ Project 12-1: Variable Consumption Rate for Water

As you are reviewing your Don Funk Music Video project plan, you realize you need to make some adjustments to the bottled water material resource. You want to use a variable rate of 0.5 cases of water per hour.

GET READY. Launch Microsoft Project if it is not already running. **OPEN Don Funk Music Video 12-1** from the data files for this lesson.

The *Don Funk Music Video 12-1* project plan is available on the companion CD-ROM.

1. On the menu bar, click **Edit**, and then click **Go To**. Key **34** in the ID box, and then click **OK**.

2. On the Standard toolbar, click the **Assign Resources** button.

3. In the Assign Resources dialog box, click the Units field for Bottled Water. Key **0.5/h** and then press **Enter**.

4. Click the **Close** button in the Assign Resource dialog box.

5. **SAVE** the project plan as **Don Funk Bottled Water** and then **CLOSE** the file.

   PAUSE. LEAVE Project open to use in the next exercise.

Project 12-2: Office Remodel Multiple Pay Rates

On the office remodel project you are currently managing, you need to set up different pay rates for one of the resources, Run Lui. He has different pay scales depending upon whether he is moving furniture and appliances or doing painting and material installation work.

OPEN *Office Remodel 12-2* from the data files for this lesson.

The *Office Remodel 12-2* project plan is available on the companion CD-ROM.

1. On the menu bar, click **View** and then click **Resource Sheet**.

2. In the Resource Sheet view, click the name of resource 3, **Run Lui**.

3. On the Standard toolbar, click the **Resource Information** button.

4. Click the **Costs** tab, if it is not already selected.

5. Under *Cost rate tables*, click the **B** tab.

6. Select the default entry of $0.00/h in the field directly below the Standard Rate column heading, key **12/h**, and then press [Enter].

7. In the Overtime Rate field, key **18.00/h**, and then press [Enter].

8. Click **OK** to close the Resource Information dialog box.

9. **SAVE** the project plan as **Office Remodel Multiple Rates** and then **CLOSE** the file.

   PAUSE. LEAVE Project open to use in the next exercise.

■ Proficiency Assessment

➔ Project 12-3: Hiring New Employee Resource Leveling

The *Hiring New Employee 12-3* project plan is available on the companion CD-ROM.

Several employees on the Hiring New Employee project plan are overallocated. Use resource leveling to resolve these overallocations.

OPEN *Hiring New Employee 12-3* from the data files for this lesson.

1. Activate the Resource Sheet view.

2. Activate the Resource Leveling dialog box.

3. In the Resource Leveling dialog box, make the selections that correspond to the following options:

   • Level manually

   • Level day by day

   • Clear leveling values before leveling

   • Level the entire project

   • Use Standard leveling order

   • Do not level within available slack

   • Allow leveling to adjust individual assignments

   • Allow leveling to create splits

4. Click the **Level Now** button.

5. Level for the entire pool.

6. Change the view to the Leveling Gantt.

7. Scroll to task 4 to view more of the leveled Gantt Chart.

8. **SAVE** the project plan as **Hiring New Employee Leveled** and then **CLOSE** the file.

   PAUSE. LEAVE Project open to use in the next exercise.

➔ Project 12-4: Employee Orientation–Specifying Conference Room Availability

The *Employee Orientation 12-4* project plan is available on the companion CD-ROM.

You have just been told that the Large Conference Room is not available for use from 9/1/09 through 9/12/09 and from 9/17/09 through 9/18/09. Although this does not immediately interfere with your current orientation schedule, you want to update the resource availability information so that you can avoid conflicts if your schedule changes.

OPEN *Employee Orientation 12-4* from the data files for this lesson.

1. Activate the Resource Sheet view.

2. Select the Large Conference Room resource.

3. Activate the Resource Information dialog box. Activate the General tab, if it is not already selected.

4. Fill in the Resource Availability table to reflect that the conference room is available until 8/31/09, from 9/13-16/09, and after 9/18/09, but that it is not

available on the dates as noted in the instructions above. Close the Resource Information box when you are finished.

5. **SAVE** the project plan as **Employee Orientation Conf Room Availability** and then **CLOSE** the file.

   PAUSE. LEAVE Project open to use in the next exercise.

■ Mastery Assessment

➔ Project 12-5: Applying a Different Cost Rate

The **Office Remodel 12-5** project plan is available on the companion CD-ROM.

On the office remodel project you are currently managing, you have set up different pay rates for one of the resources, Run Lui. Now you need to apply these pay rates to the appropriate assignments.

OPEN *Office Remodel 12-5* from the data files for this lesson.

1. For Run Lui's assignment to tasks 2 and 18, change the cost rate table to B.

2. **SAVE** the project plan as **Office Remodel Run Lui B**, and then **CLOSE** the file.

   PAUSE. LEAVE Project open to use in the next exercise.

➔ Project 12-6: Don Funk Music Video–Costs Per Use

The **Don Funk Music Video 12-6** project plan is available on the companion CD-ROM.

You need to update the Don Funk Music Video project plan to reflect several resources that have a cost associated with each use.

OPEN *Don Funk Music Video 12-6* from the data files for this lesson.

1. Enter the following cost per use information for the specified resources:
   - the musicians have a $100 travel and set-up/breakdown fee each time they are used, payable at the beginning of the session
   - the sound editing studio has a $50 cleaning fee per use, payable at the end of the session
   - the video editing studio has a $50 cleaning fee per use, payable at the end of the session

2. **SAVE** the project plan as **Don Funk Cost Per Use** and then **CLOSE** the file.

   CLOSE Project.

INTERNET READY

In this lesson you learned about resources that have a cost associated with each use, and about resources that have multiple cost rates depending upon their particular activity on a project. Both of these situations are very common occurrences in project management. Search the Internet for a project that has resources that fall into either or both categories above. You can look for an actual Microsoft Project file, a template, a story about a current event, a press release from a company, or even a project run by a local business that is of interest to you. Write a brief description of the project (enough to familiarize your instructor with it), or save a copy of the Project file. Then make a list of the resources and describe how per use costs or multiple cost rates might apply to these resources. For example:

- Resource: Concert Hall–cost per use fee for cleaning and/or setup/cleanup; may have different rates for day and night use
- Resource: limousine–cost per use fee for gas or cleaning; may have different rates for weekdays and weekends

You can put your list into a Word file or an Excel file.

Project Plan Optimization

LESSON SKILL MATRIX

SKILLS	MATRIX SKILL
Making Time and Date Adjustments	Adjust fiscal year settings within Microsoft Project
Viewing the Project's Critical Path	View the project's critical path
Delaying the Start of Assignments	Delay the start of a resource assignment
Applying Contours to Assignments	Apply a contour to a resource assignment Edit a task assignment manually
Optimizing the Project Plan	Identify the project finish date and total cost Compress the project plan to pull in the project finish date

You are a video project manager for Southridge Video, and one of your primary responsibilities recently has been to manage the new Don Funk Music Video project. Recently, you have been focusing on using some of the more advanced features of Microsoft Office Project to fine-tune your project plan prior to saving a baseline and commencing project work. In this lesson, you will wrap up the fine-tuning activities on your project plan by focusing on assignment adjustments, critical paths, and the project's finish date.

KEY TERMS
contour
crashing
optimizing
predefined contour

SOFTWARE ORIENTATION

Microsoft Project's Calendar Tab of the Options Dialog Box

The Calendar tab of the Options dialog box is used to provide basic time values, such as the hours per day or week, fiscal year settings, and the first day of the week.

Figure 13-1

The Calendar tab of the Options dialog box

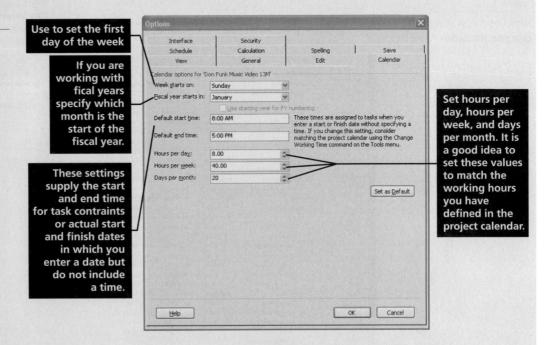

Use to set the first day of the week

If you are working with fical years specify which month is the start of the fiscal year.

These settings supply the start and end time for task contraints or actual start and finish dates in which you enter a date but do not include a time.

Set hours per day, hours per week, and days per month. It is a good idea to set these values to match the working hours you have defined in the project calendar.

Keep in mind that the Calendar tab has nothing to do with Microsoft Project's base, project, resource, or task calendars. The settings on the Calendar tab affect only the time conversions for task durations that you enter into Microsoft Project, not when work can be scheduled.

■ Making Time and Date Adjustments

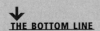
THE BOTTOM LINE

As part of its project management capabilities, Microsoft Project acts as a calculating engine that works with time. Because time is always part of the "project equation," it is critical that the project manager understand the array of time and date settings used by Microsoft Project.

The *Don Funk Music Video 13M* project plan is available on the companion CD-ROM

GET READY. Before you begin these steps, launch Microsoft Project.

OPEN the *Don Funk Music Video 13M* project plan from the data files for this lesson.

SAVE the file as *Don Funk Music Video 13* in the solutions folder for this lesson as directed by your instructor.

⊕ ADJUST FISCAL YEAR SETTINGS WITHIN MICROSOFT PROJECT

1. On the Project Guide toolbar, click the **Show/Hide Project Guide** button to close the Project Guide.

2. On the Gantt Chart, drag the divider bar (between the table portion and the bar portion of the Gantt Chart) to the right until the Start and Finish columns are visible.

3. On the menu bar, click **Tools**, and then click **Options**. The Options dialog box appears.

4. Click the **Calendar** tab.

5. In the *Fiscal year starts in:* box, select **July**, and then click **OK** to close the Options dialog box. Your screen should look similar to Figure 13-2.

Figure 13-2

Gantt Chart view showing fiscal year timescale

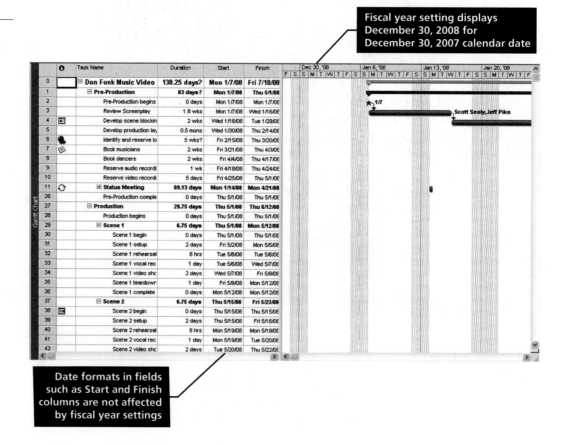

Fiscal year setting displays December 30, 2008 for December 30, 2007 calendar date

Date formats in fields such as Start and Finish columns are not affected by fiscal year settings

When you select the starting month of the fiscal year, Microsoft Project reformats the dates on the Gantt Chart timescale to use the fiscal year, not the calendar year. The months of July–December 2007 now show a 2008 year to reflect that the 2008 fiscal year runs from July 1, 2007 through June 30, 2008.

6. Click the **Undo** button to restore the dates to the calendar year format.

ANOTHER WAY

You can also restore the calendar year format by returning to the Calendar tab of the Options dialog box and selecting January in the *Fiscal year starts in:* box.

7. Drag the divider back to the right edge of the Duration column.

8. **SAVE** the project plan.

PAUSE. LEAVE Project open to use in the next exercise.

In this exercise, you changed the timescale view to accommodate a fiscal year–any 12 consecutive month period defined for accounting purposes–rather than a calendar year–a 12 month period from January to December. Using a fiscal year timescale is most appropriate if there are stakeholders who are accustomed to analyzing information in a fiscal year format. Otherwise, use the calendar year format.

There are many other options for controlling time in Microsoft Project through the Calendar tab of the Options dialog box. You use the Calendar tab to define basic time values, such as how many hours a day or a week should equal, or how many days should equal one month. You can also control other time settings, such as which day is the first day of the week (this varies from country to country).

The Calendar tab can be confusing, however, because it has nothing to do with Microsoft Project's base, project, resource, or task calendars. (You control these calendars through the Change Working time dialog box on the Tools menu.) The settings on the Calendar tab affect only the time conversions for task durations that you enter into Microsoft Project, such as how many hours equal one day–not when work can be scheduled.

The Default Start Time and Default End Time settings on the Calendar tab can also be confusing. These settings are not related to working time values for calendars. Rather, the Default Start Time and Default End Time settings have a very specific purpose. These settings supply the default start and end time for task constraints or for actual start and finish dates in which you enter a date but do not include a time. For example, if you enter a Must Start On constraint value of January 14, 2009, for a task but do not specify a start time, Microsoft Project will use the Default Start Time value that is set on the Calendar tab.

■ Viewing the Project's Critical Path

THE BOTTOM LINE   One of the most important parts of the project plan is the project's critical path. The critical path is the series of tasks which will extend the project's end date if they are delayed.

⊕ VIEW THE PROJECT'S CRITICAL PATH

USE the project plan you created in the previous exercise.

1. On the menu bar, click **View**, and then click **More Views**. The More Views dialog box appears.
2. In the More Views dialog box, select **Detail Gantt**, and then click **Apply**.
3. On the menu bar, click **View**, point to **Table: Delay**, and click **Entry**.
4. On the menu bar, click **Edit**, and then click **Go To**.
5. In the ID box, key **45**, and then click **OK**. Microsoft Project displays the Scene 3 summary task; this is a convenient location to view both noncritical and critical tasks. In the Detail Gantt view, noncritical tasks appear in blue, and critical tasks are in red. In this view, you can also see some tasks that have free slack. A thin teal line and the number next to it represent the free slack for a given task. Your screen should look similar to Figure 13-3.

Figure 13-3

Detail Gantt view showing
noncritical and critical tasks

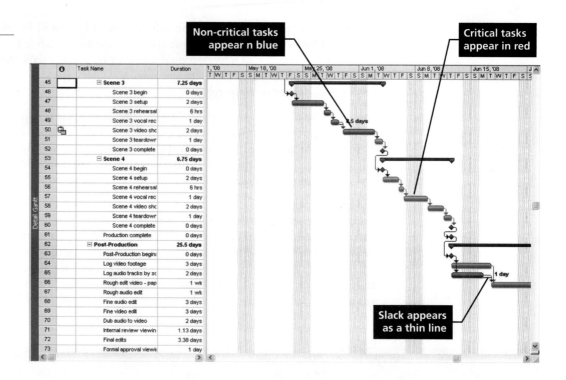

6. On the menu bar, click **View**, point to **Table: Entry** and then click **Schedule**. The Schedule table appears in the Detail Gantt view.

7. Drag the divider bar to the right until all columns in the Schedule table are visible. Your screen should look similar to Figure 13-4.

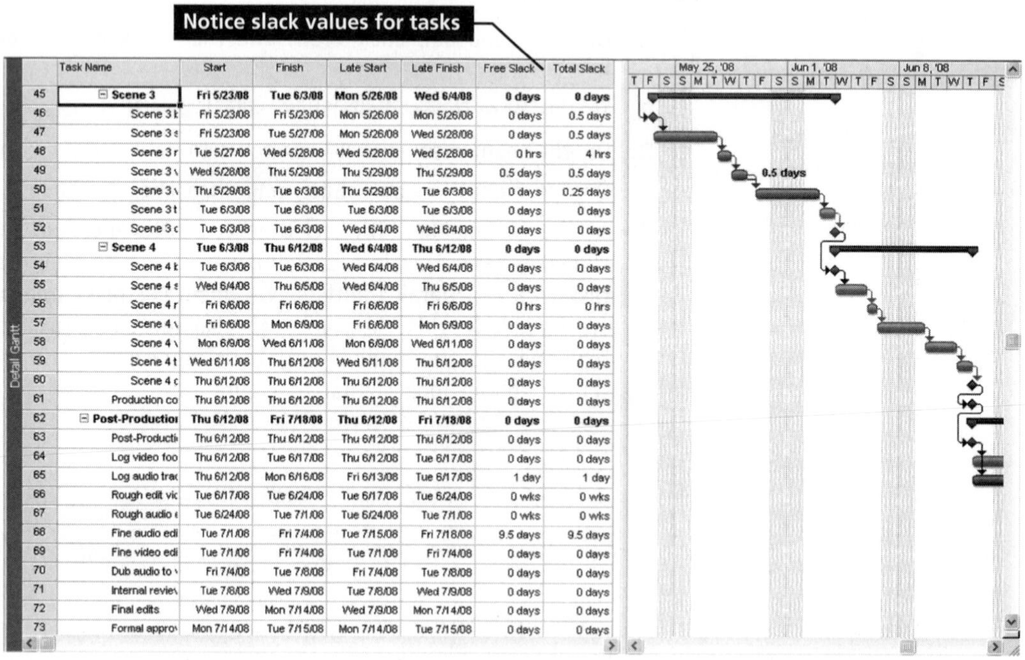

Figure 13-4

Schedule table showing free
slack and total slack for
each task

Review the free slack and total slack for each task. Recall from Lesson 4 that *free slack* is the amount of time the finish date of a task can be delayed before the start of a successor task must be rescheduled. *Total slack* is the amount of time the finish date on a task can be delayed before the completion of the project will be delayed. A task may have total slack, free slack, or both.

8. Drag the divider bar back to the left to show just the Task Name column.

9. On the menu bar, click **View**, and then click **Zoom**. Click **Entire Project**, and then click **OK**.

10. Scroll your screen up to the beginning of the project plan and click on the name of task 11, **Status Meeting**.

11. On the menu bar, click **Tools**, click **Options**, and then click the **Calculation** tab.

12. Select the **Calculate multiple critical paths** checkbox near the bottom of this dialog box, and then click **OK**. Microsoft Project reformats the tasks in the Pre-Production phase to show the critical path within this phase. Your screen should look similar to Figure 13-5.

Figure 13-5

Detail Gantt showing
Pre-Production critical path

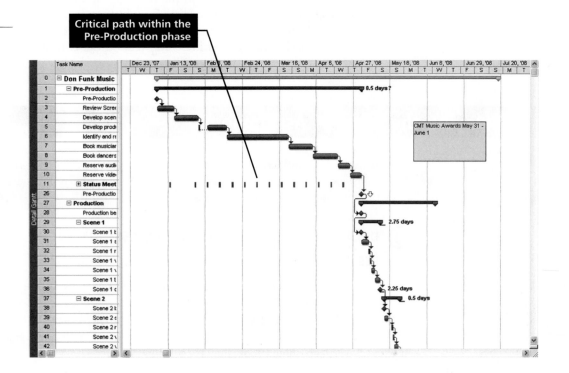

13. On the Standard toolbar, click the **Undo** button. Microsoft Project reverts to the single critical path for the project.

14. On the menu bar, click **View**, point to **Table: Schedule**, and then click **Entry**.

15. Drag the vertical divider bar to the right of the Duration column.

16. **SAVE** the project plan.

PAUSE. LEAVE Project open to use in the next exercise.

In this exercise, you reviewed the critical path of your project plan and the free and total slack for some of the tasks. As discussed in several previous lessons, one of the most important factors that should be monitored in any project plan is the project's critical path. Keep in mind that "critical" does not refer to the importance of these tasks in relation to the overall project, but rather to how their scheduling will affect the project's finish date. As a project manager, it is very important for you to understand how changes in schedule, resource assignments, constraints, etc., will affect this key series of tasks. After a task on the critical path is complete, it is no longer critical, because it can no longer affect the project finish date. During the life of the project, it is normal that the critical path will occasionally change.

In previous lessons, only a single critical path per project has been emphasized: the critical path that determines the project finish date. However, as you saw in this exercise, Microsoft Project can identify a critical path within any chain of linked tasks. This is especially useful when the project is divided into distinct phases. In this exercise, the Pre-Production critical

For a review of
critical paths and slack,
see Lesson 4.

path was made up of only the status meeting tasks. Usually, the critical path within a phase will have a much more distinct line of tasks in it.

Most projects have a specific end date. If you want to shorten the duration of the project to make the end date occur sooner, you need to begin by shortening the critical path (in project management jargon, this is called "crashing"). Prior to starting actual work on the project, it is critical that the project manager closely manage both the critical path and the slack. This involves:

- Knowing the tasks that are on the critical path and being able to evaluate the risk to project success if any of the tasks are not completed as scheduled. Any delays in completing tasks on the critical path delay the completion date of the project.

- Knowing where the slack is in the project. On a complex project, the critical path may change frequently. Tasks with very little free slack might become critical as the project begins and the actuals start to vary from the plan. In addition, tasks that had no free slack initially (and therefore were on the critical path) might get free slack as other tasks move on to the critical path.

■ Delaying the Start of Assignments

↓
THE BOTTOM LINE

If more than one resource is assigned to a task, you may not want all the resources to start working on the task at the same time. You can delay the start of work for one or more resources assigned to a task.

⊕ DELAY THE START OF A RESOURCE ASSIGNMENT

USE the project plan you created in the previous exercise.

1. On the menu bar, click **View**, and then click **Task Usage**. The Task Usage view appears.

2. On the menu bar, click **Edit and** click **Go To.** Key **74** in the ID box, and then click **OK.** Microsoft Project displays the "Duplicate audio and video masters" task. Your screen should look similar to Figure 13-6.

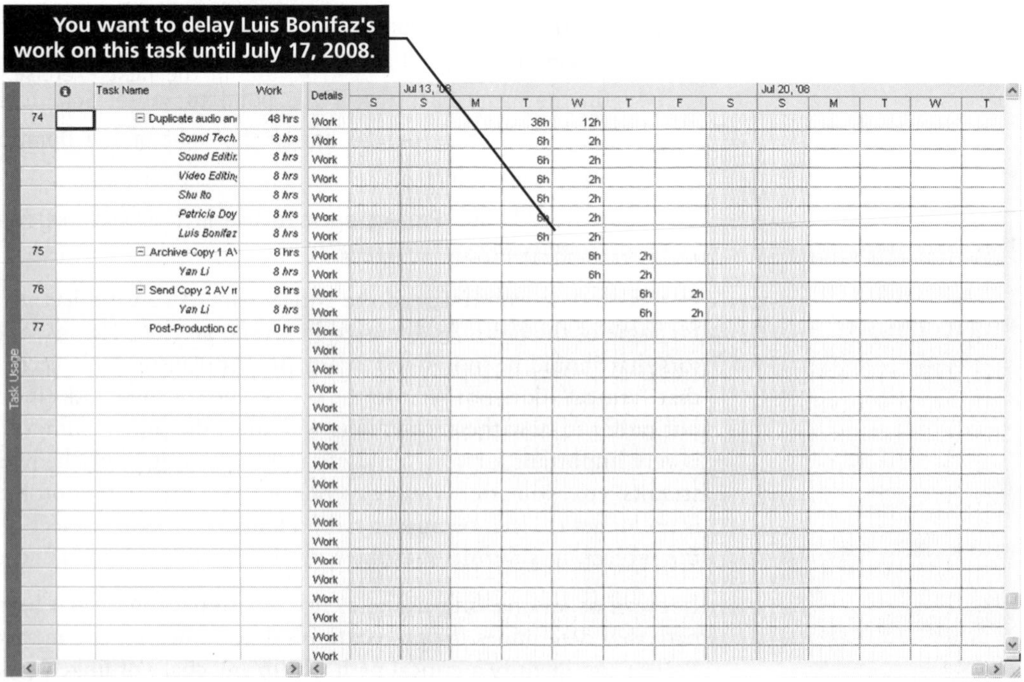

Figure 13-6

Task Usage view at task 74

Luis Bonifaz will inspect the final copies of the masters, so you want to delay his work on this task until Thursday, July 17, 2008.

3. In the Task Name column, select the name of the resource **Luis Bonifaz**.

4. On the Standard toolbar, click the **Assignment Information** button. The Assignment Information dialog box appears.

5. Click the **General** tab, if it is not already selected.

6. In the *Start* box, key or select **7/17/08**, and then click **OK** to close the Assignment Information dialog box. Microsoft Project adjusts Luis Bonifaz's assignment on this task so that he works eight hours on Thursday. The other resources assigned to this task are not affected. Your screen should look similar to Figure 13-7.

Figure 13-7

Task Usage view showing delayed assignment start for Luis Bonifaz

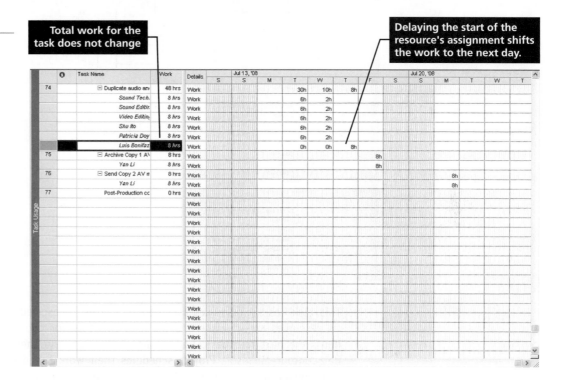

7. **SAVE** the project plan.

PAUSE. LEAVE Project open to use in the next exercise.

In this exercise, you delayed the start of work for a resource assigned to a task. You can delay the start of work for any number of resources assigned to a task. However, if you need to delay the start of work for all resources on a particular task, it may be better to just reschedule the start date of the task (rather than adjusting each resource's assignment).

■ Applying Contours to Assignments

 THE BOTTOM LINE   You can control the amount of time a resource works on a task by applying a work contour. A contour describes the way the resource's work is distributed over time.

Applying a Contour to a Resource Assignment

To optimize your project plan, you can apply a predefined contour to a task's assignments.

APPLY A CONTOUR TO A RESOURCE ASSIGNMENT

USE the project plan you created in the previous exercise.

1. On the menu bar, click **Edit** and click **Go To.** Key **67** in the ID box, and then click **OK.** Microsoft Project scrolls to task 67. Your screen should look similar to Figure 13-8.

Figure 13-8

Task Usage view showing resource assignments for task 67

> **These six resource assignments have a flat contour.**

	❶	Task Name	Work	Details	Jun 22, '08 S	S	M	T	W	T	F	S	Jun 29, '08 S	M	T	W	T
67		⊟ Rough audio edit	240 hrs	Work				12h	48h	48h	48h			48h	36h		
		Yan Li	40 hrs	Work				2h	8h	8h	8h			8h	6h		
		Sound Editir.	40 hrs	Work				2h	8h	8h	8h			8h	6h		
		Florian Voss	40 hrs	Work				2h	8h	8h	8h			8h	6h		
		Greg Guzik	40 hrs	Work				2h	8h	8h	8h			8h	6h		
		Maria Hamn	40 hrs	Work				2h	8h	8h	8h			8h	6h		
		Ido Ben-Sac	40 hrs	Work				2h	8h	8h	8h			8h	6h		
68		⊟ Fine audio edit	96 hrs	Work										8h	32h	32	
		Sound Editir.	24 hrs	Work										2h	8h	8	
		Jim Kim	24 hrs	Work										2h	8h	8	
		Greg Guzik	24 hrs	Work										2h	8h	8	
		Maria Hamn	24 hrs	Work										2h	8h	8	
69		⊟ Fine video edit	84 hrs	Work										7h	28h	28	
		Video Editin;	24 hrs	Work										2h	8h	8	
		Shu Ito	24 hrs	Work										2h	8h	8	
		Greg Guzik	24 hrs	Work										2h	8h	8	
		David Barbe	12 hrs	Work										1h	4h	4	
70		⊟ Dub audio to video	32 hrs	Work													
		Video Editin;	16 hrs	Work													
		Shu Ito	16 hrs	Work													
71		⊟ Internal review vie	57.5 hrs	Work													
		Jamie Redir.	7 hrs	Work													
		Scott Seely	5 hrs	Work													
		Jeff Pike	7 hrs	Work													
		Judy Lew	7 hrs	Work													
		Brenda Diaz	7 hrs	Work													
		Brad Sutton	7 hrs	Work													
		Annette Hill	3.5 hrs	Work													
		Ryan Ihrig	7 hrs	Work													

This task has six resources assigned to it. The timescaled data illustrates that all six resources are scheduled to work on this task for two hours the first day, eight hours the next four days, and six hours the last day. These assignments have a flat contour–Microsoft Project schedules their work based on a regular rate of eight hours per day. (The resources only work two hours the first day because they are scheduled for six hours on another task–for a total of eight.) This is the default work contour type that Microsoft Project uses when scheduling work.

You want to change Greg Guzik's assignment on this task so that he starts with a brief daily assignment and increases his work time as the task progresses. He will still be working on the task after the other resources have finished their assignments.

2. In the Task Name column under task 67, select **Greg Guzik.**

3. On the Standard toolbar, click the **Assignment Information** button. The Assignment Information dialog box appears.

4. Click the **General** tab, if it is not already selected.

5. In the *Work contour* box, select **Back Loaded**, and then click **OK** to close the Assignment Information dialog box. Microsoft Project applies the contour to Greg Guzik's assignment and reschedules his work on the task. Scroll your screen so that you can see all of Greg's assignments on this task. Your screen should look similar to Figure 13-9.

Figure 13-9

Task Usage view showing
contoured work for Greg Guzik

Contour indicator matches the type of contour applied– back loaded, in this case.

	0	Task Name	Work	Details	3 M	T	W	T	F	S	Jun 29, '08 S	M	T	W	T	F	S
67		⊟ Rough audio edit	240 hrs	Work		10.2h	40.97h	41.67h	43.5h			44.17h	36h	6.83h	8h	8h	
		Yan Li	40 hrs	Work		2h	8h	8h	8h			8h	6h				
		Sound Editir.	40 hrs	Work		2h	8h	8h	8h			8h	6h				
		Florian Voss	40 hrs	Work		2h	8h	8h	8h			8h	6h				
	.ıll	Greg Guzik	40 hrs	Work		0.2h	0.97h	1.67h	3.5h			4.17h	6h	6.83h	8h	8h	
		Maria Hamn	40 hrs	Work		2h	8h	8h	8h			8h	6h				
		Ido Ben-Sac	40 hrs	Work		2h	8h	8h	8h			8h	6h				
68		⊟ Fine audio edit	96 hrs	Work													
		Sound Editir.	24 hrs	Work													
		Jim Kim	24 hrs	Work													
		Greg Guzik	24 hrs	Work													
		Maria Hamn	24 hrs	Work													
69		⊟ Fine video edit	84 hrs	Work													
		Video Editir.	24 hrs	Work													
		Shu Ito	24 hrs	Work													
		Greg Guzik	24 hrs	Work													
		David Barbe	12 hrs	Work													
70		⊟ Dub audio to video	32 hrs	Work													
		Video Editir.	16 hrs	Work													
		Shu Ito	16 hrs	Work													
71		⊟ Internal review vie	57.5 hrs	Work													
		Jamie Redir.	7 hrs	Work													
		Scott Seely	5 hrs	Work													
		Jeff Pike	7 hrs	Work													
		Judy Lew	7 hrs	Work													
		Brenda Diaz	7 hrs	Work													
		Brad Sutton	7 hrs	Work													
		Annette Hill	3.5 hrs	Work													
		Ryan Ihrig	7 hrs	Work													

6. Point to the contour indicator in the Indicators column. Microsoft Project displays a ToolTip describing the type of contour applied to this assignment.

SHOOTING

Note that applying a contour to this assignment caused the overall duration of the task to be extended. If you do not want a contour to extend a task's duration, you need to change the Task Type (on the Advanced tab of the Task Information dialog box) to Fixed Duration before you apply the contour. When you apply a contour after changing to a task type such as fixed duration, Microsoft Project will recalculate the resource's work value so that he or she works less in the same time period.

7. SAVE the project plan.

PAUSE. LEAVE Project open to use in the next exercise.

In this exercise, you applied a predefined work contour to an assignment. A *contour* determines how a resource's work on a task is scheduled over time. In general, *predefined contours* describe how work is distributed over time in terms of graphical patterns. Some options are Bell, Front Loaded, Back Loaded, Double Peak, and Turtle. Predefined contours work best for assignments where you can estimate a probable pattern of effort. For instance, if a task might require significant ramp-up time, a back loaded contour might be beneficial, since the resource will be most productive toward the end of the assignment.

Keep in mind that because Greg Guzik's assignment to this task finishes later than the other resource assignments, Greg Guzik sets the finish date of the task. Sometimes it is said that Greg Guzik is the "driving resource" of this task because his assignment determines, or drives, the finish date of the task.

Manually Editing a Task Assignment

It is also possible to manually edit the assignment values for a resource assigned to a task, rather than applying a contour.

⊕ EDIT A TASK ASSIGNMENT MANUALLY

USE the project plan you created in the previous exercise.

1. On the menu bar, click **Edit**, and click **Go To.** Key **51** in the ID box, and then click **OK.** Microsoft Project scrolls vertically to task 51.

   You want to change Ido Ben-Sachar's assignment on the last two days of the task so that he will work part time on it.

2. Select Ido Ben-Sachar's eight-hour assignment for Tuesday, June 3, 2008.

3. Key **4h** and press [Tab].

4. In Ido Ben-Sachar's assignment for Wednesday, June 4, 2008, key **4h**, and then press [Enter]. Ido Ben-Sachar is now assigned four hours on each of these days. Your screen should look similar to Figure 13-10.

Figure 13-10

Task Usage view showing Ido Ben-Sachar's revised assignment for task 51

Work values for Tuesday and Wednesday, after editing

		Task Name	Work	Details	Jun 1, '08 S	S	M	T	W	T	F	S	Jun 8, '08 S	M	T	W	T
51		⊟ Scene 3 teardc	16 hrs	Work				12h	4h								
		Patricia	8 hrs	Work				8h									
	⚠	Ido Ben-	8 hrs	Work				4h	4h								
52		Scene 3 compl	0 hrs	Work													
53		⊟ Scene 4	156 hrs	Work						24h	24h			20h	30h	24h	22
54		Scene 4 begin	0 hrs	Work													
55		⊟ Scene 4 setup	48 hrs	Work						24h	24h						
		Brad Sut	16 hrs	Work						8h	8h						
		Chris Pr	16 hrs	Work						8h	8h						
		electrici	16 hrs	Work						8h	8h						
56		⊟ Scene 4 rehea	12 hrs	Work										12h			
		dancers	6 hrs	Work										8h			
		musiciai	6 hrs	Work										6h			
57		⊟ Scene 4 vocal	32 hrs	Work										8h	24h		
		Sound T	8 hrs	Work										2h	6h		
		Don Fun	8 hrs	Work										2h	6h		
		Luis Box	8 hrs	Work										2h	6h		
		musiciai	8 hrs	Work										2h	6h		
58		⊟ Scene 4 video	48 hrs	Work										6h	24h	18	
		Sound T	16 hrs	Work										2h	8h	6	
		DVD	2-hour disc	Work (										0.13	0.5	0.3	
		Don Fun	16 hrs	Work										2h	8h	6	
		Frank Zi	8 hrs	Work										1h	4h	3	
		David Ba	8 hrs	Work										1h	4h	3	
		Dry Ice	10 lb block	Work (										0.13	0.5	0.3	
		Bottled V	bottle case	Work (										0.13	0.5	0.3	
59		⊟ Scene 4 teardc	16 hrs	Work													4
		Patricia	8 hrs	Work													2
		Ido Ben-	8 hrs	Work													2

5. **SAVE** the project plan.

   PAUSE. LEAVE Project open to use in the next exercise.

In this exercise, you manually edited the assignment for a resource by directly changing the assignment values in the timescaled grid of the Task Usage view. You may have noticed that when you entered the four hours for the work assignment on Wednesday for Ido Ben-Sachar, the tasks after task 51 shifted to reflect the longer duration of task 51.

You can use either predefined contours or make manual edits to a resource's work assignments. How you contour or edit an assignment depends on what you need to accomplish.

■ Optimizing the Project Plan

THE BOTTOM LINE

Prior to saving the baseline project plan and tracking actuals, an important part of project planning is to verify that the project has been optimized. This might mean reducing cost, duration, scope, or any combination of these aspects of a project.

Identifying the Project Finish Date and Total Cost

In order to optimize a project plan, you must first identify and understand the project's duration, finish date, and total cost.

→ IDENTIFY THE PROJECT FINISH DATE AND TOTAL COST

USE the project plan you created in the previous exercise.

1. On the menu bar, click **View,** and then click **More Views.** The More Views dialog box appears.

2. In the More Views dialog box, select **Detail Gantt,** and then click **Apply.** The Detail Gantt view appears.

3. On the menu bar, click **Project,** and click **Project Information.** The Project Information dialog box appears. Your screen should look similar to Figure 13-11.

Figure 13-11

Project Information dialog box

Notice that the Finish Date value of 7/28/08 is formatted in gray, indicating that you cannot directly edit it. Because the Don Funk Music Video project is scheduled from a start date, the finish date is calculated by Microsoft Project based on the task durations and schedule logic in the project plan.

4. Click the **Statistics** button. The Project Statistics dialog box appears. This box provides the current calculated cost: just over $94,000. This value is the sum of all task and resource costs in the project. These include fixed costs, per-use costs, and the calculated costs of resource assignments. Your screen should look similar to Figure 13-12.

Figure 13-12

Project Statistics dialog box

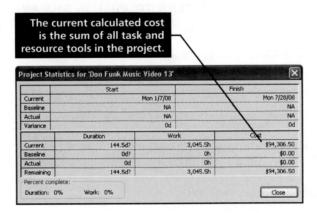

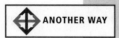ANOTHER WAY

You can also view the same details you see in the Project Statistics dialog box (and more) in the Project Summary Report. This report is helpful for communicating high-level project information to stakeholders. You can access the Project Summary Report on the Reports menu in the Overview section of reports.

5. Click **Close** to close the Project Statistics dialog box.
6. **SAVE** the project plan.

   PAUSE. LEAVE Project open to use in the next exercise.

In this exercise, you reviewed project details such as the duration, finish date, and total costs. It is helpful to review this information so that you understand the nature of your project and how it can best be optimized. Optimizing is adjusting the aspects of the project plan, such as cost, duration, and scope (or any combination of these), to achieve a desired project plan result. A desired result may be a target finish date, duration, or overall cost.

Note that in Figure 13-12 above, many of the values in the Project Statistics dialog box equal zero or NA (not applicable). Why is this? The current values are the values entered into the project plan to date. Since you have not yet saved a baseline, these values are zero or NA. In addition, since you have not started entering actual values, these are also zero or NA. There is no variance since you have no baseline or actuals. Finally, since you have no actuals, the remaining values equal the current values.

Now let's look forward to the next exercise. Assume that you have shared the project details from above with the project stakeholders, and you have all agreed to optimize the project to meet a finish date of 07/21/08. The projected cost is acceptable, and can even increase slightly, if necessary, to meet the new target finish date. Decreasing the project's duration without altering the basic sequence of activities is known as *crashing*.

Compressing the Project Plan

Now that you have reviewed the project details, you will focus on pulling in the project finish date.

⊕ COMPRESS THE PROJECT PLAN TO PULL IN THE PROJECT FINISH DATE

USE the project plan you created in the previous exercise.

1. On the menu bar, click **View**, and then click **Zoom**.
2. Click **Reset**. The Custom box adjusts to a preset number of days. Click **OK** to close the Zoom dialog box.
3. Scroll through and review the task list. Note that task 38, *Scene 2 begin*, has a Start No Earlier Than constraint date of 5/15/08 applied to it. Shortening the duration of tasks prior to task 38 will have no effect on the project finish date at this time, since those tasks are not on the critical path. They already finish prior to the earliest day on which task 38 could start. To shorten the project finish date, you must work with tasks after task 38.

TROUBLESHOOTING

The constraint on task 38 is one example of why you should limit your use of inflexible and semi-flexible constraints. The constraint has limited your means of shortening the project's duration.

4. On the menu bar, click **Edit**, and then click **Go To**.

5. In the ID box, key **67**, and then click **OK**. If necessary, scroll the Gantt Chart view to the right so that you can see the entire Gantt bar for task 67. Your screen should look similar to Figure 13-13.

Figure 13-13

Detail Gantt Chart showing task 67

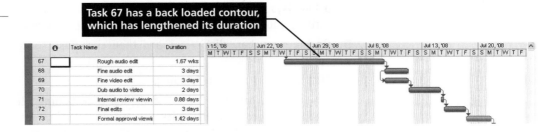

Recall that in an earlier exercise, you applied a back loaded contour to Greg Guzik's assignment to this task, lengthening its duration. To leave this assignment contour in place but start subsequent tasks earlier, you will add lead time to task 68, task 67's successor task.

6. In the Task Name column, double-click the name of task 68, **Fine audio edit**. The Task Information dialog box appears.

7. Click the **Predecessors** tab.

8. In the Lag field for the predecessor task 67, key **-50%** and press **Enter**. Click **OK** to close the Task Information dialog box.

   Applying a lead time to the task relationship between tasks 67 and 68 causes task 68 and all successor tasks to start earlier. Entering this lag causes the successor task 68 to begin when 50% of the predecessor task 67's duration has elapsed. Your screen should look similar to Figure 13-14.

Figure 13-14

Detail Gantt Chart showing task 68 with adjusted predecessor lag time

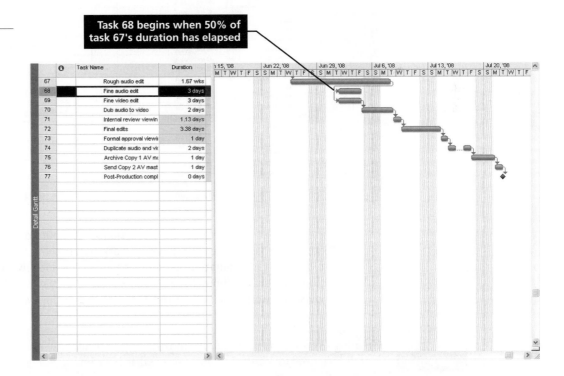

Note that task 69 has a Start-to-Start relationship with task 68, so it has the same new start date as task 68. All subsequent successor tasks were also rescheduled, resulting in a new project finish date.

You can review the Detail Gantt view (or display the Project Information dialog box) to see that the final task of the project now ends on 7/22/08. This is still a few days later than your desired finish date. To compress the project duration further, you will apply overtime work to some assignments.

9. On the menu bar, click **View**, and then click **Task Usage**. The Task Usage view appears.

10. Click the **Work** column heading.

11. On the menu bar, click **Insert**, and then click **Column**. In the *Field name* box, select **Overtime Work**, and then click **OK**. Microsoft Project inserts the Overtime Work column between the Task Name and Work columns. Drag the divider bar between the table and bar portions of the Gantt Chart to the right until the Work column is visible. The specific task for which you wish to apply overtime is task 66.

12. On the menu bar, click **Edit**, and click **Go To**. Key **66** in the ID box, and then click **OK**. Microsoft Project scrolls the Task Usage view to display the assignments of task 66. Your screen should look similar to Figure 13-15.

Figure 13-15

Task Usage view showing task 66 with assignments

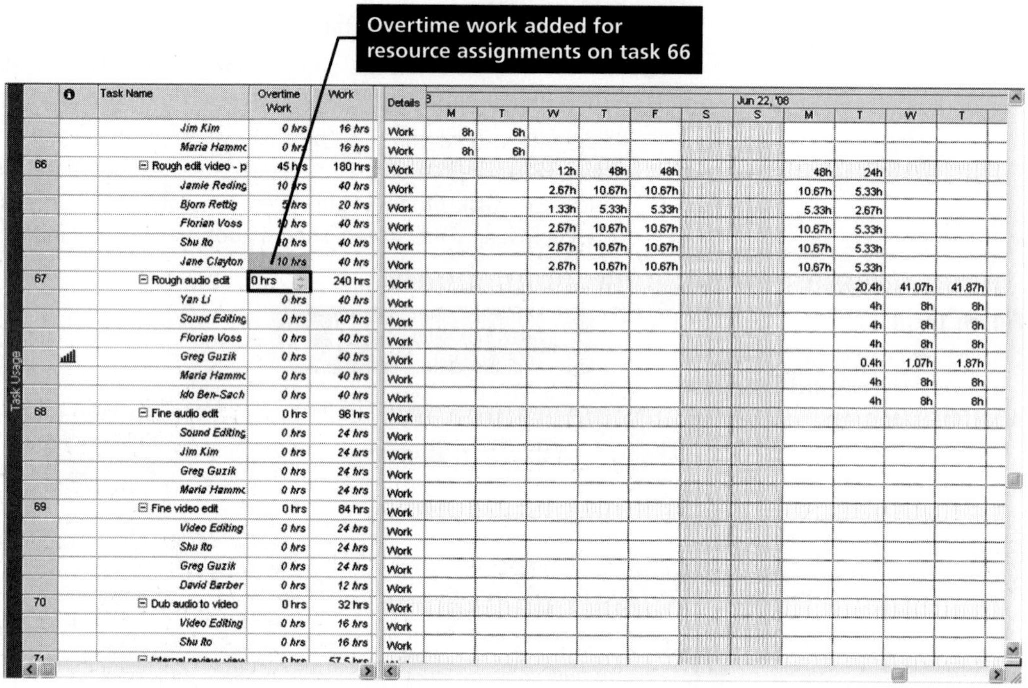

Currently, four of the resources are assigned 40 hours of regular work to this task. Bjorn Rettig is assigned 20 hours of work because his Max Units value is 50%. To shorten the task's duration without changing the total work in the task (for each assignment except Bjorn Rettig), you will record that 10 of the 40 hours of work is overtime work. You will record 5 hours of overtime work for Bjorn Rettig.

TAKE NOTE Entering overtime work for an assignment does not add work to the assignment. Rather, it indicates how much of the work assigned is overtime. Adding overtime work reduces the overall duration of the assignment.

13. Click the Overtime Work cell for Jamie Reding, the first resource assigned to task 66.

14. Key **10** and press [Enter].

15. Repeat steps 13 and 14 for Florian Voss, Shu Ito, and Jane Clayton.

16. Repeat steps 13 and 14 for Bjorn Rettig, except key **5** in the Overtime Work cell. Your screen should look similar to Figure 13-16.

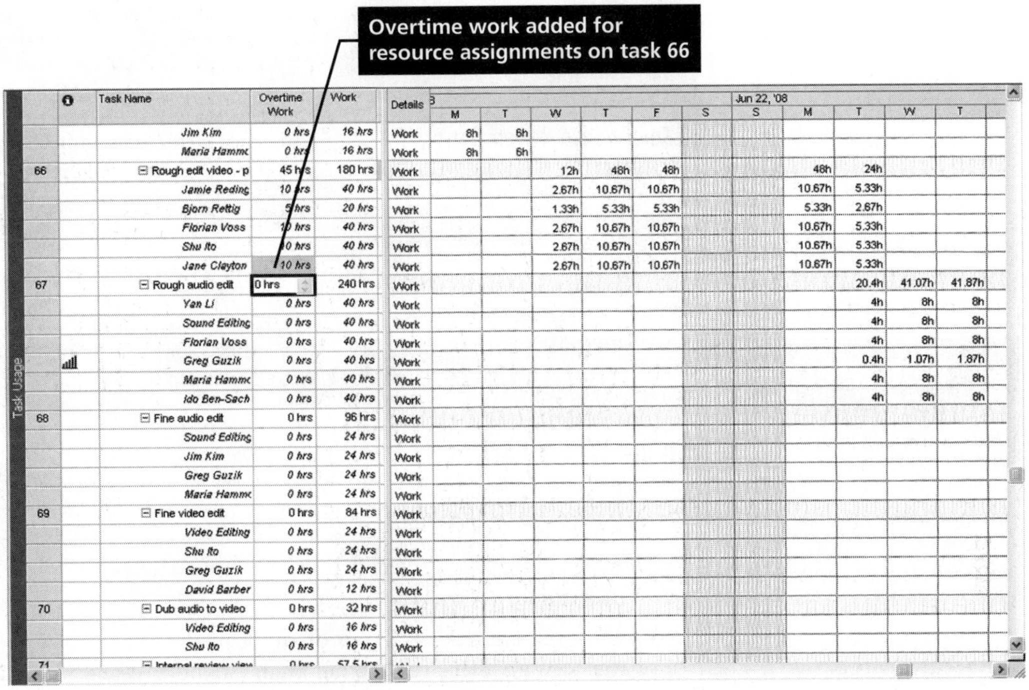

Figure 13-16

Task Usage view showing task 66 with overtime work added

17. On the menu bar, click **Project**, and then click **Project Information**. The Project Information dialog box appears. Note that the new finish date is 7/21/08. Click **OK** to close the Project Information dialog box.

The finish date is now at your target date, so you will stop your project optimization work here.

18. **SAVE** the project plan, and then **CLOSE** the file.

PAUSE. If you are continuing to the next lesson, keep Project open.
If you are not continuing to additional lessons, **CLOSE** Project.

In this exercise, you compressed a project plan by applying lead time to some tasks, and allowing overtime for another task. *Optimizing* a project plan and responding to variance are issues that Microsoft Project cannot automate. As a project manager, you must know the nature of your projects and how they should be optimized. As you saw in this exercise, you might need to make trade-offs, such as cutting scope, adding resources, allowing overtime, or adding lead time.

In this exercise, although you stopped your optimization work when you achieved your desired finish date, keep in mind that once actual work starts, variance will almost certainly appear and the critical path and project finish date are likely to change. For this reason, properly identifying and responding to variance is a key project management skill that will be addressed in a later lesson.

SUMMARY SKILL MATRIX

IN THIS LESSON YOU LEARNED	MATRIX SKILL
To make time and date adjustments	Adjust fiscal year settings within Microsoft Project
To view the project's critical path	View the project's critical path
To delay the start of assignments	Delay the start of a resource assignment
To apply a contour to a resource	Apply a contour to a resource assignment Edit assignment a task assignment manually
To optimize the project plan	Identify the project finish date and total cost Compress the project plan to pull in the project finish date

■ Knowledge Assessment

Fill in the Blank

Complete the following sentences by writing the correct word or words in the blanks provided.

1. A(n) _____ determines how a resource's work on a task is scheduled over time.

2. The _____ tab of the Options dialog box provides an option to change the view to fiscal year rather than calendar year.

3. The _____ is the series of tasks which will extend the project's end date if they are delayed.

4. Adjusting the aspects of the project plan, such as cost, duration, and scope, to achieve a desired project plan result is known as _____.

5. For a task on the critical path, critical refers to how its scheduling will affect the project's _____.

6. _____ is the amount of time that the finish date of a task can be delayed before the start of a successor task must be rescheduled.

7. A(n) _____ contour describes how work is distributed over time in terms of graphical patterns.

8. It is important to optimize your project plan prior to saving a(n) _____.

9. Decreasing the project's duration without altering the basic sequence of activities is known as _____.

10. The amount of time the finish date on a task can be delayed before the completion of the project will be delayed is known as _____.

Multiple Choice

Select the best response for the following statements.

1. Using a fiscal year view is most appropriate when

   a. you want to view the costs for individual tasks.

   b. you need to pull in the project end date.

   c. there are stakeholders who are accustomed to analyzing data in this format.

   d. you need to combine projects with other project managers.

2. Predefined contours work best when you can estimate
   a. the finish date of the task.
   b. a probable pattern of effort.
   c. the overallocation of a resource.
   d. none of the above.

3. A task may have
   a. total slack.
   b. free slack.
   c. partial slack.
   d. both A and B above.

4. A task that has free slack before a project begins
   a. might become critical as the project begins and actuals are entered.
   b. will always have free slack.
   c. cannot ever affect the critical path.
   d. should be optimized as soon as possible.

5. You cannot use the Calendar tab of the Options dialog box to
   a. define how many hours are in a day.
   b. identify which is the first day of the week.
   c. set up the base calendar.
   d. define how may days should equal one month.

6. If a resource's assignment determines the finish date of a task, it is said that the resource is the
   a. driving resource.
   b. critical resource.
   c. final resource.
   d. end resource.

7. Which of the following is not a predefined contour?
   a. Bell
   b. Half Pike
   c. Front Loaded
   d. Turtle

8. You can view the costs of a project in the
   a. Project Information dialog box.
   b. Project Cost dialog box.
   c. Project Statistics dialog box.
   d. Detailed Gantt Chart view.

9. Once work has commenced on a project
   a. the critical path cannot change.
   b. variance can no longer appear.
   c. the finish date is likely to change.
   d. a task cannot move from noncritical to critical.

10. The Default Start Time and Default End Time settings on the Calendar tab of the Options dialog box

    a. are not related to the working time values for calendars.

    b. supply the default start and end time for task constraints.

    c. supply the default start and end time for actual start and finish dates in which you enter a date but do not include a time.

    d. all of the above.

■ Competency Assessment

➔ Project 13-1: Fiscal Year View for Office Remodel

The Facility Management department would like to see the project plan for your lunchroom office remodel in a fiscal year view. For your company, the fiscal year begins on October 1.

GET READY. Launch Microsoft Project if it is not already running.

OPEN *Office Remodel 13-1* from the data files for this lesson.

The *Office Remodel 13-1* project plan is available on the companion CD-ROM.

1. Click the **Show/Hide Project Guide** button on the Project Guide toolbar.
2. On the Gantt Chart, drag the vertical divider bar to the right to expose the Start and Finish columns.
3. On the menu bar, click **Tools**, and then click **Options**.
4. Click the **Calendar** tab.
5. In the *Fiscal year starts in:* box, select **October**, and then click **OK** to close the Options dialog box.
6. **SAVE** the project plan as *Office Remodel Fiscal Year* and then **CLOSE** the file.

    PAUSE. LEAVE Project open to use in the next exercise.

➔ Project 13-2: Compressing the HR Interview Project Plan

After a team meeting regarding the HR Interview project plan, it is decided that you need to wrap up your interviewing process before the beginning of December. November 28 is your target date. Make lead time and overtime adjustments to your project plan to bring in the finish date.

The *HR Interview Plan 13-2* project plan is available on the companion CD-ROM.

OPEN *HR Interview Plan 13-2* from the data files for this lesson.

1. On the menu bar, click **View**, and then click **More Views**.
2. In the More Views dialog box, select **Detail Gantt**, and then click **Apply**.
3. Click on the name of task 1, **HR Interview Plan**, and then click the **Scroll to Task** button on the Standard toolbar.
4. Double-click the name of task 6, **Assemble potential candidate applications and resumes**.
5. In the Task Information dialog box, click the **Predecessors** tab, if necessary.
6. In the Lag field for the predecessor task 5, key **-60%** and press ⏎Enter. Click **OK**.
7. On the menu bar, click **View**, and then click **Task Usage**.
8. Click the **Work** column heading.
9. On the menu bar, click **Insert**, and then click **Column.** In the Field Name box, select **Overtime Work**, and then click **OK**.
10. On the menu bar, click **Edit**, and click **Go To.** Key **12** in the ID box, and then click **OK**.

11. Under task 12, click the Overtime Work cell for Keith Harris.

12. Key **8** and press **Enter**.

13. Repeat steps 11 and 12 for Mu Zheng and Megan Sherman.

14. On the menu bar, click **View**, and then click **More Views**. In the More Views dialog box, select **Detail Gantt**, and then click **Apply**.

15. On the menu bar, click **Edit**, and click **Go To**. Key **30** in the ID box, and then click **OK**. Point your cursor to the Interview Process Complete Milestone and note the new finish date.

16. **SAVE** the project plan as *HR Interview Compressed* and then **CLOSE** the file.

PAUSE. LEAVE Project open to use in the next exercise.

■ Proficiency Assessment

Project 13-3: Office Remodel Cost and Finish Date

The *Office Remodel 13-3* project plan is available on the companion CD-ROM.

Before you begin to optimize your Office Remodel project plan, you need to identify the project finish date and total cost.

OPEN *Office Remodel 13-3* from the data files for this lesson.

1. Activate the More Views dialog box, and then apply the Detail Gantt view.

2. Activate the Project Information dialog box.

3. In a separate Word document, document the Finish date of the project.

4. Activate the Project Statistics dialog box.

5. Continuing in the same Word document, document the current cost of the project.

6. Close the Project Statistics dialog box.

7. **SAVE** the project plan as *Office Remodel Finish-Cost*. **SAVE** the Word document as *Office Remodel Finish-Cost*. **CLOSE** both files.

PAUSE. LEAVE Project open to use in the next exercise.

Project 13-4: Don Funk Resource Assignment Contour

The *Don Funk Music Video 13-4* project plan is available on the companion CD-ROM.

You are working on the Don Funk Music Video and want to apply a predefined contour for Annette Hill's assignment to task 7, Book musicians. Because of other commitments, she will work more hours on the front end of this task.

OPEN *Don Funk Music Video 13-4* from the data files for this lesson.

1. Activate the Task Usage view.

2. Scroll to task 7.

3. Select the name **Annette Hill**.

4. Activate the General tab of the Assignment Information dialog box.

5. Apply a front loaded contour to this resource for this assignment.

6. Scroll the screen so that you can see Annette's later assignments on this task.

7. **SAVE** the project plan as *Don Funk Contour* and then **CLOSE** the file.

PAUSE. LEAVE Project open to use in the next exercise.

■ Mastery Assessment

→ Project 13-5: Employee Orientation Assignment Delay

The *Employee Orientation 13-5* project plan is available on the companion CD-ROM.

During your employee orientation, you will be presenting an overview of the profit sharing plan at your company. Kevin McDowell will talk to the new hires after Sidney Higa has finished. You need to delay the start of Kevin's assignment until after Sidney Higa has finished her assignment.

OPEN *Employee Orientation 13-5* from the data files for this lesson.

1. Switch to the Task Usage view.
2. For task 19, *Overview of profit sharing plan*, delay Kevin McDowell's 0.5h assignment from 11:00 AM until 11:30 AM.
3. **SAVE** the project plan as *Employee Orientation Manual Edit* and then **CLOSE** the file.

   PAUSE. LEAVE Project open to use in the next exercise.

→ Project 13-6: Insurance Claim Process Delayed Start

The *Insurance Claim Process 13-6* project plan is available on the companion CD-ROM.

On your Insurance Claim Process project plan, you need to edit Chris Gray's assignment on task 18, Repair performed, so that he does not start work until after the other resource assigned to the task.

OPEN *Insurance Claim Process 13-6* from the data files for this lesson.

1. Activate the Task Usage view.
2. Using the Assignment Information dialog box, edit Chris Gray's assignment on task 18 so that the start of his work on this task is delayed until Wednesday, June 18, 2008.
3. **SAVE** the project plan as *Insurance Claim Delayed Start*, and then **CLOSE** the file.
   CLOSE Project.

INTERNET READY

Although only briefly discussed in this lesson, it is important that a good project manager understand project crashing—what it really means, how it is accomplished, effects on the project plan, trade-offs that must be made, etc.

Search the Internet for articles on project crashing. Some good places to start are Microsoft's Work Essential web site or a project management web site. Read and review the articles you find. Look for detailed information above and beyond the concepts discussed in this lesson. Summarize your findings in a brief Word document or outline, and then practice by applying what you have learned to a project on which you are currently working.

Advanced Project Plan Formatting

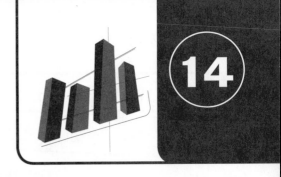

LESSON SKILL MATRIX

SKILLS	MATRIX SKILL
Customizing the Calendar View	Format bar styles for tasks in the Calendar view
Using Task IDs and WBS Codes	Work with Unique ID and WBS codes
Formatting the Network Diagram	Format items in the Network Diagram view
Customizing and Printing Reports	Create a custom report

You are a video project manager for Southridge Video, and one of your primary responsibilities recently has been to manage the new Don Funk Music Video project. In an earlier lesson, you learned about some of the basic formatting features in Microsoft Office Project that allow you to change the way your data appears. In this lesson, you will learn about some of the more powerful formatting features that enable you to organize and analyze data that otherwise would require separate tools, such as a spreadsheet application.

KEY TERMS
mask
Network Diagram
node
outline number
Unique ID
work breakdown structure
(WBS) code

■ SOFTWARE ORIENTATION

WBS Codes and Unique IDs in the Task Sheet View

Unique IDs are unique identifiers for tasks and resources. WBS codes show the outline hierarchy of a project.

Figure 14-1

WBS Codes and Unique IDs in the Task Sheet view

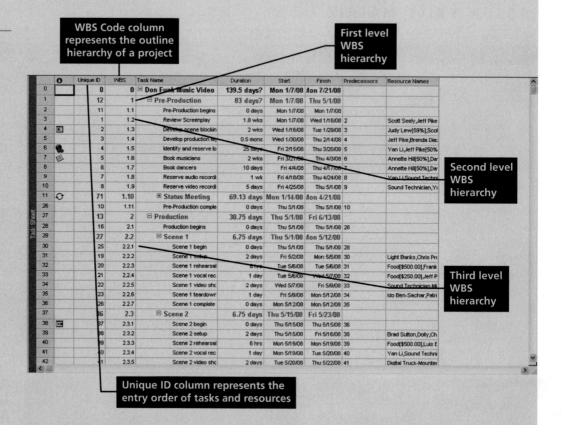

A Unique ID tracks the order in which you enter tasks and resources. WBS codes are numeric representations of the outline hierarchy of a project.

■ Customizing the Calendar View

THE BOTTOM LINE

The Calendar view is one of the simplest views available in Microsoft Project. It can be customized in several different ways.

CD

The *Don Funk Music Video 14M* project plan is available on the companion CD-ROM

GET READY. Before you begin these steps, launch Microsoft Project.

OPEN the *Don Funk Music Video 14M* project plan from the data files for this lesson.

SAVE the file as *Don Funk Music Video 14* in the solutions folder for this lesson as directed by your instructor.

➔ FORMAT BAR STYLES FOR TASKS IN THE CALENDAR VIEW

1. Click the **Show/Hide Project Guide** button on the Project Guide toolbar. The Project Guide closes.

2. On the menu bar, click **View**, and then click **Calendar**. The Calendar view appears. Your screen should look similar to Figure 14-2.

Figure 14-2

Calendar view

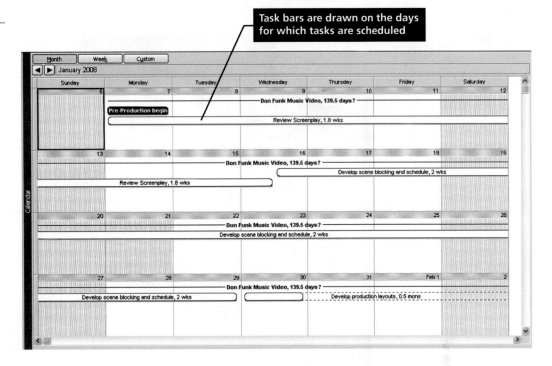

The Calendar view displays four weeks at a time and looks similar to a month-at-a-glance calendar. Task bars are drawn on the days for which tasks are scheduled.

3. On the menu bar, click **Format**, and then click **Bar Styles**. The Bar Styles dialog box appears.

4. In the *Task type* box, click **Summary**.

5. In the *Bar type* box, click **Line**. Summary tasks will be shown with a line.

6. In the *Task type* box, click **Critical**.

7. In the Pattern box, click the second option, the solid bar.

8. In the Color box, click **Red**. Critical tasks will be shown with a solid red bar.

9. Make sure that the check boxes for *Shadow* and *Bar rounding* are selected. Your screen should look similar to Figure 14-3.

Figure 14-3

Bar Styles dialog box displaying formatting selections

10. Click **OK** to close the Bar Styles dialog box.

11. On the menu bar, click **Format**, and then click **Layout Now**. Microsoft Project applies the format options to the Calendar view.

12. Move your pointer to the divider bar between the weeks of the calendar. Your pointer will change to a bar with perpendicular arrows. Your screen should look like Figure 14-4.

Figure 14-4

Calendar View with pointer positioned on divider bar

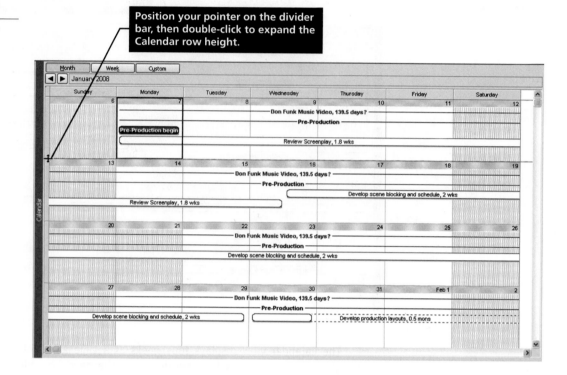

13. Double-click on the divider bar to expand the width of the calendar rows to show all tasks.

14. On the menu bar, click **Edit**, and then click **Go To**. In the Date box (not the ID box), key or select **07/11/08**, and then click **OK**. The Calendar view displays the first critical tasks using the revised formatting. Your screen should look similar to Figure 14-5.

Figure 14-5

Calendar view showing refor-matted critical tasks

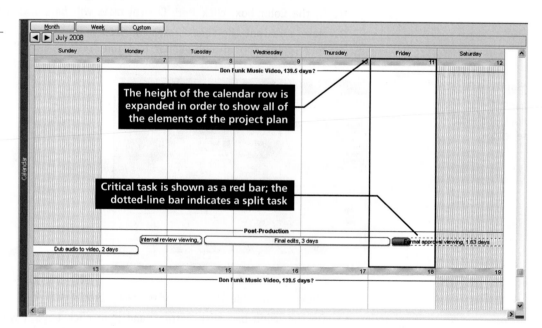

15. **SAVE** the project plan.

PAUSE. LEAVE Project open to use in the next exercise.

In this exercise, you reformatted several of the bar styles in the Calendar view. The Calendar view is one of the simplest views available in Microsoft Project, and it offers several formatting options. This view is often used for sharing schedule information with resources or other stakeholders who prefer a more traditional monthly or weekly view, rather than a detailed view such as the Gantt Chart.

■ Using Task IDs and WBS Codes

THE BOTTOM LINE

Microsoft Project organizes and tracks the tasks entered into a project plan using several unique identifiers: Task IDs, Unique IDs, and Work Breakdown Structure (WBS) codes. You can structure the Task Sheet view so that columns for these identifiers are displayed.

→ WORK WITH UNIQUE ID AND WBS CODES

USE the project plan you created in the previous exercise.

1. On the menu bar, click **View**, and then click **More Views**.

2. In the More Views dialog box, select **Task Sheet**, and then click the **Apply** button. The project appears in the Task Sheet view.

3. On the menu bar, click **View**, point to **Table: Music Video Schedule Table**, and then click **Entry**. Your screen should look similar to Figure 14-6.

Figure 14-6

Project plan in Task Sheet view

> **Project plan in Task Sheet view with Entry table**

	❶	Task Name	Duration	Start	Finish	Predecessors	Resource Names
0		⊟ Don Funk Music Video	139.5 days?	Mon 1/7/08	Mon 7/21/08		
1		⊟ Pre-Production	83 days?	Mon 1/7/08	Thu 5/1/08		
2		Pre-Production begins	0 days	Mon 1/7/08	Mon 1/7/08		
3		Review Screenplay	1.8 wks	Mon 1/7/08	Wed 1/16/08	2	Scott Seely,Jeff Pike
4	▣	Develop scene blockin	2 wks	Wed 1/16/08	Tue 1/29/08	3	Judy Lew[59%],Scot
5		Develop production lay	0.5 mons	Wed 1/30/08	Thu 2/14/08	4	Jeff Pike,Brenda Diaz
6		Identify and reserve lo	5 wks?	Fri 2/15/08	Thu 3/20/08	5	Yan Li,Jeff Pike[50%
7		Book musicians	2 wks	Fri 3/21/08	Thu 4/3/08	6	Annette Hill[50%],Da
8		Book dancers	2 wks	Fri 4/4/08	Thu 4/17/08	7	Annette Hill[50%],Da
9		Reserve audio recordi	1 wk	Fri 4/18/08	Thu 4/24/08	8	Yan Li,Sound Techni
10		Reserve video recordi	5 days	Fri 4/25/08	Thu 5/1/08	9	Sound Technician,Ya
11	↻	⊞ Status Meeting	69.13 days	Mon 1/14/08	Mon 4/21/08		
26		Pre-Production comple	0 days	Thu 5/1/08	Thu 5/1/08	10	
27		⊟ Production	30.75 days	Thu 5/1/08	Fri 6/13/08		
28		Production begins	0 days	Thu 5/1/08	Thu 5/1/08	26	
29		⊟ Scene 1	6.75 days	Thu 5/1/08	Mon 5/12/08		
30		Scene 1 begin	0 days	Thu 5/1/08	Thu 5/1/08	28	
31		Scene 1 setup	2 days	Fri 5/2/08	Mon 5/5/08	30	Light Banks,Chris Pre
32		Scene 1 rehearsal	6 hrs	Tue 5/6/08	Tue 5/6/08	31	Food[$500.00],Frank
33		Scene 1 vocal rec	1 day	Tue 5/6/08	Wed 5/7/08	32	Food[$250.00],Jeff P
34		Scene 1 video sho	2 days	Wed 5/7/08	Fri 5/9/08	33	Sound Technician,Mi
35		Scene 1 teardown	1 day	Fri 5/9/08	Mon 5/12/08	34	Ido Ben-Sachar,Patri
36		Scene 1 complete	0 days	Mon 5/12/08	Mon 5/12/08	35	
37		⊟ Scene 2	6.75 days	Thu 5/15/08	Fri 5/23/08		
38	▦	Scene 2 begin	0 days	Thu 5/15/08	Thu 5/15/08	36	
39		Scene 2 setup	2 days	Thu 5/15/08	Fri 5/16/08	38	Brad Sutton,Dolly,Ch
40		Scene 2 rehearsal	6 hrs	Mon 5/19/08	Mon 5/19/08	39	Food[$500.00],Luis E
41		Scene 2 vocal rec	1 day	Mon 5/19/08	Tue 5/20/08	40	Yan Li,Sound Techni
42		Scene 2 video sho	2 days	Tue 5/20/08	Thu 5/22/08	41	Digital Truck-Mounted

ANOTHER WAY

You can also insert a column by right-clicking a column heading, and in the shortcut menu that appears, clicking Insert Column.

4. Click on the Task Name column heading.

5. On the menu bar, click **Insert**, and then click **Column**. The Column Definition dialog box appears.

6. In the *Field name* list, click **Unique ID**, and then click **OK**. Microsoft Project inserts the Unique ID column to the left of the Task Name column. Your screen should look similar to Figure 14-7.

Figure 14-7

Task view with Unique ID column inserted

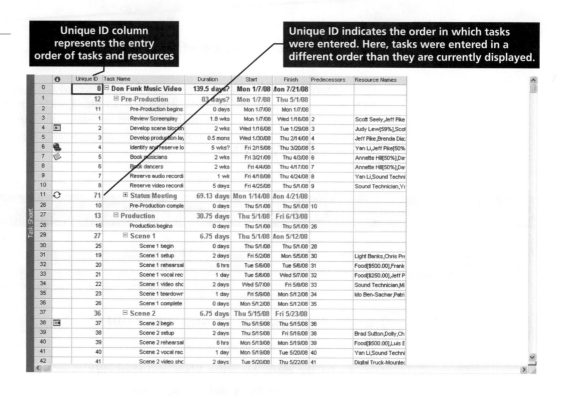

The Unique ID column indicates the order in which the tasks were entered into the project. Cutting and pasting a task causes its Unique ID value to change. You can see that the tasks in this project were entered in a different order than they are currently displayed.

7. Click on the Task Name column heading.

8. On the menu bar, click **Insert**, and then click **Column**.

9. In the *Field name* list, click **WBS**, and then click **OK**. Microsoft Project inserts the WBS column to the left of the Task Name column. WBS codes represent the hierarchy of summary and subtasks in the project. Your screen should look similar to Figure 14-8.

TAKE NOTE*

If you ever want to reorder tasks to reflect the order in which they were entered, you can sort the Task Sheet by Unique ID.

Figure 14-8

Task Sheet view with WBS column inserted

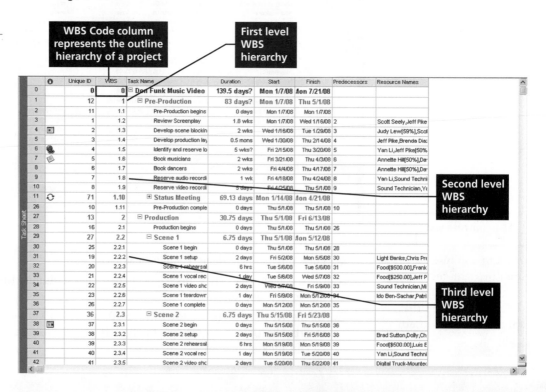

The WBS numbering system is standard in project management. You can see that in the WBS structure, the top-level summary tasks are sequentially numbered with a single digit, the second-level summary or subtasks add a period and a second digit to the first digit, and so on.

10. In the Task ID column (the left-most column), select **7** and **8**. This selects the entire rows for the tasks "Book musicians" and "Book dancers."

11. On the Formatting toolbar, click the **Indent** button. Microsoft Project makes tasks 7 and 8 subtasks of task 6. Your screen should look similar to Figure 14-9.

Figure 14-9

Task Sheet view showing reordered tasks

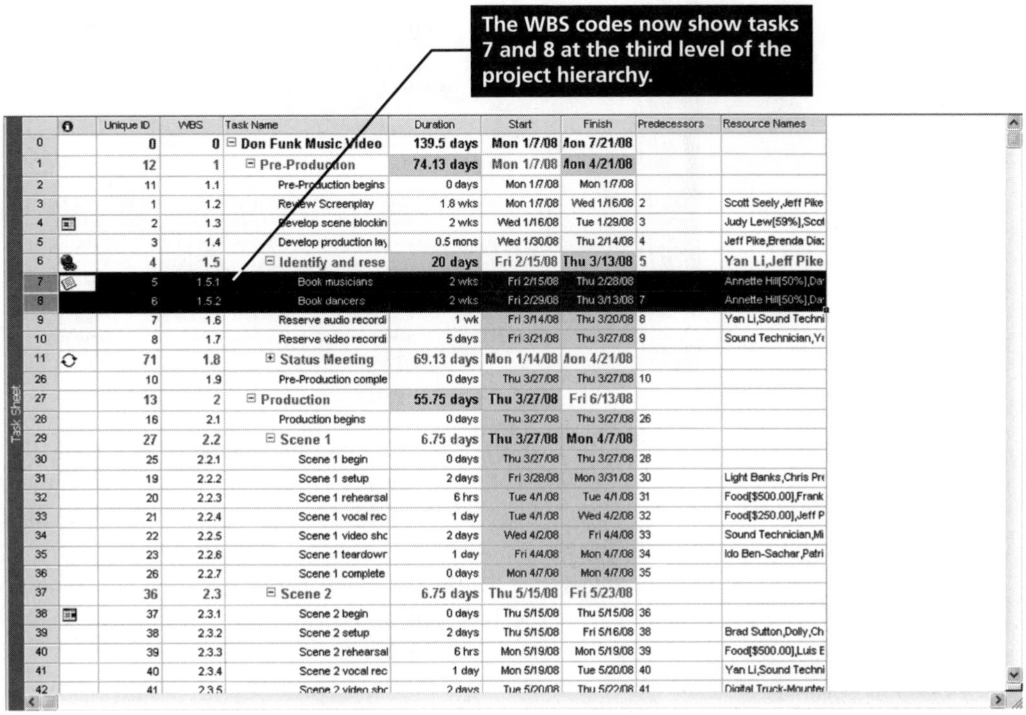

The WBS codes now show tasks 7 and 8 at the third level of the project hierarchy.

Note that the Task and Unique ID values for these tasks are not affected, but the WBS codes are. The WBS codes for tasks 7 and 8 now list them at the third level of the project hierarchy. In addition, the other tasks in the 1.x branch of the WBS are renumbered. For example, "Reserve audio recording equipment" is renumbered from 1.8 to 1.6.

12. Select task 7. On the menu bar, click **Edit**, and then click **Cut Task**. Microsoft Project cuts the selected task to the Windows Clipboard. Your screen should look similar to Figure 14-10.

Figure 14-10

Task Sheet view showing
task 7 removed

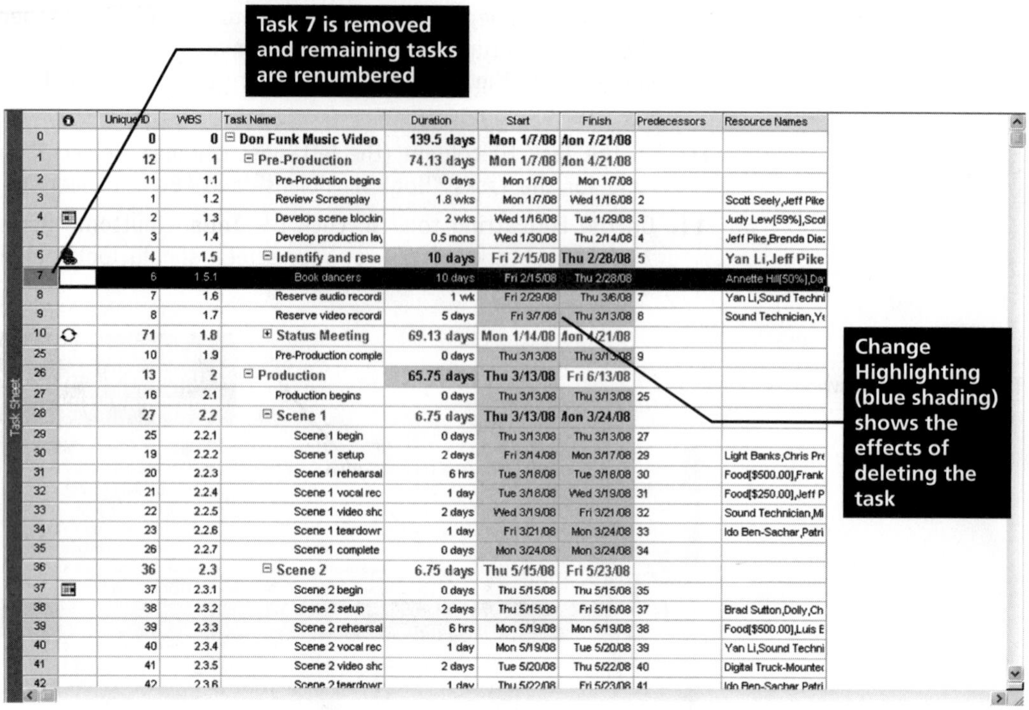

Task 7 is removed
and remaining tasks
are renumbered

Change
Highlighting
(blue shading)
shows the
effects of
deleting the
task

Note that the Task IDs are renumbered, the Unique IDs are unchanged, and only
the WBS codes in the Pre-Production phase are renumbered. The WBS codes in the
other phases of the project are unaffected because that part of the project hierarchy did not change.

13. Select task 4. On the menu bar, click **Edit**, and then click **Paste**. Microsoft Project
pastes the task you previously cut back into the task list. Your screen should look
similar to Figure 14-11.

Figure 14-11

Task Sheet view showing
reinserted task

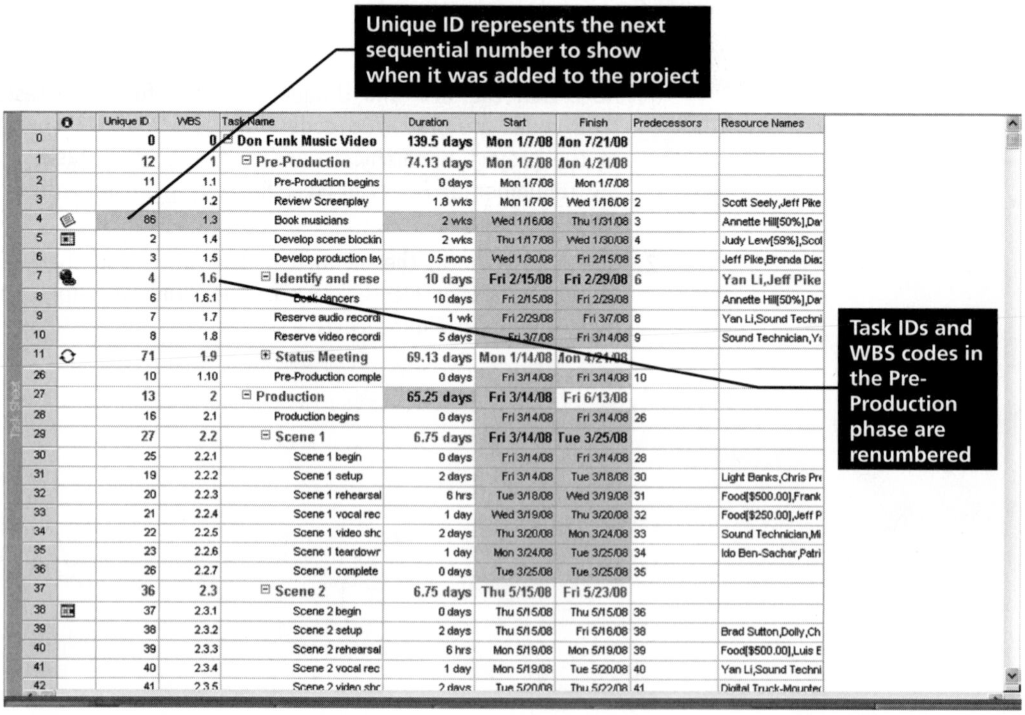

Unique ID represents the next
sequential number to show
when it was added to the project

Task IDs and
WBS codes in
the Pre-
Production
phase are
renumbered

Note that again, the Task IDs and the WBS codes in the Pre-Production phase are renumbered. The Unique ID for the pasted task is then updated with the next sequential number to specify when it was added to the project.

14. On the Standard toolbar, click the **Undo** button three times. The task list is restored to its original order.

15. SAVE the project plan.

   PAUSE. LEAVE Project open to use in the next exercise.

In this lesson, you added Unique ID and WBS code columns to the Task Sheet view, and then explored how these identifiers change when you move, delete, or add tasks. Each task in a Microsoft Project project plan has a unique identifier, called the *Task ID*. Microsoft Project assigns sequential ID numbers to each task that you enter. When you insert, move, or delete a task, Microsoft Project updates the ID numbers so that the numbers always reflect the current task order. The Task ID column appears (by default) on the left side of most task tables in Microsoft Project. Note that resources have Resource IDs assigned to them, and that they behave like a Task ID.

Microsoft Project also tracks the order in which you enter tasks and resources. The ***Unique ID*** task and resource fields store this entry order. If tasks or resources are reorganized, and you later need to see their original entry order, you can view this in the Unique ID field.

Although these identifiers uniquely identify each task, they do not give you any information about the task's place in the hierarchy of a project plan. For example, you can't tell if a task is a summary or a subtask by simply looking at a Task ID. A better way to show the hierarchy of a project plan is to display the ***outline numbers*** or ***work breakdown structure (WBS) codes*** of tasks–the numeric representations of the outline hierarchy of a project. You can change WBS codes to include any combination of letters and numbers that you desire, but outline numbers are numeric only and are generated by Microsoft Project. When working with these codes, the ***mask***, or appearance, defines the format of the code–the order and number of alphabetic, numeric, and alphanumeric strings in a code and the separators between them. Initially, outline numbers and WBS codes of tasks are identical. Microsoft Project also stores the Predecessor and Successor values for tasks' Unique IDs and WBS codes. Because the WBS codes indicate the place of every task in the project hierarchy, it is common to use WBS codes instead of Task ID or names when referencing tasks between team members on a project.

If you are working on a complex project, the WBS or standard outline options available in Microsoft Project may not be sufficient for your report or analysis requirements. If this occurs, you can investigate Microsoft Project's capabilities to handle custom outline numbers to identify a hierarchy within a project plan. For example, you can define a custom outline number that links different outline levels of a project plan with different levels of the organization's structure. (The top level might be a regional division, the second level a business unit, and the third level a local team.) You could also use custom outline numbers to associate different outline levels of a project plan with internal cost centers or job tracking codes.

After you have applied a custom outline number to your project plan, you can then group, sort, and filter tasks and resources by their outline numbers. You can apply up to ten levels of a custom outline number for tasks and ten for resources in a single Microsoft Project file.

■ Formatting the Network Diagram

 THE BOTTOM LINE   In traditional project management, a Network Diagram is a standard way for representing project activities and their relationships in a flowchart format.

➔ FORMAT ITEMS IN THE NETWORK DIAGRAM VIEW

USE the project plan you created in the previous exercise.

1. On the menu bar, click **View**, and then click **Network Diagram**. The Network Diagram view appears. Your screen should look similar to Figure 14-12.

Figure 14-12

Network Diagram view

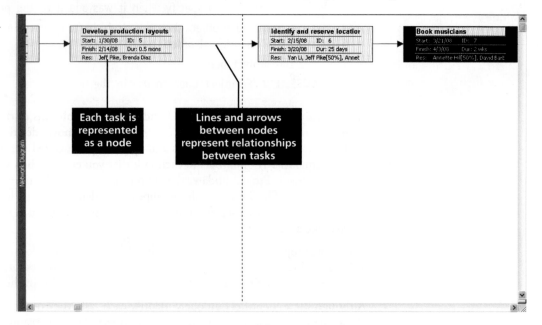

The focus of the Network Diagram is task relationships (rather than durations or sequence). Each task is represented as a box, or node, containing several pieces of information about the task. The relationships between tasks are represented as lines and arrows.

2. On the menu bar, click **Format**, and then click **Box Styles**. The Box Styles dialog box appears. Your screen should look similar to Figure 14-13.

Figure 14-13

Box Styles dialog box

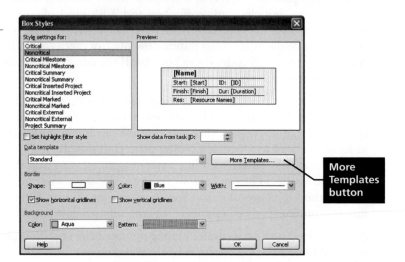

3. Click **More Templates**. The Data Templates dialog box appears.

4. In the *Templates in "Network Diagram"* list, make sure that **Standard** is selected, and then click the **Copy** button. The Data Template Definition dialog box appears. You will add the WBS code value to the lower right corner of the node.

5. In the *Template name* box, key **Standard + WBS**.

6. Below *Choose cell(s)*, click the empty cell below *Duration* and to the right of *Resource Names*.

7. In the dropdown list that becomes active, select **WBS**. This will add the WBS code to the standard box style in the Network Diagram. Your screen should look similar to Figure 14-14.

Figure 14-14

Data Template Definition box

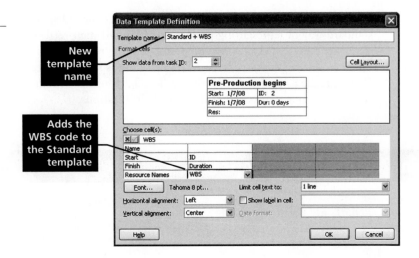

8. Click **OK** to close the Data Template Definition box. Click **Close** to close the Data Templates dialog box.

9. In the Box Styles dialog box, under *Style settings for*, click and drag to select **Critical** and **Noncritical**.

10. In the *Data template* box, click **Standard + WBS**, and then click **OK** to close the Box Styles dialog box. Microsoft Project applies the revised box style to the critical and noncritical task nodes in the Network Diagram. Your screen should look similar to Figure 14-15.

Figure 14-15

Network Diagram showing revised box style applied to critical and noncritical tasks

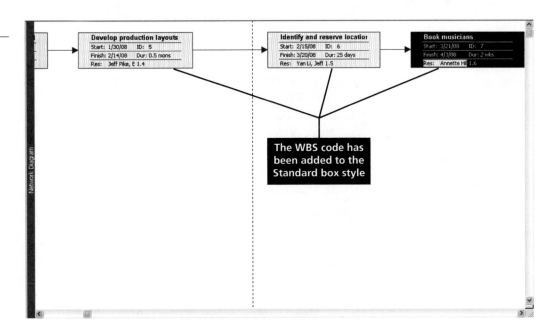

Microsoft Project adds the WBS code to the nodes for critical and noncritical tasks. Scroll left and right to review some of the other nodes in the Network Diagram. As you can see, the node representing other types of tasks, such as summary tasks, are not affected. If you want to apply the new template to other task types, you would do so in the Box Styles dialog box.

11. **SAVE** the project plan.

PAUSE. LEAVE Project open to use in the next exercise.

In this lesson, you applied and formatted the Network Diagram. The **Network Diagram** is a standard way of representing project activities and their relationships, in a flowchart format. Tasks are represented as boxes, or **nodes**, and the relationships between tasks are drawn as lines connecting nodes. The Network Diagram is not a timescaled view like the Gantt Chart. Rather, it shows project activities in a flowchart format so that you can focus on the relationships between activities rather than on their durations.

■ Customizing and Printing Reports

 **THE BOTTOM LINE**   Reports are the primary way to communicate project information among stakeholders. You can edit a report or create a new report that includes the specific table and filter you want.

CREATE A CUSTOM REPORT

USE the project plan you created in the previous exercise.

1. On the menu bar, click **Report**, and then click **Reports.** The Reports dialog box appears.

ANOTHER WAY   You can also access the Reports dialog box from the Project Guide toolbar. Click *Report*, then click the *Select or view a report* link. Click *Create a project report*, and then click the *Display Reports* link.

2. Click **Custom**, and then click **Select.** The Custom Reports dialog box appears.
3. Click **New.** The Define New Report dialog box appears.
4. In the Define New Report dialog box, make sure that **Task** is selected, and then click **OK.** The Task Report dialog box appears.
5. In the Name box, select the boilerplate text that is in the box, and then key **Music Video Schedule.**
6. In the Table box, click **Music Video Schedule Table.**
7. In the Filter box, click **Unfinished Shoots.** Your screen should look similar to Figure 14-16.

Figure 14-16

Task Report dialog box

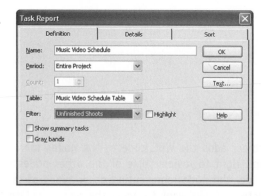

8. Click **OK** to close the Task Report dialog box.
9. In the Custom Reports dialog box, make sure that **Music Video Schedule** is selected, and then click **Preview.**
10. Move your mouse pointer over the text on the report, and click to zoom in. This is a custom report that you set up to include only uncompleted shoots and a custom table to include only the detail you see in the preview. Your screen should look similar to Figure 14-17.

Figure 14-17

Print preview of Music
Video Schedule report with
Unfinished Shoots filter applied

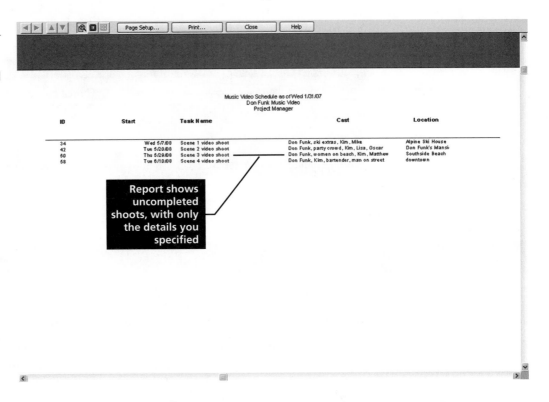

11. Click **Close** to close the Print Preview window.

12. Click **Close** two more times to close the Custom Reports and Reports dialog boxes.

13. **SAVE** the project plan, and then **CLOSE** the file.

PAUSE. If you are continuing to the next lesson, keep Project open. If you are not continuing to additional lessons, **CLOSE** Project.

REF

For a review of formatting and printing reports, see Lesson 7.

In this exercise, you created a new report that included a custom table and filter, and then viewed the report in the Print Preview window. As you learned in previous lessons, reports are a primary way that project managers can communicate project information to stakeholders. Keep in mind that reports are designed only for printing or viewing, but do not allow for any data entry or manipulation.

TAKE NOTE

You can also use a new feature in Microsoft Project called Visual Reports to create and distribute reports. The Visual Reports feature uses Microsoft Office Excel and Microsoft Office Visio Professional to produce PivotTable views, charts, graphs, and diagrams based on Project data. You can access Visual Reports from the menu bar by clicking Report and then Visual Reports. To learn more about Visual Reports and how to use them, key "visual reports" in the Search box, located in the upper right corner of the Microsoft Project window.

SUMMARY SKILL MATRIX

IN THIS LESSON YOU LEARNED	MATRIX SKILL
To customize the calendar view	Format bar styles for tasks in the Calendar view
To use Task IDs and WBS codes	Work with Unique ID and WBS codes
To format the Network Diagram	Format items in the Network Diagram view
To customize and print reports	Create a custom report

■ Knowledge Assessment

Matching

Match the term in column 1 to its description in column 2.

Column 1		Column 2
1. Task ID		**a.** a numeric-only representation of the outline hierarchy of a project, generated by Microsoft Project
2. nodes		**b.** defines the format of the outline and WBS codes
3. Unique ID		**c.** the view that looks similar to a "month-at-a-glance"
4. Network Diagram		**d.** a representation of the outline hierarchy of a project, which you can change to include any combination of letters and numbers
5. lines		**e.** a unique identifier that tracks the order in which you enter tasks and resources
6. outline numbers		**f.** represent the relationships between tasks on a Network Diagram
7. mask		**g.** a standard way of representing project activities in a flowchart format
8. reports		**h.** the boxes used to represent tasks in a Network Diagram
9. WBS codes		**i.** the primary way that project managers communicate project information to stakeholders
10. Calendar		**j.** the unique identifier that Microsoft Project assigns to each task sequentially as you enter it

True / False

Circle T if the statement is true or F if the statement is false.

T F 1. The new Visual Reports feature uses Microsoft Word and Excel to produce reports based on Project data.

T F 2. You can apply up to ten levels of a custom outline number for tasks in a single Microsoft Project file.

T F 3. Reports do not allow for any data entry or manipulation.

T F 4. WBS codes can include letters and numbers.

T F 5. The Network Diagram view is one of the simplest views available in Microsoft Project.

T F 6. If you want to reorder tasks by the order in which they were entered, you can sort by the Task ID.

T | F   **7.** In the WBS structure, top-level summary tasks are sequentially numbered with a single digit.

T | F   **8.** The Network Diagram focuses on task durations.

T | F   **9.** The Calendar view displays three months at a time.

T | F **10.** The Unique ID shows a task's place in the hierarchy of the project plan.

■ Competency Assessment

⊕ Project 14-1: WBS Codes for New Employee Orientation

You and your team are reviewing the project plan for your company's new employee orientation. You agree that it would be easier to refer to tasks by their WBS codes and so you need to change the view of your plan to reflect this. You also need to make changes in the hierarchy to a few of the tasks.

GET READY. Launch Microsoft Project if it is not already running.

OPEN *Employee Orientation Plan 14-1* from the data files for this lesson.

The *Employee Orientation Plan 14-1* project plan is available on the companion CD-ROM.

1. Click the Show/Hide Project Guide button on the Project Guide toolbar.
2. On the menu bar, click View, and then click More Views.
3. In the More Views dialog box, select Task Sheet, and then click Apply.
4. Right-click the Task Name column heading. On the shortcut menu that appears, click Insert Column.
5. In the *Field name* box of the Column Definition dialog box, select WBS from the dropdown menu, and then click OK.
6. In the Task ID column, click and drag to select tasks 22 and 23.
7. On the Formatting toolbar, click Indent.
8. SAVE the project plan as *Employee Orientation WBS* and then CLOSE the file.

   PAUSE. LEAVE Project open to use in the next exercise.

⊕ Project 14-2: Don Funk Custom Critical Task Report

One of the Finance managers on the Don Funk Music Video has asked for a report summarizing the critical tasks, as well as their start, finish, duration, and cost. You need to create and print (preview) this report for him.

The *Don Funk Music Video 14-2* project plan is available on the companion CD-ROM.

OPEN *Don Funk Music Video 14-2* from the data files for this lesson.

1. Click the Show/Hide Project Guide button on the Project Guide toolbar.
2. On the menu bar, click Report, and then click Reports.
3. In the Reports dialog box, click Custom, and then click Select.
4. Select Critical Tasks from the Reports list, and then click Copy.
5. In the Name box of the Task Report dialog box, select the displayed text and then key Custom Critical Task Report.
6. In the Table box, select Summary from the dropdown list.
7. Click the Text button on the right side of the dialog box.
8. In the Text Styles dialog box, select Critical Tasks from the *Items to Change* dropdown list.
9. In the Color box, select Red from the dropdown list.
10. In the *Font style* box, select Bold.
11. Click OK to close the Text Styles dialog box. Click OK again to close the Task Report dialog box.

12. Make sure that Custom Critical Task Report is selected in the Custom Reports dialog box, and then click **Preview** to view the report.

13. Click **Close** on the Print Preview toolbar. Click **Close** on the Custom Reports dialog box. Click **Close** on the Reports dialog box.

14. **SAVE** the project plan as *Don Funk Custom Critical Tasks* and then **CLOSE** the file.

    PAUSE. LEAVE Project open to use in the next exercise.

■ Proficiency Assessment

⊕ Project 14-3: Calendar View for Insurance Claim Process

You would like to hand out a monthly view of the insurance claim process so that agents and adjustors can keep a quick reference of this process at their fingertips. You need to change the view of your project plan to a calendar view, as well as change the bar style formatting for several task types.

The *Insurance Claim Processing 14-3* project plan is available on the companion CD-ROM.

OPEN *Insurance Claim Processing 14-3* from the data files for this lesson.

1. Click the **Show/Hide Project Guide** button on the Project Guide toolbar.

2. Change to the Calendar view on the View menu.

3. Activate the Bar Styles dialog box on the Format menu.

4. Select **Critical** in the *Task type* box. Change the pattern to the last bar (checkered) in the dropdown list and change the color to Red.

5. Select **Project Summary** in the *Task type* box. Change the bar type to None.

6. Close the Bar Styles dialog box.

7. Double-click on the divider bar between the calendar rows (weeks) to expand the row height.

8. **SAVE** the project plan as *Insurance Claim Calendar View* and then **CLOSE** the file.

   PAUSE. LEAVE Project open to use in the next exercise.

⊕ Project 14-4: New Employee Orientation Network Diagram

Because the timeline for your New Employee Orientation is so short, you would like to focus on the relationships between tasks rather than their durations. You want to change the view to the Network Diagram and reformat some of the elements of the Network Diagram.

The *Employee Orientation Plan 14-4* project plan is available on the companion CD-ROM.

OPEN *Employee Orientation Plan 14-4* from the data files for this lesson.

1. Close the Project Guide.

2. Activate the Network diagram from the View menu.

3. Activate the Box Styles dialog box from the Format menu.

4. Select **Critical Summary** from the *Style settings for* box if it is not already selected. Set the Data template for these boxes to **WBS**.

5. Select **Noncritical Summary** from the *Style settings for* box. Set the Data template for these boxes to **WBS**.

6. Close the Box Styles dialog box.

7. **SAVE** the project plan as *Employee Orientation Network Diagram* and then **CLOSE** the file.

   PAUSE. LEAVE Project open to use in the next exercise.

■ Mastery Assessment

→ Project 14-5: HR Interview Custom Critical Tasks

The *HR Interview Project 14-5* project plan is available on the companion CD-ROM.

The HR Group Manager has requested a critical task report for this project, but would like to see it using a custom Interview Schedule table that was developed earlier in the project. You need to create this report.

OPEN *HR Interview Project 14-5* from the data files for this lesson.

1. Activate the Reports dialog box, and then the Custom Reports dialog box.
2. Make a copy of the Critical Tasks report and name it **Custom Critical Task Report–HR Interview**.
3. Apply the Interview Schedule table.
4. Format the critical tasks to appear in Bold Teal.
5. Preview the report to make sure your custom changes are active.
6. **SAVE** the project plan as *HR Interview Custom Critical Tasks* and then **CLOSE** the file.
   PAUSE. LEAVE Project open to use in the next exercise.

→ Project 14-6: Insurance Claim Processing WBS Codes

The *Insurance Claim Processing 14-6* project plan is available on the companion CD-ROM.

You want to add the Unique ID and WBS columns to your Insurance Claim Processing project plan. You would also like to explore how several changes to your project plan will affect the Unique ID and WBS codes.

OPEN *Insurance Claim Processing 14-6* from the data files for this lesson.

1. Close the Project Guide.
2. Insert the Unique ID and WBS columns to the left of the Task Name column.
3. **SAVE** the project plan as *Insurance Claim WBS*.
4. In a separate Word document, explain how the Unique ID and WBS codes are affected for each of the following independent situations (*Hint*: After documenting the changes for a given situation, close the file without saving. Reopen the solution file *Insurance Claim WBS* to explore and document each situation.):

   - Tasks 7 and 8 are indented under task 3
   - Task 25 is indented under task 22
   - Task 11 is cut and then inserted below task 7 (*Hint*: Describe each part of this step separately.)

5. **SAVE** the Word document as *Insurance Claim WBS*.
6. **CLOSE** both files.
   CLOSE Project.

INTERNET READY

Search the Internet for information on using WBS codes in a project plan. Look for any documents explaining how to apply, use, format, or troubleshoot WBS codes. Review the information you have found.

Now, locate a project plan template on the Internet, or use a project plan from your personal experience. Experiment with indenting and outdenting tasks, and adding, moving, and deleting tasks. Study how WBS codes are affected with each change. Build on the knowledge you gained from this lesson, especially from Project 14-6 at the end of the lesson.

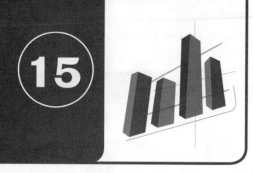

Advanced Project Plan Tracking

LESSON SKILL MATRIX

SKILLS	MATRIX SKILL
Recording Actual Start, Finish, and Duration Values of Tasks	Enter actual start date and duration for a task
Adjusting Remaining Work or Duration of Tasks	Adjust actual and remaining work for a task
Rescheduling Uncompleted Work	Reschedule incomplete work
Saving an Interim Plan	Save an interim project plan
Comparing Baseline, Interim, and Actual Plans	Compare the baseline, interim, and actual project plans
Reporting Project Status	Report project variance with a "Stoplight" view
Evaluating Performance with Earned Value Analysis	Set project status date and display the Earned Value table

KEY TERMS
actual cost of work performed (ACWP)
budgeted cost of work performed (BCWP)
budgeted cost of work scheduled (BCWS)
Cost Performance Index (CPI)
cost variance (CV)
earned value (EV)
interim plan
planned value (PV)
project triangle
Schedule Performance Index (SPI)
schedule variance (SV)

You are a video project manager for Southridge Video, and one of your primary responsibilities recently has been to manage the new Don Funk Music Video project. In an earlier lesson, you learned about some of the basic project plan tracking features in Microsoft Office Project. In this lesson, you will become familiar with some of the more advanced tracking functions that enable you to record progress details of your project.

■ SOFTWARE ORIENTATION

Microsoft Project's Earned Value Table

The Earned Value table displays a number of schedule indicator and cost indicator values that are useful in measuring the project's progress and forecasting its outcome through earned value analysis.

Figure 15-1

The Earned Value table in the Task Sheet view

	Task Name	CPI	SPI	Planned Value - PV (BCWS)	Earned Value - EV (BCWP)	AC (ACWP)	SV	CV	EAC	BAC	VAC
0	⊟ Don Funk Music Video	1	1	$29,496.75	$29,363.50	$29,446.78	($133.25)	($83.28)	$94,481.71	$94,214.50	($267.21)
1	⊟ Pre-Production	1	1	$23,529.00	$23,529.00	$23,529.00	$0.00	$0.00	$28,529.00	$28,529.00	$0.00
2	Pre-Production begins	0	0	$0.00	$0.00	$0.00	$0.00	$0.00	$0.00	$0.00	$0.00
3	Review Screenplay	1	1	$2,295.00	$2,295.00	$2,295.00	$0.00	$0.00	$2,295.00	$2,295.00	$0.00
4	Develop scene blockin	1	1	$1,560.00	$1,560.00	$1,560.00	$0.00	$0.00	$1,560.00	$1,560.00	$0.00
5	Develop production lay	1	1	$2,520.00	$2,520.00	$2,520.00	$0.00	$0.00	$2,520.00	$2,520.00	$0.00
6	Identify and reserve lo	1	1	$9,455.00	$9,455.00	$9,455.00	$0.00	$0.00	$14,455.00	$14,455.00	$0.00
7	Book musicians	1	1	$1,360.00	$1,360.00	$1,360.00	$0.00	$0.00	$1,360.00	$1,360.00	$0.00
8	Book dancers	1	1	$1,768.00	$1,768.00	$1,768.00	$0.00	$0.00	$1,768.00	$1,768.00	$0.00
9	Reserve audio recordi	1	1	$1,400.00	$1,400.00	$1,400.00	$0.00	$0.00	$1,400.00	$1,400.00	$0.00
10	Reserve video recordi	1	1	$1,680.00	$1,680.00	$1,680.00	$0.00	$0.00	$1,680.00	$1,680.00	$0.00
11	⊞ Status Meeting	1	1	$1,491.00	$1,491.00	$1,491.00	$0.00	$0.00	$1,491.00	$1,491.00	$0.00
26	Pre-Production comple	0	0	$0.00	$0.00	$0.00	$0.00	$0.00	$0.00	$0.00	$0.00
27	⊟ Production	0.99	0.98	$5,967.75	$5,834.50	$5,917.78	($133.25)	($83.28)	$23,703.07	$23,369.50	($333.57)
28	Production begins	0	0	$0.00	$0.00	$0.00	$0.00	$0.00	$0.00	$0.00	$0.00
29	⊟ Scene 1	1	1	$5,301.50	$5,301.50	$5,301.50	$0.00	$0.00	$6,051.50	$6,051.50	$0.00
30	Scene 1 begin	0	0	$0.00	$0.00	$0.00	$0.00	$0.00	$0.00	$0.00	$0.00
31	Scene 1 setup	1	1	$536.00	$536.00	$536.00	$0.00	$0.00	$536.00	$536.00	$0.00
32	Scene 1 rehearsal	1	1	$388.50	$388.50	$388.50	$0.00	$0.00	$888.50	$888.50	$0.00
33	Scene 1 vocal rec	1	1	$1,442.00	$1,442.00	$1,442.00	$0.00	$0.00	$1,692.00	$1,692.00	$0.00
34	Scene 1 video sho	1	1	$2,687.00	$2,687.00	$2,687.00	$0.00	$0.00	$2,687.00	$2,687.00	$0.00
35	Scene 1 teardowr	1	1	$248.00	$248.00	$248.00	$0.00	$0.00	$248.00	$248.00	$0.00
36	Scene 1 complete	0	0	$0.00	$0.00	$0.00	$0.00	$0.00	$0.00	$0.00	$0.00
37	⊟ Scene 2	0.86	0.8	$666.25	$533.00	$616.28	($133.25)	($83.28)	$8,004.72	$6,923.00	($1,081.72)
38	Scene 2 begin	0	0	$0.00	$0.00	$0.00	$0.00	$0.00	$0.00	$0.00	$0.00
39	Scene 2 setup	0.86	0.8	$666.25	$533.00	$616.28	($133.25)	($83.28)	$1,232.56	$1,066.00	($166.56)
40	Scene 2 rehearsal	0	0	$0.00	$0.00	$0.00	$0.00	$0.00	$824.00	$824.00	$0.00
41	Scene 2 vocal rec	0	0	$0.00	$0.00	$0.00	$0.00	$0.00	$1,440.00	$1,440.00	$0.00

The columns in the Earned Value table are:

1. **CPI**–or Cost Performance Index, the ratio of budgeted to actual cost, or BCWP divided by ACWP
2. **SPI**–or Schedule Performance Index, the ratio of performed to schedule work, or BCWP divided by BCWS
3. **Planned Value-PV (BCWS)**–the value of the work scheduled to be completed as of the status date
4. **Earned Value-EV (BCWP)**–the portion of the budgeted cost that should have been spent to complete each task's actual work performed up to the status date
5. **AC (ACWP)**–the actual cost incurred to complete each task's actual work up to the status date
6. **SV** – or Schedule Variance, the difference between the budgeted cost of work performed and the budgeted cost of work scheduled
7. **CV**–or Cost Variance, the difference between the budgeted and actual cost of work performed
8. **EAC**–Estimate at Completion, the expected total cost of a task based on performance up to the status date

9. **BAC**–Budget at Completion, the total planned cost

10. **VAC**–Variance at Completion, the difference between the BAC (Budgeted At Completion) or baseline cost and EAC (Estimated At Completion)

■ Recording Actual Start, Finish, and Duration Values of Tasks

↓
THE BOTTOM LINE

Once the details of the project plan have been finalized and work has started, the project manager can begin to track progress on the project by recording actual start, finish, and duration values.

The *Don Funk Music Video 15MA* project plan is available on the companion CD-ROM

GET READY. Before you begin these steps, launch Microsoft Project.

OPEN the *Don Funk Music Video 15MA* project plan from the data files for this lesson.

SAVE the file as *Don Funk Music Video 15A* in the solutions folder for this lesson as directed by your instructor.

⊙ ENTER ACTUAL START DATE AND DURATION FOR A TASK

1. Click the **Show/Hide Project Guide** button on the Project Guide toolbar. The Project Guide closes.

2. If the Tracking toolbar is not active, on the menu bar, click **View**, point to **Toolbars**, and click **Tracking**. The Tracking toolbar appears.

3. On the menu bar, click **Edit**, and then click **Go To.** In the ID box, key **7**, and then click **OK.** Microsoft Project displays task 7, Book musicians. This task started one day ahead of schedule, so you need to record this.

4. On the menu bar, click **Tools**, point to **Tracking**, and then click **Update Tasks.** The Update Tasks dialog box appears.

5. Under the Actual label, in the Start box, key or select **March 20, 2008.**

6. In the *Actual dur* box, key or select **2w**, and then click **OK** to close the Update Tasks dialog box. Microsoft Project records the actual start date and work for task 7. Your screen should look similar to Figure 15-2.

Figure 15-2

Gantt Chart showing actual start date and work for task 7

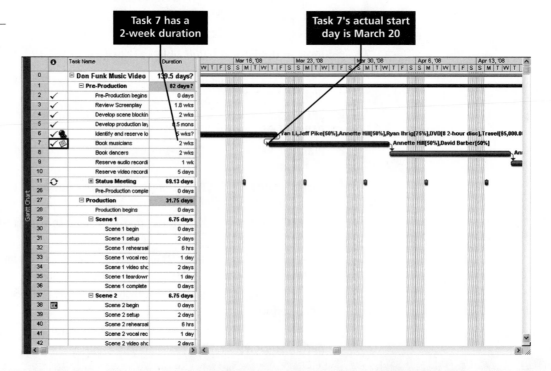

7. In the Task Name column, select the name of task 8, **Book dancers.** You need to record that task 8 started on time but took three days longer to complete.

8. Click the **Update Tasks** button on the Tracking toolbar. The Update Tasks dialog box appears.

9. In the *Actual dur* box, key **13d**, and then click **OK.**

10. Click the **Scroll to Task** button so that the Gantt bar for task 8 is visible. Your screen should look similar to Figure 15-3.

Figure 15-3

Gantt Chart showing updated progress for task 8

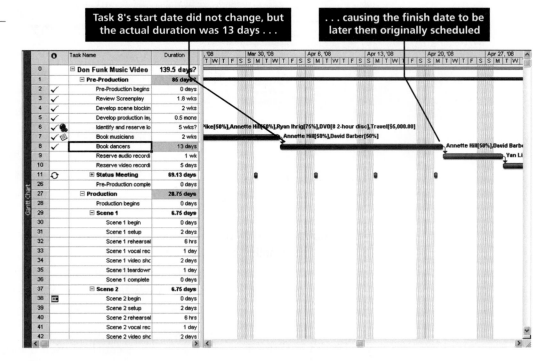

Microsoft Project records the actual duration of the task. Microsoft Project assumes that the task started as scheduled because you did not specify an actual start date. However, the actual duration that you entered causes Microsoft Project to calculate a finish date that is later than the originally scheduled finish date.

Next you will record that task 9 was completed as scheduled and that task 10 took longer than scheduled to complete.

11. In the Task Name column, select the name of task 9, **Reserve audio recording equipment.**

12. On the tracking toolbar, click the **100% Complete** button. Microsoft Project updates task 9 as 100% complete.

13. In the Task Name column, select the name of task 10, **Reserve video recording equipment,** and then click the **Update Tasks** button on the Tracking toolbar. The Update Tasks dialog box appears.

14. In the *Actual dur* box, key or select **6d**, and then click **OK.** Microsoft Project records the actual duration of the task.

15. On the Standard toolbar, click the **Scroll to Task** button. Microsoft Project scrolls the Gantt bar chart so that the bar for task 10 is visible. Your screen should look similar to Figure 15-4.

Figure 15-4

Gantt Chart showing task completion for tasks 9 and 10

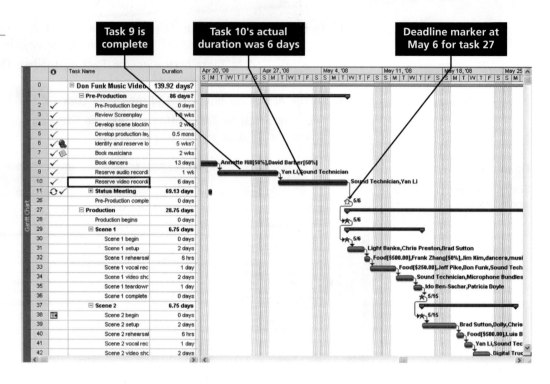

You can see that the Pre-Production phase of the Don Funk Music Video project has met its deadline of May 6, 2008.

16. SAVE the project plan, and then **CLOSE** the file.

PAUSE. LEAVE Project open to use in the next exercise.

In this exercise, you entered actual start dates and durations for several tasks. Remember, as you learned in Lesson 8, tracking actuals is essential to a well-managed project. As the project manager, you need to know how well the project team is performing and when to take action to make corrections. When you enter actual start, finish, or duration values, Microsoft Project updates the schedule and calculates the task's percentage of completion. When doing this, Microsoft Project uses the following rules:

- When you enter a task's actual start date, Microsoft Project moves the scheduled finish date to match the actual start date.

- When you enter a task's actual finish date, Microsoft Project moves the scheduled finish date to match the actual finish dates and assigns a completion percentage of 100%.

- When you enter an actual duration for a task that is less than the scheduled duration, Microsoft Project subtracts the actual duration from the scheduled duration to determine the remaining duration.

- When you enter a task's actual duration that is equal to the scheduled duration, Microsoft Project sets the task to 100% complete.

- When you enter an actual duration for a task that is longer than the scheduled duration, Microsoft Project adjusts the scheduled duration to match the actual duration and sets the task to 100%.

Evaluating the status of a project is not always easy or straightforward. Keep in mind the following issues:

- For many tasks, it is difficult to evaluate a percentage of completion. For example, when is a design engineer 75% finished designing a new production process, or a computer engineer 50% finished coding a new software upgrade? Often, reporting work in progress is a best guess and therefore carries an inherent risk.

- The portion of a task's duration that has elapsed does not always equate to a percentage accomplished. For example, a front-loaded task might require a lot of effort initially, so that when 50% of its duration has elapsed, much more than 50% of its total work will have been completed.

- The resources assigned to a task might have different criteria for what determines the task's completion than does the project manager–or the resources assigned to successor tasks.

To avoid or lessen these and other problems that arise in project implementation, a good project manager needs to carry out good project planning and communication. No matter how much planning is done, large and complex projects tend to almost always have variance from the baseline.

■ Adjusting Remaining Work or Duration of Tasks

↓ THE BOTTOM LINE While tracking actual values, it is also possible to adjust the work or duration remaining on a task.

The *Don Funk Music Video 15MB* project plan is available on the companion CD-ROM

To continue with this lesson, you will use an updated version of the Don Funk Music Video project to simulate the passage of time since you completed the previous exercise.

OPEN the *Don Funk Music Video 15MB* project plan from the data files for this lesson.

SAVE the file as *Don Funk Music Video 15B* in the solutions folder for this lesson as directed by your instructor.

➔ ADJUST ACTUAL AND REMAINING WORK FOR A TASK

1. Click the **Show/Hide Project Guide** button on the Project Guide toolbar. The Project Guide closes.

2. On the menu bar, click **View**, and then click **Task Usage**. The Task Usage view appears. Your screen should look similar to Figure 15-5.

Figure 15-5

Actual Work rows in the timephased Task Usage grid

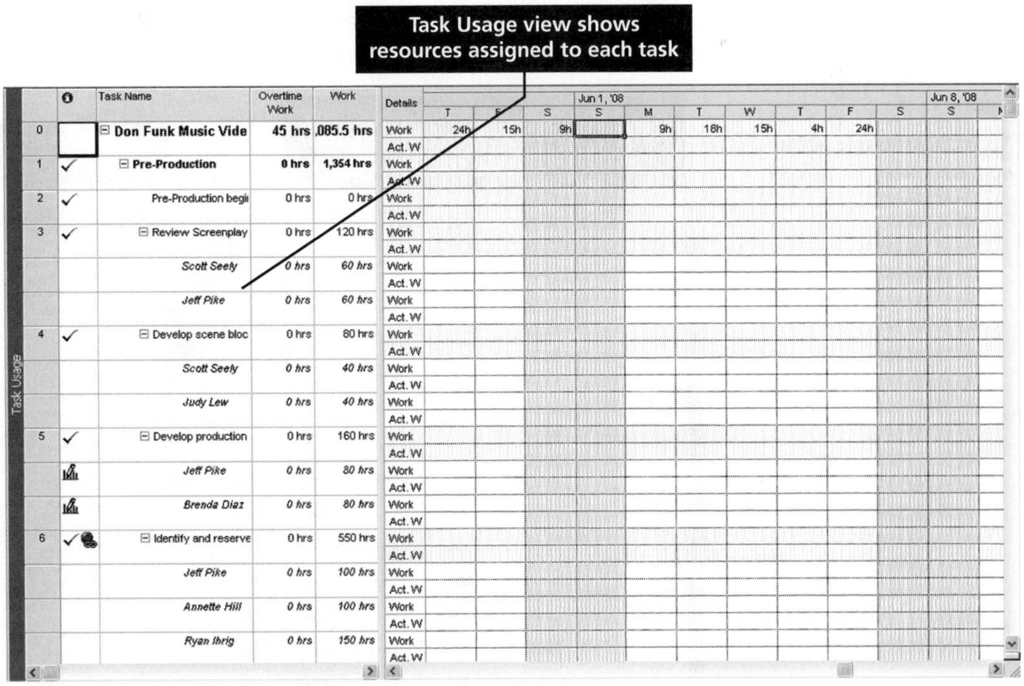

3. On the menu bar, click **Edit**, and then click **Go To**. In the ID box, key **39**, and then click **OK**. Microsoft Project scrolls the timescaled portion of the view to display the scheduled work information for task 39.

4. On the menu bar, click **View**, point to **Table: Usage**, and then click **Work**. Microsoft Project displays the Work table in the Task Usage view.

5. Click on the divider bar between the Task Usage table and the Work table, and drag the divider bar to the right until you can see all the columns in the Work table. Your screen should look similar to Figure 15-6.

Figure 15-6

Work table in the Task Usage view

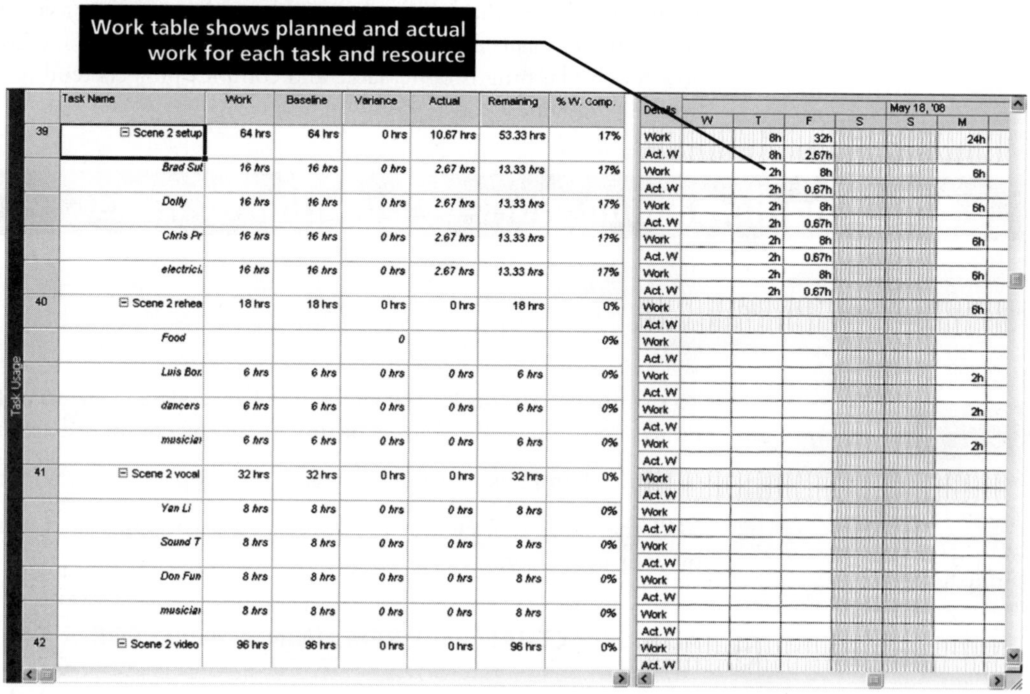

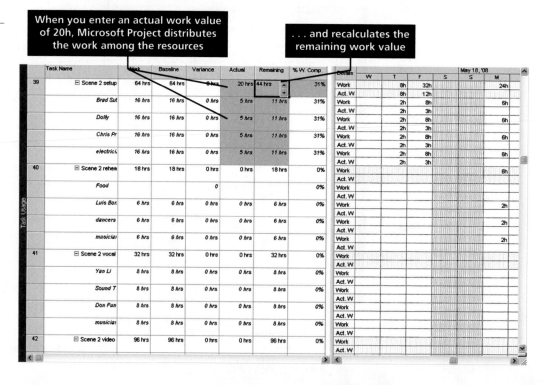

TAKE NOTE

The mouse pointer changes to a two-headed arrow (pointing left and right) when it is in the correct position to drag the vertical divider bar.

6. In the Actual column for task 39, key **20h**, and then press **Tab**. Change highlighting shows that several things have occurred (the light blue shaded cells). First, because you entered the actual work at the task level, Microsoft Project distributed it among the assigned resources. Second, Microsoft Project recalculated the remaining work value. Your screen should look similar to Figure 15-7.

Figure 15-7

Work table showing actual work completed for task 39

7. In the Remaining column for task 39, key **54h** and press $\boxed{\text{Tab}}$. Notice that the new remaining work value was distributed among the assigned resources. Your screen should look similar to Figure 15-8.

Figure 15-8

Work table showing work remaining for task 39

When you adjust the remaining work value to 54h, Microsoft Project distributes the work among the resources . . .

. . . and recalculates the new % Work Complete value

	Task Name	Work	Baseline	Variance	Actual	Remaining	% W. Comp.	Details		W	T	F	S	S	M
39	⊟ Scene 2 setup	74 hrs	64 hrs	10 hrs	20 hrs	54 hrs	27%	Work			8h	32h			32h
								Act. W			8h	12h			
	Brad Sut	18.5 hrs	16 hrs	2.5 hrs	5 hrs	13.5 hrs	27%	Work			2h	8h			8h
								Act. W			2h	3h			
	Dolly	18.5 hrs	16 hrs	2.5 hrs	5 hrs	13.5 hrs	27%	Work			2h	8h			8h
								Act. W			2h	3h			
	Chris Pr	18.5 hrs	16 hrs	2.5 hrs	5 hrs	13.5 hrs	27%	Work			2h	8h			8h
								Act. W			2h	3h			
	electricl	18.5 hrs	16 hrs	2.5 hrs	5 hrs	13.5 hrs	27%	Work			2h	8h			8h
								Act. W			2h	3h			
40	⊟ Scene 2 rehea	18 hrs	18 hrs	0 hrs	0 hrs	18 hrs	0%	Work							
								Act. W							
	Food				0		0%	Work							
								Act. W							
	Luis Bor.	6 hrs	6 hrs	0 hrs	0 hrs	6 hrs	0%	Work							
								Act. W							
	dancers	6 hrs	6 hrs	0 hrs	0 hrs	6 hrs	0%	Work							
								Act. W							
	musician	6 hrs	6 hrs	0 hrs	0 hrs	6 hrs	0%	Work							
								Act. W							
41	⊟ Scene 2 vocal	32 hrs	32 hrs	0 hrs	0 hrs	32 hrs	0%	Work							
								Act. W							
	Yan Li	8 hrs	8 hrs	0 hrs	0 hrs	8 hrs	0%	Work							
								Act. W							
	Sound T	8 hrs	8 hrs	0 hrs	0 hrs	8 hrs	0%	Work							
								Act. W							
	Don Fun	8 hrs	8 hrs	0 hrs	0 hrs	8 hrs	0%	Work							
								Act. W							
	musician	8 hrs	8 hrs	0 hrs	0 hrs	8 hrs	0%	Work							
								Act. W							
42	⊟ Scene 2 video	96 hrs	96 hrs	0 hrs	0 hrs	96 hrs	0%	Work							
								Act. W							

8. SAVE the project plan.

PAUSE. LEAVE Project open to use in the next exercise.

In this lesson, you adjusted actual and remaining work for a task in the project plan. In addition to adjusting work, as you track actuals you can also adjust duration, and start and finish dates. Remember that only an incomplete task can have a remaining work or duration value. For example:

- A task that was scheduled for 40 hours is partially completed. The resources have performed 30 hours of work and expect to finish the entire task after working 6 more hours. As you learned in this lesson, you would enter 30 hours of actual work and 6 hours of remaining work using the Work table.

- A task that was scheduled for four days duration is partially complete. Two days have elapsed, and the resources working on the task estimate they will need three additional days to complete the task. You can enter the actual and remaining duration via the Update Tasks dialog box (on the Tools menu, point to Tracking, and then click Update Tasks).

It is important to remember that whenever you enter actual work values, Microsoft Project calculates actual cost values. By default, Microsoft Project calculates actual costs, and you are not able to enter actual costs directly. If you want to enter actual cost values yourself, on the Tools menu, click Options, and then select the Calculation tab in the Options dialog box that opens. Under the *Calculation options for Microsoft Office Project* label, select the *Calculation mode* of Manual.

Once you turn off automatic calculation, you can enter or import task-level or assignment-level actual costs in the Actual Cost field. This field is available in several locations, such as the Cost table. You can also enter actual cost values on a daily or any other interval in any usage view, such as the Task Usage view. (On the Format menu, point to Details, and then click Actual Cost.) Exercise caution, though, anytime you enter costs manually: entering actual costs for tasks or assignments prevents Microsoft Project from calculating costs based on resource rates and task progress.

■ Rescheduling Uncompleted Work

↓
THE BOTTOM LINE
It is not uncommon for work delays to cause scheduling problems. As the project manager, you must understand the cause of the delays, as well as how rescheduling the work will ultimately affect the project plan.

USE the project plan you created in the previous exercise.

→ RESCHEDULE INCOMPLETE WORK

1. On the menu bar, click **View**, and then click **Gantt Chart**.
2. In the Task Name column, click the name of task 39, **Scene 2 setup**.
3. On the Standard toolbar, click the **Scroll to Task** button. Microsoft Project scrolls to task 39.
4. In the Task Name column, double-click the name of task 39. The Task Information dialog box appears.
5. Click the **General** tab, if it is not already selected.
6. In the *Percent complete* box, key or select **50%**, and then click **OK**. Microsoft Project records progress for the task and updates the progress bar in the task's Gantt bar. Your screen should look similar to Figure 15-9.

Figure 15-9

Gantt Chart showing 50% completion for task 39

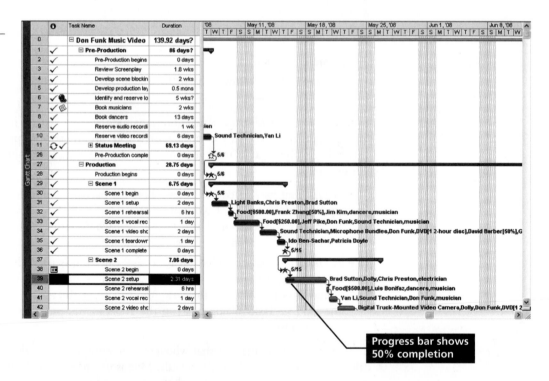

Progress bar shows 50% completion

You have just been told that on the evening of May 16, the transformer that routes electricity to the studio for Scene 2 short-circuited and now needs to be replaced. You will not be able to resume work until Tuesday, May 20.

7. On the menu bar, click **Tools**, point to **Tracking**, and then click **Update Project**. The Update Project dialog box appears.
8. Click **Reschedule uncompleted work to start after**, and in the date box, key or select **5/19/08**, and then click **OK**. Microsoft Project splits task 29 so that the uncompleted portion of the task is delayed until Tuesday. Your screen should look similar to Figure 15-10.

Figure 15-10

Gantt Chart showing split in task 39 to account for delay

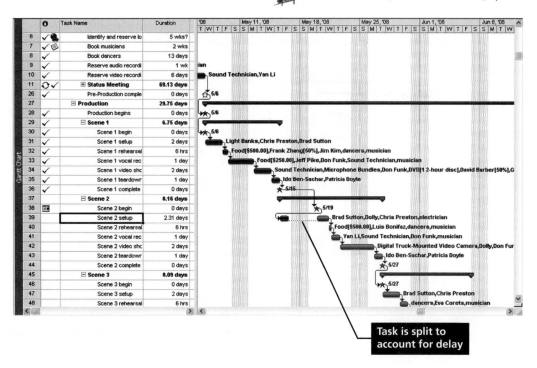

Task is split to account for delay

You can see that although the duration of task 39 remained the same, its finish date and subsequent start dates for successor tasks are now later. So, although you have resolved a specific problem, this has resulted in other potential problems in the remainder of the project.

TAKE NOTE

It is possible to disable the ability of Microsoft Project to reschedule uncompleted work on tasks that are showing any actual work. On the Tools menu, click Options. In the Options dialog box, click the Schedule tab and then clear the *Split in-progress tasks* check box. You can get more information about this and all of the options on this tab of the Options dialog box by clicking the Help button that appears at the bottom of the dialog box.

9. **SAVE** the project plan.

PAUSE. LEAVE Project open to use in the next exercise.

In this exercise, you rescheduled some work that was delayed because of a problem in the studio. Schedule variance is usually the rule rather than the exception in any complex project. As the project manager, it is important that you know when and to what extent variance has occurred, and then take prompt corrective action to stay on track.

■ Saving an Interim Plan

THE BOTTOM LINE

As you track actual values for the project plan, it is often helpful to capture a snapshot of the current values at different times in the project's progress, and to save these values in an interim plan.

USE the project plan you created in the previous exercise.

⊕ **SAVE AN INTERIM PROJECT PLAN**

1. On the menu bar, click **Tools**, point to **Tracking**, and click **Set Baseline**. The Set Baseline dialog box appears.

2. Click **Set interim plan**. The Copy and Into boxes become active. Your screen should look similar to Figure 15-11.

Figure 15-11

Set Baseline dialog box

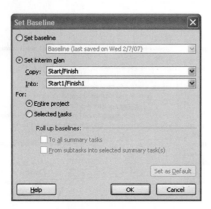

The Copy and Into boxes enable you to select start and finish values for tasks that you want to save in the specific interim start and finish fields. These fields are numbered Start1 through Start10 and Finish1 through Finish10. Because this is the first interim project plan you have saved, use the default fields that appear in the Into box.

3. Click **OK** to save the interim project plan and close the Set Baseline dialog box. Microsoft Project saves each task's current start and finish values in the Start1 and Finish1 fields.

4. **SAVE** the project plan.

PAUSE. LEAVE Project open to use in the next exercise.

In this exercise, you saved an interim baseline for your project plan. Once you have saved the original baseline and then started tracking actuals, or any time you have adjusted the current schedule, it is helpful to take a snapshot of the current values—an *interim plan.* Like a baseline, an interim plan is a set of current values from the project plan that Microsoft Project saves with the file. Unlike the baseline, however, an interim plan saves only the start and finish dates of tasks, not resource or assignment values. You can save up to 10 different interim plans during a project.

Depending on the scope and duration of the project, here are a few suggestions for times when you might want to save interim plans:

• At the end of a major phase of work
• At preset time intervals, such as weekly, bi-weekly, or monthly
• Just before or after entering a large number of actual values

■ Comparing Baseline, Interim, and Actual Plans

THE BOTTOM LINE

Once you have saved a baseline and an interim project plan, it is useful to compare the baseline, interim. and actual plans to evaluate the progress of the project and any changes that have been made.

USE the project plan you created in the previous exercise. Since it can be helpful to compare actual progress with the initial plan, you will display the current schedule along with the baseline and the interim project plan. You will begin by customizing a copy of the Tracking Gantt Chart view.

➔ COMPARE THE BASELINE, INTERIM, AND ACTUAL PROJECT PLANS

1. On the menu bar, click **View**, and then click **More Views**. The More Views dialog box appears.

2. In the Views list, select **Tracking Gantt**, and then click the **Copy** button. The View Definition dialog box appears.

3. In the Name box, key **Interim Tracking Gantt**, and then click **OK**. The new view is listed in the More Views dialog box.

4. Make sure that **Interim Tracking Gantt** is selected in the More Views dialog box, and then click **Apply**. Microsoft Project displays the new view, which is currently identical to the Tracking Gantt view.

5. On the menu bar, click **Format**, and then click **Bar Styles**. The Bar Styles dialog box appears.

6. Click the **Insert Row** button.

7. In the new cell directly below the Name column heading, key **Interim** and press **Tab**. In the same row, click the cell under the *Show For...Tasks* column heading, and then select **Normal** from the dropdown list.

8. Click the cell under the From column heading, and select **Start1** from the dropdown list. Click the cell under the To column heading, and select **Finish1** from the dropdown list. You have now instructed Microsoft Project to display the first interim project plan start and finish dates as bars.

9. On the Bars tab, in the Pattern box under the Middle label, select the sixth option–the first diagonally striped bar. In the Color box, select **Fuchsia**. Your screen should look similar to Figure 15-12.

Figure 15-12

Bar Styles dialog box

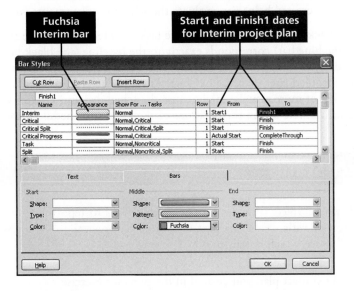

10. Click **OK** to close the Bar Styles dialog box.

11. Scroll the task list so that task 29 is the first task listed on your screen. Click on the name of task 29, **Scene 1**, and then click the **Scroll to Task** button. Your screen should look similar to Figure 15-13.

Figure 15-13

Gantt Chart view showing baseline, interim, and actual task bars

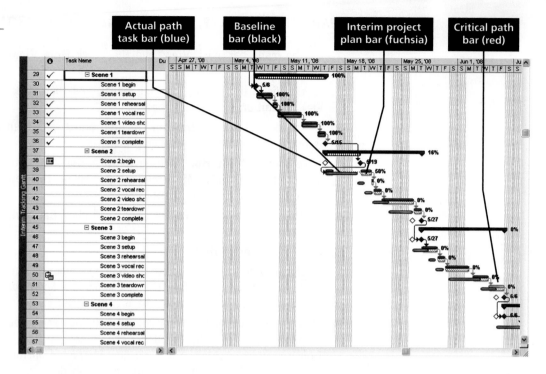

12. SAVE the project plan.

   PAUSE. LEAVE Project open to use in the next exercise.

In this exercise, you compared baseline, interim, and actual plans in a single view. The custom view you created helps you evaluate the schedule adjustments you have made.

Look back to Figure 15-13. Examine task 39. Here you can see that the first portion of task 39 (the blue bar) corresponds exactly to the baseline (the black bar), but because this task was delayed, the remaining portion of the task bar and the interim task bar (the fuchsia bar) are scheduled later than the baseline. Any additional adjustments to the schedule (such as the entering of more actuals) might cause the scheduled and interim values to differ. You would see such differences in the positions of the baseline, scheduled, and interim Gantt bars.

■ Reporting Project Status

THE BOTTOM LINE

Microsoft Project provides many different ways to report a project's status in terms of budget or variance. A key part of a project manager's job is knowing which stakeholders need to see which details in which format.

USE the project plan you created in the previous exercise.

⊙ REPORT PROJECT VARIANCE WITH A "STOPLIGHT" VIEW

1. On the menu bar, click **View**, and then click **More Views**. The More Views dialog box appears.

2. Select **Task Sheet**, and then click **Apply**. Microsoft Project displays the Task Sheet view.

3. On the menu bar, click **View**, point to **Table: Music Video Schedule Table** and then click **Cost**.

4. On the menu bar, click **Tools**, point to **Customize**, and then click **Fields**. The Customize Fields dialog box appears.

5. Under the Field label at the top of the dialog box, make sure that **Task** is selected. In the Type box, select **Number** from the dropdown list.

6. In the Field list, select **Overbudget(Number3)**.

7. Under the *Custom attributes* label, click the **Formula** button. The Formula dialog box is displayed. The formula shown in this dialog box has been pre-entered to save time and accuracy. Your screen should look similar to Figure 15-14.

Figure 15-14

Formula dialog box

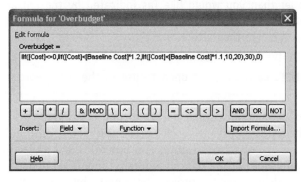

The formula evaluates each task's cost variance. If the task falls within 30 percent above baseline, the formula assigns the number 30 to the task; if within 20 percent, a 20; and if within 10 percent, a 10.

8. Click **Cancel** to close the Formula dialog box.

9. In the Customize Fields dialog box, under the *Values to display* label, click the **Graphical Indicators** button. The Graphical Indicators dialog box appears. This dialog box enables you to specify a unique graphical indicator to display, depending on the value of a field for each task. To save time, the indicators have already been selected.

10. Click the first cell under the Image column heading, and then click the dropdown arrow. Here you can see the many graphical indicators you can associate with the values of fields.

11. Click **Cancel** to close the Graphical Indicators dialog box, and then click **Cancel** again to close the Customize Fields dialog box.

12. Select the **Fixed Cost** column heading. On the menu bar, click **Insert**, and then click **Column**. The Column Definition dialog box appears.

13. In the *Field name* box, select **Overbudget (Number3)** from the dropdown list, and then click **OK**. Microsoft Project displays the Overbudget column in the Cost table. Your screen should look similar to Figure 15-15.

Figure 15-15

Cost table with Overbudget column displayed

	Overbudget	Fixed Cost	Fixed Cost Accrual	Total Cost	Baseline	Variance	Actual	Remaining
ik Music Vid		$0.00	Prorated	$94,381.06	$94,214.50	$166.56	$29,446.78	$64,934.28
Production		$0.00	Prorated	$28,529.00	$28,529.00	$0.00	$23,529.00	$5,000.00
e-Production beg		$0.00	Prorated	$0.00	$0.00	$0.00	$0.00	$0.00
view Screenpla	☺	$0.00	Prorated	$2,295.00	$2,295.00	$0.00	$2,295.00	$0.00
velop scene blo	☺	$0.00	Prorated	$1,560.00	$1,560.00	$0.00	$1,560.00	$0.00
velop productior	☺	$0.00	Prorated	$2,520.00	$2,520.00	$0.00	$2,520.00	$0.00
ntify and reserv	☺	$0.00	Prorated	$14,455.00	$14,455.00	$0.00	$9,455.00	$5,000.00
ok musicians	☺	$0.00	Prorated	$1,360.00	$1,360.00	$0.00	$1,360.00	$0.00
ok dancers	☺	$0.00	Prorated	$1,768.00	$1,768.00	$0.00	$1,768.00	$0.00
serve audio rec	☺	$0.00	Prorated	$1,400.00	$1,400.00	$0.00	$1,400.00	$0.00
serve video rec	☺	$0.00	Prorated	$1,680.00	$1,680.00	$0.00	$1,680.00	$0.00
tatus Meetin;		$0.00	Prorated	$1,491.00	$1,491.00	$0.00	$1,491.00	$0.00
e-Production cor		$0.00	Prorated	$0.00	$0.00	$0.00	$0.00	$0.00
uction		$0.00	Prorated	$23,536.06	$23,369.50	$166.56	$5,917.78	$17,618.28
oduction begins		$0.00	Prorated	$0.00	$0.00	$0.00	$0.00	$0.00
cene 1		$0.00	Prorated	$6,051.50	$6,051.50	$0.00	$5,301.50	$750.00
Scene 1 begin		$0.00	Prorated	$0.00	$0.00	$0.00	$0.00	$0.00
Scene 1 setup	☺	$0.00	Prorated	$536.00	$536.00	$0.00	$536.00	$0.00
Scene 1 rehea	☺	$0.00	Prorated	$888.50	$888.50	$0.00	$388.50	$500.00
Scene 1 vocal	☺	$0.00	Prorated	$1,692.00	$1,692.00	$0.00	$1,442.00	$250.00
Scene 1 video	☺	$0.00	Prorated	$2,687.00	$2,687.00	$0.00	$2,687.00	$0.00
Scene 1 teard(	☺	$0.00	Prorated	$248.00	$248.00	$0.00	$248.00	$0.00
Scene 1 compl		$0.00	Prorated	$0.00	$0.00	$0.00	$0.00	$0.00
cene 2		$0.00	Prorated	$7,089.56	$6,923.00	$166.56	$616.28	$6,473.28
Scene 2 begin		$0.00	Prorated	$0.00	$0.00	$0.00	$0.00	$0.00
Scene 2 setup	☺	$0.00	Prorated	$1,232.56	$1,066.00	$166.56	$616.28	$616.28
Scene 2 rehea		$0.00	Prorated	$824.00	$824.00	$0.00	$0.00	$824.00
Scene 2 vocal	☺	$0.00	Prorated	$1,440.00	$1,440.00	$0.00	$0.00	$1,440.00
Scene 2 video	☺	$0.00	Prorated	$3,345.00	$3,345.00	$0.00	$0.00	$3,345.00

The yellow indicator alerts you that the variance is higher than you would like it to be

The custom field Overbudget (Number3) displays a graphical indicator that represents one of three different levels of cost variance. The graphical indicators change, according to the ranges specified in the formula, as each task's cost variance changes. This is a useful format for identifying tasks whose cost variance is higher than you would like (as indicated by the red and yellow indicators). This makes it easy for any stakeholder to quickly scan the task list and locate tasks that need further attention.

14. SAVE the project plan.

PAUSE. LEAVE Project open to use in the next exercise.

In this lesson, you applied some custom formulas and graphical indicators to make it simple to review the status of tasks using the Task Sheet view. Communicating the project status to stakeholders is one of the most important functions of a project manager—and one that may occupy a significant portion of your working time. It is imperative that the project manager know who needs to know the project status and why, as well as in what format and level of detail these people need the information. The time to find the answers to these questions is in the initial planning stages of the project.

Once work on the project has commenced, your primary communication task will be reporting project status. This can take several forms:

- Status reports describing where the project is in terms of scope, cost, and schedule. These are often referred to as the three sides of the project triangle. The project triangle is a popular model of project management.
- Progress reports that provide the specific accomplishments of the project team.
- Forecasts that predict future project performance.

Standard report formats may already exist if your organization is highly focused on projects and project management. If your organization does not have standard reports, you may be able to introduce project status formats that are based on clear communication and project management principles. You may be able to report project status using some of the following:

- Printing the Project Summary report.
- Copying Microsoft Project data to other applications. For example, you could copy the Calendar view to Microsoft Office Word or Microsoft Office PowerPoint.
- Saving Microsoft Project data in other formats, such as HTML or GIF.

■ Evaluating Performance with Earned Value Analysis

THE BOTTOM LINE
Earned value analysis is used to measure a project's progress in terms of both schedule and budget, as well as to help predict its outcome.

USE the project plan you created in the previous exercise.

⊕ SET PROJECT STATUS DATE AND DISPLAY THE EARNED VALUE TABLE

1. On the menu bar, click **Project**, and then click **Project Information**. The Project Information dialog box appears.
2. In the *Status date* box, key or select **5/18/08**, and then click **OK**.
3. On the menu bar, click on **View**, point to **Table: Cost** and click **More Tables**. The More Tables dialog box appears.
4. In the Tables list, select **Earned Value**, and then click **Apply**. Microsoft Project displays the Earned Value table in the Task Sheet view. If necessary, double-click between column headings to display all values. Your screen should look like Figure 15-16.

Figure 15-16

Earned Value table in Task
Sheet view

Figure 15-16

Earned Value table in Task
Sheet view

Earned Value table in Task Sheet view

	Task Name	Planned Value - PV	Earned Value - EV	AC (ACWP)	SV	CV	EAC	BAC	VAC
0	⊟ Don Funk Music Vide	$29,496.75	$29,363.50	$29,446.78	($133.25)	($83.28)	$94,481.71	$94,214.50	($267.21)
1	⊟ Pre-Production	$23,529.00	$23,529.00	$23,529.00	$0.00	$0.00	$28,529.00	$28,529.00	$0.00
2	Pre-Production beg	$0.00	$0.00	$0.00	$0.00	$0.00	$0.00	$0.00	$0.00
3	Review Screenpla	$2,295.00	$2,295.00	$2,295.00	$0.00	$0.00	$2,295.00	$2,295.00	$0.00
4	Develop scene blo	$1,560.00	$1,560.00	$1,560.00	$0.00	$0.00	$1,560.00	$1,560.00	$0.00
5	Develop productior	$2,520.00	$2,520.00	$2,520.00	$0.00	$0.00	$2,520.00	$2,520.00	$0.00
6	Identify and reserv	$9,455.00	$9,455.00	$9,455.00	$0.00	$0.00	$14,455.00	$14,455.00	$0.00
7	Book musicians	$1,360.00	$1,360.00	$1,360.00	$0.00	$0.00	$1,360.00	$1,360.00	$0.00
8	Book dancers	$1,768.00	$1,768.00	$1,768.00	$0.00	$0.00	$1,768.00	$1,768.00	$0.00
9	Reserve audio rec	$1,400.00	$1,400.00	$1,400.00	$0.00	$0.00	$1,400.00	$1,400.00	$0.00
10	Reserve video rec	$1,680.00	$1,680.00	$1,680.00	$0.00	$0.00	$1,680.00	$1,680.00	$0.00
11	⊞ Status Meetin	$1,491.00	$1,491.00	$1,491.00	$0.00	$0.00	$1,491.00	$1,491.00	$0.00
26	Pre-Production cor	$0.00	$0.00	$0.00	$0.00	$0.00	$0.00	$0.00	$0.00
27	⊟ Production	$5,967.75	$5,834.50	$5,917.78	($133.25)	($83.28)	$23,703.07	$23,369.50	($333.57)
28	Production begins	$0.00	$0.00	$0.00	$0.00	$0.00	$0.00	$0.00	$0.00
29	⊟ Scene 1	$5,301.50	$5,301.50	$5,301.50	$0.00	$0.00	$6,051.50	$6,051.50	$0.00
30	Scene 1 begin	$0.00	$0.00	$0.00	$0.00	$0.00	$0.00	$0.00	$0.00
31	Scene 1 setup	$536.00	$536.00	$536.00	$0.00	$0.00	$536.00	$536.00	$0.00
32	Scene 1 rehea	$388.50	$388.50	$388.50	$0.00	$0.00	$888.50	$888.50	$0.00
33	Scene 1 vocal	$1,442.00	$1,442.00	$1,442.00	$0.00	$0.00	$1,692.00	$1,692.00	$0.00
34	Scene 1 video	$2,687.00	$2,687.00	$2,687.00	$0.00	$0.00	$2,687.00	$2,687.00	$0.00
35	Scene 1 teardo	$248.00	$248.00	$248.00	$0.00	$0.00	$248.00	$248.00	$0.00
36	Scene 1 compl	$0.00	$0.00	$0.00	$0.00	$0.00	$0.00	$0.00	$0.00
37	⊟ Scene 2	$666.25	$533.00	$616.28	($133.25)	($83.28)	$8,004.72	$6,923.00	($1,081.72)
38	Scene 2 begin	$0.00	$0.00	$0.00	$0.00	$0.00	$0.00	$0.00	$0.00
39	Scene 2 setup	$666.25	$533.00	$616.28	($133.25)	($83.28)	$1,232.56	$1,086.00	($166.56)
40	Scene 2 rehea	$0.00	$0.00	$0.00	$0.00	$0.00	$824.00	$824.00	$0.00
41	Scene 2 vocal	$0.00	$0.00	$0.00	$0.00	$0.00	$1,440.00	$1,440.00	$0.00
42	Scene 2 video	$0.00	$0.00	$0.00	$0.00	$0.00	$3,345.00	$3,345.00	$0.00

Here you can see most of the earned value numbers detailed at the beginning of
this lesson in the Software Orientation section.

5. Click on the name of the **Planned Value–PV** column to select the entire column.

6. On the menu bar, click **Insert**, and then click **Column**. The Column Definition dialog
box appears.

7. In the *Field name* box, select **SPI** from the dropdown list, and then click **OK**.
Microsoft Project displays the SPI column in the Earned Value table.

8. On the menu bar, click **Insert**, and then click **Column**. The Column Definition dialog
box appears.

9. In the *Field name* box, select **CPI** from the dropdown list, and then click **OK**.
Microsoft Project displays the CPI column to the left of the SPI column in the
Earned Value table. Your screen should look similar to Figure 15-17.

Figure 15-17

Earned Value table containing
CPI and SPI columns

**Earned value table with CPI (Cost Performance Index)
and SPI (Schedule Performance Index) columns added**

	Task Name	CPI	SPI	Planned Value - PV (BCWS)	Earned Value - EV (BCWP)	AC (ACWP)	SV	CV	EAC	BAC	VAC
0	⊟ Don Funk Music Vide	1	1	$29,496.75	$29,363.50	$29,446.78	($133.25)	($83.28)	$94,481.71	$94,214.50	($267.21)
1	⊟ Pre-Production	1	1	$23,529.00	$23,529.00	$23,529.00	$0.00	$0.00	$28,529.00	$28,529.00	$0.00
2	Pre-Production beg	0	0	$0.00	$0.00	$0.00	$0.00	$0.00	$0.00	$0.00	$0.00
3	Review Screenpla	1	1	$2,295.00	$2,295.00	$2,295.00	$0.00	$0.00	$2,295.00	$2,295.00	$0.00
4	Develop scene blo	1	1	$1,560.00	$1,560.00	$1,560.00	$0.00	$0.00	$1,560.00	$1,560.00	$0.00
5	Develop productior	1	1	$2,520.00	$2,520.00	$2,520.00	$0.00	$0.00	$2,520.00	$2,520.00	$0.00
6	Identify and reserv	1	1	$9,455.00	$9,455.00	$9,455.00	$0.00	$0.00	$14,455.00	$14,455.00	$0.00
7	Book musicians	1	1	$1,360.00	$1,360.00	$1,360.00	$0.00	$0.00	$1,360.00	$1,360.00	$0.00
8	Book dancers	1	1	$1,768.00	$1,768.00	$1,768.00	$0.00	$0.00	$1,768.00	$1,768.00	$0.00
9	Reserve audio rec	1	1	$1,400.00	$1,400.00	$1,400.00	$0.00	$0.00	$1,400.00	$1,400.00	$0.00
10	Reserve video rec	1	1	$1,680.00	$1,680.00	$1,680.00	$0.00	$0.00	$1,680.00	$1,680.00	$0.00
11	⊞ Status Meetin	1	1	$1,491.00	$1,491.00	$1,491.00	$0.00	$0.00	$1,491.00	$1,491.00	$0.00
26	Pre-Production cor	0	0	$0.00	$0.00	$0.00	$0.00	$0.00	$0.00	$0.00	$0.00
27	⊟ Production	0.99	0.98	$5,967.75	$5,834.50	$5,917.78	($133.25)	($83.28)	$23,703.07	$23,369.50	($333.57)
28	Production begins	0	0	$0.00	$0.00	$0.00	$0.00	$0.00	$0.00	$0.00	$0.00
29	⊟ Scene 1	1	1	$5,301.50	$5,301.50	$5,301.50	$0.00	$0.00	$6,051.50	$6,051.50	$0.00
30	Scene 1 begin	0	0	$0.00	$0.00	$0.00	$0.00	$0.00	$0.00	$0.00	$0.00
31	Scene 1 setup	1	1	$536.00	$536.00	$536.00	$0.00	$0.00	$536.00	$536.00	$0.00
32	Scene 1 rehea	1	1	$388.50	$388.50	$388.50	$0.00	$0.00	$888.50	$888.50	$0.00
33	Scene 1 vocal	1	1	$1,442.00	$1,442.00	$1,442.00	$0.00	$0.00	$1,692.00	$1,692.00	$0.00
34	Scene 1 video	1	1	$2,687.00	$2,687.00	$2,687.00	$0.00	$0.00	$2,687.00	$2,687.00	$0.00
35	Scene 1 teardo	1	1	$248.00	$248.00	$248.00	$0.00	$0.00	$248.00	$248.00	$0.00
36	Scene 1 compl	0	0	$0.00	$0.00	$0.00	$0.00	$0.00	$0.00	$0.00	$0.00
37	⊟ Scene 2	0.86	0.8	$666.25	$533.00	$616.28	($133.25)	($83.28)	$8,004.72	$6,923.00	($1,081.72)
38	Scene 2 begin	0	0	$0.00	$0.00	$0.00	$0.00	$0.00	$0.00	$0.00	$0.00
39	Scene 2 setup	0.86	0.8	$866.25	$533.00	$616.28	($133.25)	($83.28)	$1,232.56	$1,086.00	($166.56)
40	Scene 2 rehea	0	0	$0.00	$0.00	$0.00	$0.00	$0.00	$824.00	$824.00	$0.00
41	Scene 2 vocal	0	0	$0.00	$0.00	$0.00	$0.00	$0.00	$1,440.00	$1,440.00	$0.00

10. SAVE the project plan.

> **PAUSE. LEAVE** Project and your project plan open so that you can refer to it as you are reading the exercise discussion below.

In this exercise, you set the project status date and displayed the Earned Value table. The status date is the date you want Microsoft Project to use when calculating the earned value numbers.

Looking at task and resource variance throughout a project's duration is a key project management activity. Unfortunately, it does not give you the true picture of a project's long-term health. For example, a task might be over budget and ahead of schedule (possibly not good) or over budget and behind schedule (definitely not good). Looking at schedule and budget variance by themselves does not tell you very much about performance trends that may continue throughout the project.

Instead, earned value analysis gives you a more complete picture of overall project performance in relation to both time and cost. Earned value analysis is used to measure the project's progress and help forecast its outcome. It focuses on schedule and budget performance in relation to baseline plans. The key difference between earned value analysis and simpler budget/schedule analysis can be thought of in this way:

- "What are the current performance results we are getting?" is the question answered by simple variance analysis.
- "Are we getting our money's worth for the current performance results we are getting?" is the question answered by earned value analysis.

Although the difference is subtle, it is important. Earned value analysis allows you look at project performance in a more detailed way. It allows you to identify two important things: the true cost of project results to date, and the performance trend that is likely to continue for the rest of the project.

Review the project plan and steps you performed in this exercise. In order for Microsoft Project to calculate the earned value amounts for a project plan, you must first do the following:

- Save a baseline plan so that Microsoft Project can calculate the budgeted cost of the work scheduled before you start tracing actual work. (The baseline was already saved when you opened the file for this lesson.)
- Record actual work on tasks or assignments. (You did this in previous exercises in this lesson.)
- Set the status date so that Microsoft Project can calculate actual project performance up to a certain point in time. If you do not specify a status date, Microsoft Project uses the current date.

Earned value analysis uses the following three key values to generate all other schedule indicator and cost indicator values:

- The planned value (PV) or budgeted cost of work scheduled (BCWS). This is the value of the work scheduled to be completed as of the status date. Microsoft Project calculates this value by adding up all the timephased baseline values for tasks up to the status date.
- The actual cost of work performed (ACWP). This is the actual cost incurred to complete each task's actual work up to the status date.
- The earned value (EV) or budgeted cost of work performed (BCWP). This is the portion of the budgeted cost that should have been spent to complete each task's actual work performed up to the status date. This value is called earned value because it is literally the value earned by the work performed.

The earned value analysis schedule and the cost variance are directly related, but it is simpler to examine each independently. For clarity, Microsoft Project groups the earned value schedule indicator fields into one table, and the earned value cost indicator fields into another table. A third table combines the key fields of both schedule and cost indicators.

Using the above key values, Microsoft Project can also calculate some other important indicators of project performance:

- The project's cost variance, or CV, is the difference between the budgeted and actual cost of work performed.
- The project's schedule variance, or SV, is the difference between the budgeted cost of work performed and the budgeted cost of work scheduled.

It might seem strange to think of being ahead of or behind schedule in terms of dollars. However, keep in mind that dollars buy work, and work drives tasks to be completed. You will find that viewing both cost and schedule variance in the same unit of measure makes it easier to compare the two, as well as other earned value numbers that are also measured in dollars.

Finally, there are two other earned value numbers that are very helpful indicators:

- The Cost Performance Index, or CPI, is the ratio of budgeted to actual cost, or BCWP divided by ACWP.
- The Schedule Performance Index, or SPI, the ratio of performed to schedule work, or BCWP divided by BCWS.

The CPI and SPI allow you to evaluate a project's performance and compare the performance of multiple projects in a consistent way. In the Don Funk Music Video, the CPI and SPI provide information about each task and phase in the project and about the project as a whole:

- The CPI for the Don Funk Music Video project (as of the status date) is 1. You can interpret this as for every dollar's worth of work that has been paid for, 1 dollar's worth of work was actually accomplished.
- The SPI for the Don Funk Music Video project (as of the status date) is also 1. This can be interpreted that for every dollar's worth of work that was planned to be accomplished, 1 dollar's worth of work was accomplished.

Although both the SPI and CPI are currently 1 for the Don Funk Music Video project, keep in mind that these ratios can (and most likely will) change as work is completed and other factors change.

Earned value analysis is one of the more complicated things you can do in Microsoft Project, but it provides very valuable project status information. Earned value analysis also again illustrates why it is a good idea to enter task and resource cost information into a project plan any time you have it.

CLOSE the project plan. **PAUSE.** If you are continuing to the next lesson, keep Project open. If you are not continuing to additional lessons, **CLOSE** Project.

SUMMARY SKILL MATRIX

IN THIS LESSON YOU LEARNED	MATRIX SKILL
To record actual start, finish, and duration values of tasks	Enter actual start date and duration for a task
To adjust remaining work or duration of tasks	Adjust actual and remaining work for a task
To reschedule uncompleted work	Reschedule incomplete work
To save an interim plan	Save an interim project plan
To compare baseline, interim, and actual plans	Compare the baseline, interim, and actual project plans
To report project status	Report project variance with a "Stoplight" view
To evaluate performance with earned value analysis	Set project status date and display the Earned Value table

■ Knowledge Assessment

Fill in the Blank

Complete the following sentences by writing the correct word or words in the blanks provided.

1. The _____ is a popular model of project management that uses time, cost, and scope.

2. A snapshot of current values from the project plan that Microsoft Project saves with the file is called a(n) _____.

3. _____ is the difference between the budgeted cost of work performed and the budgeted cost of work scheduled (SV).

4. The ratio of performed to scheduled work is the _____.

5. _____ is used to measure the project's progress by giving a more complete picture of overall project performance in relation to both time and cost.

6. You specify the _____ that you want Microsoft Project to use when calculating the earned value numbers.

7. The _____ is the actual cost incurred to complete each task's actual work up to the status date.

8. The difference between the budgeted and actual cost of work performed is the _____.

9. The ratio of budgeted to actual cost is the _____.

10. You can save up to _____ different interim plans during a project.

Multiple Choice

Select the best response for the following statements.

1. The term that means the same as earned value (EV) is
   a. actual cost of work performed (ACWP).
   b. budgeted cost of work performed (BCWP).
   c. cost performance index (CPI).
   d. budgeted cost of work scheduled (BCWS).

2. Only a(n) _____ can have a remaining work or duration value.

   a. delayed task

   b. incomplete task

   c. complete task

   d. overbudget task

3. Which of the following would NOT be an optimum time to save an interim project plan?

   a. at the end of a major phase

   b. at preset time intervals

   c. at the end of the project

   d. just before entering a large number of actuals

4. The value of the work scheduled to be completed as of the status date is the

   a. ACWP.

   b. EV.

   c. BCWS.

   d. BCWP.

5. Which dialog box is used to record actual work done on a task?

   a. Update Project

   b. Project Information

   c. Task Drivers

   d. Task Information

6. By default, whenever you enter actual work values, Microsoft Project

   a. calculates actual cost values.

   b. determines estimated cost values.

   c. predicts the final project end date.

   d. all of the above.

7. The term that means the same as budgeted cost of work scheduled (BCWS) is

   a. planned value (PV).

   b. cost variance (CV).

   c. schedule variance (SV).

   d. earned value (EV).

8. Which of the following is NOT a rule used by Microsoft Project when updating the project schedule based on actual start, finish, or duration values you have entered?

   a. When you enter a task's actual start date, Microsoft Project moves the scheduled finish date to match the actual start date.

   b. When you enter a task's actual duration that is equal to the scheduled duration, Microsoft Project sets the task to 100% complete.

   c. When you enter a task's actual finish date, Microsoft Project moves the scheduled finish date to match the actual finish dates and assigns a completion percentage of 100%.

   d. When you enter an actual duration for a task that is longer than the scheduled duration, Microsoft Project subtracts the actual duration from the scheduled duration to determine the remaining duration.

9. Which of the following is NOT something that must be done in order for Microsoft Project to calculate earned value amounts for a project plan?

 a. save a baseline plan

 b. finish at least 50% of the project plan

 c. record actual work on tasks or assignments

 d. set a status date (or allow the default of the current date)

10. The portion of the budgeted cost that should have been spent to complete each task's actual work performed up to the status date is the

 a. ACWP.

 b. PV.

 c. BCWS.

 d. BCWP.

■ Competency Assessment

Project 15-1: Recording Actuals for Office Lunchroom Remodel

Work has finally started on the lunchroom remodel at your office. You need to update some of the task information to reflect actuals that have been provided to you: task 6 started one day early but took the scheduled amount of time, and task 7 started on time, but took one day longer to complete.

GET READY. Launch Microsoft Project if it is not already running.

OPEN *Office Remodel 15-1* from the data files for this lesson.

The *Office Remodel 15-1* project plan is available on the companion CD-ROM.

1. Click on the name of task 6, **Tear out inside dividing walls.**
2. On the tracking toolbar, click the **Update Tasks** button.
3. Under the Actual label, in the Start box, key or select **10/22/07.**
4. In the *Actual dur* box, key or select **2d**, and then click **OK.**
5. Select the name of task 7, **Remove drywall from main walls.**
6. On the tracking toolbar, click the **Update Tasks** button.
7. In the *Actual dur* box, key or select **3d**, and then click **OK.**
8. **SAVE** the project plan as *Office Remodel Actuals*, and then close the file.

 PAUSE. LEAVE Project open to use in the next exercise.

Project 15-2: Save an Interim Plan for HR Interview Plan

More than half of the tasks have been completed for the HR Interview project plan. You would like to save an interim plan at this point.

OPEN *HR Interview Plan 15-2* from the data files for this lesson.

The *HR Interview Plan 15-2* project plan is available on the companion CD-ROM.

1. On the menu bar, click **Tools**, point to **Tracking**, and then click **Set Baseline.**
2. Select **Set interim plan.**
3. Under *Set interim plan*, in the Into box, select **Start3/Finish3** from the dropdown list.
4. Click **OK.**
5. Click on the name of task 18, and then click the **Scroll to Task** button on the Standard toolbar.
6. **SAVE** the project plan as **HR Interview Interim3**, and then **CLOSE** the file.

 PAUSE. LEAVE Project open to use in the next exercise.

Project 15-3: Compare Baseline, Interim, and Actual Plans for the Office Lunchroom Remodel

Now that work is in progress for your office lunchroom remodel, you'd like to evaluate the progress of the project. You know that one way to do this is to compare baseline, interim, and actual plans for the project.

OPEN *Office Remodel 15-3* from the data files for this lesson.

1. Activate the Set Baseline dialog box, and set (save) an interim plan.
2. Make a copy of the Tracking Gantt view. Name the copy **Tracking Gantt–Interim**.
3. Activate the new *Tracking Gantt–Interim* view.
4. Activate the Bar Styles dialog box.
5. Insert a new row. Name the new row **Interim**, and in the *Show For...Tasks* column, select **Normal**.
6. Select **Start1** in the From column heading and **Finish1** in the To column heading.
7. On the Bars tab under the Middle label, in the Shape box, select the second bar option. In the Pattern box, select the third option. In the color box, select **Lime**. Apply your selections.
8. Scroll to task 11.
9. **SAVE** the project plan as **Office Remodel Interim**, and then **CLOSE** the file.
   PAUSE. LEAVE Project open to use in the next exercise.

Project 15-4: Don Funk Music Video Earned Value Analysis

More time has passed since you performed your previous earned value analysis on the Don Funk Music Video project, and additional tasks have been completed. You need to set a new status date and display the Earned Value Table.

OPEN *Don Funk Music Video 15-4* from the data files for this lesson.

1. In the Project Information dialog box, set a status date of 6/09/08.
2. Change the view to the Task Sheet view.
3. Apply the Earned Value table from the More Tables dialog box.
4. Insert the SPI and CPI columns to the left of the Planned Value-PV column.
5. Click on the name of task 45 and scroll your task list so that task 45 is visible in the middle of your screen.
6. **SAVE** the project plan as **Don Funk Earned Value** and then **CLOSE** the file.
   PAUSE. LEAVE Project open to use in the next exercise.

■ Mastery Assessment

Project 15-5: Rescheduled Work on Insurance Claim Process

On your Insurance Claim Process project, you have just been informed that there will be a delay in making repairs. Work has started but cannot continue because a part is backordered and will not arrive at the body shop until June 23, 2008.

OPEN *Insurance Claim Process 15-5* from the data files for this lesson.

1. Update task 18 to show that work is 30% complete.
2. Reschedule remaining work to start after 6/23/08.
3. **SAVE** the file as **Insurance Claim Process Reschedule**, and then **CLOSE** the file.
   PAUSE. LEAVE Project open to use in the next exercise.

Project 15-6: Adjusting Remaining Work and Duration on Don Funk Music Video Tasks

You now have more actuals to enter into the Don Funk Music Video project plan. Update the work (as provided below) in the Work table of the Task Usage view.

OPEN *Don Funk Music Video 15-6* from the data files for this lesson.

1. For task 47, Scene 3 setup, 34 hours of actual work have been completed and 0 hours of work are remaining.

2. For task 48, Scene 3 rehearsal, 12 hours of actual work have been completed and 8 hours of work are remaining.

3. **SAVE** the project plan as **Don Funk Adjusted**, and then **CLOSE** the file.
   CLOSE Project.

INTERNET READY

This lesson provided a brief introduction to earned value analysis. Search the Internet for more information on earned value analysis. Look for information on its history and development (i.e., who developed it and the original industry in which it was used), its integration into modern project management, and more information on the various indicators discussed in this lesson. Write a brief (1–2 page) document summarizing your research. Comment on how you might be able to use earned value analysis even as a beginning project manager.

Working with Resource Pools

LESSON SKILL MATRIX

SKILLS	MATRIX SKILL
Developing a Resource Pool	Develop a resource pool
Viewing Assignment Details in a Resource Pool	View assignment details in the resource pool
Revising Assignments in a Sharer Plan	Revise assignments in a sharer plan
Updating Resource Information in a Resource Pool	Update working time for a resource in a resource pool
Updating Working Time for All Projects in a Resource Pool	Update working time for all sharer plans via the resource pool
Adding New Project Plans to a Resource Pool	Add new files to the resource pool
Revising a Sharer Plan and Updating a Resource Pool	Revise a sharer plan and manually update the resource pool

KEY TERMS
line manager
program office
resource manager
resource pool
sharer plan

289

You are a video project manager for Southridge Video, and one of your primary responsibilities recently has been to manage the new Don Funk Music Video project. However, you also have several other projects that you manage. These projects often share resources and are worked on simultaneously. Microsoft Office Project has several features that facilitate working with multiple project plans. In this lesson, you will learn how to work with a resource pool, as well as review consolidated projects and how they relate to resource pools.

■ SOFTWARE ORIENTATION

Microsoft Project's Share Resources Dialog Box

In Microsoft Project, you can use the Share Resources dialog box to create a resource pool.

The Share Resources dialog box

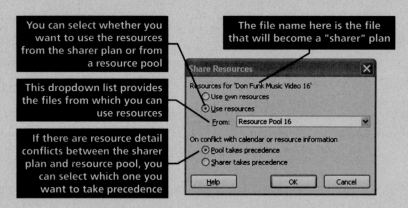

The Share Resources dialog box enables you to select the options you want when creating a resource pool, including the project plan or resource pool to which you want to add your file as a sharer plan, and whether you want the resource pool or sharer plan to take precedence in case of conflict.

■ Developing a Resource Pool

THE BOTTOM LINE

A resource pool can help a project manager to see the extent to which resources are utilized across multiple and simultaneous projects.

The **Don Funk Music Video 16M** project plan is available on the companion CD-ROM

GET READY. Before you begin these steps, launch Microsoft Project.

OPEN the **Don Funk Music Video 16M** project plan from the data files for this lesson.

SAVE the file as **Don Funk Music Video 16** in the solutions folder for this lesson as directed by your instructor.

OPEN the **Adventure Works Promo 16M** project plan from the data files for this lesson.

SAVE the file as **Adventure Works Promo 16** in the solutions folder for this lesson as directed by your instructor.

The **Adventure Works Promo 16M** project plan is available on the companion CD-ROM

➔ DEVELOP A RESOURCE POOL

1. On the Standard toolbar, click the **New** button. A blank project opens.

2. Click the **Show/Hide Project Guide** button on the Project Guide toolbar. The Project Guide closes.

3. On the menu bar, click **File**, and then click **Save As**.

4. In the *Save in* box, locate your solution folder as directed by your instructor. In the *File name* box, key **Resource Pool 16**, and then click **Save**.

> **TAKE NOTE** Although you can choose any name you want for a resource pool, it is a good idea to indicate that it is a resource pool as part of the file name.

5. On the menu bar, click **Window**, and then click **Arrange All**. Microsoft Project arranges the three project plan windows within the Microsoft Project window. (It is not necessary to arrange the project windows this way to create a resource pool, but is helpful for viewing purposes in this lesson.)

6. On the menu bar, click **View**, and then click **Resource Sheet**. Your screen should look similar to Figure 16-2.

Figure 16-2

Resource Sheet view showing resource pool

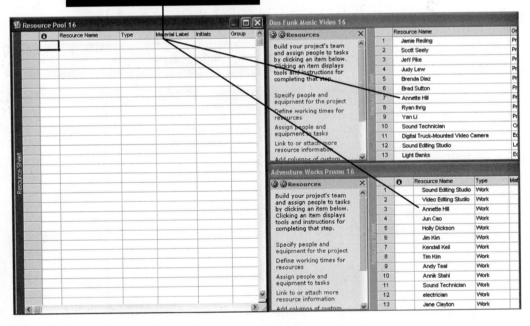

Notice that in the resource lists for the two project plans, several resources appear in both lists. These include Annette Hill, Jane Clayton, Sound Technician, electrician, and microphone bundles, among others. None of these resources are overallocated in either project.

7. Click the title bar of the Don Funk Music Video 16 window.

8. On the menu bar, click **Tools**, point to **Resource Sharing**, and then click **Share Resources**. The Share Resources dialog box appears.

9. Under *Resources for 'Don Funk Music Video 16,'* click **Use resources**. In the From list, select **Resource Pool 16** from the dropdown list if it is not already selected. Your screen should look similar to Figure 16-3.

Figure 16-3

Share Resources dialog box

10. Click **OK** to close the Share Resources dialog box. The resource information from the Don Funk Music Video 16 project plan appears in the Resource Pool 16 file.

11. Click the title bar of the Adventure Works Promo 16 window.

12. On the menu bar, click **Tools**, point to **Resource Sharing**, and then click **Share Resources**.

13. Under *Resources for 'Adventure Works Promo 16,'* click **Use resources**. In the From list, make sure that **Resource Pool 16** is selected.

14. Under the *On conflict with calendar or resource information* label, make sure that **Pool takes precedence** is selected. Selecting this option causes Microsoft Project to use resource information (such as cost rates) in the resource pool rather than in the sharer plan should it find any differences between the two project plans.

15. Click **OK** to close the Share Resources dialog box. The resource information from the Adventure Works Promo 16 project plan appears in the resource pool. Your screen should look similar to Figure 16-4.

Figure 16-4

Resource Pool 16

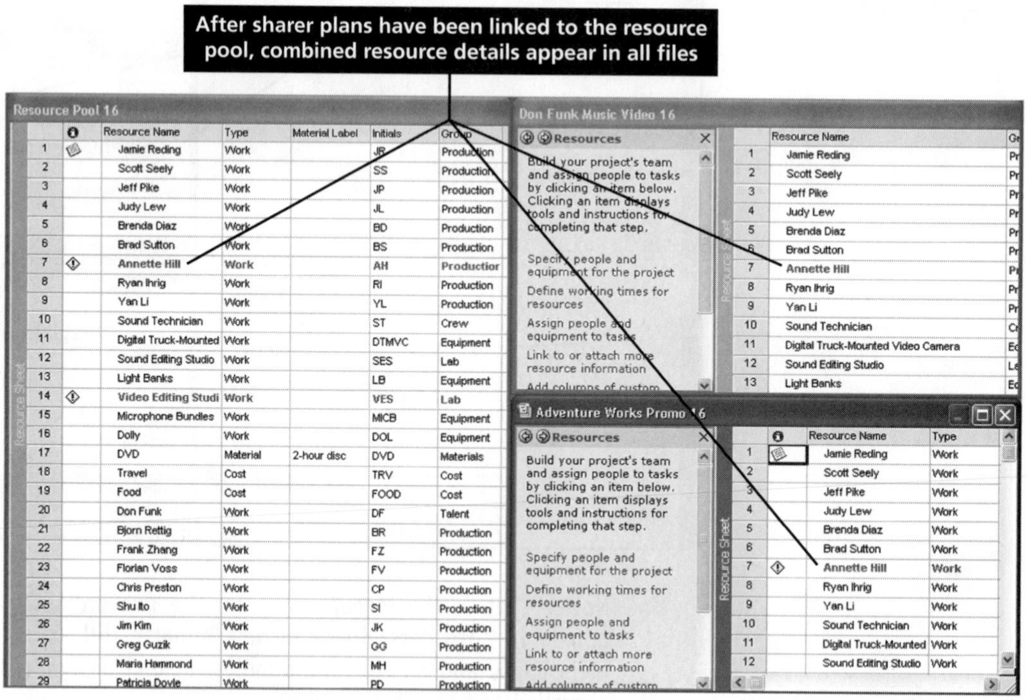

After sharer plans have been linked to the resource pool, combined resource details appear in all files

TAKE NOTE

If you decide at some point in the future that you do not want to use a resource pool with a project plan, you can break the link. On the menu bar, click Tools, point to Resource Sharing, and click Share Resources. In the Share Resources dialog box, under Resources for '<current project name>' click *Use own resources.*

16. SAVE each project plan by clicking on the title bar of each file and then clicking the Save button on the Standard toolbar.

PAUSE. LEAVE Project open to use in the next exercise.

In this exercise, you created a resource pool across two individual project plans. A **resource pool** is a project plan from which other project plans gather their resource information. As a project manager works to manage multiple projects, work resources are often assigned to more than one project at a time. It can be difficult to manage the resources' time among multiple projects, especially if different project managers are involved for each different project. For example, a technical editor might have task assignments on three different productions. In each project, the editor might be fully allocated or even underallocated, but when you add together all of the tasks from the three projects, you might find out that the editor is actually overallocated.

A resource pool can help you monitor how resources are utilized across multiple projects. It contains information about all resources' task assignments from all the project plans linked to the resource pool. If you change resource information—such as cost rates, maximum units, and nonworking time—in the resource pool, all linked project plans will use the updated information. The project plans that are linked to the resource pool are called **sharer plans**.

If you only manage one project, and your resources are not used in other projects, then using a resource pool will provide no additional benefit to you. However, if your organization must manage multiple projects at the same time, setting up a resource pool allows you to do such things as:

- Enter resource information one time, but use it in multiple project plans.
- View resources' assignment details from multiple projects in a single place.
- View assignment costs per resource across multiple projects.
- Identify resources that are overallocated across multiple projects, even if they are fully- or underallocated in individual projects.
- Enter resource information, such as nonworking time, in any of the individual plans or in the resource pool so that it is available in the other sharer plans.

A resource pool is particularly beneficial when you are working with other Microsoft Project users across a network. The resource pool can be stored in a central location—such as a network server—and the individual owners of the sharer plans share the network resource pool.

In the above exercise, the resource pool contains the resource information from both sharer plans. Microsoft Project consolidates the information from sharer plans based on the name of the resource. Annette Hill, for example, is listed only once in the resource pool, no matter how many sharer plans list her as a resource. Keep in mind, however, that Microsoft Project can't match variations of a resource's name—say, Annette Hill from one sharer plan and Annette L. Hill from another. It is good to develop a convention for naming a resource and stick with it.

Any Microsoft Project plan, with or without tasks, can serve as a resource pool. It is a good idea, though, to specify a file that does not contain tasks as the resource pool. This is because any project with tasks will come to an end at some point, and you might not want assignments for those tasks (along with their costs and other details) to be included indefinitely in the resource pool. In addition, a dedicated resource pool file without tasks allows people such as line managers or resource managers to maintain some information about their resources in the resource pool. A **line manager** is a manager of a group of resources, and is also sometimes called a functional manager. A **resource manager** oversees resource usage in project activities specifically to manage the time and cost of resources. These people might not have a role in project management, and therefore would not need to deal with task-specific details in the resource pool.

■ Viewing Assignment Details in a Resource Pool

THE BOTTOM LINE By viewing project assignments in a resource pool, you can see, in a combined format, how all the resources for the sharer projects are allocated.

USE the project plans you created in the previous exercise.

➡ VIEW ASSIGNMENT DETAILS IN THE RESOURCE POOL

1. Double-click the title bar of the Resource Pool 16 window. The resource pool window maximizes to fill the active window. In the resource pool, you can view all resources from the two sharer plans.

2. On the menu bar, click **View**, and then click **Resource Usage**. The Resource Usage view appears.

3. In the Resource Name column, scroll to select the name of resource 14, **Video Editing Studio**. Click the plus sign (+) next to Video Editing Studio's name to expand its assignment list. Your screen should look similar to Figure 16-5.

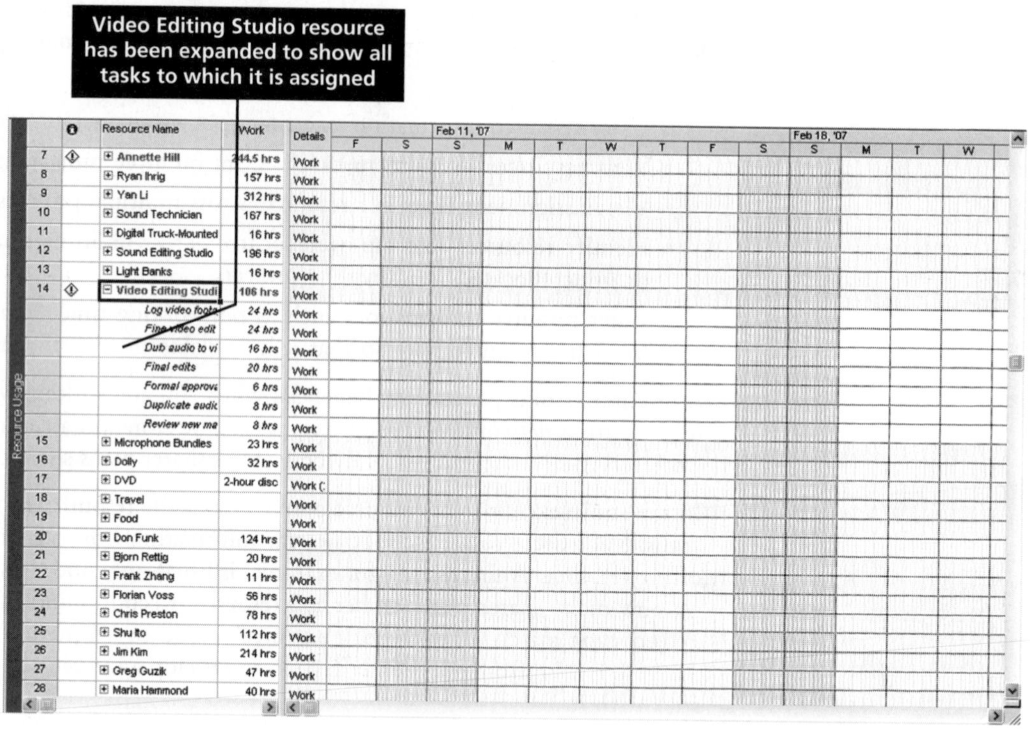

Figure 16-5

Resource Usage view showing all of Video Editing Studio's assignments

Video Editing Studio resource has been expanded to show all tasks to which it is assigned

For a review of resolving problems with resource allocation, see Lesson 12.

4. On the Standard toolbar, click the **Scroll to Task** button. The timescale details on the right side of the active window scroll horizontally to show the Video Editing Studio's earliest assignments.

5. Scroll the timescale details to the right until you can see the assignments for the Video Editing Studio during the weeks of July 6, 2008 and July 13, 2008.

6. On the menu bar, click **Window**, and then click **Split**. The Resource Usage/Resource Form combination view is activated. Your screen should look similar to Figure 16-6.

Figure 16-6

Combination view of Resource Usage view and Resource Form view for Video Editing Studio

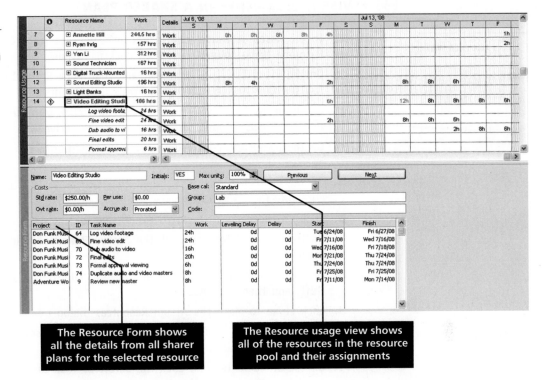

The Resource Form shows all the details from all sharer plans for the selected resource

The Resource usage view shows all of the resources in the resource pool and their assignments

In this view, you can see all of the resources in the resource pool and their assignments (in the upper pane), as well as the additional details for the resources (in the lower pane) for all sharer plans. Note, for example, that the *Fine video edit* task to which the Video Editing Studio is assigned is from the Don Funk Music Video project, and the *Review new master* task is from the Adventure Works Promo project. While the Video Editing Studio was not overallocated in either project, it is actually overallocated when you look at its assignments across projects in this way.

Take a minute to select different resource names in the Resource Usage view to see their assignment details in the Resource Form.

7. On the menu bar, click **Window**, and then click **Remove Split**.

8. SAVE the project plan.

PAUSE. LEAVE Project open to use in the next exercise.

In this lesson, you changed the view of the resource pool to be better able to view and analyze the information it contains. One of the most important benefits of using a resource pool is that it enables you to see how resources are allocated across projects. You can pinpoint resources that are overallocated across the multiple projects to which they are assigned.

■ Revising Assignments in a Sharer Plan

THE BOTTOM LINE

When you make changes to resource assignments in a sharer plan, these changes will be reflected in the resource pool as well.

USE the project plans you used in the previous exercise. Make sure that *Resource Pool 16* is the project plan in the active window.

→ **REVISE ASSIGNMENTS IN A SHARER PLAN**

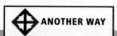
ANOTHER WAY

You can also use the Go To dialog box on the Edit menu to move the view to Arlene Huff's name.

1. In the Resource Usage view, scroll until you see resource 46, Arlene Huff, in the Resource Name column, and then click her name.

2. On the menu bar, click **Window**, and then click **Split**. In the lower window, you can see that Arlene Huff has no task assignments in either sharer plan.

3. On the menu bar, click **Window**, and then click **Don Funk Music Video 16**. The *Don Funk Music Video 16* project is in the active window.

4. On the menu bar, click **View**, and then click **Gantt Chart**. The Gantt Chart appears.

5. On the menu bar, click **Edit**, then click **Go To**. In the ID box, key **67**, and then click **OK**. The Gantt Chart view scrolls to task 67.

6. Click on the name of task 67, **Rough audio edit**.

7. On the Standard toolbar, click the **Assign Resources** button. The Assign Resources dialog box appears.

8. In the Resource Name column in the Assign Resources dialog box, select **Arlene Huff**, and then click **Assign**.

9. Click **Close** to close the Assign Resources dialog box.

10. On the menu bar, click **Window**, and then click **Resource Pool 16** to switch back to the resource pool.

11. On the Standard toolbar, click the **Scroll to Task** button. Arlene Huff's new task assignment appears in the resource pool. You may need to scroll the upper window (the Resource Usage view) to see Arlene Huff's name. Your screen should look similar to Figure 16-7.

Figure 16-7

Resource Pool 16 showing Arlene Huff assigned to task 67 of Don Funk Music Video 16

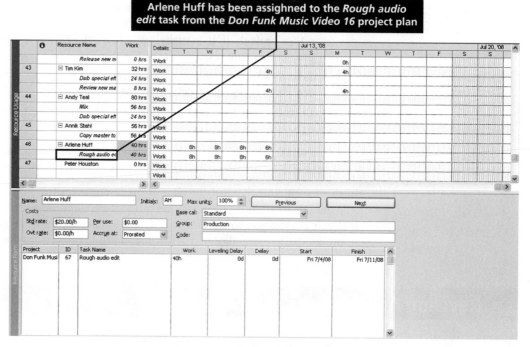

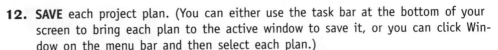

12. **SAVE** each project plan. (You can either use the task bar at the bottom of your screen to bring each plan to the active window to save it, or you can click Window on the menu bar and then select each plan.)

13. After saving the project plans, make sure that *Resource Pool 16* is in the active window.

    PAUSE. LEAVE Project open to use in the next exercise.

In this exercise, you made a resource assignment from the resource pool into a sharer plan, and then viewed the change posted to the resource pool. Recall that an assignment is the matching of a resource to a task. The resource's assignment details originate in a sharer plan, and Microsoft Project updates the resource pool with assignment details as you make them in the sharer plan.

■ Updating Resource Information in a Resource Pool

 THE BOTTOM LINE When a resource's information is updated in a resource pool, it is also updated in all of the sharer plans linked to that resource pool.

USE the project plans you used in the previous exercise.

➔ UPDATE WORKING TIME FOR A RESOURCE IN A RESOURCE POOL

You have just been told that Jim Kim is not available to work on July 10-11, 2008 because he will be attending a training program.

1. In the Resource Name column, scroll to select resource name 26, **Jim Kim**.

2. Click the plus sign (+) next to Jim Kim's name to display all of his assignments below his name. If necessary, scroll the Resource Usage view so that all of Jim Kim's assignments are visible.

3. On the Standard toolbar, click the **Resource Information** button. The Resource Information dialog box appears. Click the **General** tab, if necessary.

4. Click the **Change Working Time** button. The Change Working Time dialog box appears.

5. Drag the vertical scroll bar or click the up and down arrows next to the calendar until July 2008 appears.

6. Select the dates **July 10** and **11**.

7. On the Exceptions tab below the calendar, under the Name column heading, click on the first empty cell. Key **Training Class** and press ⟨Enter⟩. Microsoft Project fills the Start and Finish cells with 7/10/2008 and 7/11/2008 respectively, and sets these dates to nonworking time. Your screen should look like Figure 16-8.

Figure 16-8

Change Working Time
dialog box

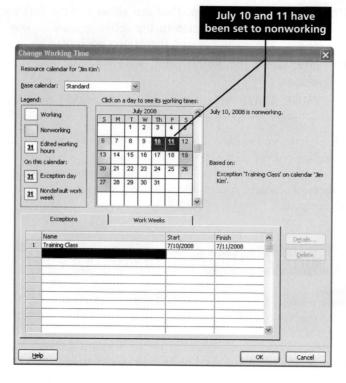

8. Click **OK** to close the Change Working Time dialog box. Click **OK** again to close the Resource Information dialog box. Scroll the screen so that July 10 and 11 are visible. Notice that Jim Kim now has no work scheduled for July 10 and July 11, 2008 (previously he had). Your screen should look similar to Figure 16-9.

Figure 16-9

Resource Usage view showing
nonworking time for Jim Kim

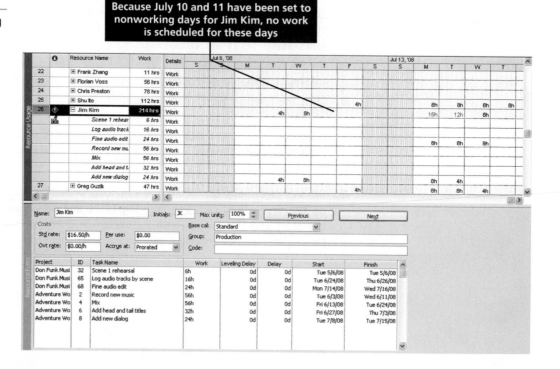

Anytime you make changes in a resource pool, make sure you have it open as read-write (as it is in this lesson). When you create a resource pool, it is automatically created as read-write. When you open any resource pool, if Microsoft Project asks whether you want to open it as read-only or read-write, select read-write.

SHOOTING

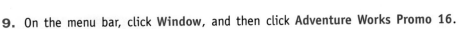

9. On the menu bar, click **Window**, and then click **Adventure Works Promo 16**.

10. In the Resource Name column, select the resource name of **Jim Kim** (resource 26).

11. On the Standard toolbar, click the **Resource Information** button. In the Resource Information dialog box that appears, click the **Change Working Time** button. The Change Working Time dialog box appears.

12. Drag the vertical scroll bar or click the up and down arrows next to the calendar until July 2008 appears. Click on the date **July 10**, and then click on **July 11**. The notes next to the calendar indicate that both of these days are nonworking.

13. Click **Cancel** to close the Change Working Time dialog box. Click **Cancel** again to close the Resource Information dialog box.

14. **SAVE** all of the project plans.

PAUSE. LEAVE Project open to use in the next exercise.

In this exercise, you updated a resource's calendar in the resource pool, and then verified that this change was reflected in the sharer plan. This is another key benefit of using resource pools–you have a central location to enter resource details, such as working time and cost rates, and any updates you make to the resource pool are made available in all of the sharer plans. This is particularly useful in organizations with large numbers of resources working on multiple projects. In larger organizations, employees such as line managers, resource managers, or even staff in a program office may be responsible for keeping general resource information updates. A **_program office_** is a group that oversees a collection of projects (such as producing doors and producing engines), each of which is part of a complete deliverable (such as an automobile) and the organization's strategic objectives.

■ Updating Working Time for All Projects in a Resource Pool

THE BOTTOM LINE

Any working time change that you make in the resource pool will update to all sharer plans.

USE the project plans you used in the previous exercise.

⊙ UPDATE WORKING TIME FOR ALL SHARER PLANS VIA THE RESOURCE POOL

The entire company (Southridge Video) will be attending a company picnic on July 18, 2008, and you want this to be a nonworking day for all sharer projects.

1. On the menu bar, click **Window**, and then click **Resource Pool 16**.

2. On the menu bar, click **Tools**, and then click **Change Working Time**. The Change Working Time dialog box appears.

3. In the _For calendar_ box, select **Standard (Project Calendar)** from the dropdown menu.

4. Drag the vertical scroll bar or click the up and down arrows next to the calendar until July 2008 appears. Click on the date **July 18**.

5. On the Exceptions tab below the calendar, under the Name column heading, click on the first empty cell. Key **Company Picnic** and press Enter. Microsoft Project fills the Start and Finish cells with 7/18/2008, and sets the time to nonworking. Your screen should look similar to Figure 16-10.

Figure 16-10

Change Working Time dialog box showing company picnic exception time

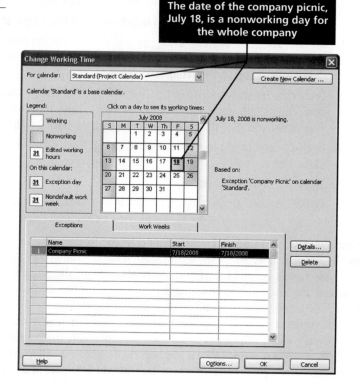

6. Click **OK** to close the Change Working Time dialog box.

7. On the menu bar, click **Window**, and then click **Don Funk Music Video 16**.

8. On the menu bar, click **Tools**, and then click **Change Working Time**. The Change Working Time dialog box appears.

9. Make sure that **Standard (Project Calendar)** is selected in the *For calendar* box, and then drag the vertical scroll bar or click the up and down arrows next to the calendar until July 2008 appears. Notice that July 18, 2008 is flagged as a nonworking day and the details are shown on the Exceptions tab below the calendar.

10. Click **Cancel** to close the Change Working Time dialog box.

If you desire, you can switch the view to the Adventure Works Promo 16 project and use the same steps to verify that July 18, 2008 is also a nonworking day for that project.

11. **SAVE** all project plans and then **CLOSE** all files.

PAUSE. LEAVE Project open to use in the next exercise.

In this exercise, you made a change to the base calendar for the resource pool, and then verified this change in one of the sharer plans. This is another key advantage of using a resource pool. By changing the base calendar for the resource pool, the change is updated for ALL sharer plans that use that calendar.

By default, all sharer plans share the same base calendars, and any changes you make in a base calendar in one sharer plan are reflected in all other sharer plans using that base calendar through the resource pool. If you have a certain sharer plan for which you want to use different base calendar working times, you must change the base calendar that sharer plan uses. This different base calendar will still be available for use in all other sharer plans through the resource pool, but will only apply to those sharer plans in which you select it as the base calendar.

SHOOTING

■ Adding New Project Plans to a Resource Pool

THE BOTTOM LINE

Project plans can be made into sharer plans for a resource pool at any time. For this reason, it is a good idea to make all project plans into sharer plans (once you have set up a resource pool).

 CD

The ***Resource Pool 16MA*** project plan is available on the companion CD-ROM

GET READY. OPEN *Resource Pool 16MA* from the data files for this lesson. When prompted, click the second option to open the file as read-write, and then click **OK**.

SAVE the file as *Resource Pool 16A* in the solutions folder for this lesson as directed by your instructor.

TAKE NOTE

The default option is for Microsoft Project to open resource pools as read-only. You might want to choose this option if you and other Microsoft Project users are sharing a resource pool across a network. However, if you store the resource pool locally, you should open it as read-write.

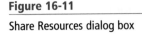 **ADD NEW FILES TO THE RESOURCE POOL**

1. On the menu bar, click **View**, and then click **Resource Sheet**. The Resource Sheet View appears.
2. On the menu bar, click **Window**, and then click **Remove Split**.
3. On the Standard toolbar, click the **New** button.
4. Click the **Show/Hide Project Guide** button on the Project Guide toolbar. The Project Guide closes.
5. On the menu bar, click **File**, and then click **Save As**. The Save As dialog box appears.
6. In the *Save in* box, locate your solution folder as directed by your instructor. In the *File name* box, key **Coho Winery Project 16**, and then click **Save**.
7. On the Standard toolbar, click the **Assign Resources** button. The Assign Resources dialog box appears.

    The Assign Resources box is currently empty because you have not yet entered any resource information into this project plan.
8. On the menu bar, point to **Tools**, point to **Resource Sharing**, and then click **Share Resources**. The Share Resources dialog box appears.
9. Under *Resources for 'Coho Winery Project 16,'* select **Use Resources**.
10. In the *From* list, make sure that **Resource Pool 16A** is selected in the dropdown list. Your screen should look similar to Figure 16-11.

Figure 16-11

Share Resources dialog box

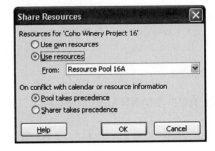

11. Click **OK** to close the Share Resources dialog box. In the Assign Resources dialog box, you can now see all of the resources from the resource pool. These resources are now ready for assignment to tasks in this project. Your screen should look similar to Figure 16-12.

Figure 16-12

Assign Resources dialog box for Coho Winery Project 16

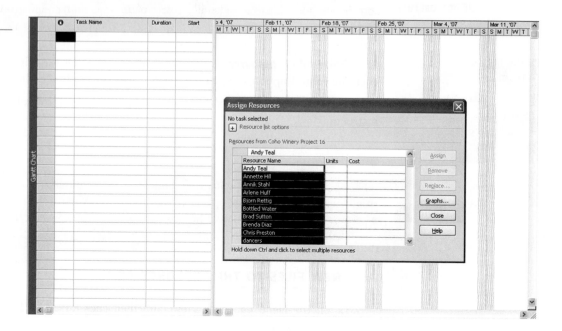

12. Click **Close** to close the Assign Resources dialog box.
13. **SAVE** the project plans, and then **CLOSE** the files.

 PAUSE. LEAVE Project open to use in the next exercise.

In this exercise, you created a project plan and made it a sharer plan for the resource pool. You can do this at any time: when initially entering the project plan's tasks, after you have assigned resources to tasks, or even after work has begun. Once you have set up a resource pool, you might find it helpful to make sharer plans of projects in progress and of all new projects. This is a good way to become accustomed to relying on the resource pool for resource information.

■ Revising a Sharer Plan and Updating a Resource Pool

THE BOTTOM LINE
Sometimes, you may have the resource pool open as read-only. In this case, you would have to manually update resource information to the resource pool.

GET READY. OPEN *Adventure Works Promo 16* from your solution files for this lesson (this is a project plan you used in a previous exercise, but we want to open it now as read-only). Select the **Open resource pool to see assignments across all sharer files** option, and then click **OK**.

⊕ **REVISE A SHARER PLAN AND MANUALLY UPDATE THE RESOURCE POOL**

1. On the menu bar, click **View**, and then click **Gantt Chart**.
2. In the Task Name column, click on the name of task 6, **Add head and tail titles**.

3. On the Standard toolbar, click the **Assign Resources** button. The Assign Resources dialog box appears.

4. In the Resource Name column in the Assign Resources dialog box, select the name of **Frank Zhang**, and then click the **Assign** button.

5. In the Task Name column, click the name of task 9, **Review new master**.

6. In the Resource Name column in the Assign Resources dialog box, select the name of **Holly Dickson**, and then click the **Remove** button.

    You have made two assignment changes in the sharer plan. Because the resource pool is open as read-only, these changes were not automatically saved in the resource pool. You need to manually update the resource pool.

7. On the menu bar, click **Tools**, point to **Resource Sharing**, and then click **Update Resource Pool**. Microsoft Project updates the assignment information in the resource pool file with the new details from the sharer plan. If anyone opens or refreshes the resource pool from now on, the updated assignment information will be available.

> **TAKE NOTE**
> Keep in mind that only assignment information is saved to the resource pool from the sharer plan. Any changes you make to resource details, such as cost rates or Max. units, in the sharer plan are not saved in the resource pool when you update. If you want to change resource details, you must open the resource pool as read-write. Once it is open as read-write, you can change resource details in either the resource pool or the sharer plan, and Microsoft Project will update the other file.

8. In the Task Name column, click on the name of task 3, **Sync Sound**.

9. In the Resource Name column in the Assign Resources dialog box, select **Arlene Huff**, and then click the **Assign** button.

10. Click the **Close** button to close the Assign Resources dialog box. Your screen should look similar to Figure 16-13.

Figure 16-13

Adventure Works Promo 16 project plan with revised resources

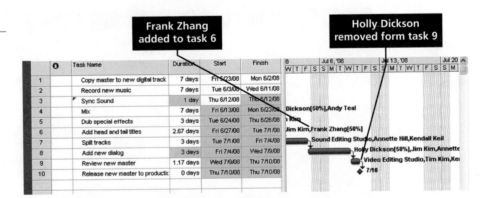

11. On the menu bar, click **File**, and then click **Close**. When prompted to save changes, click **Yes**. Microsoft Project determines that because the resource pool was opened as read-only, the assignment changes you just made in the sharer plan have not been updated in the resource pool file. A dialog box appears, and you are offered a choice as to whether or not you want to update the resource pool. Your screen should look similar to Figure 16-14.

Figure 16-14

Microsoft Office Project
dialog box

12. After you review the options in the dialog box, click **OK**. Microsoft Project updates the assignment information with the new details from the sharer plan. The resource pool remains open as read-only.

13. On the menu bar, click **File** and then click **Close**. Since the resource pool was opened as read-only, Microsoft Project closes it without prompting you to save changes.

PAUSE. If you are continuing to the next lesson, keep Project open. If you are not continuing to additional lessons, **CLOSE** Project.

In this exercise, you made changes to a sharer plan and updated a resource pool that had been opened as read-only (as if you were on a network, rather than working with local files). This is an important concept because if you are sharing a resource pool with other Microsoft Project users across a network, whoever has the resource pool open as read-write prevents others from updating resource information. For this reason, it is a good idea to open the resource pool as read-only and to use the Update Resource Pool command only when you need to update the resource pool with assignment information. Once this is done, anyone else who opens the resource pool will see the latest assignment information.

SUMMARY SKILL MATRIX

IN THIS LESSON YOU LEARNED	MATRIX SKILL
To develop a resource pool	Develop a resource pool
To view assignment details in a resource pool	View assignment details in the resource pool
To revise assignments in a sharer plan	Revise assignments in a sharer plan
To update resource information in a resource pool	Update working time for a resource in a resource pool
To update working time for all projects in a resource pool	Update working time for all sharer plans via the resource pool
To add new project plans to a resource pool	Add new files to the resource pool
To revise a sharer plan and update a resource pool	Revise a sharer plan and manually update the resource pool

■ Knowledge Assessment

Matching

Match the term in column 1 to its description in column 2.

Column 1

Column 2

1. line manager

a. project plans that are linked to the resource pool

2. resource pool

b. a group that oversees a collection of projects, each of which is part of a complete deliverable

3. assignment

c. the work assigned to a resource is more than can be done within the normal work capacity of the resource

4. program office

d. a manager of a group of resources

5. underallocated

e. dialog box that enables you to specify how resources will be used across project plans

6. resource manager

f. a project plan from which other project plans gather their information

7. split view

g. the matching of a resource to a task

8. Share Resources

h. the active view is composed of two views which divide the screen horizontally

9. overallocated

i. the work assigned to a resource is less than the resource's maximum capacity

10. sharer plan

j. a manager who oversees resource usage in project activities to manage the time and cost of resources

True / False

Circle T if the statement is true or F if the statement is false.

T F **1.** You can link a maximum of three sharer plans to a resource pool.

T F **2.** Any Microsoft Project plan can serve as a resource pool.

T F **3.** If you decide that you do not want to use a resource pool with a project plan, it is possible to break the link between the resource pool and sharer plan.

T F **4.** If you have a resource pool open as read-only and make changes to a sharer plan, only assignment information is saved to the resource pool from the sharer plan.

T F **5.** Microsoft Project does not update the resource pool with assignment details as you make them in the sharer plan.

T F **6.** When you save a resource pool, you must use 'resource pool' as part of the file-name.

T F **7.** A project plan can be made into a sharer plan for a resource pool only before work has started.

T F **8.** For a resource pool on a network, multiple users can simultaneously have the resource pool open as read-write.

T F **9.** If you change resource information, such as costs rate, in the resource pool, all linked projects will use the updated information.

T F **10.** By default, all sharer plans use the same base calendar.

■ Competency Assessment

⊕ Project 16-1: Adding a Sharer Plan to the Southridge Video Resource Pool

You have created a resource pool for two of the Southridge Video projects on which you are working. You have been assigned to work on another project, and want to add this sharer plan to the resource pool.

GET READY. Launch Microsoft Project if it is not already running.

The *Southridge Video Resource Pool 16-1* and *Gregory Weber Biography 16-1* project plans are available on the companion CD-ROM.

OPEN *Southridge Video Resource Pool 16-1* from the data files for this lesson. When prompted, click the second option to open the file as read-write, and then click **OK. OPEN** *Gregory Weber Biography 16-1* from the data files for this lesson.

SAVE the files as *Southridge Video Resource Pool* and *Gregory Weber Biography*.

1. On the menu bar, click **Window**, and then click *Gregory Weber Biography*.
2. On the menu bar, click **View**, and then click **Resource Sheet**.
3. Click the **Show/Hide Project Guide** button on the Project Guide toolbar.
4. On the menu bar, click **Tools**, point to **Resource Sharing**, and then click **Share Resources**.
5. Under *Resources for 'Gregory Weber Biography,'* select the **Use resources** option.
6. In the *From* list, make sure that **Southridge Video Resource Pool** is selected from the drop-down list, and then click **OK**.
7. **SAVE** the project plans.
8. **CLOSE** the *Gregory Weber Biography* project plan. Leave the *Southridge Video Resource Pool* project plan open.

   PAUSE. LEAVE Project open to use in the next exercise.

⊕ Project 16-2: Updating Working Time in the Southridge Video Resource Pool

Arlene Huff has just informed you that she is unable to work on June 17, 2008 due to a personal commitment. You need to update her resource information to reflect this date as non-working time.

SAVE the open *Southridge Video Resource Pool* as *Southridge Video Resource Pool 2*.

1. On the menu bar, click **View** and then click **Resource Usage**.
2. In the Resource Name column, select the name of **Arlene Huff**.
3. On the Standard toolbar, click the **Resource Information** button.
4. In the Resource Information dialog box, click the **Change Working Time** button.
5. Drag the vertical scroll bar or click the up and down arrows next to the calendar until June 2008 appears.
6. Select the date **June 17**.
7. On the Exceptions tab below the calendar, under the Name column heading, click on the first empty cell. Key **Vacation Day** and press Enter.
8. Click **OK** in the Change Working Time dialog box.
9. Click **OK** in the Resource Information Dialog box.
10. **SAVE** the project plan, and then **CLOSE** the file.

    PAUSE. LEAVE Project open to use in the next exercise.

■ Proficiency Assessment

➔ Project 16-3: Revising the Employee Orientation Sharer Plan and Updating the HR Resource Pool.

You need to make several changes to the Employee Orientation Plan, but want to open the HR Resource Pool as read-only so that others can still read the file while you are using it. You will then need to update the resource pool with your changes.

(To set up this exercise, you will first need to build a resource pool from the Employee Orientation Plan and HR Interview Plan projects. After creating and saving the resource pool and sharer files, you will reopen the necessary files for this exercise.)

The *Employee Orientation Plan 16-3* and *HR Interview Plan 16-3* project plans are available on the companion CD-ROM.

OPEN *Employee Orientation Plan 16-3* and *HR Interview Plan 16-3* from the data files for this lesson.

SAVE the project plans as *Employee Orientation Plan 3* and *HR Interview Plan 3*.

1. OPEN a new, blank project plan. Once the plan is open, close the Project Guide, if necessary.
2. SAVE the new file as *HR Resource Pool 3*.
3. Change the view to the Resource Sheet.
4. Arrange all three open files in the active window.
5. Use the Share Resources dialog box to add the resources from *HR Interview Plan 3* to *HR Resource Pool 3*.
6. Use the Share Resources dialog box to add the resources from *Employee Orientation Plan 3* to *HR Resource Pool 3*.
7. SAVE all three open files, and then CLOSE the files.
8. OPEN *Employee Orientation Plan 3* from *your* solution file location. When prompted, select the option to open the resource pool.
9. Make sure that the *Employee Orientation Plan* project fills the active window. Change the view to the Gantt Chart.
10. Select the name of task 11, **Tour Customer Service Center.**
11. Activate the Assign Resources dialog box.
12. Assign Jason Watters to this task.
13. Select the name of task 10, **Measuring for uniforms.**
14. Assign Britta Simon to this task.
15. Close the Assign Resources dialog box.
16. Activate the Resource Sharing options on the Tools menu, and then update the resource pool.
17. CLOSE *Employee Orientation Plan 3*. When you are prompted to save, click **Yes.** In the dialog box that appears, click **OK.**
18. CLOSE *HR Resource Pool 3*.

    PAUSE. LEAVE Project open to use in the next exercise.

The *Southridge Video Resource Pool 16-4, Don Funk Music Video 16-4,* and *Adventure Works Promo 16-4* project plans are available on the companion CD-ROM.

Project 16-4: Updating Working Time for All Projects in Southridge Video Resource Pool

You need to make a change to working time for all employees of Southridge Video to reflect two days that everyone will be spending at the National Videographer's Conference. You need to reflect this as nonworking time in all sharer projects.

OPEN *Southridge Video Resource Pool 16-4* from the data files for this lesson. When prompted, click the second option to open the file as read-write, and then click **OK.** OPEN *Don Funk Music Video 16-4* and *Adventure Works Promo 16-4* from the data files for this lesson.

SAVE the files as *Don Funk Music Video 4*, *Adventure Works Promo 4*, and *Southridge Video Resource Pool 4*.

1. Expand the *Southridge Video Resource Pool 4* to fill the active window, if it is not already expanded.

2. Activate the Change Working Time dialog box from the Tools menu.

3. Select the **Standard (Project Calendar)** as the calendar to which you want to apply your change.

4. Select the dates of **March 20-21, 2008**.

5. Add the National Videographers' Conference to the Exceptions tab.

6. Close the Change Working Time dialog box.

7. Verify the working time change in the two sharer files.

8. **SAVE** all open project plans, and then **CLOSE** the files.

   PAUSE. LEAVE Project open to use in the next exercise.

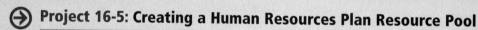

■ Mastery Assessment

The *Employee Orientation Plan 16-5* and *HR Interview Plan 16-5* project plans are available on the companion CD-ROM.

➔ Project 16-5: Creating a Human Resources Plan Resource Pool

You have several human resources project plans that are active in your department. You need to create a resource pool and link these plans to it.

OPEN *Employee Orientation Plan 16-5* and *HR Interview Plan 16-5* from the data files for this lesson.

SAVE the files as *Employee Orientation Plan* and *HR Interview Plan*.

1. Open a new file and save it as *HR Resource Pool*.

2. Link the *Employee Orientation Plan* to the resource pool using the Share Resources dialog box.

3. Link the *HR Interview Plan* project to the resource pool using the Share Resources dialog box. Make sure that the pool takes precedence.

4. **SAVE** all three project plans.

   PAUSE. LEAVE Project and all three plans open to use in the next exercise.

➔ Project 16-6: Updating Assignments in a Sharer Plan to the HR Resource Pool

You now need to make several updates to the sharer plans linked to the HR Resource Pool.

GET READY. SAVE the open plans from the previous exercise as *HR Resource Pool 6, HR Interview Plan 6,* and *Employee Orientation Plan 6*.

1. In the *HR Interview Plan 6* project plan, for task 6, replace Keith Harris with Garth Fort using the Assign Resources dialog box.

2. In the *HR Interview Plan 6* project plan, for task 19, remove Keith Harris' assignment to this task using the Assign Resources dialog box.

3. In the *Employee Orientation Plan 6* project plan, for task 12, assign Karen Berg to this task using the Assign Resources dialog box.

4. **SAVE** all of the project plans, and then **CLOSE** the files.

   CLOSE Project.

INTERNET READY

Search the Microsoft Office Online Website (or any other site you find helpful) for more information on ways to share resources across projects (resource pool). Consider how this information might be applied to your department at work, a community or volunteer group with which you are involved, or a school group. Write a memo to your manager detailing how and why it would be useful to implement a resource pool across projects in your department (or community, volunteer, or school group). If possible, create some simple project plans that relate to current activities, and link them to a resource pool to use as an example.

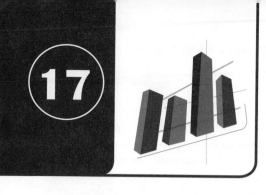

Customizing Microsoft Project

LESSON SKILL MATRIX

SKILLS	MATRIX SKILL
Defining General Preferences	Specify the default path for use in the Open and Save As dialog boxes
Working with Templates	Create a new template based on a current project plan
Working with the Organizer	Copy a custom view from one project plan to another using the organizer
Working with Macros	Record and run a macro

Now that you have worked with project plans extensively, it is time to learn about some of the ways you can customize Microsoft Office Project to fit your own preferences. Some of the customization options you see in Microsoft Project are similar to those you see in other Microsoft Office programs, such as Microsoft Word or Microsoft Excel. In this lesson, you will learn how to customize some general settings, how to use a macro, and how to use the Organizer.

KEY TERMS
global template
macro
Organizer
shortcut
template
Visual Basic for
    Applications

■ SOFTWARE ORIENTATION

Microsoft Project's Organizer Dialog Box

In Microsoft Project, the Organizer is the feature that enables you to share elements between Microsoft Project files.

Figure 17-1

The Organizer dialog box

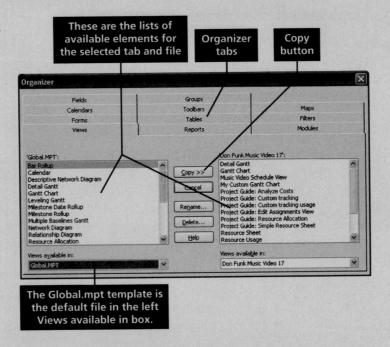

The Organizer dialog box enables you to copy views, tables, filters, and other items between the Global.mpt template and other Microsoft Project files, or between two different Microsoft Project files.

■ Defining General Preferences

THE BOTTOM LINE

You are able to make choices that will customize Microsoft Project. These choices enable you to specify personal preferences regarding how Microsoft Project will operate.

CD

The *Don Funk Music Video 17M* project plan is available on the companion CD-ROM.

GET READY. Before you begin these steps, launch Microsoft Project.

OPEN the *Don Funk Music Video 17M* project plan from the data files for this lesson.

SAVE the file as *Don Funk Music Video 17* in the solutions folder for this lesson as directed by your instructor.

⊙ SPECIFY THE DEFAULT PATH FOR USE IN THE OPEN AND SAVE AS DIALOG BOXES

1. On the menu bar, click **Tools**, and then click **Options**. The Options dialog box appears.
2. In the Options dialog box, click the **Save** tab. The Save tab is displayed. Your screen should look similar to Figure 17-2.

Figure 17-2

The Save tab in the Options dialog box

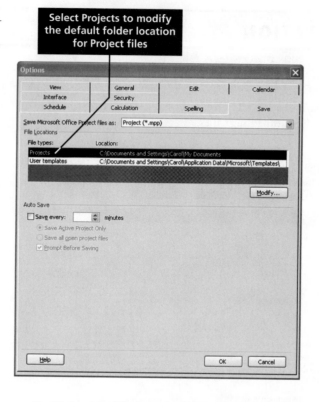

Select Projects to modify the default folder location for Project files

3. Under the File Locations label, select **Projects**, and then click the **Modify** button. The Modify Location dialog box appears.

4. Select your desired folder location as directed by your instructor, and then click **OK**. If you are not changing your file location, click **Cancel**.

TAKE NOTE
Specifying the folder you want to open by default in the Open and Save As dialog boxes can be very helpful if you usually keep all of your Microsoft Project files in one location.

5. Click **OK** again to close the Options dialog box.

   To verify that the new location you have selected is now the default folder location, you can view the Open dialog box.

6. On the menu bar, click **File**, and then click **Open**. The Open dialog box appears, using the path you specified.

7. Click **Cancel** to close the Open dialog box.

8. **SAVE** the project plan.

   PAUSE. LEAVE Project open to use in the next exercise.

In this exercise, you specified the folder that you wanted to open as the default in the Open and Save As dialog boxes. This can be quite helpful if you tend to keep most or all of your Microsoft Project files in one location. Like many other Microsoft Office applications, you have the capability within Microsoft Project to make choices about how you work with this application. By selecting these preferences, the person working with Microsoft Project (such as the project manager or the organization) can personalize the software to fit their needs.

■ Working with Templates

THE BOTTOM LINE   A template provides the basic structure of a new project plan. It may include information such as resources, tasks, assignments, views, tables, and more.

USE the project plan you created in the previous exercise.

⊕ CREATE A NEW TEMPLATE BASED ON A CURRENT PROJECT PLAN

1. On the menu bar, click **File**, and then click **Save As**. The Save As dialog box appears.
2. In the *File name* box, key **Music Video Template**.
3. In the *Save as type* box, select **Template**.
4. In the *Save in* box (located at the top of the Save As dialog box), select the Lesson 17 solutions folder as directed by your instructor.
5. Click the **Save** button. The Save As Template dialog box appears.

   The **Don Funk Music Video 17** file contains both baseline and actual values, and you do not want to include these with the template.
6. Select the **Values of all baselines**, **Actual Values**, and **Fixed Costs** check boxes. You are indicating that these items should be removed from your template. Your screen should look like Figure 17-3.

Figure 17-3

Save As Template dialog box

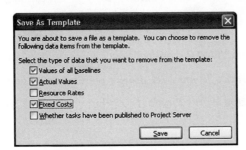

7. Click the **Save** button. Microsoft Project creates a new template based on the **Don Funk Music Video 17** file.

   Based on the options you selected in the Save As Template dialog box, Microsoft Project removes the data you chose not to include with the template. However, the task list, relationships, resources, and assignments are conserved as entered in the original **Don Funk Music Video 17** file. If Southridge Video has a similar project in the future, you could start with this template and modify it to fit the new project.

SHOOTING   When you create a new project file based on a template, you may need to adjust more than the project start date to preserve the task relationships and schedule logic. For example, if the template contains hard constraints with dates prior to the current date, Microsoft Project may not be able to properly schedule tasks. You can use the Adjust Dates macro to schedule such a project with the correct start and finish dates for tasks. To run the Adjust Dates macro, click Adjust Dates on the Analysis toolbar. To display the Analysis toolbar, on the View menu, point to Toolbars, and then click Analysis. (If you do not see the Analysis toolbar on your View menu, key Analysis Toolbar into the Help box and look for information on how to reinstall it.)

8. Make sure that the *Music Video Template* file is in the active window. On the menu bar, click **File**, and then click **Close**. If prompted to save changes to the *Music Video Template*, click **Yes**.

9. On the menu bar, click **File**, and then click **Don Funk Music Video 17**. Microsoft Project reopens the *Don Funk Music Video 17* file, just as you left it.

10. **SAVE** the project plan.

   PAUSE. LEAVE Project open to use in the next exercise.

In this exercise, you saved your current project plan as a template. A ***template*** is a Microsoft Project file format that lets you reuse an existing project plan as the basis for a new project plan. Templates can include any of the types of information you might expect to find in a Microsoft Project plan, including task and resource lists, assignments, customized views, tables, filters, and macros.

As you saw in this exercise, you can save any Microsoft Project file, at any time, as a template to use in the future. When saving a template from a current file, you usually exclude baseline and actual values, as these would not be useful as part of a template. You can also exclude things such as resource cost rates and fixed costs, if there is a need to protect this information as confidential.

■ Working with the Organizer

THE BOTTOM LINE

The Organizer is a feature in Microsoft Project that enables you to reset custom elements or to copy elements (such as views, reports, tables, etc.) from one project plan to another.

USE the *Don Funk Music Video 17* project plan you opened in the previous exercise.

OPEN the *Adventure Works Promo 17M* project plan from the data files for this lesson.

SAVE the file as *Adventure Works Promo 17* in the solutions folder for this lesson as directed by your instructor.

The *Adventure Works Promo 17M* project plan is available on the companion CD-ROM.

➔ COPY A CUSTOM VIEW FROM ONE PROJECT PLAN TO ANOTHER USING THE ORGANIZER

1. On the menu bar, click **Window**, and then click **Don Funk Music Video 17**. The *Don Funk Music Video 17* project plan is brought into the active window.

2. On the menu bar, click **View**, and then click **More Views**.

3. Select **Music Video Schedule View**, and then click **Apply**. Your screen should look similar to Figure 17-4.

Figure 17-4

Don Funk Music Video 17 project plan with Music Video Schedule View applied

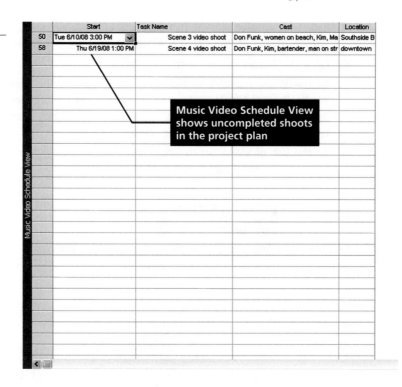

You'd like to copy this custom view to the Adventure Works Promo 17 project plan, using the Organizer.

4. On the menu bar, click **Tools**, and then click **Organizer**. The Organizer dialog box appears. Your screen should look similar to Figure 17-5.

Figure 17-5

Organizer dialog box

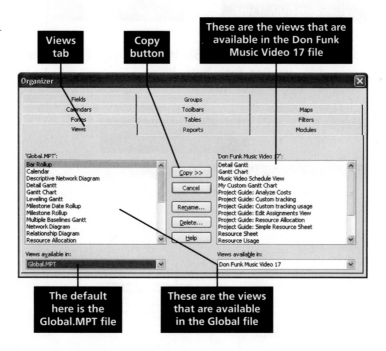

5. Click several of the tabs in the dialog box to get an overview of the available options.

Notice that each tab of the Organizer dialog box is structured in the same way: elements such as views and tables appear on the left and right sides of the dialog box. The element on the left are from one file, and the elements on the right are from another file. By default, the elements from the Global.mpt file appear on the left side of the dialog box, and the corresponding elements from the active project file appear on the right.

TAKE NOTE*

The global template is a Microsoft Project template named Global.mpt.

TAKE NOTE*

Notice that the two arrow symbols (>>) beside the Copy button switch direction (<<) when you select an element on the right side of the dialog box.

Selecting an element on the left side of the dialog box and then clicking the Copy button will copy that element to the file listed on the right, and vice versa.

6. Click the **Views** tab, if it is not already selected.

7. In the *Views available in* list on the left side of the dialog box, select **Adventure Works Promo 17**. The names of the views in the *Adventure Works Promo 17* file appear on the left. Note that the *Adventure Works Promo 17* file does not contain the Music Video Schedule View.

8. In the list of views on the right side of the dialog box, click **Music Video Schedule View**. Your screen should look similar to Figure 17-6.

Figure 17-6

Organizer showing views in both project plans

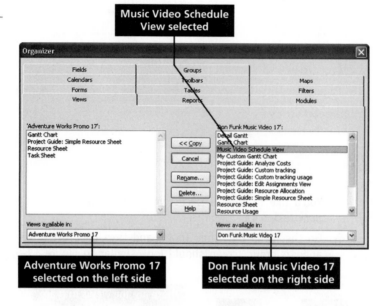

9. Click the **<<Copy** button. Microsoft Project copies the Music Video Schedule View from the *Don Funk Music Video 17* project plan to the *Adventure Works Promo 17* project plan. Your screen should look similar to Figure 17-7.

Figure 17-7

Organizer showing Music Video Schedule View in both project plans

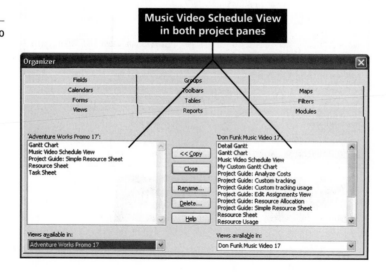

10. Click Close to close the Organizer.

11. SAVE both project plans.

PAUSE. LEAVE Project open to use in the next exercise.

In this exercise, you used the Organizer to share a table between two Microsoft Project files. The *Organizer* is a feature you use to organize elements between Microsoft Project files so that they can be shared, edited, and reset. The names of the tabs in the Organizer dialog box indicate the elements you can copy between project plans.

One feature of Microsoft Project that you can work with via the organizer is the global template, a Microsoft Project template named Global.mpt. The *global template* provides the default views, tables, and other elements in Microsoft Project, and includes:

- Calendars
- Filters
- Forms
- Groups
- Import/export maps
- Menu bars
- Reports
- Tables
- Toolbars
- VBA Modules (macros)
- Views

At first, the specific definitions of all views, tables, and other elements are contained in the global template. The first time you display a view, table, or similar element in a Microsoft Project file, it is copied from the global template to that file. From then on, the element resides in the Microsoft Project file. If you customize that element in the Microsoft Project file (for example, you change the columns displayed in a table), the changes apply only to the Microsoft Project file, and not to the global template.

It is possible to use Microsoft Project extensively and never need to use the global template. If you do need to work with the global template, however, there are two primary actions you can accomplish with it:

- Create a customized element, such as a custom table, and make it available in all project plans with which you work by copying the custom view into the global template.
- Replace a customized element, such as a custom table in a project plan, by copying the original, unmodified element from the global template to the project plan in which you've customized the same element.

Take note that customized data maps, VBA modules, and toolbars are not normally stored in individual Microsoft Project plans, unlike other elements with which you work via the Organizer. Instead, these elements are stored in the global template, and are available for the global template for all Microsoft Project plans with which you work. If you want to share a data map, VBA module, or toolbar with another Microsoft Project user, you need to copy it from the global template to a Microsoft Project plan, and then send the project plan to the other user.

VBA will be discussed in more detail in the next section of this lesson.

When using the Organizer, if you attempt to copy a view, table, or other element from a project plan to the global template, Microsoft Project alerts you if you will overwrite that same element in the global template. If you choose to overwrite it, that customized element (such as the Music Video Schedule View in this exercise) will be available in all new project plans, and any other project plans that do not already contain that element. If instead you choose to rename the customized element, it becomes available in all project plans, but does not affect the existing elements already stored in the global template. It is a good idea to give

■ Working with Macros

THE BOTTOM LINE

Repetitive series of actions performed in Microsoft Project can be recorded (saved) as a macro to save time.

your customized elements unique names, like Music Video Schedule View, so that you can keep the original element intact.

 USE the project plan you used in the previous exercise. Make sure that *Don Funk Music Video 17* is in the active window.

RECORD AND RUN A MACRO

1. On the menu bar, point to **View**, and then click **Gantt Chart**.
2. On the menu bar, click **Tools**, point to **Macro**, and then click **Record New Macro**.

TAKE NOTE*

Macro names must begin with a letter and cannot contain spaces. If you want to improve the readability of your macro names, use an underscore (_) where you would use a space.

The Record Macro dialog box appears.

3. In the *Macro name* box, key **Zoom_Entire_View**.

TROUBLESHOOTING

A *shortcut* is one or more keys that you press on the keyboard to complete a task. The shortcut takes less key strokes than it would normally take to complete the task. (For instance, *Ctrl+S* saves a file.) For this exercise, you did not designate a shortcut key. However, when recording other macros, keep in mind that you cannot use a Ctrl+ key combination already reserved by Microsoft Project, such as Ctrl+G (Go To..). If you do select a shortcut that is already reserved, when you click the OK button to close the Macros dialog box, Microsoft Project will alert you that you need to choose a different key combination.

4. Leave the *Shortcut key* box blank. In this exercise, you will not specify a shortcut key.
5. In the *Store macro in* box, select **This Project** to store the macro in the active project for use only in this project.
6. In the Description box, select the existing text and replace by keying **Zooms to view the entire project**. Your screen should look similar to Figure 17-8.

Figure 17-8

Record Macro dialog box

7. Click **OK**. Microsoft Project will begin to record the new macro. Microsoft Project does not actually record and play back every mouse movement like a video camera, but records only the results of the keystrokes and actions you make. You do not need to rush to complete the macro.

8. On the menu bar, click **View**, and then click **Zoom**.

9. In the Zoom dialog box, select **Entire Project**, and then click the **OK** button. Microsoft Project adjusts the timescale to display the entire project. Now you are ready to stop recording the macro.

10. On the menu bar, click **Tools**, point to **Macro**, and then select **Stop Recorder**.

   To verify that the macro functions correctly, you will return the zoom setting to its original setting and then run the macro you just recorded.

11. On the menu bar, click **View**, and then click **Zoom**.

12. In the Zoom dialog box, click **Reset**, and then click **OK**. Microsoft Project restores the timescale to its previous setting.

13. On the menu bar, click **Tools**, point to **Macro**, and then click **Macros**. The Macros dialog box appears.

14. In the Macro name box, select **Don Funk Music Video 17.mpp!Zoom_Entire_View**, and then click the **Run** button. Microsoft Project carries out the macro and adjusts the timescale to display the entire project. Your screen should look similar to Figure 17-9. Note that the timescale is condensed (zoomed) so that entire project can be viewed in the width of one screen.

Figure 17-9

Gantt Chart showing entire project

	ℹ	Task Name	Duration	Start
50		Scene 3 video shoot	2 days	Tue 6/
51		Scene 3 teardown	1 day	Thu 6/
52		Scene 3 complete	0 days	Fri 6/
53		⊟ Scene 4	6.75 days	Fri 6/
54		Scene 4 begin	0 days	Fri 6/
55		Scene 4 setup	2 days	Fri 6/
56		Scene 4 rehearsal	6 hrs	Tue 6/
57		Scene 4 vocal recordin	1 day	Wed 6/
58		Scene 4 video shoot	2 days	Thu 6/
59		Scene 4 teardown	1 day	Mon 6/
60		Scene 4 complete	0 days	Tue 6/
61		Production complete	0 days	Tue 6/
62		⊟ Post-Production	25.25 days	Tue 6/
63		Post-Production begins	0 days	Tue 6/
64		Log video footage	3 days	Tue 6/
65		Log audio tracks by scene	2 days	Tue 6/
66		Rough edit video - paper	1 wk	Fri 6/
67		Rough audio edit	1 wk	Fri 7
68		Fine audio edit	3 days	Fri 7/
69		Fine video edit	3 days	Fri 7/
70		Dub audio to video	2 days	Wed 7/
71		Internal review viewing	1.13 days	Fri 7/
72		Final edits	3 days	Mon 7/
73		Formal approval viewing	1 day	Wed 7/
74		Duplicate audio and video m	1 day	Thu 7/
75		Archive Copy 1 AV master:	1 day	Fri 7/
76		Send Copy 2 AV master an	1 day	Mon 7/
77		Post-Production complete	0 days	Tue 7/

15. SAVE all open project plans, and then CLOSE all files.

PAUSE. If you are continuing to the next lesson, keep Project open. If you are not continuing to additional lessons, CLOSE Project.

In this exercise, you recorded a simple macro to save time when you want to zoom the view in Microsoft Project to the entire project. A *macro* is a recorded or programmed set of instructions that carry out a specific action when initiated. Macros in Microsoft Project use Visual Basic for Applications (VBA). *Visual Basic for Applications (VBA)* is the built-in programming language of the Microsoft Office family of desktop applications. VBA enables you to do sophisticated things, but if you are not familiar with VBA, you can record and play back simple macros in a project plan without ever directly seeing or working with VBA code.

By default, the macros you create are stored in the global template, which means they are available to you whenever Microsoft Project is running. If you want, you can use the Organizer to copy the macro from the global template to another project plan to give it to someone else, as discussed in the "Working with the Organizer" section earlier in this lesson.

SUMMARY SKILL MATRIX

IN THIS LESSON YOU LEARNED	MATRIX SKILL
To define general preferences	Specify the default path for use in the Open and Save As dialog boxes
To work with templates	Create a new template based on a current project plan
To work with the organizer	Copy a custom view from one project plan to another using the organizer
To work with macros	Record and run a macro

■ Knowledge Assessment

Fill in the Blank

Complete the following sentences by writing the correct word or words in the blanks provided.

1. The file name of the global template is _____.
2. A(n) _____ is a Microsoft Project file format that lets you use an existing project plan as the basis for a new project plan.
3. The _____ allows you to share elements between Microsoft Project files.
4. Macro names must begin with a(n) _____.
5. The names of the _____ in the Organizer dialog box indicate the elements you can copy between project plans.
6. The _____ provides the default views, tables, and other elements in Microsoft Project.
7. A(n) _____ is a recorded set of instructions that carry out a specific action when initiated.

8. The _____ tab in the Options dialog box enables you to specify where you want your files to be saved.

9. VBA stands for _____.

10. One or more keys that you press on the keyboard to complete a task is a(n) _____.

True / False

Circle T if the statement is true or F if the statement is false.

T F **1.** Your Microsoft Project files must always be stored in the default file folder.

T F **2.** When you create a template, you can choose not to include information such as baseline and actual values.

T F **3.** The two primary actions you can accomplish with a global template are to create a customized element and to replace a customized element.

T F **4.** A macro must start with a letter and can contain spaces.

T F **5.** You can save a Microsoft Project file as a template only if a baseline has not yet been saved.

T F **6.** You must know VBA code in order to create a macro.

T F **7.** By default, macros are stored in the active project plan.

T F **8.** Templates can include information such as task and resource lists, assignments, customized views, tables, filters, and macros.

T F **9.** It is not possible to overwrite elements in the global template.

T F **10.** The Organizer enables you to reset custom elements in a project plan.

■ Competency Assessment

⊙ Project 17-1: Copy the Critical Tasks report to the Office Remodel Project Plan

You want to copy the Critical Tasks report from the global template for use in the Office Remodel project plan. Use the Organizer to do this.

GET READY. Launch Microsoft Project if it is not already running.

OPEN *Office Remodel 17-1* from the data files for this lesson.

SAVE the file as *Office Remodel Critical Tasks Report*.

The ***Office Remodel 17-1*** project plan is available on the companion CD-ROM.

1. On the menu bar, click **Tools**, and then click **Organizer**.

2. Click the **Reports** tab, if it is not already selected.

3. Make sure that in the *Reports available in* box on the left side of the dialog box, Global.MPT is selected. Make sure that in the *Reports available in* box on the right side of the dialog box, Office Remodel Critical Tasks Report is selected.

4. In the list of reports on the left side of the dialog box, click **Critical Tasks**.

5. Click the **Copy>>** button.

6. Click **Close**.

7. **SAVE** the project plan, and then **CLOSE** the file.

   PAUSE. LEAVE Project open to use in the next exercise.

➔ Project 17-2: **HR Interview Template**

Because your department is currently in a hiring mode, you want to save the HR Interview project plan as a template so that it can be used by anyone in your department to develop an interview plan. You do not want to save baselines, cost rates, and fixed cost data in the template.

The *HR Interview 17-2* project plan is available on the companion CD-ROM.

OPEN *HR Interview 17-2* from the data files for this lesson.

1. On the menu bar, click **File**, and then click **Save As**.
2. In the *File name* box, key *HR Interview Template*.
3. In the *Save as type* box, select **Template**.
4. In the *Save in* box, locate and select your Lesson 17 solution folder (or as otherwise directed by your instructor).
5. Click the **Save** button.
6. In the Save As Template dialog box, select the **Values of all baselines, Actual Values,** and **Fixed Costs** check boxes.
7. Click **Save**.
8. **CLOSE** the file.

   PAUSE. LEAVE Project open to use in the next exercise.

■ Proficiency Assessment

➔ Project 17-3: **Recording a Macro to Change a View**

Whenever you want to add resource information to a project plan, you switch to the Resource Sheet view and the Entry table. Record a macro to change the view to the Resource Sheet view with the Entry table.

The *Don Funk Music Video 17-3* project plan is available on the companion CD-ROM.

OPEN *Don Funk Music Video 17-3* from the data files for this lesson.

1. Activate the Record Macro dialog box from the Tools menu.
2. Name the macro **Change_To_Resource_Sheet_View**.
3. Store the macro in this project.
4. Enter a description of **Changes view to Resource Sheet view with Entry table**.
5. Close the Record Macro dialog box to begin recording the macro.
6. Activate the Resource Sheet view.
7. Activate the Entry table.
8. Stop the macro recording via the Tools menu.
9. **SAVE** the file as *Don Funk Change View Macro*, and then **CLOSE** the file.

   PAUSE. LEAVE Project open to use in the next exercise.

➔ Project 17-4: **Restoring a Customized Table to the Default Settings**

While you were working with the Litware project plan, you accidentally customized the default Usage table, rather than making a copy of the default table and then customizing the copy. You want to restore the customized Usage table by replacing it with the default "factory settings" Usage table from the Global.mpt file.

OPEN *Litware 17-4* from the data files for this lesson.

The *Litware 17-4* project plan is available on the companion CD-ROM.

1. Change the view to the Task Usage view.
2. Activate the Organizer dialog box.
3. Activate the Tables tab.
4. Make sure that the Global.mpt table list is on the left side of the dialog box and that the Litware 17-4 table list is on the right side of the dialog box.

5. Copy the Usage table from the Global.mpt list to the Litware 17-4 list.

6. Select **Yes** when you are alerted that you are about to replace the Usage table and then close the Organizer.

7. Activate the new Usage table from the Tables list on the View menu.

8. **SAVE** the file as *Litware New Usage*.

   PAUSE. LEAVE Project open to use in the next exercise.

■ Mastery Assessment

➔ Project 17-5: Copying a Custom Report Using the Organizer

The *Gregory Weber Biography17-5* and the *HR Interview 17-5* project plans are available on the companion CD-ROM.

You have several custom views and reports already defined in the HR Interview project plan. You want to copy the Custom Critical Task Report from the HR Interview plan to the Gregory Weber Biography plan

OPEN *Gregory Weber Biography 17-5* and *HR Interview 17-5* from the data files for this lesson.

1. Use the Organizer to copy the Custom Critical Task Report from the *HR Interview 17-5* project plan to the *Gregory Weber Biography 17-5* project plan.

2. **SAVE** the project plans as *HR Interview Custom Critical* and *Gregory Weber Custom Critical,* and then **CLOSE** the files.

   PAUSE. LEAVE Project open to use in the next exercise.

➔ Project 17-6: Defining General Preferences

You want to set some more preferences for how Microsoft Project looks and works for you. In a separate Word or WordPad document, explain the steps you would follow to set the following preferences. Use any Microsoft Project file with which you are familiar to explore these options. DO NOT make the actual changes in the file; just explain in a separate document how you would set these preferences.

1. Use the Options dialog box to:
   - Set the number of Undo levels to 25
   - Have Microsoft Project prompt you for project information for new projects
   - Have Microsoft Project automatically save your active project every 10 minutes, prompting you before saving

2. **SAVE** the Word document as *Defining General Preferences.*
   CLOSE Project.

INTERNET READY

In this lesson, you learned how to save your project plan as a template for use on other projects. Many Microsoft Project experts have saved their project plans as templates and shared them on the Internet for public use. Search the Internet to find Microsoft Project templates that may be useful to you – either at work, at school, at home, or in your community. Microsoft offers many templates from the Project home page, but many other sites offer templates also. Download several templates and save them to your local drive. Explore what information has been provided with the template, such as general resources (HR Manager, Line Supervisor, etc.) and task durations, as well as what information was removed by the author before saving as a template (baselines, cost rates, etc.). If possible, post one of your own project plans (saved as a template) to the Internet to share with others.

✳ Workplace Ready

COMPARING BASELINE, INTERIM, AND ACTUAL PLANS

Tracking actuals is vital to properly managing a project. A project manager must understand how well (or poorly) the project team is performing and know when to take action to correct problems and realign the project. By tracking project performance and comparing it against the original plan, a project manager can keep a close eye on how the start and finish dates of tasks will affect the overall project finish date; how much time resources are taking to complete tasks; and how much money is being spent to complete tasks.

As a project manager for a commercial real estate and construction firm, you know that after you have started tracking actual values, as well as any time you make changes to your schedule, it is very helpful to take a "snapshot" of the current values in your project plan. You do this with an interim plan. Some of the key times that you save interim plans are at the end of each building phase—site prep, foundation, structural skeleton, plumbing and electrical, etc.—as well as at the end of each month, when you provide a report to your manager.

You also know that comparing these interim plans to the baseline and actual plans helps you to evaluate your progress, including any changes to the schedule that you make along the way. For instance, after you saved the initial baseline, a schedule change pushed out the scheduled start date of the foundation task. The foundation task was started and completed on time according to the revised dates. When you compare the baseline, actual, and interim plans in a Gantt Chart view, you can see that bars representing the interim and actual foundation tasks match each other, but have a later start date than the baseline. Any additional adjustments you make to the schedule (such as changing task information or entering actuals) may cause the scheduled and interim values for other tasks to be different.

By monitoring the differences that appear in the positions of the baseline, scheduled, and interim Gantt bars, you know that you can evaluate the progress of your project and any schedule adjustments you make.

Figure 17-10

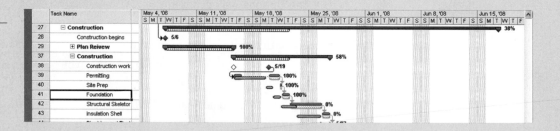

↻ Circling Back

Mete Goktepe is a project management specialist at Woodgrove Bank. He is managing a project plan for a Request for Proposal (RFP) process to evaluate and select new commercial lending software. This process entails determining needs, identifying vendors, requesting proposals, reviewing proposals, and selecting the software.

Now that Mete has established the foundation of the project plan, he will begin using some of the more advanced features of Microsoft Office Project to fine-tune the tasks and resources and to format the project plan.

⊙ Project 1: SETTING DEADLINES AND ESTABLISHING MULTIPLE PAY RATES

Acting as Mete, you need to set a deadline for one of the tasks in the project. You then need to establish and apply multiple pay rates for a resource.

GET READY. Launch Microsoft Project if it is not already running.

OPEN *RFP Bank Software Project Plan* from the data files for this lesson.

The *RFP Bank Software Project Plan* is available on the companion CD-ROM.

1. In the Task Name column, click on the name of task 3, **RFP Creation**.
2. If the *Tasks* pane is not already displayed, click **Tasks** on the Project Guide toolbar.
3. In the *Tasks* pane, click the **Set deadlines and constrain tasks** link.
4. In the drop-down date box under *Set a deadline*, key or select **6/6/08**, and then press Tab.
5. Scroll the Gantt bar chart to the right to view the deadline marker.
6. Click the **Done** link in the *Deadlines and Constraints* pane.
7. On the menu bar, click **View** and then click **Resource Sheet**.
8. In the Resource Name column, click on the name of resource 9, **Marc J. Ingle**.

   Because Marc J. Ingle's rate differs depending on whether he is doing document preparation or meeting facilitation, you need to enter a second rate for him.
9. On the Standard toolbar, click the **Resource Information** button. Click the **Costs** tab, if it is not already selected.
10. Under Cost rate tables, click the **B** tab.
11. Select the default entry of **$0.00/h** in the field directly below the Standard Rate column heading, key **1200/w**, and then press Enter. Click **OK**.
12. On the menu bar, click **View** and then click **Task Usage**.
13. On the menu bar, click **Edit**, and then click **Go To**. In the ID box, key **5**, and then click **OK**.
14. On the menu bar, click **View**, point to **Table:Usage**, and then click **Cost**.
15. Under task 5, click the row heading directly to the left of Marc J. Ingle so that Marc J. Ingle's entire assignment is selected.
16. Drag the divider bar between the Cost table and the Work table to the right until the Total Cost column is visible.
17. Click the **Assignment Information** button on the Standard toolbar. Click the **General** tab, if it is not already selected.
18. In the Cost rate table box, key or select **B**, and then click **OK**.
19. **SAVE** the project plan as *RFP Bank Software Multiple Rates* in the solutions folder for this lesson as directed by your instructor.

    PAUSE. LEAVE Project and the project plan open to use in the next exercise.

⊙ Project 2: **Contours, WBS Codes, and Interim Plans**

Next, you want to apply a work contour to one of Mike Tiano's assignments. You will then add Unique ID and WBS columns to help you track and analyze your project data. Then you will update the project to reflect some progress made, and set an interim plan.

GET READY. SAVE the open project plan as *RFP Bank Software Interim* in the solution folder for this lesson as directed by your instructor.

1. On the menu bar, click View, point to Table: Cost, and then click Usage.
2. On the menu bar, click Edit and then click Go To. Key 6 in the ID box, and then click OK.
3. In the Task Name column under task 6, select Mike Tiano.
4. On the Standard toolbar, click the Assignment Information button. Click the General tab, if it is not already selected.
5. In the *Work contour* box, select Front Loaded, and then click OK.
6. On the menu bar, click View, and then click More Views. In the More Views dialog box, select Task Sheet, and then click Apply.
7. Click on the Task Name column heading.
8. On the menu bar, click Insert, and then click Column. In the *Field Name* list, click Unique ID, and then click OK.
9. Click on the Task Name column heading.
10. On the menu bar, click Insert, and then click Column. In the *Field Name* list, click WBS, and then click OK.
11. If necessary, activate the Tracking toolbar: on the menu bar, click View, point to Toolbars, and then click Tracking.
12. Select the names of tasks 4 through 8. Click the 100% Complete button on the Tracking toolbar.
13. Click on the name of task 9, and then click the Update Tasks button on the Tracking toolbar.
14. Under the Actual label, in the Start box, key or select 5/29/08. In the *Acutal dur* box, key or select 2d, and then click OK.
15. Click on the name of task 10, and then click the Update Tasks button on the Tracking toolbar.
16. In the *Acutal dur* box, key or select 3d, and then click OK.
17. Select the name of task 11. Click the 100% Complete button on the tracking toolbar.
18. On the menu bar, click Tools, point to Tracking, and click Set Baseline.
19. Click Set interim plan, and then click OK.
20. On the menu bar, click View, and then click More Views. In the Views list, select Tracking Gantt, and then click the Copy button.
21. In the Name box, key Interim Tracking Gantt, and then click OK.
22. Make sure that Interim Tracking Gantt is selected in the More Views dialog box, and then click Apply.
23. On the menu bar, click Format, and then click Bar Styles. Click the Insert Row button.
24. In the new cell directly below the Name column heading, key Interim and press ⏀Tab⏀. In the same row, click the cell under the Show For... Tasks column heading, and then select Normal from the drop-down list.
25. Click the cell under the From column heading, and select Start1 from the drop-down list. Click the cell under the To column heading, and select Finish1 from the drop-down list.

26. On the Bars tab, in the Pattern box under the Middle label, select the third option. In the Color box, select Green. Click OK.

27. Click the Show/Hide Project Guide button to close the Project Guide. Slide the divider bar between the Entry Table and the Gantt bar chart to the right until the Task Name column is visible.

28. Click on the name of task 8, and then click the Scroll to Task button.

29. SAVE the project plan.

   PAUSE. LEAVE Project and the project plan open to use in the next exercise.

⊕ Project 3: Creating a Resource Pool and Applying a New View

You have decided to create a resource pool, using another project from within the bank as an additional sharer file. While you have the additional sharer file open, you will copy a view from the file using the Organizer and you will apply this view to your project.

GET READY. SAVE the open project plan as *RFP Bank Software Organizer* in the solution folder for this lesson as directed by your instructor.

OPEN the *Check Processing Rework* project plan from the data files for this lesson.

SAVE the newly opened file as *Check Processing Rework Pool* in the solution folder for this lesson as directed by your instructor.

The *Check Processing Rework* project plan is available on the companion CD-ROM.

1. Make sure that the *RFP Bank Software Organizer* file is in the active window.

2. On the menu bar, click View, and then click Resource Sheet.

3. On the Standard toolbar, click the New button.

4. Click the Show/Hide Project Guide button on the Project Guide toolbar.

5. On the menu bar, click File, and then click Save As. In the *Save in* box, locate the solution folder for this lesson as directed by your instructor. In the *File name* box, key Bank Resource Pool, and then click Save.

6. On the menu bar, click View, and then click Resource Sheet.

7. On the menu bar, click Window, and then click Arrange All.

8. Click the title bar of the RFP Bank Software Organizer window.

9. On the menu bar, click Tools, point to Resource Sharing, and then click Share Resources.

10. In the Share Resources dialog box, under *Resources for 'RFP Bank Software Organizer,'* click Use resources. In the From list, select Bank Resource Pool, if it is not already selected. Click OK.

11. Click the title bar of the Check Processing Rework Pool window.

12. On the menu bar, click Tools, point to Resource Sharing, and then click Share Resources.

13. In the Share Resources dialog box, under *Resources for 'Check Processing Rework Pool,'* click Use resources. In the From list, select *Bank Resource Pool*, if it is not already selected. Under the *On conflict with calendar or resource information* label, make sure that Pool takes precedence is selected. Click OK.

14. SAVE the *Bank Resource Pool* project plan.

15. Expand the *RFP Bank Software Organizer* project plan to fill the active window.

16. On the menu bar, click Tools, and then click Organizer.

17. Click the Views tab, if it is not already selected.

18. In the *Views available in* list on the left side of the dialog box, select *Check Processing Rework Pool*. In the *Views available in list* on the right side of the dialog box, select RFP Bank Software Organizer, if it is not already selected.

19. In the list of views on the left side of the dialog box, click **My Custom Gantt Chart.**

20. Click the **Copy>>** button, and then click **Close.**

21. On the menu bar, click **View,** and then click **My Custom Gantt Chart.**

22. SAVE and then CLOSE the *RFP Bank Software Organizer* file.
SAVE and then CLOSE the *Check Processing Rework Pool* file.
SAVE and then CLOSE the *Bank Resource Pool* file.

CLOSE Project.

COMPONENT	REQUIREMENT
Computer and processor	500 megahertz (MHz) processor or higher[1]
Memory	256 megabyte (MB) RAM or higher[1, 2]
Hard disk	2 gigabyte (GB); a portion of this disk space will be freed after installation if the original download package is removed from the hard drive.
Drive	CD-ROM or DVD drive
Display	1024x768 or higher resolution monitor
Operating system	Microsoft Windows(R) XP with Service Pack (SP) 2, Windows Server(R) 2003 with SP1, or later operating system[3]
Other	Certain inking features require running Microsoft Windows XP Tablet PC Edition or later. Speech recognition functionality requires a close-talk microphone and audio output device. Information Rights Management features require access to a Windows 2003 Server with SP1 or later running Windows Rights Management Services.
	Connectivity to Microsoft Exchange Server 2000 or later is required for certain advanced functionality in Outlook 2007. Instant Search requires Microsoft Windows Desktop Search 3.0. Dynamic Calendars require server connectivity.
	Connectivity to Microsoft Windows Server 2003 with SP1 or later running Microsoft Windows SharePoint Services is required for certain advanced collaboration functionality. Microsoft Office SharePoint Server 2007 is required for certain advanced functionality. PowerPoint Slide Library requires Office SharePoint Server 2007. To share data among multiple computers, the host computer must be running Windows Server(R) 2003 with SP1, Windows(R) XP Professional with SP2, or later.
	Internet Explorer 6.0 or later, 32 bit browser only. Internet functionality requires Internet access (fees may apply).
Additional	Actual requirements and product functionality may vary based on your system configuration and operating system.

[1] 1 gigahertz (GHz) processor or higher and 512 MB RAM or higher recommended for Business Contact Manager. Business Contact Manager not available in all languages.

[2] 512 MB RAM or higher recommended for Outlook Instant Search. Grammar and contextual spelling in Word is not turned on unless the machine has 1 GB memory.

[3] Office Clean-up wizard not available on 64 bit OS

A

actual cost The cost that has been incurred so far (after the indicated total work has been completed).

actual cost of work performed (ACWP) The actual cost incurred to complete each task's actual work up to the status date.

actuals Project work completed and recorded in a Microsoft Project file.

allocation The portion of a resource's capacity devoted to work on a specific task.

assignment The matching of a specific resource to a particular task to do work.

AutoFilter A quick way to view only the task or resource information that meets the criteria you choose.

availability Determines when and how much of a resource's time can be assigned to work on tasks.

B

base calendar Can be used as both a task and project calendar and specifies default working and nonworking times for a set of resources.

baseline A collection of key values in the project plan, such as the planned start dates, finish dates, and costs of the various tasks and assignments. A baseline allows you to begin the tracking phase of project management.

baseline cost The total planned cost of the project when the baseline was saved.

bottom-up planning Develops a project plan by starting with the lowest level tasks before organizing them into higher level phases or summary tasks. This approach works from specific to general.

budgeted cost of work performed (BCWP) The portion of the budgeted cost that should have been spent to complete each task's actual work performed up to the status date. This value is called earned value because it is literally the value earned by the work performed. Also known as earned value (EV).

budgeted cost of work scheduled (BCWS) The value of the work scheduled to be completed as of the status

date. Microsoft Project calculates this value by adding up all the timephased baseline values for tasks up to the status date. Also known as planned value (PV).

C

calendar A scheduling tool that determines the standard working time and nonworking time (such as evening or holidays) for the project, resources, and tasks. Calendars are used to determine how tasks and resources assigned to these tasks are scheduled.

chart A view or part of a view that presents project information graphically, such as the Network Diagram.

consolidated project A Microsoft Project file that contains other Microsoft Project files, called inserted projects.

constraint A restriction that you or Microsoft Project set that controls the start or finish date of a task.

contour Determines how a resource's work on a task is scheduled over time.

Copy Picture Enables you to take a snapshot of a view. With Copy Picture, you have several options when taking snapshots of the active view: (1) You can copy the entire view that is visible on the screen, or just selected rows of a table in a view. (2) You can copy a range of time that you specify or show on the screen.

cost Refers to how much money will be needed to pay for the resources on a project.

Cost Performance Index (CPI) The ratio of budgeted to actual cost, or BCWP divided by ACWP.

cost rate table Resource pay rates that are stored on the Costs tab of the Resource Information dialog box. For a given resource you can enter up to five cost rate table.

cost resource A resource that doesn't depend on the amount of work on a task or the duration of a task.

cost variance (CV) The difference between the budgeted and actual cost of work performed.

crashing Decreasing the project's duration without altering the basic sequence of activities.

critical path The series of tasks whose scheduling directly affects the project's finish date.

current cost The sum of the actual and remaining cost values.

D

data maps Allow you to specify how you want individual fields in the source program's file to correspond to individual fields in the destination program. Once you set up an import/export map, you can use it over and over again.

deadline A date value you enter for a task that indicates the latest date by which you want the task to be completed, but the deadline date itself does not constrain the task.

deliverable The final goal of a project.

dependency Controls the start or finish of one task relative to the start or finish of another task. There are four types of dependencies in Microsoft Project: finish-to-start, start-to-start, finish-to-finish, and start-to-finish.

duration The amount of working time required to complete a task.

E

earned value (EV) The portion of the budgeted cost that should have been spent to complete each task's actual work performed up to the status date. This value is called earned value because it is literally the value earned by the work performed. Also known as budgeted cost of work performed (BCWP).

earned value analysis Used to measure the project's progress and help forecast its outcome. It gives you a more complete picture of overall project performance in relation to both time and cost.

effort-driven scheduling A scheduling method in which the duration of a task increases or decreases as you remove resources from or assign resources to a task; the amount of work needed to complete the task does not change.

elapsed duration The total length of working and nonworking time you expect it will take to complete a task.

Entry table The default table in the Gantt Chart view, used for entering basic data in a project.

export map Specifies the exact data to export and how to structure it.

F

field The intersection of a row and a column in a table. A field represents the lowest-level information about a task, resource or assignment. Another name for a field is a cell.

filter A tool that enables you to see or highlight in a table only the task or resource information that meets criteria you choose. Filtering doesn't change the data in your project plan–it only changes the data's appearance.

fixed consumption rate A resource consumption rate in which an absolute quantity of the resources will be used, no matter the duration of the task to which the material is assigned.

fixed duration A task type in which the duration value is fixed.

fixed units A task type in which the units value does not change.

fixed work A task type in which the work value is held constant.

flexible constraint A constraint type that gives Microsoft Project the flexibility to change start and finish dates of a task. No constraint date is associated with a flexible constraint.

form A type of view that presents detailed information in a structured format about one task or resource at a time, such as the Task Form.

free slack The amount of time a task can be delayed before it will delay another task.

fully allocated The condition of a resource when the total work of its task assignments is exactly equal to that resource's work capacity.

G

Gantt Chart view A view in Microsoft Project that consists of a table (the Entry table by default) on the left side and a graphical bar chart on the right side.

ghost task A task relationship between project files. A ghost task is similar to a link between tasks within a project file, except that external predecessor and successor tasks have gray task names and Gantt bars. Ghost tasks are not linked to tasks within the project file, only to tasks in other project files.

GIF Graphics Interchange Format, is an image format used for storing images and pictures.

global template A template that provides the default views, tables, and other elements in Microsoft Project, and includes: Calendars, Filters, Forms, Groups, Import/Export maps, Menu Bars, Reports, Tables, Toolbars, VBA Modules (macros), and Views.

group A way to reorder task or resource information in a table and to display summary values for each group according to various criteria you can choose. Grouping goes a step beyond sorting in that grouping your project data will add summary values, called "roll-ups," at customized intervals.

H

hyperlink A portion of text that contains a link to another file, a portion of a file, a page on the Internet, or a page on an intranet.

I

import map Specifies the exact data to import and how to structure it.

inflexible constraint A constraint type that forces a task to begin or end on a certain date, completely preventing the rescheduling of a task. Inflexible constraints are sometimes called hard constraints.

inserted project The Microsoft Project file that is inserted into another Microsoft Project file.

interim plan A snapshot of current values from the project plan that Microsoft Project saves with the file. Unlike the baseline, however, an interim plan saves only the start and finish dates of tasks, not resource or assignment values. You can save up to 10 different interim plans during a project.

L

line manager A manager of a group of resources, also sometimes called a functional manager.

link A logical connection between tasks that controls sequence and dependency.

M

macro A recorded or programmed set of instructions that carry out a specific action when initiated.

mask When working with outline or WBS codes, the mask, or appearance, defines the format of the code–the order and number of alphabetic, numeric, and alphanumeric strings in a code and the separators between them.

master project Another name for a consolidated project.

material resource Consumable items used up as the tasks in a project are completed. Unlike work resources, material resources have no effect on the total amount of work scheduled to be performed on a task.

maximum units The maximum capacity of a resource to accomplish tasks. The default value for maximum units is 100%.

milestone Represents a significant event reached within the project or imposed upon the project. Milestones are often represented as a task with zero duration.

N

negative slack The amount of time that tasks overlap due to a conflict between task relationships and constraints.

Network Diagram A standard way of representing project activities and their relationships, in a flowchart format.

nodes The boxes that represent tasks in a Network Diagram. The relationships between tasks are drawn as lines connecting nodes.

noncritical task A task that has slack greater than zero.

note Supplemental text that you can attach to a task, resource, or assignment.

O

OLE A protocol that allows you to transfer information, such as a chart or text (as an OLE object), to documents in different programs.

optimizing Adjusting the aspects of the project plan prior to saving a baseline, such as cost, duration, and scope (or any combination of these), to achieve a desired project plan result. A desired result may be a target finish date, duration, or overall cost.

Organizer A feature you use to organize elements between Microsoft Project files so that they can be shared, edited, and reset. The names of the tabs in the Organizer dialog box indicate the elements you can copy between project plans.

outline number A numeric representation of the outline hierarchy of a project. Outline numbers are numeric only and are generated by Microsoft Project.

overallocated The state of a resource when it is assigned to do more work than can be done within the normal work capacity of the resource.

P

phases A group of closely related tasks that encompass a major section of your project.

planned value (PV) The value of the work scheduled to be completed as of the status date. Microsoft Project calculates this value by adding up all the timephased baseline values for tasks up to the status date. Also known as budgeted cost of work scheduled (BCWS).

planning Developing and communicating the details of a project before actual work begins.

predecessor A task whose start or end date determines the start or finish of another task or tasks. Any task can be a predecessor for one or more tasks.

predefined contour Describes how work is distributed over time in terms of graphical patterns. Some options are Bell, Front Loaded, Back Loaded, Double Peak, and Turtle. Predefined contours work best for assignments where you can estimate a probable pattern of effort.

program office A group that oversees a collection of projects (such as producing doors and producing engines), each of which is part of a complete deliverable (such as an automobile) and the organization's strategic objectives.

progress bar The bar in the Gantt Chart view that shows how much of each task has been completed.

project calendar The base calendar that provides default working times for an entire project.

Project Guide A wizard-like interface that is divided into four subject areas: Tasks, Resources, Track, and Report. Each area guides you through the steps to create or update your project plan.

project plan A model of a real project—what you want to happen or what you think will happen. The plan contains tasks, resources, time frames, and costs that might be associated with such a project.

project triangle A popular model of project management in which time, cost, and scope are represented as three sides of a triangle. A change to one side will affect at least one of the other two sides.

R

recurring task A task that is repeated at specified intervals, such as daily, weekly, or monthly.

remaining cost The difference between the current cost and actual cost.

report A predefined format intended for printing Microsoft Project data.

resource calendar Defines the working and nonworking time for an individual resource. A resource calendar applies only to people and equipment (work) resources–not to material resources. When you establish resources in your project plan, a resource calendar is created for each resource.

resource leveling The process of delaying a resource's work on a task to resolve an overallocation. Depending on the options you choose, resource leveling might delay the start date of an assignment or an entire task, or splitting up the work on a task.

resource manager A manager who oversees resource usage in project activities specifically to manage the time and cost of resources.

resource pool A project plan from which other project plans gather their resource information.

resources The people, equipment, and materials used to complete the tasks in a project.

risk In a project, risk decreases the likelihood of completing the project on time, within budget, and to specification.

S

Schedule Performance Index (SPI) The ratio of performed to scheduled work, or BCWP divided by BCWS.

schedule variance (SV) The difference between the budgeted cost of work performed and the budgeted cost of work scheduled.

scheduling formula The formula Microsoft Project uses to calculate work: Duration × Units = Work.

semi-flexible constraint A constraint type that gives Microsoft Project the flexibility to change the start and finish dates (but not the duration) of a task within one date boundary.

sequence The chronological order in which tasks must occur.

sharer plans The project plans that are linked to the resource pool.

sheet A table view that presents task or resource information in rows and columns, such as the Task Sheet.

shortcut One or more keys that you press on the keyboard to complete a task.

slack The amount of time a task can be delayed without causing a delay to a task or the overall project. Slack is also known as float.

sort A way of ordering task or resource information in a view by the criteria you specify. You can sort tasks or resources using predefined criteria, or you can create your own sort order with up to three levels (a group within a group within a group).

split An interruption in a task, represented in the Gantt bar by a dotted line between the two segments of the task.

sponsor The individual or organization that provides financial support and supports the project team within the larger organization.

stakeholders All people or organizations that might be affected by project activities, from resources working on the project to customers receiving the end result of the project.

status date The date you specify (not necessarily the current date) that you want Microsoft Project to use when calculating earned value numbers.

subproject Another name for an inserted project.

subtasks The detail tasks that fall below a summary task.

successor A task whose start or finish is driven by another task or tasks.

summary task A task that is made up of and summarizes all of the detail tasks that fall below it. You cannot directly edit a summary task's duration, start date, or other calculated values.

T

table A spreadsheet-like presentation of project data, organized in vertical columns and horizontal rows. Each column represents a field in Microsoft Project, and each row represents a single resource or task.

task Represents the actual individual work activity that must be done to accomplish the final goal of a project. The tasks contain the details about each activity or event that must occur in order for your project to be completed. These details include the order and duration of tasks, critical tasks, and resource requirements.

task calendar The base calendar that is used by a single task. It defines working and nonworking times for a task, regardless of settings in the project calendar.

Task ID A unique number that is assigned to each task in the project. It appears on the left side of the task's row.

task priority A numeric ranking between 0 and 1000 of a task's importance and appropriateness for leveling.

task type Determines which of the three scheduling formula variables remains the same if the other two values change.

template A Microsoft Project file format that lets you reuse an existing project plan as the basis for a new project plan. Templates can include any of the types of information you might expect to find in a Microsoft Project plan, including task and resource lists, assignments, customized views, tables, filters, and macros.

timephased fields Task, resource, and assignment values distributed over time.

timescale The band across the top of the Gantt Chart grid that denotes units of time.

top-down planning Develops a project plan by identifying the highest level phases or summary tasks before breaking them into lower level components or subtasks. This approach works from general to specific.

total slack The amount of time a task can be delayed without delaying the project end date.

tracking The collecting, entering, and analyzing of actual project performance data, such as work on tasks, resource costs, and actual durations.

U

underallocated The work assigned to a resource is less than the resource's maximum capacity.

Unique ID An identifier that Microsoft Project uses to track the order in which you enter tasks and resources.

units The capacity of a resource to work when you assign that resource to a task.

V

variable consumption rate A resource consumption rate in which the amount of the material resource consumed is dependent upon the duration of the task.

variance A deviation from the established schedule or budget.

view A window through which you can see the various elements of a project plan in a way that is helpful to the viewing audience. There are three types of views: charts or graphs, sheets, and forms.

Visual Basic for Applications (VBA) The built-in programming language of the Microsoft Office family of desktop applications.

W

work The total amount of effort a resource or resources will spend to complete a task.

work breakdown structure (WBS) code A numeric representation of the outline hierarchy of a project. You can change WBS codes to include any combination of letters and numbers that you desire.

work resource The people and equipment that do work to accomplish the tasks of the project. Work resources use time to accomplish tasks.

Index

A

Abbreviations, for time, 13
Actual cost of work performed (ACWP), 282–283
Actual costs (AC), 156, 267, 273
Actual project plans, 276–278, 324
Actuals, 149–150, 155–156, 324
As Late as Possible (ALAP) constraint, 80, 198
Assignment fields, 149
Assignments. *See* Tasks
Assign Resources dialog box, 49–50, 77, 209
As Soon as Possible (ASAP) constraint, 79–80, 198, 201
AutoFilter option, 99
Availability, of resources, 32, 214–215

B

Back Loaded contours, 237
Bar styles, 114–116, 250–253
Base calendars, 9, 40–41, 66, 300
Baseline, for tracking, 147–150
Baseline costs, 156
Baseline project plans, 276–278, 324
Bell contours, 237
Best Fit button, 97
Bottom-up planning, 16
Budget at completion (BAC), 268
Budgeted cost of work performed (BCWP), 282–283
Budgeted cost of work scheduled (BCWS), 282–283
Business startup, 28

C

Calendars
  base, 9, 40–41, 66, 300
  create new base calendar dialog box and, 66
  defining, 7–9
  options dialog box and, 11
  for resource pools, 300
  start dates on, 6
  task, 66–69
Calendar tab of Options dialog box, 229
Calendar view, 250–253
Capacity, 33, 53, 215
Change management, 64
Change Working time dialog box, 66, 231
Chart view, 114, 116. *See also* Gantt Chart view
Circling Back feature, 109–112, 192–194, 325–328
Column Definition dialog box, 117

Completion percentage, 150–152, 270
Compressing project plans, 240–243
Consolidated Project Gantt Chart view, 166
Consolidated project plans, 166–169
Constraints
  on calendar tab, 231
  compressing projects and, 240
  effort-driven scheduling and, 55
  leveling and, 223
  in project plans, 77–81
  scheduling effects of, 196–199
Consumption, units of, 38
Consumption rates, material, 209–210
Contouring, 74, 235–237
Copying and pasting, 182–184, 280
Copy Picture dialog box, 179–182
Cost
  actual, 267
  fixed, 36–37
  of over-budget tasks, 156
  rate of, 213–214
  of resources, per use, 32, 210–211, 227
  total, 239–240
  variance in, 267, 283
Cost performance index (CPI), 267, 283
Cost resources, 36–37, 59–60
Crashing project plans, 234, 240, 248
Create new base calendar dialog box, 66
Critical path, 81–82, 90, 231–234
Cross-project links, 171–172
Current costs, 156
Custom filters, 101–102
Custom views, 126–127
CV (cost variance), 267, 283

D

Data maps, 186
Deadline dates, 199–201
Default paths, 311–312
Deliverables, of projects, 9
Dependencies
  in multiple projects, 169–172
  scheduling effects of, 196–199
  of tasks, 17–18
Documenting tasks, 20–22
Double Peak contours, 237
Durations
  adjusting, 271–273
  on calendar tab, 229
  description of, 10–13

fixed, 71
leveling and, 223
of project plan, 22–23
in scheduling formula, 54, 57–58, 69
short, 155
of split tasks, 74
tracking, 268–271

E

Earned Value analysis, 267–268, 280–283, 288
Effort-driven scheduling, 53, 55–56, 58, 71–72
Elapsed duration, 12–13
Entering tasks, 9–10
Entry table, 3
Equipment resources, 33–35
Estimate at completion (EAC), 267
Export maps, 186

F

Fields, 123, 149, 215
Filtering, 99–102, 137
Financial obligations. *See* Cost resources
Finish dates of projects, 6
  identifying, 239–240
  pulling in, 240–243
  recording actual, 268–271
Finish-no-earlier-than (FNET) constraint, 80, 198
Finish-no-later-than (FNLT) constraint, 198
Finish-to-finish (FF) dependencies, 17–18, 198
Finish-to-start (FS) dependencies, 17–20, 198
Fiscal year settings, 229–231
Fixed consumption rates for materials, 210
Fixed costs, 36–37
Fixed duration task type, 71
Fixed unit quantities, of materials, 59
Fixed units task type, 71
Fixed work task type, 71
Flexible constraints, 79, 198
Forecasts, 280
Formatting, 113–131, 249–265
  Bar Styles dialog box for, 114–116
  Calendar view, 250–253
  custom views, 126–127
  drawings in Gantt Charts, 119–121
  Gantt Charts, 114–119
  network diagrams, 257–260
  reports, 260–261

tables, 124–125
Task Sheet view for, 250
templates, 131
text, 121–123
Unique IDs and WBS codes for, 253–257, 265
Forms view, 116
Free slack, 82, 220, 232, 234
Front Loaded contours, 237
Fully allocated resources, 86, 219

G

Gantt, Henry, 116
Gantt Chart view
  adjusting, 99
  baseline, interim, and actual plans in, 324
  Calendar view *versus*, 253
  Consolidated Project, 166
  copying and pasting, 183
  drawings in, 119–121
  formatting, 114–119
  milestone links on, 20
  in opening screen, 3
  printing, 133–137
  progress bar in, 150
  project duration on, 22–23
  task dependencies on, 18
  task splits on, 74
  task type on, 71
  timescale on, 73
Gantt Chart Wizard, 117–119
Ghost tasks, 170, 172
GIF images, 179–182, 280
Global templates, 318
Grouping data, 96–98
Group resources, 32–33

H

Hyperlinking, 20, 22

I

Import maps, 186
Import Wizard, 184–185
Inflexible constraints, 79, 198–199, 201, 240
Inserted project, 168
Integrating with other programs, 178–194
  copying and pasting for, 182–184
  Copy Picture dialog box for, 179
  Excel files as, 184–186, 191
  GIF image in, 179–182
  Word files as, 191
Interim project plans, 275–278, 324
Internet Ready feature
  business startup projects, 28
  change management, 64

costs of resources, 227
critical path, 90
earned value analysis, 288
integrating with Word and
    Excel, 191
managing multiple projects, 177
project crashing, 248
Project Management Institute
    (PMI), 145
project plans, 131
resource pools, 309
resource table, 47
scheduling, 106
task priorities, 207
templates, 323
tracking, 164
WBS codes, 265

L

Legacy file formats, 184
Leveling of resources, 74, 202,
    220–223
Line managers, 293
Linking
    to documentation, 20–22
    tasks, 16–20
    two project plans, 169–172
List Tasks pane, 9

M

Macros, 313, 318–320
Managers, 293
Managing multiple projects,
    165–177
    Consolidated Project Gantt
        Chart view for, 166
    consolidated project plan in,
        166–169
    dependencies in, 169–172
    examples of, 177
Masks, of codes, 257
Master project file, 166, 168.
    See also Managing
        multiple projects
Material consumption rates, 209–210
Material resources, 35–36, 38, 58–59
Maximum Units field, 33, 53, 215
Microsoft Excel, 184–186, 191,
    227, 261, 310
Microsoft Office Online, 107
Microsoft Outlook, 31
Microsoft PowerPoint, 280
Microsoft Visio Professional, 261
Microsoft Website for Work
    Essentials, 64, 248
Microsoft Word, 122, 191, 227,
    280, 310
Milestones, 13–14, 19–20, 100
More Groups dialog box, 97
Multiple Level Undo function, 96
Multiple pay rates for resources,
    211–214
Multiple projects. *See* Managing
    multiple projects
Multiyear projects, 13
Must Finish On (MFO)
    constraint, 198
Must Start On (MSO) constraint,
    80, 198, 231

N

Negative slack, 80, 199
Network diagrams, 137, 257–260
New Project task pane, 3–4
Nodes, on network diagrams, 260
Noncritical tasks, 82
Nonworking times, 39–40
Notes, 21–22, 42

O

OLE objects, 183–184
Opening screen, 2–3
Open Internet Address dialog
    box, 181
Options dialog box, 11, 229
Organizer, 311, 314–318
Organize tasks pane, 15
Outline numbers of tasks, 257
Overallocation of resources
    definition of, 53
    identifying, 83–86
    leveling of, 220–223
    manually resolving, 216–219
    task priorities and, 201–202
Over-budget tasks and resources,
    156–159
Overtime, 243

P

Page Setup dialog box, 133
Pay rates for resources, 37–38,
    211–214
People resources, 31–33, 35
Percentage of completion,
    150–152, 270
Phases of tasks, 14–16
Planned value (PV), 282
Planning, 16, 149
Planning Wizard dialog box, 197
Predecessor tasks, 18–19, 172
Predefined contours, 235–237
Printing, 132–145
    Gantt Chart view, 133–137
    Page Setup dialog box for, 133
    reports, 137–140
Print Preview feature, 134, 136
Priorities for tasks, 201–202, 207
Program office, 299
Progress bar, in Gantt Chart, 150
Progress reports, 280
Project 2007, basics of, 1–28
    duration of project plan in,
        22–23
    opening project plan in, 5–6
    opening screen of, 2–3
    project calendars in, 7–9
    saving project plan in, 6–7
    starting, 3–5
    tasks in, 9–22
        documenting, 20–22
        entering, 9–10
        estimating durations of, 11–13
        linking, 16–20
        milestones for, 13–14
        phase organization of, 14–16
Project 2007, customizing, 310–328
    baseline, interim and actual plans
        in, 324
    macros for, 318–320

Organizer for, 311, 314–318
specifying default paths in,
    311–312
templates for, 313–314, 323
Project calendars, 9, 40
Project Guide, 3, 5, 97, 152
Project Management Institute
    (PMI), 145
Project plans, 65–90. *See also*
    Formatting; Resource
    pools; Tracking
    actual, 276–278
    baseline, 276–278
    change working time dialog box
        and, 66
    changing task types in, 69–72
    constraints in, 77–81
    create new base calendar dialog
        box and, 66
    critical path in, 81–82, 90
    interim, 275–278
    on Internet, 131
    opening, 5–6
    recurring tasks in, 74–77
    resource allocations over time in,
        83–86
    saving, 6–7
    splitting tasks in, 72–74
    task calendar applications in,
        66–69
Project plans, optimizing, 228–248
    Calendar tab of Options dialog
        box for, 229
    compressing for, 240–243
    contours for, 235–237
    crashing for, 240, 248
    critical path and, 231–234
    delaying resource assignment
        starts for, 234–235
    editing task assignments for,
        237–238
    finish dates and total cost in,
        239–240
    time and date adjustments for,
        229–231
Project Statistics dialog box,
    239–240
Project triangle, 280
Project Working Times task pane, 7
Pulling-in finish dates, 240–243
PV (planned value), 267, 282

R

Ramp-up time, 237
Recurring tasks, 74–77
Relationships, task, 16, 198, 223.
    See also Constraints;
    Dependencies; Linking
Remaining costs, 156
Report button, 83
Reports
    actuals in, 156
    formatting, 260–261
    printing, 137–140
    Report pane for, 134
Request for proposal (RFP) process,
    109–112
Resource calendars, 9, 40–41
Resource fields, 149

Resource Leveling dialog box,
    220–223
Resource managers, 293
Resource pools, 289–309
    adding project plans to, 301–302
    assignment details in, 294–295
    developing, 290–293
    Share Resources dialog box
        for, 290
    sharer plans for, 295–297, 302–
        304, 309
    updating working time in,
        297–300
Resources, 29–47. *See also* Cost
    resources; Material resourc-
    es; Tasks; Work resources
    allocations of, 83–86
    delaying assignment starts of,
        234–235
    equipment, 33–35
    leveling of, 74, 202
    nonworking times for, 39–40
    notes for, 42
    overallocation of, 201
    over-budget, 156–159
    pay rates for, 37–38
    people, 31–33
    recurring task assignment of,
        76–77
    resource sheet view of, 30
    table of, 47
    work schedule for, 40–41
Resources, fine-tuning, 208–227
    availability in, 214–215
    costs per use of, 210–211, 227
    material consumption rates for,
        209–210
    multiple pay rates for, 211–214
    overallocation of, 216–219,
        221–223
    Resource Leveling dialog box for,
        220–223
Resource Usage view, 83–84, 155
Risk, in estimating durations, 13

S

Schedule performance index (SPI),
    267, 283
Scheduling
    constraint and dependency effects
        on, 196–199
    critical path and, 233
    deadlines dates and, 200
    effort-driven, 53, 55–56, 58,
        71–72
    example of, 106
    from finish dates, 6
    incomplete work, 274–275
    linking tasks and, 17–18
    people versus equipment, 35
    resources, 39–41
    tracking as per, 150–151
    tracking problems in, 159–160
    uncompleted work, 159–160
    variance in, 267, 283
Scheduling formula, 54, 69–71
Scope of projects, 64
Screen, opening, 2–3
ScreenTips, 73, 197

Security settings, 184
Semi-flexible constraints, 79–80, 198–199, 201, 240
Sequences of tasks, 17
Share Resources dialog box, 290, 292
Sharer plans for resource pools
 definition of, 293
 on Internet, 309
 revising, 302–304
 revising assignments in, 295–297
 updating working time for, 299–300
Sheet view, 116
Shortcuts, 318
Slack, 80, 82, 199–200, 220, 232, 234
Smart tags, 55–58, 70–71
Software Orientation feature
 Assign Resources dialog box, 49
 Bar Styles dialog box, 114
 Calendar tab of Options dialog box, 11, 229
 Consolidated Project Gantt Chart view, 166
 Copy Picture dialog box, 179
 Earned Value table, 267–268
 Opening Screen, 2–3
 Options dialog box, 229
 Organizer, 311
 Page Setup dialog box, 133
 Resource Leveling dialog box, 220–223
 Resource Sheet view, 30
 Share Resources dialog box, 290
 Sort dialog box, 92
 Task Information dialog box, 196
 Task Usage view, 147
 WBS codes and Unique IDs in Task Sheet view, 250
Sort dialog box, 92
Sorting data, 92–96
SPI (schedule performance index), 267, 283
Splitting tasks, 72–74, 221
Sponsors, of projects, 150
Stakeholders, 137, 150, 159, 240, 280
Start dates, 5–6, 268–271
Starting businesses, 28
Start-no-earlier-than (SNET) constraint, 77–81, 198
Start-no-later-than (SNLT) constraint, 198
Start-to-finish (SF) dependencies, 17–18, 198
Start-to-start (SS) dependencies, 17–18, 198
Statistics, project, 22–23, 239–240
Status date, 280–283
Status reports, 280

"Stoplight" view of variance, 278–280
Subphases, of projects, 14
Subprojects, 168
Subtasks, 16
Successor tasks, 18–19, 55, 172
Summary tasks, 15–16, 20, 200
SV (schedule variance), 267, 283

T
Tables
 Earned Value, 267–268, 280–283
 entry, 3
 formatting, 124–125
 of resources, 47
 variance, 148
 in views, 123
Tasks, 9–22, 48–64. See also Leveling; Tracking; Tracking, advanced
 Assign Resources dialog box and, 49–50
 bar styles for, 250–253
 change management and, 64
 changing types of, 69–72
 completion percentage of, 150–152
 cost resources assigned to, 59–60
 documenting, 20–22
 editing assignments of, 237–238
 entering, 9–10
 estimating durations of, 11–13
 ghost, 170, 172
 linking, 16–20
 material resources assigned to, 58–59
 milestones for, 13–14
 noncritical, 82
 over-budget, 156–159
 phase organization of, 14–16
 recurring, 74–77
 smart tags and, 55–58
 splitting, 72–74
 summary, 15–16, 20, 200
 Update Tasks dialog box for, 152
 work resources assigned to, 50–55
Tasks, fine-tuning, 195–207
 constraints and dependency effects on, 196–199
 deadline dates for, 199–201
 priorities for, 201–202, 207
Task Information dialog box for, 196
Task calendars, 9, 66–69
Task Drivers, 80–81
Task fields, 149
Task IDs, 10, 250, 253–257
Task Information dialog box, 71–72, 196
Task Sheet view, 250

Task Usage view, 147, 155
Templates
 customizing, 313–314, 323
 examples of, 107–108
 formatting, 131
 global, 318
 on Internet, 90
 project plans from, 4–5
Text, 119–123
Text Style dialog box, 123
Time. See also Durations
 abbreviations for, 13
 adjusting, 229–231
 change working time dialog box, 66
 nonworking, 39–40
 ramp-up, 237
 resource availability over, 214–215
 slack, 80, 82, 199–200, 220, 232, 234
 tracking, 150, 159–160
 updating working, 297–300
Timephased actual work, 147, 149, 153–156
Timescale view, 73, 85, 137, 230
Top-down planning, 16
Total slack, 82, 232
Tracking, 146–164
 actuals, 324
 baseline for, 147–150
 example of, 164
 over-budget tasks and resources, 156–159
 as scheduled, 150–151
 task completion percentage for, 151–152
 Task Usage view for, 147
 time and schedule problems, 159–160
 timephased actual work, 153–156
Tracking, advanced, 266–288
 actual and remaining work, 271–273
 actual task start date and duration, 268–271
 baseline, interim, and actual project plans, 276–278
 Earned Value table for, 267–268, 280–283, 288
 interim project plans and, 275–276
 rescheduling incomplete work and, 274–275
 variance, with "stoplight" view, 278–280
Track pane, 69
Turtle contours, 237

U
Underallocated resources, 86, 219
Unique IDs, 253–257

Units of consumption, 38
Unlink tasks button, 18
Unsorting data, 95
Update Tasks dialog box, 152

V
Variable consumption rates, 209–210
Variable unit quantities, 59
Variance
 cost, 267, 283
 in short-duration tasks, 155
 simple analysis of, 282
 "stoplight" view of, 278–280
 table of, 148
Variance at completion (VAC), 268
Views. See also Gantt Chart view
 Calendar, 250–253
 chart, 114, 116
 custom, 126–127
 fields in, 123
 form, 116
 resource sheet, 30
 Resource Usage, 83–84, 155
 sheet, 116
 "stoplight," 278–280
 tables in, 123
 Task Sheet, 250
 Task Usage, 147, 155
 timescale, 73, 85, 137, 230
Visual Basic for Applications (VBA), 320
Visual Change Highlighting, 96
Visual Reports, 261

W
WBS (work breakdown structure) codes
 columns for, 253–257
 Internet information on, 265
 in Task Sheet view, 250
Work
 actual and remaining, 271–273
 assignment-level, 150
 fixed, 71
 scheduling incomplete, 159–160, 274–275
 timephased actual, 147, 149, 153–156
 updating time for, 297–300
Working Times task pane, 7
Workplace Ready feature, 107–108, 324
Work resources
 definition of, 32
 nonworking times for, 39–40
 task assignments of, 50–55

Y
Year, fiscal, 229–231

Photo Credits

Lesson 1
"PhotoDisc, Inc./Getty Images"

Lesson 2
Corbis Digital Stock

Lesson 3
"PhotoDisc, Inc./Getty Images"

Lesson 4
"PhotoDisc, Inc./Getty Images"

Lesson 5
"PhotoDisc, Inc./Getty Images"

Lesson 6
© IT Stock

Lesson 7
"PhotoDisc, Inc."

Lesson 8
Digital Vision

Lesson 9
"PhotoDisc, Inc./Getty Images"

Lesson 10
"Thomas Barwick/PhotoDisc, Inc./Getty Images"

Lesson 11
Corbis Digital Stock

Lesson 12
"Photodisc, Inc."

Lesson 13
Digital Vision

Lesson 14
Digital Vision

Lesson 15
© IT Stock

Lesson 16
© IT Stock

Lesson 17
StockByte/Getty Images

Microsoft Office Ultimate 2007

To use Microsoft Office Ultimate 2007, you will need:

COMPONENT	REQUIREMENT
Computer and processor	500 megahertz (MHz) processor or higher[1]
Memory	256 megabyte (MB) RAM or higher[1, 2, 3]
Hard disk	3 gigabyte (GB); a portion of this disk space will be freed after installation if the original download package is removed from the hard drive.
Drive	CD-ROM or DVD drive
Display	1024x768 or higher resolution monitor
Operating system	Microsoft Windows(R) XP with Service Pack (SP) 2, Windows Server(R) 2003 with SP1, or later operating system[4]
Other	Certain inking features require running Microsoft Windows XP Tablet PC Edition or later. Speech recognition functionality requires a close-talk microphone and audio output device. Information Rights Management features require access to a Windows 2003 Server with SP1 or later running Windows Rights Management Services.

Connectivity to Microsoft Exchange Server 2000 or later is required for certain advanced functionality in Outlook 2007. Instant Search requires Microsoft Windows Desktop Search 3.0. Dynamic Calendars require server connectivity.

Connectivity to Microsoft Windows Server 2003 with SP1 or later running Microsoft Windows SharePoint Services or Office SharePoint Server 2007 is required for certain advanced collaboration functionality. PowerPoint Slide Library requires Office SharePoint Server 2007. Connectivity to Office SharePoint Server 2007 required for browser-enabled InfoPath forms and additional collaboration functionality. Groove Messenger integration requires Windows Messenger 5.1 or later or Communicator 1.0 or later. Includes a 5 year subscription to the Groove relay service.

Some features require Microsoft Windows Desktop Search 3.0, Microsoft Windows Media Player 9.0, Microsoft DirectX 9.0b, Microsoft Active Sync 4.1, microphone[1], audio output device, video recording device (such as a webcam), TWAIN-compatible digital camera or scanner, Windows Mobile 2003 powered Smartphone or Windows Mobile 5 powered Smartphone or Pocket PC, or a router that supports Universal Plug and Play (UPnP). Sharing notebooks requires users to be on the same network.

Internet Explorer 6.0 or later, 32 bit browser only. Internet functionality requires Internet access (fees may apply). |
| Additional | Actual requirements and product functionality may vary based on your system configuration and operating system. |

[1] 2 gigahertz (GHz) processor or higher and 1 GB RAM or higher recommended for **OneNote Audio Search**. Close-talking microphone required. Audio Search not available in all languages.

[2] 1 gigahertz (GHz) processor or higher and 512 MB RAM or higher recommended for **Business Contact Manager**. Business Contact Manager not available in all languages.

[3] 512 MB RAM or higher recommended for **Outlook Instant Search**. Grammar and contextual spelling in *Word* is not turned on unless the machine has 1 GB memory.

[4] Send to **OneNote 2007** print driver not available on a 64 bit operating system. Groove Folder **Synchronization** not available on 64 bit operating system. Office Clean-up wizard not available on 64 bit OS.